Some Excerpts from Within

"[That] every movement in the stock market must have a rational foundation . . . is one of the greatest errors in the history of economic thought."

Robert Shiller, Yale University, author of *Irrational Exuberance*

"After the Ethiopian war and the fascist intervention in the Spanish Civil War, I began to develop a strong antifascist sentiment and the intent to leave Italy, but the final step was the close alliance of Mussolini with Hitler, which resulted in anti-Semitic laws, [and] made it impossible to live in Italy in a dignified way."

Franco Modigliani, Nobel Laureate, MIT

"Trade is confirmed to be a substitute for massive immigration from poor to rich countries. U.S. labor has lost its old monopoly on American advanced know-how and capital . . . Nowadays every short-term victory by a union only speeds up the day that its industry moves abroad . . . A 'cowed' labor force runs scared under the newly evolved form of ruthless corporate governance."

Paul Samuelson, Nobel Laureate, MIT

"I had a session with Nixon sometime in 1970 . . . , in which he wanted me to urge Arthur [Burns] to increase the money supply more rapidly [*laughter*] and I said to the President, 'Do you really want to do that? The only effect of that will be to leave you with a larger inflation if you do get reelected.' And he said, 'Well, we'll worry about that after we get reelected.' Typical. So there's no doubt what Nixon's pleasure was."

Milton Friedman, Nobel Laureate, Hoover Institution, Stanford University

"One of my close friends was not only arrested, but tried and executed. Many of my best friends were arrested . . . I was attacked as a 'traitor' to socialism . . . the horrible crimes the system had committed—the imprisonment, torture, and murder of innocent people—made my most sincere beliefs seem naïve and shameful."

János Kornai, Harvard University and Collegium Budapest, Hungary

"Like number theory, knot theory was totally, totally useless. So, I was attracted to knots . . . Fifty years later, the 'absolutely useless'—the 'purest of the pure'—is taught in the second year of medical school."

"Kennedy was influenced by the game-theoretic school . . . [and he] is now praised for his handling of that [Cuban missile] crisis . . . Kissinger spoke about game-theoretic thinking in Cold War diplomacy . . . People were really afraid that the world was coming to an end."

Robert Aumann, Nobel Laureate, Hebrew University of Jerusalem

Praise for *Inside the Economist's Mind*

"A tour de force."
> **Oded Galor**, Brown University, Providence and Hebrew University
> of Jerusalem, Israel, Editor, *Journal of Economic Growth*

". . . a unique insider view . . . fascinating reading to anyone interested in contemporary economics and its role in modern society."
> **Seppo Honkapohja**, University of Cambridge, Cambridge, UK

". . . an intellectuals' *People Magazine*—complete with !%$!!'s and pictures."
> **Roger Farmer**, University of California at Los Angeles

"These remarkably candid interviews are exemplars . . . this superb collection is mandatory reading."
> **Adrian Pagan**, Australian National University, Australia

"They curse. They dish on their colleagues. They give the inside scoop."
> *Lawrence Journal World*

INSIDE THE ECONOMIST'S MIND

Conversations with Eminent Economists

Edited by

Paul A. Samuelson and William A. Barnett

Blackwell
Publishing

© 2007 by Blackwell Publishing Ltd

BLACKWELL PUBLISHING
350 Main Street, Malden, MA 02148-5020, U.S.A.
9600 Garsington Road, Oxford OX4 2DQ, U.K.
550 Swanston Street, Carlton, Victoria 3053, Australia

The right of Paul A. Samuelson and William A. Barnett to be identified as
the Authors of the Editorial Material in this Work has been asserted in
accordance with the U.K. Copyright, Designs, and Patents Act 1988.

First published 2007 by Blackwell Publishing Ltd

1   2007

Library of Congress Cataloging-in-Publication Data

Inside the economist's mind: conversations with eminent economists /
edited by Paul A. Samuelson and
William A. Barnett.—1st ed.
      p. cm.
   Includes bibliographical references.
   ISBN-13: 978-1-4051-5715-5 (hardcover : alk. paper)
   ISBN-10: 1-4051-5715-1 (hardcover : alk. paper)
   ISBN-13: 978-1-4051-5917-3 (paperback : alk. paper)
   ISBN-10: 1-4051-5917-0 (paperback : alk. paper) 1. Economists—
Interviews. 2. Economists—Biography. 3. Economics. 4. Economics—
History—20th century. I. Samuelson, Paul Anthony, 1915–
II. Barnett, William A. III. Title: History of modern economic thought.

   HB76.157 2007
   330.092'2—dc22

                                                         2006017115

A catalogue record for this title is available from the British Library.

Set in 10/12.5pt Galliard
by Graphicraft Limited, Hong Kong
Printed and bound in the United Kingdom
by TJ International Ltd

The publisher's policy is to use permanent paper from mills that operate
a sustainable forestry policy, and which has been manufactured from pulp
processed using acid-free and elementary chlorine-free practices. Furthermore,
the publisher ensures that the text paper and cover board used have met
acceptable environmental accreditation standards.

For further information on
Blackwell Publishing, visit our website:
www.blackwellpublishing.com

Contents

About the Editors

William A. Barnett is Oswald Distinguished Professor of Macroeconomics at the University of Kansas. He was previously Research Economist at the Board of Governors of the Federal Reserve System in Washington, DC; Stuart Centennial Professor of Economics at the University of Texas at Austin; and Professor of Economics at Washington University in St. Louis. William Barnett has been a leading researcher in macroeconomics and econometrics. He is one of the pioneers in the study of chaos and nonlinearity in socioeconomic contexts, as well as a major figure in the study of the aggregation problem, which lies at the heart of how individual and aggregate data are related. He is Editor of the Elsevier monograph series *International Symposia in Economic Theory and Econometrics*, and Editor of the journal *Macroeconomic Dynamics*, published by Cambridge University Press. He received his BS degree from MIT, his MBA from the University of California at Berkeley, and his MA and Ph.D. from Carnegie Mellon University. He has published 17 books (as either author or editor) and over 130 articles in professional journals.

Paul A. Samuelson was the first American to win the Nobel Prize in Economics. He is Professor Emeritus of Economics and Institute Professor at the Massachusetts Institute of Technology; Institute Professor is the highest rank awarded by MIT. His landmark 1947 book, *Foundations of Economic Analysis*, based upon his Ph.D. dissertation at Harvard University, established him as "the economists' economist" by raising the standards of the entire profession. Paul Samuelson's classic textbook, *Economics*, first published in 1948, is among the most successful textbooks ever published in the field. The book's 16 editions have sold over four million copies and have been translated into 41 languages. He received his BA degree from the University of Chicago and his MA and Ph.D. from Harvard University. As one of the profession's most productive scholars for over a half-century, he remains an intellectual force of towering stature.

Coeditor's Foreword

Reflections on How Biographies of Individual Scholars Can Relate to a Science's Biography

Paul A. Samuelson

This book adds up to more than the sum of its parts. When W. Somerset Maugham opined that "to know one country you must know two countries," he was saying in a different way that 1 + 1 can exceed 2. Adam Smith and Allyn Young categorized this as "increasing returns to scale."

When a discipline—economics, chemistry, or acupuncture—is in a dynamic stage of rapid growth, its up-front cyclists care little whether it was Newton or Leibniz who "invented" the calculus. The economics profession is in such a dynamic stage of rapid growth, as made clear by the interviews in this book. The book permits us to step back and view the whole of the field in a revealing context that otherwise is easily missed in the narrow focus of individual expert researchers. The twenty-first century's go-getters in economics go whole hours ignoring what more John Bates Clark did for marginal productivity theorizing, than Johann Ludwig von Thünen had not already done.

This helps explain the historical fact that the role in the graduate curriculum once played by "History of Economic Thought" has eroded down to a narrow cadre of learned experts. An unearned snobbery ensues, as is well illustrated by Bernard Shaw's canard: "Those who can, do. Those who can't, teach." Good history of science deserves a non-zero weight in the university curriculum. The dynamic growth in individual subfields of the economics profession needs to be supplemented by overviews of the whole, not just as the sum of its normally separated parts. This book provides such a view of the whole of the modern field of economics and the connection of that whole with the life experiences of famous economists whose work was seminal to the field.

Returning to the theme of how multiplicity of cases can be fruitful, let's test an alleged dictum of Socrates: "The unexamined life is not worth living." When I once read an excellent book about the principal philosophers, all the usual suspects were there: Spinoza, Kant, Hegel, Wittgenstein, Russell, ... My inductive finding was that Socrates had it completely wrong. An unhappier gaggle of misfits could hardly be imagined. Suicides abounded, melancholies persisted, celibacies and divorces competed for frequencies. A vulgar explanation would nominate as a common cause that the study of philosophy destroys the joy of life. Perhaps a better explanation would be that becoming an orphan early, or being born dyslexic, et cetera, predisposes one to choose philosophy over being a cheerful bartender. Acquiring an objective and insightful overview of the whole in any area of understanding is important, but less easily and enjoyably acquired than the skills of a bartender.

I return to economics and to economists, and to the question of why the profession's directions have evolved in the manners evident from this book. A major conservative economist once explained that a source of his antipathy to government traced back to the defeat of his southern ancestors by a larger north economy. Here is a similar factoid. Joan Robinson once wrote that her opposition to having the U.K. enter the European Market was due to the fact that she "had more friends in [Nehru's] India than on the continent." Yes, it is a banality that personal piffle can affect ideology. But can we take autobiographical judgments as most accurate judgments? The Robinson I knew could well have thought back in the 1960s that her kind of post-Fabian socialism would flourish better in India than on the continent. And, alas, she may have been right in so thinking.

Published scientific research, by its very nature, is designed not to identify any personal motives of the authors. In understanding what is in this revealing book, need we be concerned with the personal motives for the directions taken by these eminent economists? If so, is this interviews format the best way to gain insight into those motives?

I conclude with an unworthy hypothesis regarding past and present directions of economic research. Sherlock Holmes said, "*Cherchez la femme.*" When asked why he robbed banks, Willie Sutton replied, "That's where the money is." We economists do primarily work for our peers' esteem, which figures in our own self-esteem. When post-Depression Roosevelt's New Deal provided exciting job opportunities, first the junior academic faculties moved leftward. To get back ahead of their followers, subsequently the senior academic faculties shoved ahead of them. As post-Reagan, post-Thatcher electorates turned rightward, follow the money pointed, alas, in only one direction. So to speak, we eat our own cooking.

We economists love to quote Keynes's final lines in his 1936 *General Theory*—for the reason that they cater so well to our vanity and self-importance. But to admit the truth, madmen in authority can *self-generate* their own frenzies without needing help from either defunct or avant-garde economists. What establishment economists brew up is as often what the Prince and the Public are already wanting to imbibe. We guys don't stay in the best club by proffering the views of some past *academic* crank or academic sage.

Indeed, this book adds up to more than the sum of its parts. It provides a rare overview of the economics profession in a manner that reveals the relevancy of the personal motives and experiences of some of its leading modern contributors.

Coeditor's Preface

An Overview of the Objectives and Contents of the Volume

William A. Barnett[1]

This collection of interviews contains unique insights into the thinking of some of the world's most important economists, whose work contributed to the evolution of modern economic thought. What makes this collection so unusual is the source of these interviews. They first were published in a highly regarded, peer-reviewed, Cambridge University Press journal, *Macroeconomic Dynamics*, of which I am Editor. Publication in scientific peer-reviewed journals normally is subject to refereeing, which constrains authors to publish only what is deemed to be acceptable to the referees, associate editors, and editors of those journals. These constraints do not permit casual, freewheeling discussion of the sort more commonly found in the popular press. But it is publication in those professional journals that is most highly regarded by scientists, since only publication in those journals has the stamp of approval of the profession, as being consistent with the rigorous standards of science. Hence it is through publication in such journals that scientists speak to each other in a manner that commands the respect of their peers.

To the layman, it may seem odd that even the world's most famous Nobel Prize winners are not permitted to speak to their profession within scientific journals in a manner that is free from the constraints of peer review. With recognition of this communication problem, I instituted an interview series within the journal, *Macroeconomic Dynamics*.[2] That journal never publishes more than one interview in any issue, since the journal is otherwise a rigorously refereed scientific journal. But it has been made clear to the journal's publisher, Cambridge University Press, that an interview is entirely a quotation and cannot be touched by referees, associate editors, copy editors, the publisher, or me. It is a matter of freedom of speech and freedom of the press that quotations cannot be altered.

From the startup of the journal, interviewers and interviewees have been informed that they can say whatever they want in these interviews, despite the fact that publication is within an otherwise peer-reviewed scientific journal. As a result, the leaders of the field can openly reveal any matters that they may wish to share with the profession, whether personal, religious, or political. Personal attacks; claims of unfairness or prejudice, of religious persecution, or of political oppression; and unvarnished strong statements about politicians, administrators, and public policy, while normally excluded from professional journals, are not excluded from these interviews. Participants in an interview are free to put such matters "on the record." The nature of the fireworks contained in some of these interviews cannot be found in other professional economics journals. Nothing is removed from those interviews by the journal's editorial board or by Cambridge University Press, although in one interview, Cambridge University Press did replace an Anglo-Saxon expletive with the abbreviation "f—."

The participants in these interviews include eight Nobel Laureates, Wassily Leontief, Robert Lucas, Franco Modigliani, Robert Solow, Milton Friedman, Paul Samuelson, Robert Aumann, and James Tobin; two central bank governors, Paul Volcker (former Chairman of the Federal Reserve Board) and Stanley Fischer (Governor of the Bank of Israel); and a Chairman of the Council of Economic Advisors, Martin Feldstein. Robert Aumann won his Nobel Prize as this book was in preparation. Some of the other participants in these interviews are high on most economists' lists for possible future Nobel Prizes in Economics. Despite the fame of the interviewers and interviewees, you will not find comparably candid insights into their lives and views anywhere else but in this book or in the original interviews in *Macroeconomic Dynamics*.

The following equally important interviews, which have appeared in *Macroeconomic Dynamics*, are planned to be included in the anticipated volume 2 of this book, along with other important interviews that now are in process. Each of the two books will be balanced in content to be comparably as informative and to reflect a broad spectrum of views of many of the world's most influential economists.

Allan Meltzer interviewed by Bennett McCallum (*Macroeconomic Dynamics*, vol. 2, no. 2, 1998)
Elhanan Helpman interviewed by Daniel Trefler (*Macroeconomic Dynamics*, vol. 3, no. 4, 1999)

William Brock interviewed by Michael Woodford (*Macroeconomic Dynamics*, vol. 4, no. 1, 2000)
Karl Shell interviewed by Steven Spear and Randall Wright (*Macroeconomic Dynamics*, vol. 5, no. 5, 2001)
Axel Leijonhufvud interviewed by Brian Snowdon (*Macroeconomic Dynamics*, vol. 8, no. 1, 2004)
Anna Schwartz interviewed by Edward Nelson (*Macroeconomic Dynamics*, vol. 8, no. 3, 2004)
Guillermo Calvo interviewed by Enrique Mendoza (*Macroeconomic Dynamics*, vol. 9, no. 1, 2005)
Assar Lindbeck interviewed by Thorvaldur Gylfason (*Macroeconomic Dynamics*, vol. 10, no. 1, 2006)

In keeping with the high standards of the profession, we invited an introduction by one of the world's leading authorities on the history of economic thought, E. Roy Weintraub. Weintraub's Introduction follows this Preface. In addition, Paul Samuelson, who is a coeditor of this book, contributed the book's thought-provoking Foreword, which precedes this Preface.[3] To emphasize the colorful nature of much that appears in these interviews and the unusual insights available herein, a few of the more striking statements are briefly quoted below. These quotations are taken out of context and are no substitute for the full interviews, but are an indication of the unusual nature of this collection of important and fascinating interviews.

All of the interviews published in this book are reprinted in their entirety from the *Macroeconomic Dynamics* originals, although some of the photographs have been removed. The following are samples of some of the quotations and observations that can be found in this book.

1 Wassily Leontief interviewed by Duncan K. Foley

Wassily Leontief, best known as the originator of the fundamental planning tool, input–output analysis, won the Nobel Prize in Economics in 1973, while a professor at Harvard University. He was born in the Soviet Union. The following quotations are indicative of the insights about his life and views that can be found in his interview:

> Marx was not a very good mathematician. He was always mixed up in math, and the labor theory of value didn't make much sense.

I left the Soviet Union in 1925. I got in trouble with the government, actually.

Richard Goodwin was my student. . . . He couldn't get tenure. And this was the reason why he went to England . . . I think possibly it was politics. He was on the left.

Regarding his views about the distant future, Leontief explains:

I think problems of income distribution will increase in importance. As I mentioned before, labor will be not so important, and the problem will be just to manage the system. People will get their income allocated through social security—already now we get it through social security, and we try to invent pretexts to provide social security for people. Here, I think, the role of the government will be incredibly important, and those economists who try to minimize the role of the government, I fear, show a superficial understanding of how the economic system works. My feeling is, if we abolished the government now, already there would be complete chaos . . . it would be horrible.

Wassily Leontief died in 1999, a year after the publication of his interview in *Macroeconomic Dynamics*.

2   David Cass interviewed jointly by Steven E. Spear and Randall Wright

David Cass has produced some of the deepest theoretical insights in the field of economics, including the discovery of "sunspot equilibria" in his joint research with Karl Shell. Cass, along with Hirofumi Uzawa and Karl Shell, has influenced economic dynamics in ways that have been pivotal in the history of economic thought. In keeping with that depth of intellect, this interview is uncompromising in its emphasis on technical advances in economics. Although his time on the faculty of Carnegie Mellon University overlapped with mine, as a graduate student there, one of my disappointments was that he did not stay. He moved to the University of Pennsylvania, for reasons made clear in this interview.

There is another more colorful side to Cass. That side is well known in the profession and clearly displayed in this interview by such statements as the following:

We had to hire a new Dean. At Carnegie, the faculty was very involved in this process . . . we settled on Arnie Weber . . . That turned out to be, from Carnegie's viewpoint and my own viewpoint, a disaster . . . Arnie called me into his office for some reason, and I had an interview with him. He told me that I was a luxury good and that I didn't do business. I did theoretical economics and it wasn't something that business schools could really support, and he did it in a very obnoxious way that really pissed me off. And I said "f— you, Arnie." . . . Yeah, I said "f— you."

Cass says the following about Nobel Laureate Robert Lucas, who was on the faculty at Carnegie Mellon University at that time:

> Bob was in the Chicago tradition and was very concerned about empirical testing—whatever the hell that means—something that I have little sympathy for and very little interest in, to be perfectly honest.

Although himself a pioneer in real business cycle theory via the Cass–Koopmans model, Cass says,

> the thing about real business-cycle theory, I suppose, is that it is almost like a religion.

3 Robert E. Lucas, Jr. interviewed by Bennett T. McCallum

Robert Lucas won the Nobel Prize in Economics in 1995, while a professor at the University of Chicago. In his introduction to this interview, Bennett T. McCallum writes that,

> Bob Lucas is widely regarded as the most influential economist of the past 25–30 years, at least among those working in macro and monetary economics.

In this interview, you will learn how Lucas was motivated at age of seven or eight to be interested in economics by his father's stories about the economics of milk truck deliveries under socialism. About his later years as a graduate student at the University of Chicago, Lucas states that,

> The atmosphere at Chicago, when I was a student, was so hostile to any kind of planning that we were not taught to think: How *should* resources be allocated in this situation? How *should* people use the information available to them to form expectations? But these *should* always be an economist's first questions. My Dad was wrong to think that socialism would deliver milk efficiently, but he was right to think about how milk *should* be delivered.

Among his other statements are:

I am happy about the successes of general equilibrium theory in macro and sad about the de-emphasis on money that those successes have brought about.

Regarding the importance of technology shocks, he comments:

If we are discussing the U.S. Depression in the 1930s or the depression in Indonesia today or Mexico five years ago, I would say that technology shocks are a minor part of the picture. On the other hand, . . . in the postwar United States the relative importance . . . is much larger.

In response to the question, "is price stickiness an important economic phenomenon?" Lucas replies:

Yes. In practice it is much more painful to put a modern economy through a deflation than the monetary theory we have would lead us to expect.

Lucas says the following about monetary policy:

I am concerned about the kind of bad dynamics that Wicksell, and more recently Peter Howitt, worried about.

He further observes,

My claim is not that monetary instability is incapable of causing great harm, but only that it has not done so over the past 50 years in the United States.

Lucas states the following about modern microeconomics:

In the past 15 years, microeconomics has come to be synonymous with game theory in many places (not including Chicago!), and that is unfortunate.

4   János Kornai interviewed by Olivier Blanchard

To many in the economics profession, János Kornai is a true hero. While living in his home country of Hungary under communism, he became famous among economists in the West, against the odds and at considerable danger to himself. As explained by Olivier Blanchard in his introduction to this interview,

These difficulties have not prevented him from giving us the most informed and deepest critique of the socialist system to date.

At present, Kornai shares his time between Harvard University and Collegium Budapest. Among the statements in this interview are the following:

One of my close friends was not only arrested, but tried and executed. Many of my best friends were arrested . . . I was attacked as a "traitor" to socialism. I was fired.

I still admire Marx as an intellectual genius; he had many ideas which are still useful. He was, however, absolutely wrong on many fundamental issues.

Before 1963, I had been denied a passport. I had a standing invitation to the London School of Economics for years, for instance, and I couldn't go.

Regarding his early book, *Overcentralization*, and the events that led up to it, Kornai observes:

My disappointment began in 1953 . . . , when many facts that had previously been hidden, became known . . . the horrible crimes the system had committed—the imprisonment, torture, and murder of innocent people— made my most sincere beliefs seem naïve and shameful. Also, I began to recognize that the regime was economically dysfunctional and inefficient, created shortages, and suppressed initiative and spontaneity.

He continues,

Overcentralization . . . got worldwide attention because it was the first critical book written by a citizen living inside the Bloc.

He further observes that in the preface of the second edition of that book, he

described the Kornai of 1954–56 as a "naïve reformer."

About his book *Anti-Equilibrium*, he states:

I feel slightly bitter about its getting hardly any attention. The first, and nearly the last, people who gave it any credit were Arrow and Koopmans; then it somehow disappeared . . . it seems to me that asking relevant questions doesn't give you much reputation, at least not in our profession.

With respect to his book *Economics of Shortage*, he states:

The dysfunctional properties of socialism are systemic . . . I was rather isolated from the rest of the so-called reformers who were working on small changes to the Communist system. In that sense, it's a revolutionary book . . . You have to change the system as a whole to get rid of the dysfunctional properties

Changing the subject to his book *The Socialist System*, he states that,

The central idea of the book was to show that the classical Stalinist system, however repressive and brutal it was, was coherent, while the more relaxed, half-reformed Gorbachev-type of system was incoherent, and subject to erosion. I foresaw the erosion.

Kornai comments on the current post-communist Eastern Europe:

I think people belonging to the elite of the former socialist regime have, with few exceptions, totally forgotten the Communist Manifesto, but they have a network of friends from the old days. Right now these relations are extremely powerful in business, in politics, in cultural life. People who knew each other in the old system, know exactly who is a friend and who is an enemy.

5   Franco Modigliani interviewed by William A. Barnett and Robert Solow

Franco Modigliani won the Nobel Prize in Economics in 1985, while a professor at MIT. This interview was conducted jointly by the 1987 MIT Nobel Laureate, Robert Solow, and me. Since my initial interest in economics was motivated by Modigliani's graduate course, which I took while an undergraduate student in engineering at MIT, I felt a particular responsibility to assure that Modigliani's remarkable life and contributions would be adequately covered in this interview. Many of the questions that I asked were based upon longstanding rumors heard by Modigliani's students. In this interview, you will learn the truth about those rumors.

Modigliani and his parents left Italy, while under Mussolini's fascist rule. As he explains in this interview,

After the Ethiopian war and the fascist intervention in the Spanish Civil War, I began to develop a strong antifascist sentiment and the intent to leave Italy, but the final step was the close alliance of Mussolini with Hitler, which resulted in anti-Semitic laws, which made it impossible to live in Italy in a dignified way.

As explained in some detail in the interview, he and his family first moved to France and then to the U.S. He briefly returned from Paris to Rome, still under fascist rule, to defend his dissertation. As he explains,

> that operation was not without dangers, because by that time I could have been arrested. I had kept my contacts with antifascist groups in Paris, so there was the possibility of being harassed or being jailed.

He describes a code that he used with his father-in-law as a warning, while he was in Rome. It has been widely rumored, that Franco Modigliani was related to the famous painter and sculptor, Amedeo Modigliani. But that story seems not to have been true.

Modigliani's first position in the United States was at the New School University in New York City. He received an offer from Harvard, which he surprisingly turned down. His explanation is the following:

> Because the head of the department, Professor Burbank, whom I later found out had a reputation of being xenophobic and anti-Semitic, worked very hard and successfully to persuade me to turn down the offer.

Having turned down the Harvard offer, Modigliani moved to the University of Illinois, where the salary was higher than at Harvard. Regarding his years at Illinois, he observes the following:

> The president of the university brought in a new wonderful dean, Howard H. Bowen. But the old and incompetent faculty could not stand the fact that Bowen brought in some first-rate people . . . The old faculty was able to force Bowen out, as part of the witch hunt that was going on under the leadership of the infamous Senator Joseph McCarthy. The leader of the McCarthyite wing of the elected trustees was the famous [football player] Red Grange. I then quit in disgust with a blast that in the local press is still remembered: "There is finally peace in the College of Commerce, but it is the peace of death." My departure was greeted with joy by the old staff, proportional to their incompetence. But 40 years later, the university saw fit to give me an honorary degree!

The interview was conducted shortly before the stock market bubble burst in 2000, and contains the following statement by Modigliani,

> I believe that indeed the stock market in the United States is in the grips of a serious bubble. I think the overvaluation of stocks is probably on the order of 25%. . . . In my view, there will be a collapse, because if there is a marked overvaluation, as I hold, it cannot disappear slowly.

In this interview, he is on the record with that forecast, and indeed he was right. No wonder one of Modigliani's students, Robert Shiller, of *Irrational Exuberance* fame, has said of Modigliani that he is "my hero."

Modigliani says the following about Robert Barro, who also was in some of Modigliani's classes:

> In my view, Barro's theorem, despite its elegance, has no substance. I don't understand why so many seem to be persuaded by a proposition whose proof rests on the incredible assumption that everybody cares about his heirs as if they were himself.

Modigliani is referring to Barro's view on Ricardian-equivalence and its implication of the irrelevance of government debt financing. About monetary policy and Friedman's rule, Modigliani says:

> in the battle between my recommendation to make use of discretion (or common sense) and Friedman's recommendation to renounce discretion in favor of blind rules . . . , my prescription has won hands down. There is not a country in the world today that uses a mechanical rule.

Franco Modigliani died in 2003.

6   Milton Friedman interviewed by John B. Taylor

Milton Friedman won the Nobel Prize in Economics in 1976, while a professor at the University of Chicago. Alan Greenspan, former Chairman of the Board of Governors of the Federal Reserve System, has said of Milton Friedman,

> His views have had as much, if not more, impact on the way we think about monetary policy and many other important economic issues as those of any person in the last half of the twentieth century.

Regarding the "Great Inflation" in the 1970s, Friedman states:

> I believe that Arthur Burns deserves a lot of blame . . . From the moment Burns got into the Fed, I think politics played a great role in what happened. So far as Nixon was concerned, there is no doubt, as I know from personal experience. I had a session with Nixon sometime in 1970—I think it was 1970, might have been 1971—in which he wanted me to urge Arthur to increase the money supply more rapidly [laughter] and I said to the President, "Do you really want to do that?

The only effect of that will be to leave you with a larger inflation if you do get reelected." And he said, "Well, we'll worry about that after we get reelected." Typical. So there's no doubt what Nixon's pleasure was.

In this regard, I can mention that I was myself on the staff of the Federal Reserve Board from July 1973 to December 1981, which overlapped part of Burns's term as Chairman. I also met with him at the American Enterprise Institute, at his request, following the end of his term at the Board. He stated that he indeed did deserve a lot of the blame, but he denied that the reason was political pressure. He maintained that it was an honest mistake by him, based upon failure to recognize that the "natural rate" of unemployment had increased. He said that that failure resulted in a misguided attempt to lower unemployment to unsustainably low levels. But, of course, if political pressure from the White House really had played a role, it is unlikely that Burns would have admitted it to me.

Other interesting statements in Friedman's interview include:

Nixon had a higher IQ than Reagan, but he was far less principled; he was political to an extreme degree.

Friedman reveals the following about Burns as a Ph.D. student:

Burns. . . . was living in Greenwich Village. He had long hair, long fingernails. You know, he was a different character than he was later on.

Friedman says of himself as an undergraduate,

I probably would have described myself as a socialist, who knows.

In reply to a question about the use of mathematics in economics, Friedman states,

I go back to what Alfred Marshall said about economics: Translate your results into English and then burn the mathematics.

On the subject of the euro currency, Friedman says,

I think it will be a miracle—well, a miracle is a little strong. I think it's highly unlikely that it's going to be a great success.

In addition, at the time of the interview, Friedman said in this interview,

The euro is undervalued; the U.S. dollar is overvalued ... Relative to the dollar, the euro will appreciate and the dollar will depreciate.

And indeed it has, in spades.

7   Paul A. Samuelson interviewed by William A. Barnett

Paul Samuelson won the Nobel Prize in Economics in 1970, while a professor at MIT. I was an undergraduate engineering student at MIT from 1959 to 1963. To all students at MIT in all fields, there were two "gods" who loomed over the rest of the faculty: the great mathematician, Norbert Wiener, and the great economist, Paul Samuelson. At MIT, where all the tenured professors are world-renowned research stars, to loom over the rest is possible only in the rarest of cases from any generation of scholars.

To this day I think that many economists feel intimidated by Samuelson's awesome intellect. In fact, I was surprised by the difficulty that I had in finding an economist who was willing to take on the job of serving as interviewer of Samuelson. I did finally find one (V.V. Chari at the University of Minnesota). But he brought the tapes of the interview back with him on an airplane, after running them through the X-ray luggage scanner at an airport. The tapes were destroyed by the scan. So in this one case, rather than trying to find another willing interviewer, I conducted the interview entirely myself. Indeed, it was an experience.

During his career, Paul Samuelson has averaged almost one technical paper per month. He once said,

Let those who will—write the nation's laws—if I can write its textbooks.

It is widely reported that at the end of Samuelson's dissertation defense at Harvard, the great economist Joseph Schumpeter turned to the Nobel Laureate, Wassily Leontief, and asked, "Well, Wassily, have we passed?"

Regarding Leijonhufvud's interpretation of Keynes, Samuelson said in this interview that, "I knew [him] to have it wrong."

In this interview, you can find Samuelson's views on the "... rash Reagan fiscal deficit."

Changing the topic to his first economics teacher, Aaron Director, Samuelson says,

He was the only man alive who could . . . speak of "my radical brother-in-law Milton Friedman."

Discussing his years as a student during the Depression, with Frank Knight as one of his professors, Samuelson says,

the only present choice was between communism and fascism. And for himself, Knight would not choose the latter. Later, understandably, he recovered from that failure of nerve and reneged on his circulated text. Somewhere in my files will be found a copy of his doomsday text.

With respect to his years as a student at the University of Chicago, he characterizes that economics department as "dogmatically conservative." He then moved to Harvard University as a graduate student, and he comments on those years as follows:

Anti-Semitism was omnipresent in pre-World War II academic life, here and abroad.

Samuelson comments on the faculty at Harvard as follows:

Hitler (and Lenin) did much for American science. Leontief, Schumpeter, and Haberler brought Harvard to life after a lean period.

He continues that, upon completion of his studies,

When MIT made a good offer, we thought this could test whether there was great enthusiasm for my staying at Harvard. When Harvard's revealed preference consisted of no majority insistence that I stay, we moved three miles down the Charles River.

Characterizing the nature of his influence on Washington during Camelot, Samuelson comments that,

With great reluctance, I let Senator John F. Kennedy recruit me to his think tank . . . Only when they needed my extra heavy lifting from Cambridge did I weigh in.

On the subject of globalization, Samuelson comments that,

Trade is confirmed to be a substitute for massive immigration from poor to rich countries. U.S. labor has lost its old monopoly on American advanced know-how and capital . . . Free trade need not help *everybody* *everywhere* . . .

> Nowadays every short-term victory by a union only speeds up the day that its industry moves abroad . . . A "cowed" labor force runs scared under the newly evolved form of ruthless corporate governance.

As should be no surprise from these comments, Samuelson goes on to observe that,

> Probably as a syndicated columnist, I have published at monthly intervals a couple of thousand different journalistic articles.

8   Paul A. Volcker interviewed by Perry Mehrling

Paul Volcker was President of the Federal Reserve Bank of New York from 1975 to 1979 and Chairman of the Board of Governors of the Federal Reserve System from 1979 to 1987 under both Presidents Carter and Reagan.

With respect to Arthur Burns's views about suspending convertibility of the dollar into gold, Volcker says,

> Burns didn't want to do any of this. He was holding out to the end. I didn't think he had any realistic ideas as to how to reform the system, except he seemed to think we could negotiate a change in the price of gold without suspending convertibility.

About his own experience during that period of needed reform, he says,

> It's a sad story, engraved on my mind . . . I was the American negotiator for reforming the system. I don't know how close we really came to an agreement. It was very difficult. But about the time when maybe an agreement was in sight, the oil price shock was used as an excuse to end the effort.

I was myself on the staff of the Federal Reserve Board during much of the "monetarist experiment" years of 1979–82, and it was very clear to me that Volcker was sincere in his wish to try a monetarist policy to tame the double digit inflation that existed in the late 1970s. But when that new policy produced a recession, it became fashionable among the monetarists of the time to say that the Board really was not following a monetarist policy, and was just using that claim as a cover-up for continuation of the old policy. I never agreed with that interpretation of what I saw, and indeed Volcker in this interview makes clear what really happened, in the following statement:

I used to rankle when some of the members of the Board who were all enthusiastic about this turn of policy would say, "Isn't this just a kind of public relations ploy to avoid being blamed for the rise in interest rates?" I never thought it was that, but a lot of people did think it was largely that. It was a very common thing to say that we just did it to obfuscate.

About the objective of controlling the money growth rate during that three-year period, Volcker explains further,

we had no other good benchmark for how much to raise interest rates in the midst of a volatile inflationary situation.

On the subject of credit controls, Volcker comments:

There was a law that had been passed in the early 1970s to embarrass President Nixon, authorizing the president to call for credit controls. It was a two-stage thing. He could call for controls, but the Federal Reserve would have to implement them. So Carter took the view that he wanted credit controls. I didn't like the idea . . . But President Carter wanted to do something . . . I said to the Board, "Let us do as little as we possibly can, consistent with the request or demand that we have some credit controls" . . . It shouldn't have done anything, logically . . . Consumption just collapsed . . . We took the controls off as soon as we could.

On the controversies regarding floating exchange rates versus a possible future single international currency, Volcker comments that,

for many countries, particularly small and open countries, a floating currency is more trouble than the independent monetary policy is worth . . . We will need to think in terms of some truly international standard, the role that gold used to play.

Volcker says the following about deregulation:

I think that financial deregulation has been another big strand of what I've been concerned about . . . When I was in the Treasury in the sixties, Wright Patman, an extreme populist from Texas and chairman of the House Banking Committee, made a speech complaining that we had too few bank failures and too little risk taking. Well, we have fixed that problem!"

Volcker reveals his views on modern risk management in the statement,

The whole concept rests on the idea of normal distribution curves, but there ain't no normal distribution when it comes to financial crises.

On the subject of the Russian central bank, Volcker says that it

> is pretty well destroyed by accusations, rightly or wrongly, that they are
> corrupt in the most egregious sense.

It is perhaps interesting to observe that this interview was acquired
following a somewhat unusual exchange. I wrote to Paul Volcker on
August 10, 1999, inviting him to be interviewed for publication in
Macroeconomic Dynamics. He replied in a letter on January 5, 2000
agreeing, but with the following qualification:

> I apologize for a long delayed response. Perhaps it was my allergy to
> "Divisia monetary aggregates" that accounts for the lapse.[4]

The reason for his hesitancy is not difficult to understand. I originated
the Divisia monetary aggregates at the end of the 1970s, while on the
staff of the Federal Reserve Board (in the Special Studies Section).
During the "monetarist experiment" of 1979–82, my aggregates were
growing at half the rate of the official simple sum monetary aggregates.
I advised repeatedly that the official aggregates were not accurately
reflecting the restrictiveness of policy, and that the policy would result
in a recession. Perhaps the recession that followed, as I had warned, is
the source of Volcker's "allergy." I subsequently published that data
and documentation in a paper in the American Statistical Association's
journal, the *American Statistician*. When I submitted the paper to that
journal, its editor, Gary G. Koch, had the paper refereed by an astonish-
ing six referees. In addition on the telephone, he informed me he was
worried that publishing my results would cause his journal to be overwhelmed by angry letters to the editor. I assured him that the kinds of
people who would send such letters do not likely read his journal. The
article appeared in Barnett (1984). But there is more. After the economy had recovered from the recession (and I had left the Board for a
professorship at the University of Texas), there was a huge spike in the
simple sum monetary aggregates, but no spike in my Divisia monetary
aggregates. On September 26, 1983, the world's leading "monetarist,"
Milton Friedman, in a full page article in *Newsweek* magazine (p. 84),
wrote,

> The monetary explosion from July 1982 to July 1983 leaves no satisfactory
> way out . . . The result is bound to be renewed stagflation—recession
> accompanied by rising inflation and high interest rates . . . The only real
> uncertainty is when the recession will begin.

But *on the exact same day*, September 26, 1983, I said in a full page article in *Forbes* magazine (p. 196),

> people have been panicking unnecessarily about money supply growth this year . . . The Divisia aggregates are rising at a rate not much different from last year's . . . the 'apparent explosion' can be viewed as a statistical blip.

The stagflation never developed, as anticipated by my published analysis. To this day the monetarists have not recovered from the two successive public embarrassments. An overview of these events and the evidence can be found in Barnett (1997).[5]

9   Martin Feldstein interviewed by James M. Poterba

Martin Feldstein spent two years as the Chairman of the Council of Economic Advisers during Ronald Reagan's administration, while on leave from his professorship at Harvard University. As explained by James Poterba in his introduction to this interview,

> he warned frequently of the long-term economic costs of large budget deficits, even though this was a very unpopular view on political grounds.

Poterba continues that,

> His 1995 Ely Lecture to the American Economic Association was a clarion call drawing economic researchers to the analysis of Social Security reform proposals, and it anticipated the very active policy debate of the last half decade.

Feldstein has had more than 60 Ph.D. students at Harvard, and has been President of the National Bureau of Economic Research, since 1977. In 1992, he was elected President of the American Economic Association.

Regarding his research on American health care, he observes that

> there was a dynamic in which the higher the price, the more insurance you wanted, and the more insurance you had, the higher the equilibrium market price . . . my estimates implied that the existing system was on an explosive path in which some exogenous force would be needed to stop the rise in the relative cost of hospital care . . . more co-payment and deductibles would make the health care market work better.

When asked about his time as Chairman of the Council of Economic Advisors in 1982–84 under the Reagan administration, Feldstein comments that,

> it soon became clear that the budget deficit was going to be an enormous problem.

In this interview, you will also learn of Feldstein's weekly breakfasts with Paul Volcker.

10 Christopher A. Sims interviewed by Lars Peter Hansen

Chris Sims has been President of the Econometric Society and is a member of the National Academy of Sciences. His role in the development of multivariate time-series methodology is fundamental to modern econometrics.

In my opinion, one of the most brilliant publications in the fields of econometrics and statistics is Sims (1971). About that paper, Sims states the following:

> Since the work on infinite-dimensional spaces was technically beyond what was appearing in economics journals, I sent Sims (1971) to the *Annals of Mathematical Statistics* . . . the editor wrote, "Sorry it's taken so long. I had a hard time finding any referees. Here's a referee report." The referee report said, "I really don't understand what this paper is about, but I've checked some of the theorems and they seem to be correct, so I guess we should publish it."

Among his other comments on applied econometrics are the following:

> . . . specifications in which responses to what are purported to be monetary policy shocks are clearly ridiculous, tend not to be reported. This informal aspect has bothered some people.

He also says,

> I argue . . . that econometricians have failed to confront the problems of inference that are central to macroeconomic policy modeling.

Revealing his views on macroeconometric policy models, Sims states,

The models are now in a sorry state.

11 Robert J. Shiller interviewed by John Y. Campbell

Robert Shiller is known to almost everyone because of his famous popular book, *Irrational Exuberance*, which was astonishingly prescient about the stock market bubble that burst shortly after the appearance of the book. That book came out in March 2000, at the top of the market. As he explains in his interview, he "wrote that book at breakneck speed." In his interview, Shiller comments that the view that

> every movement in the stock market must have a rational foundation . . . is "one of the greatest errors in the history of economic thought."

He further comments on

> the expected present-value model for aggregate stock prices, that is egregiously wrong.

In his interview, you will learn about the influence on his thinking of his psychologist wife, Ginny, and her associates in psychology. On the general subject of the economics profession, Shiller comments that,

> Economists themselves are herd-like in their research directions, and so there is a lot to be gained by staying away from these common topics.

12 Stanley Fischer interviewed by Olivier Blanchard

Stanley Fischer has been Governor of the Bank of Israel since May 2005. He was interviewed by Olivier Blanchard, Professor of Economics at MIT. The interview was completed while the two of them were running together in Central Park, New York. Stanley Fischer was previously Chief Economist at the World Bank, First Deputy Managing Director of the International Monetary Fund, President of Citigroup International, and Professor of Economics at MIT. According to Olivier Blanchard, Stanley Fischer, while a professor at MIT, had "acquired near-guru status," and now has become "a Master of the Universe, and world VIP." In his interview, you will learn about Stanley Fischer's youth in Southern Rhodesia, now called Zimbabwe.

Included among the statements in his interview is the following:

> When I was in high school, Dag Hammarskjold was this great man. Then he was killed in the then-Belgian Congo, right next door. I knew he had done good in the world and my parents had brought me up to believe I should do good in the world. I realized that economics would help you do good . . . That factor was probably there and moved me over the course of time.

13   Jacques Drèze interviewed by Pierre Dehez and Omar Licandro

Jacques Drèze is one of Europe's most famous and deeply respected economists. Having received his Ph.D. from Columbia University in 1958 and being a founder of Belgium's eminent economics research center, the Center for Operations Research and Econometrics, his insights into the evolution of economic thought, and of his own contributions therein, span both sides of the Atlantic. He has received 15 honorary doctorates from universities on both sides of the Atlantic. From this interview, you can learn about the Louvain Bayesian School, the Belgian –French research on general equilibrium under price rigidities and quantity rationing, and other areas of economic research and policy less well known in the U.S. than in Europe.

Of particular interest is his commentary on the difference in policy influence of economists in the U.S. versus those in Europe. On that subject, he observes:

> It is indeed the standard view that economists are less influential in Europe than in the United States. Two comments on that issue. First, in Europe there is no economic authority comparable to the U.S. government. Why? Because Europe is a Union, a confederation of states, so the prerogatives at the level of the Union are limited; the decision process at that level is complicated and carries limitations. Economic advisers to the Commission are remote from the decision-making body, namely the Council of Ministers. In contrast, in the United States, the chief economic adviser attends the meetings of the cabinet where the decisions are made. So, there is no chain of communications; the economic adviser is right there. In addition, the cabinet in the United States has much more direct authority than the Council of Ministers in Europe. In that sense, there is much less influence of economic advisers on policy decisions in Europe than in the United States.

14   Thomas J. Sargent interviewed by George W. Evans and Seppo Honkapohja

As Samuelson's book, *Foundations of Economic Analysis,* mathematized neoclassical microeconomics and educated a generation of economists in rigorous microeconomic analysis, Sargent's books mathematized modern macroeconomics and educated a generation of economists in rigorous macroeconomic analysis. In keeping with the deep insights evident in all of his published research, his interview is penetrating.

For example, on the evolution of calibration methodology in empirical economics and its relationship with formal statistical theory, Sargent observed the following:

> Calibration is less optimistic about what your theory can accomplish, because you'd only use it if you didn't fully trust your entire model, meaning that you think your model is partly misspecified or incompletely specified, or if you trusted someone else's model and data set more than your own. My recollection is that Bob Lucas and Ed Prescott were initially very enthusiastic about rational expectations econometrics. After all, it simply involved imposing on ourselves the same high standards we had criticized the Keynesians for failing to live up to. But after about five years of doing likelihood ratio tests on rational expectations models, I recall Bob Lucas and Ed Prescott both telling me that those tests were rejecting too many good models. The idea of calibration is to ignore some of the probabilistic implications of your model, but to retain others. Somehow, calibration was intended as a balanced response to professing that your model, though not correct, is still worthy as a vehicle for quantitative policy analysis.

He continues that,

> In the 1980s, there were occasions when it made sense to say, "It is too difficult to maximize the likelihood function, and besides if we do, it will blow our model out of the water." In the 2000s, there are fewer occasions when you can get by saying this.

Regarding Neil Wallace, Sargent observes:

> Neil thinks that cash-in-advance models are useless and gets ill every time he sees a cash-in-advance constraint. For Neil, what could be worse than a model with a cash-in-advance constraint? A model with *two* cash-in-advance constraints.

Sargent further observes,

Except for our paper on commodity money, not our best in my opinion, Neil asked me to remove his name from every paper that he and I wrote together.

Of course Neil's name was not removed from all those papers, Sargent said the following about the introduction to one of the papers that they did coauthor:

After he read the introduction to one of our *JPE* papers, Bob Lucas told me that no referee could possibly say anything more derogatory about our paper than what we had written about it ourselves. Neil wrote those critical words.

15 Robert Aumann interviewed by Sergiu Hart

Robert Aumann won the Nobel Prize in Economics in 2005, while a professor at the Hebrew University of Jerusalem, one month before his interview appeared in *Macroeconomic Dynamics*. Aumann is widely viewed as one of the world's most brilliant mathematicians, at the forefront of advances in economic game theory. Born in Germany and educated in America, he is an Israeli who is deeply orthodox in his Jewish religion. His doctorate is in algebraic topology from MIT, and his postdoc was at Princeton. In his interview, he explains that his

interest in mathematics actually started in high school—the Rabbi Jacob Joseph Yeshiva (Hebrew Day School) on the lower east side of New York City . . . I did a bit of soul-searching when finishing high school, on whether to become a Talmudic scholar, or study secular subjects at a university. For a while I did both. . . . I did this for one semester, and then it became too much for me and I made the hard decision to quit the yeshiva and study mathematics.

About his study and research as a Ph.D. student at MIT, Aumann observes:

. . . like number theory, knot theory was totally, totally useless. So, I was attracted to knots . . . Fifty years later, the "absolutely useless" —the "purest of the pure"—is taught in the second year of medical school.

He reveals the following about a conference in 1961:

Kissinger spoke about game-theoretic thinking in Cold War diplomacy
. . . People were really afraid that the world was coming to an end.

Regarding the Cuban missile crisis, Aumann states,

Kennedy was influenced by the game-theoretic school . . . Kissinger and
Herman Kahn were the main figures in that. Kennedy is now praised for
his handling of that crisis; indeed, the proof of the pudding is in the eating.

On the subject of "rationality," Aumann comments,

One big mistake is to say that war is irrational. . . . We take all the ills of the
world and dismiss them by calling them irrational. They are not necessarily
irrational. Though it hurts, they may be rational. Saying that war is irrational may be a big mistake . . . If we simply dismiss it as irrational, we
can't address the problem.

In reply to a question about religion, Aumann states,

Religion is very different from science. The main part of religion is not about
the way that we model the real world . . . Religion is an experience—mainly
an emotional and esthetic one . . . When you play the piano, when you climb
a mountain, does that contradict your scientific endeavors? . . . It doesn't
contradict; it is orthogonal . . . in science we have certain ways of thinking
about the world, and in religion we have different ways of thinking about
the world. Those two things coexist side by side without conflict.

In an interesting commentary on his move with his family out of
Germany in the 1930s, Aumann explains:

We got away in 1938. Actually we had planned to leave already when
Hitler came to power in 1933, but for one reason or another we didn't.
People convinced my parents that it wasn't so bad; it will be okay, this
thing will blow over. The German people will not allow such a madman to
take over, et cetera, et cetera. A well-known story. But it illustrates that
when one is in the middle of things, it is very, very difficult to see the
future. Things seem clear in hindsight, but in the middle of the crisis, they
are very murky.

By analogy, Aumann similarly comments on the Six-Day War in 1967:

In hindsight it was "clear" that Israel would come out on top of that
conflict. But at the time . . . it wasn't at all clear that Israel would
survive . . . Prime Minister Eshkol was very worried. He made a broadcast

in which he stuttered and his concern was very evident, very real . . . Herb Scarf was here during the crisis. When he left, about two weeks before the war, we said goodbye, and it was clear to both of us that we might never see each other again.

On another subject, he states,

I have serious doubts about behavioral economics, as it is practiced. Now, *true* behavioral economics does in fact exist; it is called empirical economics. This really is behavioral economics. In empirical economics, you go and see how people behave in real life.

16   James Tobin and Robert J. Shiller interviewed by David Colander

James Tobin won the Nobel Prize in Economics in 1981, while a professor at Yale. This joint interview of James Tobin and Robert Shiller at Yale was different from the others published in *Macroeconomic Dynamics* and was characterized as a "dialogue" rather than an "interview" in the journal. The other interviews were of one person and focused exclusively on the work and life of that one economist. This interview was in the form of a dialogue among two persons and a moderator on a particular topic, "The Yale School of Economics." While Tobin is clearly central to this dialogue, it is interesting to contrast Shiller's part of this interview with the interview of Thomas Sargent. While the Shiller and Sargent interviews are in many ways very different, both provide deep, penetrating, and clearly contrasting insights into modern macroeconomics.

In this dialogue, there seems to be more sympathy for the Milton Friedman version of the conservative "Chicago school" than for the more recent real-business-cycle approach. In response to the moderator's question, "How about the real-business-cycle theorists?", Tobin replies,

Well, that's just the enemy . . . That's what we've been fighting about all these years, and that's just a repetition of the conflict between Keynes himself and the economists he regarded as Classicals.

He continues,

The New Classicals and the real-business-cycle believers are much more extreme than the people that Keynes was arguing with in his day, but it's the same argument over again. Actually, Pigou was a much more reasonable, plausible economist than Lucas and some of the other New Classicals.

In Shiller's part of this dialogue, he says,

the Yale school must be thought of as politically much more liberal than the conservative Chicago school . . . What image do we have of Tobin? To me, he comes through as a very moral person and who has genuine sympathy for others. That means he sees what other people are suffering and he wants to correct that. You get that sense more from him than from very many economists.

James Tobin died in 2002.

NOTES

1. I wish to thank Bill Cooper, at the University of Texas at Austin, from whom I first got the idea for this book.
2. Interviews of statisticians can be found in the journal *Statistical Science*, and interviews of econometricians can be found in the journal *Econometric Theory*. But those interviews tend to focus on the more technical objectives of those two journals, rather than on the general evolution of economic thought.
3. In a letter to me, Paul Samuelson wrote that, "I never mind it when my prose targets the most erudite of those who read it. Robert Browning said, 'Ah, but a man's reach should exceed his grasp, or what's a heaven for?'" In that context, Paul explained that his Foreword, "on purpose . . . did not include the exact famous final words in *The General Theory*." Nevertheless, for the benefit of those who do not meet Paul's high standards of erudition, I here provide Keynes's (1936, pp. 383–384) statement, to which Paul alludes in his Foreword: "Practical men, who believe themselves to be quite exempt from any intellectual influences, are usually the slaves of some defunct economist. Madmen in authority, who hear voices in the air, are distilling their frenzy from some academic scribbler of a few years back. I am sure that the power of vested interests is vastly exaggerated compared with the gradual encroachment of ideas . . . Sooner of later, it is ideas, not vested interests, which are dangerous for good or evil."
4. An interesting contrast is Lucas's (2000, p. 279) more recent statement, "I share the widely held opinion that M1 is too narrow an aggregate for this period [the 1990s], and I think that the Divisia approach offers much the best prospects for resolving this difficulty."
5. There also is an online press report from the Royal Economic Society's *Economic Journal* at http://www.res.org.uk/society/mediabriefings/pdfs/1997/July/barnett.asp

REFERENCES

Barnett, W.A. (1984) Recent monetary policy and the Divisia monetary aggregates. *American Statistician* 38, 165–172. Reprinted in W.A. Barnett &

A. Serletis (eds.) (2000) *The Theory of Monetary Aggregation*, Ch. 23, pp. 563–576. Amsterdam: Elsevier.

Barnett, W.A. (1997) Which road leads to stable money demand? *The Economic Journal* 107, 1,171–1,185. Reprinted in W.A. Barnett & A. Serletis (eds.) (2000) *The Theory of Monetary Aggregation*, Ch. 24, pp. 577–592. Amsterdam: Elsevier.

Keynes, J.M. (1936) *The General Theory of Employment, Interest, and Money.* New York: Harcourt, Brace & World.

Lucas, R.E. (2000) Inflation and welfare. *Econometrica* 68(2), 247–274.

Sims, C. (1971) Distributed lag estimation when the parameter space is explicitly infinite-dimensional. *Annals of Mathematical Statistics* 42, 1,622–1,636.

History of Thought Introduction

Economists Talking with Economists, An Historian's Perspective

E. Roy Weintraub

The ambitious and long-running project initiated by William A. Barnett, Editor of *Macroeconomic Dynamics*, has produced a number of conversations in which eminent economists are interviewed by other economists well informed about the interviewee's work. What we have then is a collection of conversations about both economics and the economists' lives and about, in a larger sense, how a community of modern social scientists conducts its business.

The conversations are unusual records. Though they provide the reader with a privileged seat at conversations with the eminent, and they enhance our understanding of those eminences, they are not themselves a history of economics, even as the conversationalists appear to be talking over their shoulders to "the historical record." Yet there is a difference between what historians of economics consider to be historically useful and what their scientist–economist subjects find historically useful. The interviewees seek to construct a particular interested interpretation of the historical record, one in which they are featured,[1] and being interviewed by a former student or present colleague, senior or junior, accentuates this problem. I say "problem" because "scientists and historians tend to find different things interesting about the past, to want to use their history for different purposes, and to select their sources and write their accounts accordingly" (Hughes 1997, 26). This point is well understood by historians of science, and to a lesser degree by scientists themselves. It is not so well understood by most economists:

There are two principal issues of concern. First, there is the issue of contested interpretation and the difficulty of grounding historical analysis in the face of what might be a well-entrenched actors' history (and, indeed, in the face of potentially litigious actors) . . . [Second] there are those scientists who wish to retain such control over their history that they will not tolerate anything that departs from the "official" (heroic/celebratory/whiggish?) line. (ibid., 27)

Both these issues surface in the conversations. As an example of the former, consider the interchange in the Milton Friedman interview about his work during World War II as a member of the Statistical Research Group. Friedman there presents a view of the economists' ideas about optimization as having shaped the military's understanding, whereas many historians who write about that period see the cause–effect nexus reversed. And as an amusing (at least to me) example of the second, I note the place in the Paul Samuelson interview where he wonders whether his own understanding of his writings on some biological topics might be reinterpreted by "future Philip Mirowskis and Roy Weintraubs."

Noninterested conversations, though, may produce emotionally complex interview situations:

For some scientists, moreover, history is so valuable a resource that to write history which doesn't legitimate science in some way is actually seen as positively *de-legitimating*—in other words, as "undermining" science in some cases—which can generate a profound hostility toward professional historians of science and their writings. (ibid., 28)

We have some of these issues involved in the Robert Aumann interview, where it is noted that a lot of work in game theory was done as part of the Cold War enlistment of mathematicians and economists in that war. The hypothesis of the politically disinterested scientist–economist is falsified by such work, and in Aumann's case additionally by the connection of Israel's defense-military needs and its large number of game theorists, but these are questions that cannot be raised (especially by Hart, Aumann's former student) without its being said that such a line of questioning appears designed to "de-legitimize" some serious work in game theory.

As documents that form part of the historical record, the conversations collected in this volume share some features with more traditional oral history. But they do have their limitations:

In the mere act of historian meeting scientist, and making the scientist aware that his or her opinions and recollections will be preserved and may be exploited by future historians, scientists may be prompted to adopt a public image, even a mask, if you will, that reflects what do they want to have remembered about themselves, their life and their accomplishments. (DeVorkin 1990, 47)

Put another way, and with respect to the collection of conversations that follow, the fact that the materials were edited with the approval of (and in some cases rewritten by) the various subjects suggests that the economists themselves were effectively in charge of the interviews, and no material that undermined their own understandings of their work would be developed in the conversation.

Even with that in mind,

> Underneath the intensions of the scientists, memory is faulty to start with, and imperfectly designed questions posed by historians stimulate improper responses, and therefore falsely distorted visions of history. In fact, there is good reason to suppose that the mere act of asking a question influences a reply. It is not unusual to find that an historian, already deep into his or her subject, may have a broader and quite different perspective on a scientist's life and the scientist being interviewed, especially if that scientist did not work in isolation but within a larger structural or organization, as most do today. (ibid., 48)

What I am suggesting, of course, is that these conversations are proto-oral histories for the very obvious reason that, with two exceptions, they were not conversations conducted by historians in a standard oral history format. A feature of a conversation in which an eminent economist is interviewed by another well-known economist who has a direct familiarity with a subject area of the interviewee's work introduces various biases into the record. One difference, for example, between a historian interviewing a subject, and a colleague interviewing that same subject, is that the subject will likely assume that the historian does not have a detailed understanding of the particular ideas, topics, analyses that the subject believes are his or her own contribution. With a colleague, the interview subject is much more likely to move quickly over technical material, and is much less likely to attempt to justify, let alone explain, an interest in working with that material in the first place.[2] Thus in reading the conversations it will become more difficult for a nonspecialist reader to understand the intricacies of what might appear to be a code-laden discussion between two colleagues than would be the case were that discussion conducted by a historian. Moreover, the questions that the historian would wish to address are seldom similar to the questions about which an economist would seek illumination.

It is for this reason that the extensive record of the development of modern physics has been put together not by physicists but by the American Institute of Physics Center for the History of Physics in New York. This long-running program has its transcribed interviews on deposit at the Niels Bohr Library of the AIP in New York City. This project is conducted by professional historians, all of whom are specially trained as oral historians; and because of the cross-connections of the interview subjects and the work they did, those historians are fully informed about the nature and scope of the interviewees' work.

We have no such organization in economics.[3] The work of historians of economics is carried out by "lone" individuals, and there is no funding source available to sponsor such a large project. Instead, the historians who do conduct interviews prepare as best they can by studying reports about what constitute good oral histories, and perhaps consulting one of several manuals on how to conduct an oral history in the history of science—see, for example, DeVorkin (1990) and Everett (1992).

The conversations in this volume were not done in such a unified fashion: the editor did not require the interviewers to attend "oral history school"; nor did he require their accounts to be homogenized in the same way that the accounts done by the AIP reflect a particular set of questions that are asked of all subjects, albeit with flexibility to move off those topics as the interview develops.

This tension between scientists as historians, and historians of science is nicely described by Stephen Brush (1995), who points out that the conflicts range all the way from the belief among some historians that scientists are incapable of historical writing because of the necessary "presentism" and whiggishness, to the view of some scientists that only those who have participated in the construction of science have the competence to evaluate that which is important for the historical record. This position was starkly presented by Andre Weil (1978), the distinguished mathematician, who argued in a plenary lecture at the World Congress of Mathematics that, "The craft of mathematical history can best be practiced by those of us who are or have been active mathematicians or at least are in close contact with active mathematicians" (440).

However, the instincts and socialization of economists and historians of economics lead them to ask different kinds of questions about the past. Most economists will see the development of economics as a sequence of problems thrown up either by the world, called the economy, or by the development of tools, techniques, and theorizations. That is, most economists see economics as a problem-solving activity and the history of economics as a sequence of problems posed, solved, re-described, and further re-posed and resolved. For them, the economist is a figure who is trained and socialized to recognize these economic problems and to operate in a world in which framing and solving such problems defines the profession of economists. Certainly in the interviews that follow we hear the interviewer asking about the origination of a particular problem, and the mindset and tools that were necessary to solve that problem which represented the contribution of the interviewee. The interviewers and the interviewees are in effect acting as economists, collaborating by stabilizing the community's understanding of the emergence of the problems, and the development of the tools and expertise that were needed to solve them. Topics like the interviewees' education, professional working environment, and so on are all associated with constructing the interviewee as well placed both intellectually, and emotionally, to answer the particular questions that the economy and the economic profession "put on the table." This is fully consistent with a writing of the history of economics that historians have called OTSOG-ery, an acronym for "On the Shoulders of Giants," reflecting the apocryphal statement by Isaac Newton that he could see farther, do better science, because he stood on the shoulders, and so on. This perspective is widely shared among scientists and is reflected in the process and result of the awarding of the Nobel Memorial Prize in Economic Science, where the award citations speak of specific contributions. Thus it is the contributions that are the focus of the discussion and the contributors are in effect "channeling" the contribution to the larger economic community.

It should be apparent, however, that the historian's interest is different.[4] For historians, context is everything, so they would treat the conversations as partial source material of some limited use in constructing a serious history. The historical narrative is not a succession of this, then that, then that, then that. Rather, it is an interweaving of many stories in a tapestry involving the local, and contingent, in a contextualization of all the this-s and that-s. The historian is interested in a larger story, a more multi-layered story[5] than "I came, I saw the problem needed to be solved, I figured out the way to do it."

Let me now look more directly at the conversations to suggest how the particularities of these individuals and their experiences connect to some larger narratives that historians of economics have been developing over the past couple of decades.

First, it should be recognized that Samuelson, Friedman, Leonteif, and Modigliani are of a different generation from most of the other interviewees. These individuals came of age intellectually from the late 1930s through the 1940s. That period saw the two most important contingencies for the development of economics in the twentieth century, the Great Depression and World War II. (James Tobin, just a few years younger, likewise might be associated with this group.)

Historians now are coming to understand that the story of the development of neoclassical economics as a progressive march, from the marginalist revolution of the late nineteenth century to today, is a fiction. It is especially a fiction with respect to economics in the United States. A number of recent studies have demonstrated quite convincingly to historians that what emerged as neoclassical (mainstream) economics in the postwar period was but one of a number of different approaches to doing economics (see Morgan and Rutherford 1998; Weintraub 2002; Mirowski 2002; Yonay 1998). It was not simply that institutionalism, an American kind of economics, was gradually pushed out by neoclassical economics but, rather, there were a number of variants of neoclassical economics all competing for economists' attention as late as the late 1930s. Moreover, the theoretical contributions of Keynes in his 1936 book were playing out side by side with a more general understanding that the policy recommendations that flowed from Keynes's general theory had been part of public policy discussions much earlier (Hutchison 1968; Davis 1971; Howson and Winch 1977).

But the development of economics is also a small part of a larger story, one in which, over the course of the twentieth century, economics became a scientific discipline in a very particular sense. The characteristic that most people think of when they associate economics with science involves the organized presentation of the core of the discipline, generally in a mathematical form. That is, individuals associate a science with various theories and laws that can be expressed mathematically, and that are derived from, or that confront, data that is separately generated although conceptually linked with the theories. Of course, much of economics does have this kind of resemblance to work done in other scientific disciplines. But the characteristics of a science, at least a developed science, go far beyond the way its "texts" appear. These days, one doesn't do an experiment in particle physics in one's basement lab. One doesn't attempt controlled fusion experiments out in the garage. Science is characterized by an enormity of scale, of funding, and of human numbers. It's a long way from a time when one could walk around a 1930s university campus and find the Chemistry Department sharing space with both the Economics Department and the French Department. If one looks around at a modern university, especially one engaged in biological science work perhaps connected to an academic medical center, one sees how the scale has changed. We think of the Manhattan Project and understand the origins of "big science," but it is not often appreciated just how the scale of "doing economics" has changed as well since World War II. These days, when many graduate Ph.D. programs admit from one to two dozen or more students annually, it is hard to look back and see that Ph.D. study before the 1960s was a very unusual activity. There were simply not many graduate students. But in the post-Sputnik era with more students, and more mentors for those students, specialization and the division of labor produced research done by "the labor group" at university X or "the public economics group" at university Y. Ph.D. students are products of these groups much as Ph.D. students in the sciences come from Professor X's lab or that of Professor Y. Generally gone are the days when an economics professor might supervise dissertations from many different areas over the course of a decade. That doesn't happen anymore, just as a theoretical physicist these days does not supervise an experimental dissertation.

Big science emerged during World War II with the immense activity of building the atomic bomb, and the direct engagement of scientists in the war effort. Aircraft design and production, radar, sonar, guidance systems, computation systems, all emerged in that war time period through the collaboration of scientists, engineers, military planners and strategists, and social scientists, particularly economists. The kinds of tools and symmetries in analysis that Samuelson had explored in his prewar doctoral dissertation were fully in play during the war as optimization analysis became central to the work of the research groups involving economists linked by the Applied Mathematics Panel to the RAD Lab at MIT, the Statistical Research Group at Columbia, and the soon to emerge RAND in Santa Monica. It is not just that economics became more scientific through these interconnections but, rather, that science became more like what we now think of as science. The public relations call to continue public support of science at such a high (wartime) level was made by Vannevar Bush (1945) in his *Science: The Endless Frontier*,[6] but of course economics was on that frontier. That economics eventually was to partake of the largesse of the National Science Foundation was one result, as was the support of economists through the Army, the Air Force, and the Office of Naval Research.

In the conversations presented in this volume one does not find much of an emphasis on particular technical details, technical innovations and analysis, as much as a sense of the "rootedness" of the contributions in larger problems. Indeed, in the Leontief interview we find even a series of complaints about the increasingly technical nature of economic theory. Nevertheless, the technical details of economic analysis are not totally absent from the conversations. Listening in on the younger economists like Fischer and Cass and Lucas, we hear scientific–technical conversation, in which matters at issue are problems, and problems are meant to be solved. To some degree of course, this is a particularly American perspective. The career problems faced by Jacques Drèze and János Kornai are systematically quite different from those faced by economists working in the United States. Nevertheless, the perspective of this volume confirms that mainstream economics is pretty much an American invention, and has been sustained in its intellectual vigor by the American higher education system, specifically the rise of a large number of research universities in the postwar period. Though Volcker had long spells in government service, and in recent years Fischer has worked in the private sector, scientific economics is a university discipline, and is not simply something that, because of its public policy importance, is merely taught within universities. This of course reflects a change from earlier times. For what these conversations record are the careers of individuals who have made contributions to economic *research* and that research is the coin of the realm in particular academic communities. Teaching, mentoring graduate students, and developing new economic analyses for emerging economic problems are by and large activities that are carried out in universities, not in think tanks, and not in government agencies.

Yet another feature of these conversations that would interest historians is that while research in economics is carried on in universities, much of this research engages a larger public through the efforts of these very same researchers. It is as if the nuclear physicists took their concerns, at the same time they were scientifically active, to larger public discussions. Here particularly one needs to take note of the work done by Martin Feldstein at the National Bureau of Economic Research, and Paul Volcker in his many roles both in and outside of government. Kornai as well has important stories to tell about the connection between economics and politics, stories that are increasingly recognizable as it is understood by historians that the history of economics is not simply a recounting of how great ideas came to be understood and developed and promulgated, but how ideas moved across the boundaries of tightly organized professional communities into the larger community interested in economics. This is a story of the increasing importance of economists in public life, a process that was heavily influenced by Roosevelt's years and moved quickly in the 1940s with the creation of the Council of Economic Advisors following on the Employment Act of 1946. Historians have begun to see that the history of economics is not just the history told by the research scientists themselves, but it is a history of the import and impact of ideas (see Bernstein 2001).

In this passage of ideas, what is termed the transmission of economic knowledge, it is not only government and the military who are the receivers. There are also large numbers of foundations which have helped to support economics and economic research for particular purposes of their own, over a long period of time. The story of the Rockefeller Foundation's support of business-cycle research internationally in the interwar period is well known, and of course much of the modern work on business cycles, and indeed econometric models, dates from those years. The Volker Fund (not associated with Paul Volcker) in the 1940s supported the reconstruction of the University of Chicago Economics Department and helped *Capitalism and Freedom*'s author publish that volume; moreover, it provided the funding/impetus for Hayek's position at Chicago. All of which is a way of noting that economists' ideas ramify: as Keynes famously remarked, "indeed, the world is ruled by little else" (Keynes 1936, 383). And thus any enhanced understanding of the genesis of economists' ideas, as may be gleaned from the set of interviews collected here, should serve to make our world more comprehensible.

NOTES

1. This issue is readily apparent in an earlier collection of interviews of macro-economists, conducted by Arjo Klamer (1984) on the subject of what was called at the time the New Classical Economics, but which now is associated with Keynesian versus real-business-cycle approaches to macroeconomics.
2. I note that although both Perry Merhling and David Colander might be considered historians of economics, they each consider themselves to be primarily economists.
3. A partial exception involves the professional oral history interviews of economists who worked for various U.S. Presidential administrations. In this case, the historians at the National Archives often interview or supervise the interviewing of economists and place the tapes and transcripts in the appropriate Presidential Library. For instance, there is a set of interviews done in 1964 and recorded by Joseph Pechman (from the Brookings Institution) with Walter Heller, Kermit Gordon, James Tobin, Gardner Ackley, and Paul Samuelson for the Kennedy Library Oral History Program (Barber, 1975).
4. Although I will not develop the point here, I must note that the interviews generally restrict the development of the subject's autobiographical material to the circumstances of the economist's contributions *qua* economist. We thus do not find the usual recollection "bump" for memories of the early adult years (Weintraub, 2005).
5. For a fuller discussion of the alternative ways historians of economics might construct such histories, see Weintraub (1999) and Weintraub (2002, pp. 256–272).
6. I note, from the Samuelson interview, his particular connection to the Bush report.

REFERENCES

Barber, W.J. (1975) The Kennedy years: purposeful pedagogy. In C.D. Goodwin (ed.), *Exhortation and Controls: The Search for a Wage–Price Policy 1945–1971*. Washington, D.C.: The Brookings Institution

Bernstein, M. (2001) *A Perilous Progress: Economists and Public Purpose in Twentieth-Century America*. Princeton, NJ: Princeton University Press.

Brush, S.G. (1995) Scientists as historians. *Osiris* 10, 215–231.

Bush, V. (1945) *Science: The Endless Frontier*. Washington, D.C.: Government Printing Office.

Davis, J.R. (1971) *The New Economics and the Old Economists*. Ames, IA: University of Iowa Press.

DeVorkin, D.H. (1990) Interviewing physicists and astronomers: methods of oral history. In J. Roche (ed.), *Physicists Look Back: Studies in the History of Physics*, pp. 44–65. Bristol and New York: Adam Hilger.

Everett, S.E. (1992) Oral History: Techniques and Procedures, U.S. Army Center for Military History; available at www.army.mil/cmh-pg/books/oral.htm

Gaudillière, J.-P. (1997) The living scientist syndrome: memory and history of molecular regulation. In T. Söderqvist (ed.), *The Historiography of Contemporary Science and Technology*. Amsterdam: Harwood Academic Publishers.

Howson, S. & D. Winch (1977) *The Economic Advisory Council, 1930–1939: A Study in Economic Advice During Depression and Recovery*. Cambridge, U.K.: Cambridge University Press.

Hughes, J. (1997) Whigs, prigs, and politics: problems in the contemporary history of science. In T. Söderquist (ed.), *The Historiography of Contemporary Science and Technology*. Amsterdam: Harwood Academic Publishers.

Hutchison, T.W. (1968) *Economics and Economic Policy in Britain, 1946–1966: Some Aspects of their Interrelation*. London: George Allen & Unwin.

Keynes, J.M. (1936) *The General Theory of Employment, Interest, and Money*. New York: Harcourt, Brace & World.

Klamer, A. (1984) *Conversations with Economists*. Totowa, NJ: Rowman & Allanheld.

Kragh, H. (1987) *An Introduction to the Historiography of Science*. New York: Cambridge University Press.

Mirowski, P.E. (2002) *Machine Dreams*. Cambridge, MA: Harvard University Press.

Morgan, M.S. & M. Rutherford (eds.) (1998) *From Interwar Pluralism to Postwar Neoclassicism*. Durham, NC: Duke University Press.

Weil, A. (1978) *History of Mathematics: Why and How*. International Congress of Mathematicians, Helsinki, Academia Scientiarum Fennica.

Weintraub, E.R. (1999) How should we write the history of twentieth century economics? *Oxford Review of Economic Policy* 15(4), 139–152.

Weintraub, E.R. (2002) *How Economics Became a Mathematical Science*. Durham, NC: Duke University Press.

Weintraub, E.R. (ed.) (2002a) *The Future of the History of Economics*. Durham, NC: Duke University Press.

Weintraub, E.R. (2005) Autobiographical memory and the historiography of economics. *Journal of the History of Economic Thought* 27(2), 1–11.

Yonay, Y.P. (1998) *The Struggle over the Soul of Economics: Institutionalist and Neoclassical Economics in America between the Wars*. Princeton, NJ: Princeton University Press.

The Interviews

1

An Interview with Wassily Leontief

Interviewed by Duncan K. Foley

BARNARD COLLEGE OF COLUMBIA UNIVERSITY

April 14, 1997

Wassily Leontief is one of the central creators and shapers of twentieth-century economics. He invented input–output theory and the techniques for constructing input–output tables from economic and technological data and was responsible for making input–output tables the most powerful and widely used tool of structural economic analysis. The theory of input–output matrices played an important role in the clarification of general equilibrium theory in the 1940s and 1950s as well. Leontief has also made fundamental and seminal contributions to the theories of demand, international trade, and economic dynamics. His research interests include monetary economics, population, econometric method, environmental economics, distribution, disarmament, induced technical change, international capital movements, growth, economic planning, and the Soviet and other socialist economies. Leontief has played a vigorous part in formulating national and international policies addressing technology, trade, population, arms control, and the environment. He has also been a well-informed and influential critic of contemporary economic method, theory, and practice. Leontief received the Nobel Memorial Prize for Economics in 1973.

I met Wassily Leontief on April 14, 1997, at his apartment high above Washington Square Park in New York City. Leontief reclined on a sofa in the living room, with Mrs. Leontief going about her business in the

Reprinted from *Macroeconomic Dynamics*, 2, 1998, 116–140. Copyright © 1998 Cambridge University Press.

Figure 1.1   Wassily Leontief.

background, occasionally asking after Leontief's comfort. Leontief's voice on the tape ranges from an assertive *forte* to a whispery *piano*. He is by turns animated, thoughtful, puzzled, inspiring, and charming. A chiming clock marking the passage of quarter-hours and characteristic New York street noise occasionally obscure his words on the tape. I have edited the transcript for continuity and clarity.

Foley: There has been considerable discussion about the relation between input–output analysis and Marx's schemes of reproduction from Volume II of *Capital*. What was the role, if any, of Marx in your education as an economist? Were Marx's schemes of reproduction an inspiration or influence on your development?

Leontief: I did my undergraduate work in Russia, and that's where I learned Marx, but I am not a militant Marxist economist. When I developed input–output analysis it was as a response to the weaknesses of classical–neoclassical supply-and-demand analysis. It was terribly disjointed essentially, I always thought. You read my Presidential Address, I think? I felt that general equilibrium theory does not see how to integrate the facts and I developed input–output analysis quite consciously to provide a factual background, to register the facts in a systematic way, so it would be possible to explain the operation of this system.

Foley: So, did the structure of Marx's schemes of reproduction play any role in forming your ideas?

Leontief: No. Not really. No. Marx was not a very good mathematician. He was always mixed up in math, and the labor theory of value didn't make much sense, but essentially I interpret Marx and am interested in Marx only as a classical economist. And it is possibly Quesnay, the ideas of Quesnay, that influenced me. It is very difficult to say what influenced you. I got my training as an economist as an undergraduate. Already I read systematically all economists beginning with the seventeenth century. I just read and read, so I had a pretty good background in the history of economic thought, and my feeling is that I understand the state of the science.

Foley: You were in the Soviet Union in the very first years of the Soviet experiment?

Leontief: I left the Soviet Union in 1925. I got in trouble with the government, actually. I had to go away in order to be able to work.

Foley: Was anyone at that time thinking about a statistical basis for planning in the Soviet Union?

Leontief: No. The first thing which had some relation to it was essentially a national income analysis. Like all national income analyses, it was not very disaggregated. Everything gives you one figure, while I thought that to understand the operation of the system, one figure is not enough. You want to see how it disaggregates. I was not interested in improving the system; I was just concentrating on understanding how it works. Of course, it's nice to understand before you improve, but my feeling is that to understand the economic system is the first job of the economist.

Foley: Then, in 1925, you moved to Berlin?

Leontief: To Berlin. I got my Ph.D. very quickly, and I had two professors. I was research assistant of Professor Sombart, who was a quite interesting historical economist, and Bortkiewicz, who was a mathematical economist. But Professor Sombart didn't understand mathematics.

Foley: Were they particularly interested in the statistical side of input–output tables?

Leontief: No, and economists in their empirical efforts must be factual. But there is a tendency to be abstract, theoretical, particularly among the better economists.

Foley: How long did you stay in Berlin?

Leontief: About two years. I got my Ph.D. very quickly. Then I was in the Institute for World Economics—a big Institute in Kiel—and I was invited to be a member of the staff, and this is essentially where I developed my idea of the input–output approach.

Foley: Were there other scholars at Kiel working on that general line, or anything related to that type of thing?

Leontief: No. I was isolated.

Foley: It must have been a tremendous job to do the statistical groundwork for input–output analysis.

Leontief: Yes, it was. I decided the only thing was practically to show how to do it, and I did this with one assistant. I was invited to the United States by the National Bureau of Economic Research. I received some foundation money and my assistant and I worked very hard, I mean, using all kinds of information—technological information, naturally, beginning with the Census. The U.S. Census was the best statistical record of an economy. From there I was invited to Harvard, where I spent 45 years. When the war began, interest in input–output analysis grew. I was kind of a consultant on economic planning. It was for the Air Force, which of course was very important during the war. The best input–output matrix was computed by the Air Force. They had also an input–output table of the German economy, because it enabled them to choose targets. Usually I'm not very pragmatic, but if you want to do something, you have to understand what you're doing, and for the Air Force that was the committed choice of targets and so on, so input–output analysis was very interesting to them.

Foley: What was your reaction to Keynes's work during the 1930s? Have you changed your mind since then?

Leontief: No, not at all. My attitude was rather critical because I felt that he developed his theory to justify his political advice. Keynes was more of a politician than an analyst. I never became a Keynesian, although I wrote some of the first criticisms of Keynes. If you look at my bibliography you'll find them. But I tried to do it systematically; that is, not so much the political side but just the approach, which was for me too pragmatic. Now, you improve the system, all right, but first describe the system in order to improve it.

Foley: Did you have an alternative theory of the Depression at that time?

Leontief: No. My feeling is that the fundamental theoretical understanding of economic fluctuations is as a dynamic process. I still believe, what explains the fluctuations of economies is some kind of difference, differential equations. Of course, structural change is very important, particularly now. It's always dynamic. It's a system of interrelationships, a system of equations, but still the quantitative approach is important. Since I paid so much attention to the relationship between observation and theory, at the same time I developed a theory of input–output analysis which is really mathematical, and tried myself to collect data. I think I influenced the course of economic statistics.

Foley: Yes. Input–output analysis and national income analysis are the two major systems that came into place in the 1940s and 1950s.

Leontief: Right. I don't think there is really a dichotomy. I think input–output analysis is just much more detailed. Stone, for example, who was commissioned to develop the statistical economic system for the United Nations, assigned a very great role to input–output analysis, as a foundation for the aggregation to national income.

Foley: In a system of that kind, there's usually some attempt to model both supply-side effects and demand-side effects.

Leontief: I was always slightly worried about having demand analysis as a separate thing. My feeling is that households are an element of the system. In a good theoretical formulation, households are just a large sector of the economy.

Foley: This echoes the classical idea that the reproduction of the population is an aspect of the reproduction of the economic system.

Leontief: Exactly. This goes back to Quesnay.

Foley: I've also talked with Richard Goodwin about this theme of the interplay between structural change and fluctuations.

Leontief: Richard Goodwin was my student. He studied with me, he was my assistant. He couldn't get a permanent appointment at Harvard and then went to England. He was a good friend. He was very interesting.

Foley: I talked with Goodwin about this at one time. He did have a job at Harvard in the late 1940s, but it was an untenured job, right?

Leontief: Yes. He couldn't get tenure. And this was the reason why he went to England.

Foley: Yes, that's what he told me as well, but I was somewhat puzzled as to why someone who had been doing the kind of work he was doing in the late 1940s would not have been a shoo-in for tenure.

Leontief: I think possibly it was politics. He was on the left.

Foley: So that shaded the evaluation of his scientific work?

Leontief: Yes. That was it, frankly.

Foley: So you would still now look for the major cause of business-cycle fluctuations in lags, but the impulses in supply-side structural change?

Leontief: Yes, structural changes, but be very careful, because a system, a dynamic system, without structural change would have lags, and latent eigenroots that create fluctuations. Of course, at the present time, technological change is very important. Technological change is the driving force of economic change and the cause of social change.

Foley: To come to a slightly more technical issue, what about the question of whether the fluctuations are damped or undamped?

Leontief: They don't have from a mathematical point of view necessarily to be damped. This raises the problem, why don't we explode? And there are some forces which prevent them from exploding, including economic forces, such as policy and other nonlinear effects.

Foley: In the 1930s, you had a controversy with Marschak over demand analysis.

Leontief: Yes, now I do not remember the details, but I think there was a logical flaw in Marschak's position.

Foley: Did this have anything to do with the development of input–output analysis?

Leontief: That was already after I developed input–output analysis, which I really developed when I was in Kiel, and at the National Bureau. In the National Bureau, I was very subversive, because the National Bureau under Mitchell was extremely empirical, while I on the other side had a very strong theoretical intuition. To understand the process you have to have a theory. I organized an underground theoretical seminar in the National Bureau. It was underground, because it was against the principle of the National Bureau.

Foley: In the 1940s, there was a rather sharp controversy between the Cowles Foundation and the National Bureau around issues of empirical method and theory. Koopmans wrote a very sharp paper at that time.

Leontief: Since I thought mathematics plays a great, important role, I would of course be on the side of the Cowles Commission.

Foley: But you found yourself institutionally associated with the National Bureau.

Leontief: Exactly. Because I always felt, as I explained in my Presidential Address, if you want to really understand an empirical science, you must have the facts. And the problem is how to organize the facts. Essentially, theory organizes facts.

Foley: So your position was a kind of synthesis of these two points of view.

Leontief: Yes. Right.

Foley: The Cowles Commission developed a very characteristic approach to econometrics and measurement problems in the 1940s. Did you find yourself sympathetic to that way of doing it?

Leontief: No. I criticized it very early.

Foley: Did you foresee that there would be a role for input–output analysis in guiding government policy after the Second World War? This is an interesting period because it set the pattern for the next decades.

Leontief: Not only in government, but also in industry. I remember when the question arose much later about the position of the automobile industry in the American economy, there was some kind of association of industrialists who said "go to Leontief," because I published some work using the example of the auto industry. I published empirical work, and my principle always, though I could not always adhere to it, was always, when I made some theoretical observation to use the data—not just to say it, but really to see how it works.

Foley: And so you used input–output analysis, say, to study the future of the auto industry or prospects for specific industries?

Leontief: Right, right. During the Cold War, there was an economist by the name of Hoffenberg. He did a lot of empirical analysis. In constructing an input–output table of the United States, he played a very important role. He was a really excellent intuitive statistician. And, you must understand, it takes a particular knack to understand statistics. When I constructed the first input–output table, which was very early, I often used the telephone. I called up industries, particularly firms which were engaged in the distribution of commodities, and got the data from them.

Foley: So you would ask the distributors what their customers' proportions were in terms of the sectors?

Leontief: Exactly! I just went straight to them.

Foley: Did the U.S. government have a functioning input–output table in 1946?

Leontief: Yes, yes. In the Department of Commerce, in the Bureau of Economic Analysis. National income computations were conducted in the Bureau of Economic Analysis, and they had an input–output table. Although the best input–output table was constructed by the Department of Labor. Roosevelt's Secretary of Labor, Frances Perkins, wrote to me that the President had asked her the question, what will happen to the American economy after the war? She said, we don't know how to do it. We tried to look at the literature, but we don't know how to study this type of thing, and then one of my first articles appeared and they said, all right, we thought possibly you could tell us how to do it. They sent a representative, and I said, get the facts and good theory; and, as a matter of fact, at that time under Roosevelt the government was very active and intelligent. Yes, they told me, all right, collect the facts. Come to Washington and collect the facts. I said, no. One cannot collect facts in Washington. I must do it at Harvard. And they opened a division of the Bureau of Labor Statistics at Harvard, at the Littauer School, and I hired people, not many economists, mostly engineers, and we constructed an input–output table. The next detailed input–output table was constructed with the money of the Defense Department. And they had a lot. Without money it's very difficult to construct an input–output table; it's a resource-intensive activity.

Foley: After the war, was there a competition between Keynesian demand management and a more structurally oriented input–output approach to economic policy?

Leontief: Oh, I think the Keynesian approach definitely took over. I don't think there was much competition. Keynes took over.

Foley: Why did that happen?

Leontief: Because Keynes was very pragmatically oriented. In spirit, he was very much a politician, an excellent politician. I think he developed his theory essentially as an instrument to support his policy advice. He was incredibly intelligent.

Foley: Well, it sounds as if you had your political contacts, too, in the Labor Department and the Defense Department, and the Commerce Department.

Leontief: Oh, yes, but you know it was different. It was much more modest. The Labor Department studied the problem of the supply of labor, different skills and so on. It was much more technical. They still have an input–output division in the Labor Department—the Bureau of Labor Statistics.

Foley: The late 1940s, as we look back on it, seems to be the time when a methodological synthesis took place in economics. How did you view the relation of input–output to the developing methodological consensus in economics and econometric theory? Did you see it as part of it or as a different path?

Leontief: You see, I was somewhat skeptical of the whole curve-fitting notion. I thought of technological information. The people who know the structure of the economy are not statisticians but technologists, but of course to model technological information is very difficult. My idea was not to infer the structure indirectly from econometric or statistical techniques, but to go directly to technological and engineering

Figure 1.2 Members of Professor Leontief's seminar of the August 1948 Salzburg Seminar in American Studies. 1, Friedrich G. Seib (Germany); 2, Bjarn Larsen (?) (Norway); 3, Helge Seip (Norway); 4, Leendert Koyck (?) (Holland); 5, Gérard Debreu (France); 6, Paul Winding (Denmark); 7, Robert Solow (U.S.A.); 8, Mrs. Robert Solow (U.S.A.); 9, Mario Di Lorenzo (Italy); 10, Arvo Puukari (Finland); 11, Jacques D. Mayer (France); 12, Odd Aukrust (Norway); 13, Professor William G. Rice (U.S.A.); 14, Joseph Klatzmann (France); 15, unknown (Germany); 16, Bjarke Fog (Denmark); 17, Professor Leontief Wassily (U.S.A.); 18, Per Silve Tweite (Norway).

sources. I had some proposals to this effect, which could not be realized because there was no money. Empirical analyses are extremely expensive.

Foley: And the input–output type is more expensive than the indirect statistical investigation.

Leontief: Oh yes, much more. It was indirect statistical methods that were used. I think I have a very strong theoretical streak. I am essentially a theorist. But I felt very strongly that theory is just construction of frameworks to understand how real systems work. It is an organizing principle, while for many economists theory is a separate object.

Foley: Some economists think of theory as predictive or behavioral.

Leontief: Yes. I think if one knows, or one agrees, what the formal nature of a mathematical system is, one can do certain predictions because of the general nature of the system. I published a couple of articles on prediction. There are short-run problems and long-run problems in quantitative analysis, and I have a feeling that conventional prediction is good for short-run problems; but technological change, which is the driving force of all economic development, is a long-run process.

Foley: So, from this point of view, specific hypotheses about human behavior, or expectation formation, or preferences would play a subsidiary role.

Figure 1.3 Joseph Schumpeter, Wassily Leontief, and Paul Sweezy at Harvard in the late 1940s.

Leontief: A subsidiary role. I think so, because my feeling is that, particularly under a market system, a capitalist system, the big industrialists play a really big role, and they try to make profits, to choose technologies which maximize profits—essentially in the short run. Of course, national policy has to be taken into account, but business is certainly a short term type of system.

Foley: In sectors like transportation or power generation where you have long-term investments, this can create problems.

Leontief: I agree. There you need long-run engineering, power generation, and—I suppose—environment, which is important now.

Foley: You talked about the money and resource problem. Was there a competition for resources between national income approaches and input–output approaches in the United States during the 1950s?

Leontief: I have a feeling that, at least in the Department of Commerce, they realized input–output was very useful for national income computations. As a matter of fact, there was a period of time—possibly even now—when the national income computation essentially summarized the results of the input–output analysis. Funding is always a problem. For input–output analysis, particularly analysis of technological change, we need more of an engineering understanding, because scientific progress is now the driving force in technological change.

Foley: Do you see any feedback in the other direction, to the priorities in scientific research from economic bottlenecks?

Leontief: Oh, no doubt, no doubt. First of all, it was always true of the war industry. Scientific progress helped the military.

Foley: In the 1960s and early 1970s, there was another major change in economic doctrine, a shift from a Keynesian consensus to what's now called rational-expectations models and the notion of market clearing and perfect foresight. You were a professor at Harvard at that time. How did you see that happening in the profession? What factors determined that change?

Leontief: In the earlier times, Keynes dominated economic thinking. I do not know to what extent the whole expectations revolution made any headway. It is a very delicate thing mathematically, and I do not follow the literature closely now, but I think there was not so much analysis about expectations. There was just talk about it. I did not see any material contribution to the theory of expectations, except the very short run, naturally, for the business cycle, which is important.

Foley: So you don't think that was the result of any empirical superiority of this new approach?

Leontief: No, I don't think so.

Foley: Was it just that Keynesianism ran out of steam?

Leontief: I think so.

Foley: You said that you were not that taken with the Keynesian point of view to begin with, so I suppose you observed this with some equanimity.

Leontief: Yes. I'm not a monetary economist, but I think that deeper analysis of the flow of money might give a little more meat to this field.

Foley: There has been the development of the flow of funds accounts.

Leontief: Yes, but it was very aggregative. For our understanding how the economic system works, disaggregation is very important.

Foley: Would it make sense to try to link flow of funds with input–output analysis at the same levels of disaggregation?

Leontief: Oh, yes, but I didn't see anybody try to do it. Of course, there's no money there, but I think the money flows are important. I sometimes suggested the possibility of aligning money flows from micro up rather than from macro down, because I think in every corporation there is some high functionary who is in charge of money flows—budgets, credit, and so on—and he has to make a plan. The only planning that exists is for money flows, and there is his counterpart in a bank, who is close to operations and, if I'm not mistaken, there is a cooperation between the official in the company who sees to it that they have enough credit, and the credit manager in the bank, who is very often in charge of separate corporations. I made a couple of proposals to work on this. The interesting thing is to have the same figures from two points of view. It might be very helpful to understand how they interact to determine the short-run path of investment.

Foley: There's not been a lot of economic theorizing in that area. Most of the models assume some kind of equilibrium conditions, but you said that it was a mistake to start from equilibrium as opposed to explicit dynamics.

Leontief: Exactly, exactly.

Foley: When you resigned from Harvard in 1974, soon after you received the Nobel Memorial Prize, you sharply criticized the direction of economics as a discipline and called for a reevaluation and redirection of research methodology in economics. Do you think that redirection has taken place?

Leontief: No.

Foley: Would you have the same view on the success of economics as a science now?

Leontief: Yes. My feeling is we require patient, practical economic advice. Our basis of understanding how the economy works is not very strong. Practical advice could and should be more based on understanding how the system works.

Foley: We've mentioned several times this afternoon the role of mathematics. Some people argue that economics has become too dominated by mathematical formalism.

Leontief: I completely agree. Very many mathematical economists were simply mathematicians who were not good enough to become pure mathematicians, so mathematical economics, which had always been dull, gave them a marvelous pretext to become economists.

Foley: But on the other hand, you've strongly supported the role of mathematics in theory in economics. When is mathematics fertile and when does it become just a formalism?

Leontief: My feeling is that mathematics is simply logic. The general insights are the most important. For example, I think mathematics gives us good reason to feel that all fluctuations are due to lags—it's dynamics. This is a real mathematical insight. Mathematicians know it. As a matter of fact, one of the problems I had in my theoretical work was how to avoid explosive fluctuations, because there are so many eigenvalues in those big matrices, and some explode.

Foley: What was your own training as a mathematician?

Leontief: I took mathematics courses, but I tried to improve my range of mathematics very early, when I realized that mathematical argument was of great importance for economics. I read a lot. I took basic courses in the university. My tendency was always to combine the empirical and theoretical. In economics that combination requires mathematical concepts, such as systems analysis.

Foley: But you're also saying that the vision of the economic structure and relations has to come first.

Leontief: I think, together, because if we have only that vision, it never adds up to anything. When I developed input–output analysis before going to the National Bureau of Economic Research, I felt it terribly important to have a good insight into the mathematical relationships. I think that the mathematics which economics used are not of a particularly high order. For example, those who translated neoclassical economics into mathematics didn't develop any very interesting insights. They obviously developed some things, but didn't come to any very interesting insights into how the economic system works, and they were, on the whole, not interested in empirical analysis.

Foley: From having talked with other people about that, I think there were very high hopes that the formalization of economics would yield some substantive insights.

Leontief: Without data you couldn't do it. Absolutely, without data it couldn't work. It can just establish certain principles of equilibrium and nonequilibrium.

Foley: You think that more or less exhausted the real scientific contribution of the program?

Leontief: I think so. They would have made more progress if they really had good, very detailed, empirical information. For example, it would be very interesting to see how modern technological change has affected the demand for labor. It might reduce the demand for labor, and even create a social problem, because labor isn't just one more factor of production. Then you will have to support labor. My speculative intuition is that the government now has to support a large part of income through education expenditure, health expenditure, and of course social security—and possibly a kind of welfare—but social security is more important. My feeling is that ultimately the transfer of income so as to provide people money to buy consumers' goods will become part of social security. It's already very large—I'm amazed how large my family social security is.

Foley: This is a Keynesian theme, the support of demand through government subsidies.

Leontief: Yes, Yes, but it's not only supporting demand. Keynes was supporting employment, which this does not do. Just demand. You feed people. Technology will reduce employment, or certainly not increase employment. Certainly I think that technology competes with labor, ordinary labor. If you produce everything automatically naturally you're not going to employ so much labor.

Foley: So this is an example of your sense that there should be a substantive foundation for the investigation in the real structure of what's going on?

Leontief: Yes. Technological change was always the driving force for economic development beginning in prehistorical time, but now, when technological change has become propelled by scientific investigation, this type of analysis is extremely important. Economists attempted to do it, but mostly by making general statements. The moment energy becomes cheaper, technological change becomes important. Production now requires much more energy.

Foley: Do you think the establishment of the Nobel Memorial Prize in Economics has, on the whole, fostered a better atmosphere for research in economics?

Leontief: You know, there's a problem. I think they'll soon run out of candidates for Nobel Prizes in economics. I think we have already problems now.

Foley: Did the Nobel Prize have any particular impact on your work or your life as a scientist?

Leontief: On my life, some. Not on my work. Naturally, it was easier to get jobs. Not necessarily easier to get financing. Now, for example, I cannot get any financing. So, I suppose my academic life got easier, but, as I said, there is a problem how the Nobel committee can continue. I think they have already begun to shift from theoretical to institutional economists. Now there is a problem because in technical economics at least you can point out some hierarchy, and also major steps forward, breakthroughs, while in institutional economics I don't really see any large breakthroughs. As a matter of fact, I am concerned that economists are not sufficiently interested now in institutional changes brought about by the development of new technologies, which I think is definitely the driving force.

Foley: There's been a lot of discussion about whether economics should take any other science as its model, in particular physics or biology, and, if so, which one. Did you ever think in those terms, that economics should be like a physics of society or a biology of society?

Leontief: I think it doesn't help much. Naturally, mathematical economists like to look to physics. I think it was the Darwinian approach that was really interesting, and I think that in one way the great intellectual revolutionary was Darwin. Incredible revolution, not only in biology, but in the analysis of all living processes. I think Darwin—it was Newton and Darwin who I think were the great contributors to the understanding of social change. Darwinism is very important, although, of course, it is interesting that Darwin was influenced by Malthus. What are you interested in?

Foley: One of the things I've been spending some time on recently is evolutionary modeling of technical change. The issue of global warming evolves over the kind of very long timescale on which changes in technology will be decisive.

Leontief: Oh, yes. I completely agree. Technology is terribly important.

Foley: If you look over a shorter time horizon, substitution of existing technologies might be important, but I think over a long time period, it's going to be the direction of technological change, and the bias of technological change. The question is whether there's any way to control it.

Leontief: Exactly. Not necessarily consciously, but. . . . Now, of course, there is a much closer link between scientific change and technological change. One hardly even can visualize technological change without science, and, with global warming, these things are terribly important. And what can we do? We can do many things. Slow down, for one.

Foley: That's not popular in a world anxious to develop as fast as it can.

Leontief: It is remarkable how technologically backward many less-developed economies are. Once you begin to cut trees, you can do it very quickly.

Foley: If you were encountering a younger scholar who had some innovative but expensive idea like input–output, how would you recommend that person proceed?

Leontief: He has to publish something. I do not know who gets money nowadays. I haven't been following the development of the field recently. I'm, after all, over 90 years old, but, of course, big money is spent not on research, but on data collection. Some people have good ideas and can really do something with the data, but economics has come closer and closer to technology now. To exploit the influence of technological change on economic change, you just can't compute some supply curve; you must really have a mass of information. I wrote up how it can be done, and I nearly succeeded in getting money to do it. My feeling is one could even do some anticipation, prediction, if one had really detailed data. I got in touch with engineering societies, the society of mechanical engineers, and they were ready to provide information. I think this is the future of the work, in the interaction between economics and engineering, science, and the substructure of production.

Foley: Did you ever have any personal or scientific contact with Piero Sraffa, the Anglo-Italian who worked on linear models?

Leontief: No. I never met him. But I think he was a very interesting man. His vision was interesting. In general, I think the input–output analysis is not necessarily linear. I would interpret it as an outgrowth of neoclassical theory. Sraffa was interested in something slightly different, the indirect relationships. I don't insist on linear relationships, only I'm conscious of the fact that dealing with nonlinear systems is terribly complicated; and even in computations, what do mathematicians do? Linearize the system in pieces, and then put it together. This is the way most of us use mathematics in a field in which data is important.

Foley: I was going to ask you about the relationship between production-function analysis and input–output. Production functions seem to have taken over the economics of production.

Leontief: Oh, yes. The production function is too flexible. First of all, continuity is silly. I visualize different methods of production as cooking recipes, including even such things as temperature and so forth, and what must be known in order to be able to cook the dish. This approach might enable us to analyze technological change. The technological production function was essentially an attempt not to go into empirical analysis. You see, given production functions, you don't need that. You guess at a few parameters, instead of having to look in detail at what's happening, and if you try to generalize production functions, it's dangerous, very dangerous.

Foley: What are your thoughts on the advantages and disadvantages of linking sectoral and establishment- or firm-level data?

Leontief: I think the institutional organization of production through the establishment in some way reflects technology, but it is a very delicate situation, because it's not very simple, how economic activities are distributed to different human organizations. It has some relation to what is actually being done, but it's very delicate. Human organizations are very complicated. You can accomplish this linkage in some respects and not some other respects, but I agree with both approaches, particularly since the establishment is not enough. Even establishments are now institutional organizations.

Foley: One practical problem is that, as you disaggregate the input–output structure, you find that one firm begins to appear in several different sectors. This also touches on the theme you were talking about earlier of finance. Finance comes at the firm level.

Leontief: I completely agree, and here, we agree with the need for continuity. Institutional organizations change very easily. So far as top management is concerned, the firm doesn't reflect technology at all. You can have the same corporation making ice cream and making steel. This is, I think, unavoidable, but, possibly because of my interests, I would rather favor establishments first, and then corporations, because the establishment is a homogeneous concept. It is quite an interesting problem.

Foley: Where do you think the future of economics, and macroeconomics in particular, lies?

Leontief: I think problems of income distribution will increase in importance. As I mentioned before, labor will be not so important, and the problem will be just to manage the system. People will get their income allocated through social security—already now we get it through social security, and we try to invent pretexts to provide social security for people. Here, I think, the role of the government will be incredibly important, and those economists who try to minimize the role of the government, I fear, show a superficial understanding of how the economic system works. My feeling is, if we abolished the government now, already there would be complete chaos. Now, planning plays a role, naturally, but I don't emphasize just planning as a role for the government, which is I think extremely important, and its importance is bound to increase because of technological change. If one asks oneself, what will happen to the system if we abolished completely the government, it would be horrible.

Foley: But you think that's particularly true because of the pressures technological change in capitalism are putting on the social fabric, and a weakening of the nexus between labor and income?

Leontief: Oh yes. Absolutely. The labor market is not a sufficient instrument to move from production to consumption.

Foley: I'm just going to ask you one more question. You've been a lifetime participant observer in the subculture of American economics and the larger world of American science and politics. If you were an anthropologist, how would you characterize economists as a tribe or a culture compared to the physicists or biologists?

Leontief: It depends what economists you have in mind. Academic economists are just part of the academic establishment, but I suppose we economists are as indispensable as accountants. In managing a system, you have to have represented the point of view and principle which managers have, and economists are just a particular type of management, if you disregard academic economists, who are a special type.

Foley: Within academics, do you see any difference between economists and their counterparts in science or the engineers that you work with?

Leontief: You see different tendencies in economics. Some prominent economists have just proved a couple of theorems, or codified classical and neoclassical textbooks.

Foley: You're suggesting that economists value classificatory or formal contributions more than finding out something about the world itself?

Leontief: Yes. My observation was a critical one. Particularly since I am interested in society, I see economics as a social science. Certainly economists should contribute something to understanding how human society developed, and here, economists have to cooperate with anthropologists and others.

2

An Interview with David Cass

Interviewed by Stephen E. Spear

CARNEGIE MELLON UNIVERSITY

and

Randall Wright

UNIVERSITY OF PENNSYLVANIA

February 13, 1998

David Cass is undoubtedly one of the central contributors to modern dynamic economics. His fundamental contributions include work on optimal growth problems, overlapping-generations models, sunspot equilibria, and general equilibrium models with incomplete markets. His research has shaped in profound ways the manner in which we do both micro- and macroeconomics. From laying the foundations of real business-cycle theory via the Cass–Koopmans model, to providing us with general tools and techniques to analyze dynamic economic models, to furthering our understanding of monetary economics, to making fundamental contributions to the economics of extrinsic uncertainty, Cass's work has played a major part in the development of much of modern macroeconomic theory. In addition to being a first-class scholar, Cass is also truly his own man and a free spirit of the highest order.

In this interview, we tried to gain some insights into the story of David Cass and his approach to economic theory. Also, given the title as well as the intended readership of *Macroeconomic Dynamics*, we made a real

Reprinted from *Macroeconomic Dynamics*, 2, 1998, 533–558. Copyright © 1998 Cambridge University Press.

Figure 2.1 David Cass, June 3, 1994, on the occasion of receiving an honorary degree ("docteur ès sciences economiques honoris causa") from the University of Geneva.

effort to get him to discuss modern macroeconomics and the influence his work has had on its development. We edited out some parts of the discussion in the interests of space, but what remains is essentially unedited. As most readers will know, David Cass has collaborated extensively with Karl Shell over the years.

We met with Dave in his office at the University of Pennsylvania's Economics Department just before noon. Amid the boxes and piles of articles, books, and CDs, he sat in his standard jeans and T-shirt, looking about as disheveled as he usually does. We chatted there for a while, went out and continued over lunch, and then returned to complete the interview several hours later. It was an unseasonably warm day in February, and Friday the 13th to be exact. That is traditionally an unlucky day, but one that turned out in this case to be a real treat, at least for us! We hope that you get as much out of this conversation with Dave as we did.

MD (Macroeconomic Dynamics): Let's begin by talking about graduate school and your adviser, [Hirofumi] Uzawa. How did you first hook up with him?

Cass: Okay. I viewed Stanford's graduate program as being completely chaotic. I'll give you an example. The first year I went to Stanford, they had a qualifying oral in the first semester and everybody had realized that this was patently absurd. So they had abolished the requirement, but they'd scheduled the orals already, so they decided to hold them. My oral—and I didn't even know people on the Stanford faculty very well at the time—my oral was composed of Ken Arrow and somebody else. When I found out about Arrow, I was terrified. So I went in and Ken asked me a question and I gave some half-assed answer, and he has this capability of taking someone's answer and then reframing it in a way that makes a lot of sense. So, my qualifying exams consisted of my short responses to Arrow and then him elaborating to make sense of them.

But the point is, they had this requirement that they abolished but they scheduled, and that was typical. So basically, at Stanford you were kind of left on your own as a graduate student. There was just no coherence in the program. Now, I don't remember exactly how I first met Uzawa, but there was a mathematical economics group who had offices separate from the department in a little house on campus called Serra House, and that is where what I consider the really good people at Stanford were: Arrow, Uzawa , Scarf. We had other kinds of mathematical social scientists there. And somehow, Karl [Shell] knew about Serra House right away, and we had our offices there.

MD: Did you and Karl enter in the same year?

Cass: Yeah, and somehow Karl introduced me to Serra House. I don't remember how we got involved with Uzawa, but we just got involved with him. Maybe he ran a seminar or something. I don't really remember how we met, but it was clear that this guy was really into research and very good at directing people, so we hooked up with him. Then, the last two years at Stanford (I stayed four years), I basically spent at Serra House working with Uzawa. He always had seminars going. Uzawa, in my view, by conventional standards, is a terrible lecturer, but he is an awesome teacher. His greatest virtue is that when he lectures he shows you how he does research. If he doesn't prepare, he will tell you about a paper he is working on, and he gets up and basically re-creates the mistakes that he made and corrects them. He explains why he decided to do this and that, and it is just like you are taught by doing research.

So, I took a couple of courses from him and found them great, but from conventional standards they were probably a disaster. He taught econometrics, and he wanted to calculate some estimator, probably a limited information maximum likelihood estimator, but he didn't really remember anything about it. Half of the course consisted of Uzawa coming in and starting to prove a theorem about this estimator, and he would go on for about an hour or an hour and a half, and then he would realize that he had gone off on the wrong track again and he would say "Oh, sorry." Next time he would start up again—it was really incredible! But it was interesting. He has a really good mind for working from first principles and for working out how you solve a problem.

Uzawa was a marvelous person to work with. I model my career in terms of working with graduate students after the experience I had working with Uzawa. He treats them exactly as equals and he spends a hell of a lot of time one-on-one with them in all kinds of situations. Don't think it was only in the office—it could be going to a bar, or any of that. He just spent an enormous amount of time. Now Uzawa probably never read anything that I wrote. I am sure he didn't. But he always wanted to talk about it. He'd always force his students to deal with that, and he had a group of students in seminars, so that all the students knew what the other students were doing. Of course, we had a focused subject—growth theory and, more particularly, applications of a fancy version of the calculus of variations, the maximum principle, to growth models. So we all had a common background but, actually, that personal thing is one of the reasons I got into trouble with the Penn administration. One of the basic issues I had about dealing with graduate students here was that somehow the administration wanted me to distinguish very carefully between my professional activities and my social activities, and I told them that wasn't consistent with my idea of how you deal with graduate students, and it isn't. So this is all in response to the question of how did you meet Uzawa—and the actual details about meeting Uzawa I do not remember.

MD: Did you know that you wanted to do growth theory?

Cass: Not at all.

MD: What was your undergraduate training?

Cass: I was a joint Economics–Russian Studies major.

MD: Russian Studies?

Cass: Yeah. Very anomalous because languages were probably my weakest suit.

MD: Where was that?

Cass: The University of Oregon. I always thought that I was to become a lawyer because that's a tradition in my family. I spent a year at the Harvard Law School and hated every minute of it. I spent most of my time re-reading great Russian literature, and I learned how to answer exams just by deductive logic. I'd memorize a few definitions and go from there, which got me through. Then I went in the army and I decided that what I really wanted to do was to go back to graduate school in Economics, and I decided to stay on the West Coast. I was very lucky. I didn't know anything about graduate schools but it seemed like the major choices were Berkeley and Stanford. Just by chance I decided Stanford rather than Berkeley, and I think it was a hell of a good decision, because the faculty that I got inspired by are really world class.

MD: So why did you decide to go to graduate school in economics?

Cass: I liked economics, and I realized that my undergraduate degree was the tip of the iceberg. They were just barely getting into the use of equations in class and it was kind of fascinating to me—the idea of being formal about a social science.

MD: So you probably had very little mathematics training when you went to grad school.

Cass: I had virtually no math training. I had taken college trig, algebra, geometry, and that was it. In fact, I remember the first day of class at Stanford there was a guy teaching a macro course; his name was Bob Slighton. The first day of class he wrote down a general equilibrium model and decided that he was going to calculate a multiplier, which is just a derivative of the model. He filled the blackboard in the front of the room and the side of the room and I didn't understand a word of this. I knew what a derivative was but I didn't know what a partial derivative was. He was doing all this partial differentiation. Of course, in those days, in terms of partial differentiation, people didn't really understand what they were doing. They would write down differential forms, what in differential topology are called the tangent spaces, and they'd be dealing with calculus on manifolds but didn't really understand it. The technique was kind of incomprehensible.

I went home from that class and I said, "Well, you're not really prepared to sit in graduate classes in economics," so I basically re-registered for calculus and statistics and I think I sat through Slighton's class, which was excellent. The micro class was more problematic. It was taught by a guy named Melvin Reder, a labor economist, and he came in the first day of class and put his feet on the chalkboard and said something deprecating about economic theory, so I never went back. The first term I spent learning introductory calculus and probability theory. The probability theory was actually taught by a guy whom I later learned was a world-class probabilist. It was marvelous because he introduced everything via examples, and then you could study for the exam because you had a good feel for what probability theory was all about.

MD: Did you and Karl work together at Stanford?

Cass: No. One of the funny things about Stanford, and this may be true in other graduate programs too, they preselected people that they assumed were going to be stars. Karl was an undergraduate math major at Princeton who basically went to Stanford because he knew about Ken Arrow, and Karl was a preselected star. (He was not selected as top star of the class; I forgot the name of the guy who was, but he turned out to be a real bust.) Since I decided not to take economics the first year I was there, I really didn't have much to do with economics students, and I only got to know Karl probably toward the end of my second year. He introduced me to Serra House, and there Uzawa's students all worked together because we all knew each others' problems, so we could communicate very quickly. But none of us actually wrote papers together. Karl and I started collaborating on papers much later, in the early 1970s, but, again, Karl knew my thesis and I knew Karl's thesis throughout the whole development phase, so basically who contributed what to what as graduate students with Uzawa was always up in the air.

MD: And how were you led to your thesis topic?

Cass: Optimal growth? Well, it was basically the fascination Uzawa had with the maximum principle.

MD: What growth theory did you know before that?

Cass: At that period there was a distinction between what we wanted to do, optimal or prescriptive growth, and descriptive growth à la Solow. He wrote a ton of papers, starting with the very famous paper on the one-sector model, and then he wrote many others describing competitive growth models that had more goods, and maybe some specialized technology, and he kept repeating how you describe a competitive equilibrium and its efficiency properties (something Malinvaud did much more elegantly in his justifiably famous *Econometrica* paper). So that's descriptive growth theory. Then there was this famous paper by Ramsey, and Uzawa was clearly fascinated by two-sector versions of the neoclassical growth model. He wrote several papers on that. Then he decided to go into optimal growth theory and produced a paper which was essentially a two-sector model with a linear objective function. Basically, he re-created the calculus of variations himself—he is a very original guy—and then he discovered the maximum principle and became fascinated with it. Uzawa also gave a seminar on economic history in which he went back and took all the great names in economics, starting with Ricardo, Marx, . . . and reproduced what they were doing as a growth model. I was very influenced by Uzawa's work. I didn't even know about Ramsey at the time.

MD: That is interesting because sometimes one hears about Ramsey as this hidden classic. But didn't some people know about Ramsey? Didn't Uzawa?

Cass: No, I don't think so, because I didn't find out about Ramsey until after I had written the first chapter of my thesis on optimum growth. And then I was, to be perfectly honest, I was a bit embarrassed about it.

MD: How did you discover Ramsey?

Cass: I don't remember now. Maybe somebody mentioned it; maybe Uzawa knew about it, but not really, because he thought my contribution was absolutely seminal. In a way it is not at all. In fact I always have been kind of embarrassed because that paper is always cited although now I think of it as an exercise, almost re-creating and going a little beyond the Ramsey model.

MD: Ramsey had no discounting and you did have discounting. That's one difference, right?

Cass: Ramsey had no discounting. He made a big point of talking about the correctness of the social welfare function from a moral viewpoint, I believe, maybe in his side remarks. Tjalling Koopmans was very sensitive to this issue, too, when he wrote a paper of this sort. It turns out to be much harder to solve the problem with no discounting because, even if the objective is written as a function of a functional, it is not well-defined because it may be infinite-valued, and you have to use a trick to make sense out of it. You have to take the difference between utility of consumption and utility of the golden rule consumption so that you get a function that is well defined. As a technical aside, it is very interesting that the Ramsey problem is a counterexample to something which people now always do. I think they do it in macro without even thinking about it, when they do dynamic optimization, and they write down transversality conditions as necessary, which I also said something about in my thesis, and this is dead wrong. The Ramsey problem is a counterexample to this: You have an optimum, but it doesn't satisfy the transversality condition.

MD: Is this an issue only in the no-discounting case?

Cass: Yeah, that's in the undiscounted case. It has to do with the condition in capital theory that is called nontightness, which is a sufficient condition for the transversality condition to be necessary, and basically is an interiority condition that enables you to use a separating hyperplane theorem. Now I have forgotten what the original question was!

MD: How you came to the optimal growth problem.

Cass: Actually, even though Uzawa always went back and read literature and was always motivated by literature, I didn't pick that up from him at all; I just decided to work on this problem because the techniques were new and exciting and it seemed like an interesting problem. So I taught myself the maximum principle, some differential equations, and so on, by talking to people, seeing Uzawa working, and basically reading math books. Our bible at the time was Pontryagin's original book on the maximum principle. That is really interesting too, because that book is very geometric, and Pontryagin's blind.

MD: Was it in Russian? You would have had a natural advantage there.

Cass: I could have read a little bit of Russian, but it was translated. Anyway, he's blind, and yet all of his thinking is purely geometric; he pictures things. So I just put the two together, and then Uzawa thought this was great. I'm not sure why, I guess probably because Tjalling Koopmans was working on this problem and Tjalling was a bit of an idol for Uzawa. Actually, Uzawa liked to one-up people. At some point he was talking to Tjalling about the problem, and Tjalling was describing what he was doing and Uzawa interrupted and said, "Well, I have a graduate student who did that problem." Then Tjalling got very nervous about it, he was always very nervous about . . . , oh, authorship and who was first and that sort of thing, and we had some correspondence. Koopmans was also very interested in the no-discounting case, so he solved the much harder problem in some ways, in addition to solving the problem with discounting. Tjalling did all his analysis from first principles; he derived all of the conditions.

MD: Then you went on the job market.

Cass: I'll tell you a story about the job market that reflects the character, the idiosyncratic character, of Uzawa. Uzawa originally engineered for me to have a postdoc at Purdue, which was a pretty good department, but then he had contact with Koopmans at the Cowles Foundation, who were interested in doing some hiring. Uzawa decided that would be a better job, but his idea of supporting a student on the market was that it was immoral to have more than one offer. So I went to the winter meetings in Boston with just an interview with the Cowles Foundation, and a couple more that I had arranged that turned into disasters. I spent most of the time in the hotel room watching football, and I was rooming with Karl who had a million interviews! It came down to the last day of interviews and everything depended on my passing an interview with the Cowles Foundation, which was a lunch with Tjalling and Herb Scarf and I don't remember who else, very likely Jim Tobin. I talked a little about my thesis, but Tjalling already knew about it, and he decided to question me with "What will you be working on 10 years from now?" As with any graduate student, I couldn't even think two months ahead. I had no idea what I would be doing!

For some reason, they couldn't make me a regular appointment, and I remember Tjalling had obligated himself to make an appointment that it turned out he couldn't make, so he signed me as a research associate at the Cowles Foundation for one year, on a one-year appointment, with the promise that it would be extended and I'd become an assistant professor as well as research associate. You can't believe salaries in those days, even adjusted for inflation. My salary when I started was $8,000.

MD: Tell us about Yale.

Cass: Yale was a great postgraduate education. The Cowles Foundation, at that point, had a lot of money, and a policy of hiring or having in residence lots of junior faculty. The physical setting was in a separate building, in a separate little house. People like Tobin, in particular, really encouraged us. I really remember my days at Yale very fondly. When I was first there I talked a lot with Ned Phelps. Then of course I met Manny Yaari, and Manny and I talked a lot and ended up writing papers just based on these conversations. The consumption loan paper came about this way.

MD: And that was when you got into overlapping-generations models?

Cass: Yeah, overlapping generations was with Manny.

MD: Was the overlapping-generations model something many people were interested in then, in the late 1960s? Presumably not, since

Samuelson's paper was published in the 1950s and then sat there for a long time without attracting much additional attention.

Cass: Yeah, it sat there for a long time. The Cass and Yaari paper used to have a lot of cites, and I think the main reason for that was it revivified interest in the overlapping-generations model. That's not a paper that I think of as a great paper because we were really struggling. I don't want to be quoted on this, but in my opinion I don't think that there is much in that paper that survives.

MD: So you and Yaari were chatting about things and began talking about overlapping generations. Had you and Karl talked about it previously?

Cass: No, I don't think so. My recollection is that I really first thought about it the first year I was at Cowles.

Going on about Cowles, my second year and into my third year, there was this big influx from MIT: Joe Stiglitz, Marty Weitzman, Bill Nordhaus, and others, too, and the environment was just great. Hell, I shared offices with Joe Stiglitz. I probably never would have gotten to know Joe and take him very seriously, because he is so quick and so sloppy, except that we shared an office together. Joe used to come in and sit down in the morning and say, "I am going to write a paper today." And he'd sit at his typewriter and write a paper. This just drove me nuts because I am very deliberate. So I got into a habit, when Joe would tell me he was going to write a paper about something, of talking with him about it. He would come up with some point and I would say, "Well, Joe, how do you know that's true?" Actually, we ended up writing a lot of papers together based on the fact that I would ask Joe, "How do you know that that is true?" One of those papers is still cited a lot. It is about portfolio choice—the reduction to choice between two assets. I think that was a hard paper and we have really cool results from it, but it's just to justify a simplification. In order to justify the simplification, it turns out you have to make extremely strong assumptions about preferences.

Anyway, Cowles was extraordinary. Very stimulating. For the most part, nobody was proprietary about sharing ideas. Nobody would try to protect their ideas. They talked about them.

MD: Was Yaari there as a visitor?

Cass: No, Manny had had his first appointment with Cowles. He was promoted to, I suppose, associate without tenure, a standard step. I was too, while I was there. Then he came up for tenure, and he had to decide whether he was going to go back to Hebrew University in Israel or stay at Cowles. Yale actually made some, I thought, really stupid personnel decisions. Partly it was motivated by the fact that they wanted to keep a throughput of junior faculty; they didn't want to get a large senior group. So they turned down Manny. Another example of a serious mistake is that they turned down Ned Phelps. Hey, he has got an extraordinarily creative mind. So does Yaari. I have tremendous feeling and respect for both of them. And they were turned down flat

I was also one of the young people that was throughput at Yale, if you will. I don't think that they were seriously considering giving me tenure and, to be honest, I didn't have a lot of publications when I would have come up for tenure, maybe a half dozen. I remember, I was on the market and I went to Johns Hopkins, and the department chair there told me they couldn't seriously consider me because I didn't have enough publications. But for some reason Dick Cyert had decided several years before that he really wanted me to come to Carnegie. Cyert is nothing if not tenacious—he kept after me every year. Originally (you probably don't want to repeat this exactly), my view of Carnegie was that it was a serious place but that the typical paper was just to apply the Kuhn–Tucker Theorem to some problem, and I didn't find that very exciting. But then I went to Carnegie and met some of the junior faculty. I knew Bob Lucas very well and he was a big draw.

MD: How did you know Lucas?

Cass: Well, Bob was at Chicago, probably just finishing up, when Uzawa moved from Stanford to Chicago. Bob never worked with Uzawa, but Bob's work was probably also not particularly fashionable with any other faculty there because he was interested in doing the kind of things Uzawa did. So he became sort of a semiprotégée of Uzawa. I don't want to exaggerate that, but anyway, I remember my first encounter with Bob intellectually. He gave some version of a dynamic IO problem, something about industrial structure, firms entering and exiting, as I remember. Anyway, I met Bob because Uzawa kept track of his graduate students and he used to hold conferences when he was in Chicago, where he had also built up a group of graduate students. One of the first conferences I went to, Bob Lucas was there and that is how I met him. He was obviously very smart, very serious, and we got along very well and so he was quite a draw to go to Carnegie. I knew he was not the kind of guy to just apply Kuhn–Tucker conditions, so he clearly did not fit my stereotype.

So I went to visit and I met other people at Carnegie. Len Rapping, for example, was a very interesting person. He was originally a die-hard Chicago market-oriented person who had a complete change of heart during the Vietnam War, but still a very interesting and smart guy. The other person that I remember who really impressed me was Herb Simon, who was clearly a really interesting and creative individual. And I said, "Well, your stereotype is wrong, and that might be a very interesting place to go." When I went to Carnegie it was a very good place. It was not a business school; even though they had a Master in Business Administration program, it was just not a traditional business school.

MD: This would have been around 1970?

Cass: Yes, this was in 1970. It was a small faculty and a relatively small number of MBAs. We taught the MBAs the same as we taught the Ph D 's almost, and at that point, unlike today, the MBAs came and they were expected to perform, and they didn't raise questions about whether the stuff was too hard or didn't have anything to do with business. Carnegie was an absolute innovator in introducing quantitative techniques, and especially economics as kind of a broad basis for most fields in business. In fact, a great example of that was the development of finance as something serious. The finance people won't like this but, to learn finance, you basically learn economic techniques, and that originally took place at Carnegie and took place in the standard way that Carnegie operated. If they had a course to teach, they would just assign somebody to teach the course. Merton Miller was one of the people assigned to teach a course on finance along with Franco Modigliani, and so: Modigliani–Miller. They were puzzled by something, and used economic methodology to solve it.

Carnegie was really a great place. They used the MBA program also to find good Ph.D. students. You didn't mind teaching MBAs at Carnegie because you could teach them a serious course. You didn't have to pull your punches because they were expected to learn programming, expected to learn serious economics, serious econometrics, and so on. The other thing about Carnegie is that it had a very good system for supporting and encouraging young faculty to interact and to have time to do research. They were really good, as Cowles had been, about teaching loads, summer support, secretarial support, and support for travel until you were well enough recognized that you could go out and raise your own money. So I had nothing but respect for Carnegie Mellon, GSIA at Carnegie Mellon, and the team run by Dick Cyert. I have enormous respect for Dick.

MD: What were you working on in those days?

Cass: One of the nice things about Cyert was that he basically paid for a year's leave between being at Cowles and being at Carnegie, so I spent that year in Tokyo, and I wrote several papers there. One I really liked the best, I think it is one of my best papers, and I don't think that it is one that is very widely read. It is solving the following problem: In the neoclassical growth model, you can have competitive equilibria which are not optimal, not efficient, if you use consumption as the criterion. You can basically overaccumulate capital. The best example of that —an example by Ned Phelps—is if you look at the same neoclassical model and you look at a steady state that is above the golden-rule path, you can move from that steady state and take one step back to the golden-

Figure 2.2 A conference at Carnegie Mellon University in honor of Dick Cyert, September 11, 1993. Pictured (from left to right) are Dave Cass, Robert Lucas, Dick Cyert, Allan Meltzer, Edward Prescott, and Timothy McGuire.

rule capital stock, and get a consumption bonus and have higher consumption ever after that. Being at the upper point you still have competitive prices, they are just not efficiency prices. If you look at those competitive paths, you can rule out the ones that are inefficient if you impose the transversality condition. So the transversality condition is a sufficient condition for ruling out capital overaccumulation.

I found this to be a very interesting problem: What is a necessary and sufficient condition? The transversality condition is a sufficient condition for efficiency, but is not necessary. The golden-rule path itself is a counterexample, as I said earlier. The golden-rule path is efficient, and for some criterion is also Pareto optimal, but there the transversality condition is not satisfied since the interest rate is identically zero. Manny Yaari and I had started working on this problem two years before, and we got one solution for it that was in terms of a condition that wasn't that interpretable. Now I know why I didn't like the condition. I wanted a condition on the price path itself that was necessary and sufficient, so I worked all year in Japan on that and got a complete solution. I really like that paper.

So I spent a year in Japan working on that problem, and then I wrote a couple of other papers on things I wanted to write about. One of them was actually very much Solow-like. I took the Wicksellian model, the point-input/point-output model and analyzed competitive equilibrium. I like that paper a lot, too, but it's very specialized. I doubt anyone has ever read it. And Joe and I finished our paper on portfolio choice that year. The biggest stumbling block for that was that in the paper itself there are computations for specific parametric forms and neither Joe nor I was that excited about, or that careful sometimes, dealing with parametric forms. So we really had a hell of a lot of trouble agreeing upon what was the correct way to write down these examples to illustrate our theorem. In the final version of that paper there were still algebraic errors; somehow neither of us took the responsibility for proofreading it.

Then I kind of fished around for a while. I worked more on growth theory. I got interested in the general problem, which was then very unfashionable because it was at the tail end of the neoclassical growth period, of the stability of competitive dynamical systems more generally. Karl and I produced a paper that I like a lot, although it might have been a little archaic even then, on this problem.

MD: Was that the first time you worked with Karl?

Cass: That was the first time Karl and I really worked together on a paper. Karl was at Penn at that time. Anyway, back at Carnegie I wrote some minor papers, like on the Hamiltonian representation of efficient production, a paper on duality; these were not major papers. Probably I got to talking with programmers and got back to doing things with programming at Carnegie. The guy I really talked to a lot was—I remember him well, in fact he died some years ago—a guy named Bob Jeroslow, who was really a mathematical logician turned programmer. He was extraordinarily clever. The big thing in programming then was integer programming, finding algorithms that would solve integer programming problems. There were lots of algorithms but people didn't have any idea of why they worked, and Bob was really good at constructing for any algorithm a counterexample that would never converge. I used to talk to him a lot. He started to get interested in economics and I got interested in programming again, so I wrote some programming papers.

After that, Karl and I got into the stability thing, which we spent a couple of years finishing up. Then at some point—I don't now how this should appear in this interview—the Dean, Cyert, became President and we had to hire a new Dean. At Carnegie the faculty was very involved in this process, and we actually talked a lot about the kind of person we wanted. For some reason we settled on Arnie Weber, who was a Chicago Business School labor economist. That turned out to be, from Carnegie's viewpoint and my own viewpoint, a disaster, because the guy had no feel for the Carnegie tradition at all. He did not understand the fact that Carnegie was quantitative, and that the quantitative emphasis was on

economics, and that meant that you were going to have a lot of economists around. An example of this, a personal example, is that very early on
Arnie called me into his office for some reason, and I had an interview
with him. He told me that I was a luxury good and that I didn't do
business. I did theoretical economics and it wasn't something that business schools could really support, and he did it in a very obnoxious way
that really pissed me off. And I said "f— you, Arnie."

MD: Literally?

Cass: Yeah, I said "f— you," and I decided that since I was working
with Karl it might make sense to come to Penn, even though I had a few
reservations about Penn because I knew it was very econometric-model
oriented. But they made me a good offer so I couldn't turn it down.

MD: Could we stay on your time at Carnegie for a while?

Cass: Yeah, we could do that.

MD: Okay. Ph.D. students: One of the prominent ones you worked
with there was Finn Kydland.

Cass: Finn Kydland, yeah, I was on his committee, and actually worked
with him a lot on one or two chapters, but not most of his thesis. His
thesis was all programming. Another one was Bill Barnett. I don't remember if I was formally on Barnett's committee. I know I talked to him a lot
but I may have left before he finished or he may have just drifted off. The
main group I worked with includes people who came my first year at
Carnegie, such as John Donaldson and Bob Forsythe. Those two stand
out in my mind.

MD: Kydland's work with Ed Prescott began the development of real
business-cycle theory, and the workhorse model in real business-cycle
theory is the Cass–Koopmans model. Did you and Finn ever talk about
growth theory?

Cass: No, as I said, Finn when he was a graduate student was doing
programming.

MD: Let's talk about Lucas's use of the overlapping-generations
model.

Cass: I'll tell you, that is an interesting paper we're talking about, in
Journal of Economic Theory, an interesting paper. I wasn't so interested in
the macro, but what struck me, and this is related to some of my later work,
was the assumption that Bob made to solve for equilibrium, that the
state variables were obvious (that is actually the first time that I thought
about the sunspot idea). Bob and I had some long discussions, and I
would say, "Well Bob, why is this the actual state space in this model?"
That question came up—and now I am jumping ahead—after I came
to Penn. At some point Karl and I started talking about that and we
developed what we called the idea of sunspots. But the initial impetus
toward that for me was talking to Lucas.

MD: Also, technically, Lucas's paper was one of the first uses in economics of contraction mappings.

Cass: Well, Bob was very fixated on using contraction mappings to get fixed points. I think maybe he always uses that technique. I don't think he even knows Brouwer's Theorem! No, actually he does. He just likes contraction mappings. Anyway, the view in capital theory, as I understood it, was that you could treat, from a fundamental state space, uncertainty as well as time. So a commodity index could represent time, uncertainty, and commodity characteristics like location, whatever you wanted. But the viewpoint in growth theory is precisely that equilibrium is just prices that depend on the underlying state space. Bob went a step further and— I'm not even sure how I would say it—it is more like a function of the underlying state variables, or to put it more accurately, the state space itself is generated via some underlying process through observed variables. So that's what the state space itself is, for instance, money and some actual random shocks. Money is one of the state variables, though it's actually defined on the underlying state space. The states of the world are described by money and a random variable that has to do with island-specific shocks.

The ultimate question is, "What is a state space?"

MD: Brock and Mirman was another seminal paper.

Cass: Brock and Mirman was kind of a milestone because they focused on introducing uncertainty into the neoclassical model. Where did I meet Buzz Brock? Somehow, Buzz was a student at Berkeley and I think his thesis had to do with optimal growth in a multisector model. That is probably when I first met him. Our careers overlapped in several dimensions, for instance, when Jan and I spent the year later visiting Cal Tech and Buzz spent part of the year there. We had quite a bit of contact when Brock was working on growth theory, and then we just kind of drifted apart. He is still very active. I just haven't kept up with him or much of his work.

MD: When you were at Carnegie and people like Lucas and Prescott were working on the new macro stuff, were you paying attention?

Cass: Not really.

MD: Or do you think that this work is more microeconomics?

Cass: It was clearly micro and was being called macro, and you know, actually, for some reason, I never talked a lot with Bob about it. I don't know why. We had a great personal relationship, but somehow we didn't talk much about that. Our styles are really different, so we didn't talk a lot about that work, except we would go to lunch together and we would talk about it more on a casual level, but it was not at the blackboard level. It probably had to do with the fact that Bob was in the Chicago tradition and was very concerned about empirical testing—whatever the hell that means—something that I have little sympathy for and very little interest in, to be perfectly honest. So there was quite a difference in viewpoints about why you did theory and what the relevance of theory is, and I am still of the opinion that theory is more a way of organizing your thoughts, how you think about the world. And it's strongest in providing counterexamples when people confidently claim that something is true in general. If you can construct a not-unreasonable model in which this phenomenon is not true, then [*Bronx cheer*]. You can't assert with any confidence that some proposition is true. Now this clearly does go over to the question of when an assertion is true or not true if you want to quantify it. You can stay at the qualitative level—like the Laffer curve, an idea that was by example. Then you can construct models, plausible models, where you can get either result, and that makes his proposition absolutely dubious. I don't know how the data look. Probably most regressions are very mixed: Take a bunch of data and fit some curve to it and then claim that you summarize the data with some curve and that's a dubious claim.

MD: This is probably a good point to ask you how you feel about calibration, as pushed by Prescott and others over the past decade or so.

Cass: The main problem I have with calibration is the level of abstraction of the models that are being calibrated. I mean, if you are calibrating something that is essentially like a neoclassical model, then I kind of wonder what the hell that means. I suppose when I thought about it (and I haven't thought in great detail about it, to be honest), the whole notion of calibration and how you say that you've got a model that fits the data well is pretty amorphous. For example, to say that it generates time series for certain parameter values that share certain characteristics with the observed time series, I think you have to have a formal methodology for talking about what it means for two time series to be close. I thought that when I paid attention to the real business-cycle stuff, the idea of what to calibrate or what a good model is was pretty vague. Now I am probably being unfair to the real business-cycle people, because there are some really smart people working in the area, and they've probably refined the idea of calibration and gone beyond the simple calculations of the original neoclassical growth model; but probably not very far beyond, because you're still dealing with aggregate time series. My student John Donaldson, who works in the area, is very good and I have a lot of respect for him.

But the thing about real business-cycle theory, I suppose, is that it is almost like a religion. I have talked quite a bit with Victor [Rios-Rull], whom I have a lot of respect for, who has this view, this view that he is convinced quite strongly about, that this is the only way to look at the world, to look at economics. When anybody tells me it's the only thing, I'm skeptical. I don't believe that using general equilibrium theory is the only way of looking at the world. I think I have learned a lot from game theory, focusing on strategic ideas, the importance of strategy, and imperfect information.

MD: Isn't that general equilibrium?

Cass: It can be, but there are other ways of looking at imperfect information and all these ways are important. But I also think that the general equilibrium model itself has a role, that it is still an important benchmark, and that there are still a lot of interesting things that can be done with that theory.

MD: That is one thing that you do have in common with Prescott.

Cass: Yeah, absolutely. But, if anything, maybe Prescott is more extreme. I have learned a hell of a lot being at Penn, where there are good game theorists. I mean, I have really learned a lot. I could probably teach a

Figure 2.3 Cass singing with Randy Wright's band (The Contractions) at the Penn Economics department's "skit night," at which economics graduate students lampoon the department faculty, and vice versa, March 3, 1998. Pictured (from left to right) are Randy Wright, Dave Cass, Andrei Shevchenko (a Penn Economics graduate student), Gwen Eudey (Georgetown University, visiting at the Research Department, FRB of Philadelphia), and Boyen Jovanovic (at piano).

game theory course without ever having read more than a dozen articles, just from having been here.

MD: Let's talk more about the Penn years, which are tied in with overlapping-generations models.

Cass: Karl and I got back, if my memory serves, into thinking about the overlapping-generations model sometime in the middle to late 1970s. If I had to pinpoint a date I would peg the year about 1977. I'll tell you the genesis, to my recollection. Karl and I were having a discussion because there was a seminar here run by more junior faculty, and we participated, and we would go back and read some classics in macro that people wanted to read. One of the papers people wanted to talk about was Lucas 1972. I don't remember why one of us decided to present it, but it got me to thinking again about this issue I'd raised with Bob about the state space, and Karl and I talked about it. Karl was astute enough to observe that we could formalize the idea of having arbitrary variables in the state space. So Karl constructed the first example of sunspot equilibrium, and I think it is the one that appeared in his so-called Malinvaud lecture. It's a linear OLG model where households' allocations but not their welfare depend on sunspots, and so I objected to the example. I said, "Karl, that's not a convincing example. It doesn't matter from a welfare viewpoint."

We were going to a conference that Karl and I had organized at Squam Lake in New Hampshire on growth theory, and after this discussion, I spent most of the conference closeted in my room trying to construct an example of a sunspot equilibrium in an overlapping-generations model where sunspots mattered for allocations. The first example I came up with was with quadratic utility. It was laborious as holy hell! So Karl and I were going to talk about this at this conference, and nobody understood the idea at all. They just didn't understand, until that last day when we actually gave the paper, and Steve Salop was the only person who understood the idea. This was sort of discouraging.

MD: Was this an overlapping-generations problem?

Cass: This was an overlapping-generations model, but in the overlapping-generations model (as Steve Spear will attest, because his thesis is about this), you have to be careful picking your utility function. I do remember that I decided that I couldn't get sunspot equilibria for the standard parametric forms, and I was going to need cross-product terms, so . . . anyway, Karl and I came back and we knew this was a great idea, but somehow the reception that it got was a little discouraging, so we didn't really start working on it until much later. Karl's enthusiasm for the idea was extraordinarily high, and he talked about it a lot. He went to Paris in the late 1970s where he gave his Malinvaud lecture, which he always cites because he wants us to claim priority, correctly.

One of the other people he talked to a lot about it was Costas Azariadis. My view is that Karl explained the idea to Costas a number of times, and Costas finally picked up on it and he wrote a paper about it. He realized, not from a utility approach, but by having a first-order Markov system of probabilities, that one can get sunspot equilibria. Steve's thesis actually develops the general story, and he solved that problem long before, for example, Azariadis and Guesnerie did. But I have to credit Costas with something. When Costas produced a working paper or maybe even before that we realized that if we were going to develop the idea we'd better get to it.

MD: And this led to the *Journal of Political Economy* paper?

Cass: The *JPE* paper constructs a standard simple example that didn't require using the overlapping-generations structure, although we built on one of the properties of the overlapping-generations model, the friction you get by restricting participation on certain markets. Much later we wrote a paper showing that there's another aspect of the overlapping-generations model, that somehow the open-endedness of time also plays a role. We constructed an example where there were complete markets and unrestricted participation—it is something like the following. This is basically an overlapping-generations model where the uncertainty is all in the first period, you either get an alpha or a beta, and you can buy insurance against that, but because of the infinite structure of the model, you would still have sunspot equilibria. So there are two causes for sunspot equilibria: One of them has to do with the time structure of overlapping generations; the other has to do with not having enough access to asset markets.

MD: Didn't Jim Peck pick up on the second thing in his thesis?

Cass: Yeah, yeah, that's right. I haven't thought much about sunspots, especially in the overlapping-generations model, for quite a while, but he develops a generalization about nonstationary sunspot equilibria in the OLG model. I think sunspots are really interesting, but even when Karl and I wrote that *JPE* paper, my interests had already diverged to thinking the way I did on the general equilibrium problem, in which you can actually do a finite-dimensional model. Of course, we have this simple but important theorem which says that if you have all the hypotheses that are necessary, stated and unstated, to get the First Welfare Theorem, then you can't have sunspots. Then we have what Karl used to call the Philadelphia Pholk theorem, which is that if you violate any of these hypotheses you can get sunspot equilibria. It's not quite true, because all it is saying is that if you have a theorem that says A, B, and C imply D, it's likely to be the case that if you drop one of the assumptions the conclusion is not going to be true. But, of course, it may be that it can still be true. I guess that is where Karl and I diverged on this a little, but he's gotten very interested in the absence of convexity. Now, his examples are perfectly okay, but it is not quite true to say that if you have some nonconvexity then you have sunspots, because—as Heracles Polemarchakis and I pointed out—you can have nonconvexity in production and, since profit maximization is relative to a hyperplane, you can substitute everything under the hyperplane and call that the production set, and you get the first welfare theorem back.

The *JPE* example is a real simple example where there are two states of the world and we interpret it, in the structure of the overlapping-generations model, as two classes of households. One class can trade assets against the state of the world, while the other can't because it is born later, so it has to trade just on the spot market. That is one kind of example. But I got interested in constructing other examples of sunspot equilibria. In particular, in the early 1980s, I went to spend a year in Paris, and the first project I wanted to work on was to construct a sunspot example where there was a missing market. Somehow I decided the way to do that was in a model where you had assets, and not enough assets to span the states of the world. That's how I got interested in incomplete markets. That's another paper I like a lot, "The Leading Example" paper. I had real trouble getting it published because I wrote it precisely in the *JPE* style, a kind of a followup to the first paper but, to the Chicago mind, sunspots are irrelevant, just not interesting. Ironic as holy hell.

MD: In the famous Kareken and Wallace volume, one thing Cass and Shell say is that by definition the overlapping-generations model is the only dynamic disaggregated model, which one may take to mean it is the only interesting macro model.

Cass: I have to get back now to the train of thought about the overlapping-generations model. I got interested in the overlapping-generations model because of sunspots. And then Okuno and Zilcha—this may have even been at the same conference at Squam Lake—presented a paper which was an attempt to prove that if you introduced money into the overlapping-generations model, then equilibrium where money had a nontrivial price would necessarily be Pareto optimal. There was a flaw in their proof.

MD: Neil Wallace was always inclined to say that in Minnesota.

Cass: Their work was based on trying to verify formally what Neil believed. I saw their proof, read their proof very carefully, and it had an error in it. I decided that it probably wasn't true, depending on some characteristics of the utility functions, and so on, so I decided to work on a counterexample. Basically, I constructed a lot of counterexamples, where you can introduce money and, for one reason or another—heterogeneity, nonstationarity, and so on—you will not get Pareto optimality. I got interested in the overlapping-generations model again. Karl and I really did believe in it, and we started working more generally on the overlapping-generations model after we'd worked on sunspots. We really did believe at that time that it was the only serious model where money played a role. Of course, subsequently you have some very famous papers which present other basic paradigms in which money plays a basic role.

MD: Although mathematically those structures maybe aren't so different?

Cass: Well, I was going to talk about that. The Kiyotaki–Wright model I like a lot, but as I have pointed out to you, Randy, I think that the ultimate principle in both of those models is that the horizon is indefinite. If you truncated your search model, you wouldn't get a role for money either. So even though we didn't have the imagination to think of another model, and this, for example, would be your model with search, in which there would be an infinite horizon, I think you were right in asserting that the underlying time structure of the overlapping-generations model is what provides a reason for having money. I still think that the ultimate thing is that money has value because people believe it is going to have value, and the only way they'll consistently believe it will have value is if they're never forced to put up. And that's common to Kiyotaki–Wright and the overlapping-generations model.

MD: Well, it's interesting, because there are some infinite horizon models in which money has no role. So the infinite horizon isn't a sufficient condition.

Cass: Just the infinite horizon does not necessarily give you a role for money. In addition, you have to have some type of imperfection, some violation of the hypotheses of the first welfare theorem, like restricted participation (overlapping generations), or noncompetitive behavior (the search model).

MD: Do you agree that there are still many issues in monetary economics that are yet to be sorted out?

Cass: Oh absolutely. It would be nice but probably impossible to have a consistent model where we could get away from having to have an indefinite future to give value to money, but it is hard to conceive of how you would do that. John Geanakoplos has a model, it's an incomplete markets model with money and cash-in-advance constraints, where he gets value for money because money is issued by a bank and you have to repay the bank. But, ultimately, the bank is just throwing money away at the end of the day, and somehow the model is not really closed. It's a little unsatisfying.

MD: What are the issues with an infinite horizon?

Cass: I changed my mind sometime in the 1980s about the infinite horizon. I suppose ultimately the reason that I object to it relates to rational expectations, although I would define rational expectations in a more general equilibrium than a macro way. I define rational expectations to mean that you have a well-defined state space, and that in those states every individual has common beliefs about the prices that will prevail. For those beliefs about future prices, today's markets will clear, and when tomorrow's state rolls around, given the plans, one equilibrium in the realized spot market will be at the prices that they forecast. Now there's a little problem in that there could be other equilibria. No equilibrium model that I'm aware of has a sensible process for actually achieving equilibrium prices, so it's not clear why the particular prices they forecast are going to be the ones that occur. Getting back to the issue, I can kind of understand why I might want to use rational expectations as a benchmark when the predictions that we're making are not too far ahead. But this is generally a question of assuming that you know what the structure of the world is. There's a big difference in my mind between that and assuming implicitly that you know this forever. I have become very uncomfortable with that.

MD: Is your view that for some relevant questions it may be more appropriate to use a short-run model?

Cass: I think you can use a short-run model, but the objection there is exactly the motivation behind the overlapping-generations model, that when you reach a certain period, if you reach that period, then it is reasonable for people to expect that there will be a period to follow. It's sort of like an induction argument. You can't cut the world off because, in the last period, people are still going to be looking ahead one period. I mean, I understand that argument, I'm just uncomfortable with the conclusion that the model has to be infinite dimensional. I guess in my experience, except for these paradoxes of infinity, I find that infinite-dimensional and finite-dimensional models are isomorphic. But they aren't isomorphic on this one dimension of providing a role for fiat money and I'm uncomfortable with that. So I'm willing to introduce one of the artifacts I used to scoff at, that people, for example, get utility from holding money, or that they're constrained to hold money, in order to close the model. I am more comfortable with that artifact than with the artifact of introducing the infinite horizon. I have come full circle. I am sure that Karl and I in our defense of the overlapping-generations model scoffed a lot at these other artificial ways of closing the model, but I'm more sympathetic to that now.

MD: Continuing on with incomplete markets, one of the things that has been happening in macro is the integration of the finance side.

Cass: Introducing finance into macro more generally, I think, is key, and I also think that macro fundamentally is going to be dealing with missing markets.

MD: Some people find incomplete markets models to be a little ad hoc because some subset of the markets is simply shut down.

Cass: It is very ad hoc, but the first step to understand the problem is to build a model where you assumed it. There is a lot of work now going on in which you try to justify missing markets, for example, along the line of, if you have a complete state space then idiosyncratic variables should appear as part of the definition of the state space. Then you won't have markets for the idiosyncratic risk because of the problem of moral hazard. Small numbers is another possibility. People are now trying to build more formal models that start out with some kind of standard information imperfection that would drive you to have incomplete markets. They want to make the incompleteness endogenous.

Another way of doing this is to maintain the structure of the incomplete markets model, but then to introduce agents who are optimizing the structure of the assets. I don't think those models have been very successful, probably because they require, for example, that the agents who are going to create the instruments have to be able to forecast (since it's a Nash equilibrium) what the other agents are introducing and then doing, what the equilibria are. You have to make this very strong informational assumption in order to get a formal model. This is an example of the kinds of problems that occur. You know, people are very aware of that, although I still think that a lot of things that are true in the model where incomplete markets are simply assumed will then be true in models where you explain why you have incompleteness. I have this belief. One of the results in incomplete markets that I like a lot was a result that I worked out in kind of a crude way, and then Yves Balasko and I wrote a paper about, and John Geanakoplos and Andreu Mas-Colell wrote a paper about at the same time, that shows that with incomplete markets you get a huge indeterminacy of equilibria in a real sense. I think that result is going to be robust.

MD: And that actually feeds back into monetary models since it implies nonneutral monetary policies when markets are incomplete.

Cass: Yes, and I am going to go a step further than that. The simplest version of indeterminacy comes about because you can pick different price numeraires, like price numeraires period by period, with incomplete markets. But another cause of indeterminacy, which creates even more indeterminacy, is that you can make the asset structure a parameter of the model.

MD: Haven't you made the point that one of the things about sunspots or dynamics is that market clearing and rational expectations are not enough to pin down very much?

Cass: Right. This is kind of self-destructive in a way.

MD: Some people say similar things because of fundamental belief in Keynesian macro—is that why you do it?

Cass: No, it isn't. I have to admit that this is kind of an anomaly, because what it is ultimately is destructive. I've been using a competitive equilibrium model as a benchmark and it has no predictive power, so in a way it is kind of self-destructive. I'm very interested in that. Intellectually, it interests me to try to figure out what it is that will pin down equilibrium. I am still at the stage where I don't know what the answer is.

MD: It's certainly a clear intellectual challenge for the future.

Cass: Well, it is an intellectual puzzle. And I must admit that in my career in economics I have always been interested in an intellectual puzzle, even though it's not fashionable, it may have no practical relevance—God knows what—you can criticize it on a million grounds. A good example of that is spending a couple of years working on this problem of characterizing Pareto optimality and efficiency in an infinite-dimensional growth model.

MD: What is in the future for micro, macro, general equilibrium, game theory? What lies ahead?

Cass: I have a very short work horizon. I always have. I think ahead to the next problem I am going to work on. I have always been penalized greatly when applying for grants, because I haven't the foggiest idea of what I will be working on in the future!

MD: It goes back to the question you told us Koopmans asked on the job market, doesn't it?

Cass: Maybe that's the whole problem, yeah! We've come full circle. But I actually know that there is a big component of serendipity in research. I mean, if you told me 15 years ago that I would be doing general equilibrium with incomplete markets, I would have said "Are you crazy?" The serendipity there is that I wanted to construct examples of sunspot equilibria with missing markets, and I realized that there were a lot of interesting questions about the model that I wanted to use for that purpose. In particular, the reason that I got into indeterminacy is that, in the sunspot model, if you have a missing financial instrument, then you get a continuum of sunspot equilibria; that turns out to be a general property of incomplete markets. The question I am pursuing now is what will actually cut down the set of equilibria. The best you could hope for is a finite number of equilibria, and I don't think the answer is that you have to introduce money in a way that normalizes prices spot by spot, because there is still something that is given as a primitive in the model that should be endogenous, and that's the asset structure. That needs to be endogenized. Now, the question is, whether when you put things in that framework, you still get indeterminacy. I'm interested in that question.

MD: So you want to endogenize the asset structure.

Cass: Yeah, you endogenize the asset structure. There are examples when you endogenize the asset structure that you do pin down the equilibrium, in a sense, but you really don't. A good example is work by Alberto Bisin, in his thesis, where he introduces basically this game theoretic idea where some households introduce new financial instruments and the way that they do it is in the Nash way. They take as given what all the other households are doing and they look at how the equilibrium is going to vary across their actions and they optimize. Now the problem with that is that we know with Nash equilibrium typically there's a plethora. What this cuts down on is the number of equilibria after the set of financial instruments is determined. Somehow, in his model, there is a section which deals with real indeterminacy which shows that you don't have a lot of equilibria associated with a given asset structure. But you do have a lot of equilibria associated with the Nash equilibrium. You've just moved the indeterminacy back one step.

MD: You were saying something a few minutes ago about the way you do research—about looking at the model as well as the questions that you think the model may help us answer. Can you expand on that?

Cass: Well, what drives me to do research is not what drives an awful lot of people to do research. I mean, I'm never much motivated by what some people call real-world problems. I am much more of a structuralist. I have pursued some questions just because they are interesting puzzles to me, not because of any economic relevance.

MD: One thing interesting about your career is that you may have worked on these things for whatever reason—independent of any interest in, say, real-world policy—and yet the Cass–Koopmans model is the foundation for modern business-cycle theory, your work on overlapping-generations models is related to much practical research in monetary economics, and your sunspot stuff also has macro policy relevance.

Cass: That is the beauty of a true intellectual discipline. It has room for people like me.

MD: Somewhere down the food chain?

Cass: Well, no, . . . you just learn something! You should never scoff at an intellectual's looking at a question, because you never know when what they are going to come up with will be actually interesting for other reasons.

MD: It may take 20 or 30 years, too.

Cass: It may take forever. And it may not ever happen.

3

An Interview with Robert E. Lucas, Jr.

Interviewed by Bennett T. McCallum
CARNEGIE MELLON UNIVERSITY
Summer 1998

Bob Lucas is widely regarded as the most influential economist of the past 25–30 years, at least among those working in macro and monetary economics. His work provided the primary stimulus for a drastic overhaul and revitalization of that broad area, an overhaul that featured the ascendance of rational expectations, the emergence of a coherent equilibrium theory of cyclical fluctuations, and specification of the analytical ingredients necessary for the use of econometric models in policy design. These are the accomplishments for which he was awarded the 1995 Nobel Prize in Economic Sciences. In addition, he has made outstanding contributions on other topics—enough, arguably, for another prize. Among these are seminal writings on asset pricing, economic growth and development, exchange-rate determination, optimal fiscal and inflation policy, and tools for the analysis of dynamic recursive models.

Clearly, Bob Lucas is very much a University of Chicago product; he studied there both as an undergraduate and as a Ph.D. student and has been on the faculty since 1975. Also, he has served as chairman of the Chicago Department of Economics and two terms as an editor of the *Journal of Political Economy*. Nevertheless, I and several colleagues at Carnegie Mellon like to point out that Bob was a professor here in the Graduate School of Industrial Administration from 1963 until 1974, during which time he conducted and published the central portions of

Reprinted from *Macroeconomic Dynamics*, 3, 1999, 278–291. Copyright © 1999 Cambridge University Press.

the work for which he was awarded the Nobel Prize. Consequently, I could not resist asking Bob a few questions about his GSIA years in the interview.

Many researchers in the economics profession have been impressed and inspired by Lucas's technical skills, but the clarity and elegance of his writing style also deserve mention, plus his choice of research topics. The latter is reflective of Bob's utter seriousness of purpose. Each of his projects attacks a problem that is simultaneously of genuine theoretical interest and also of considerable importance from the perspective of economic policy. There is nothing frivolous about Lucas's research, as he had occasion to remind me during our interview.

As is well known to those who have been around him, Bob Lucas is a person who never uses three words when one will suffice—but that one will usually be carefully chosen. This characteristic shows up in the interview below. As a departure from standard MD Interview practice, and with the Editor's permission, this interview was conducted at a distance—i.e., via mail and e-mail. It yielded a smaller number of pages than have previous interviews, but I think that readers will find them stimulating. The process of obtaining them was somewhat challenging but highly informative and thoroughly enjoyable for me.

McCallum: Let me begin by asking how and when you got interested in economics, both generally and as the subject for a career.

Lucas: When I was seven or eight, my father asked me if I had noticed how many different milk trucks stopped at our block: Darigold delivered to some houses, Carnation to others, and so on. We counted to five or six. He asked me if I thought there were any differences in the milk provided by these dairies. I thought not. He then told me that under socialism only one truck will deliver to all the houses on each block, and the time and gasoline wasted in duplicating routes will be used for something else.

I doubt very much that this was my first discussion of economics, but it is the earliest I can

Figure 3.1   Robert E. Lucas, Jr.

remember. My parents had come of age politically in the 1930s, and the virtues of free markets were not right at the front of their thinking, or mine. We took it for granted that an economic system should be intelligently managed, and we debated every day over the details of how this could and should be done.

As an undergraduate at Chicago in the 1950s, I got the idea that an intellectual career was a possibility, and knew that was what I wanted for myself. In college, these interests and prejudices led me to history. Early in graduate school, I shifted to economics.

McCallum: And how did you happen to go to Chicago as an undergraduate?

Lucas: My alternative was to stay at home and attend the University of Washington in Seattle. Chicago gave me a full-tuition scholarship, which was the ticket I needed to move out on my own. This was something I needed to do.

McCallum: Then as a graduate student in history? Can you tell us a bit about your reasons for shifting to economics?

Lucas: I drifted into economics from economic history, with no idea of what economics is or what economists do. This was just luck, but I soon discovered the essential role that mathematical reasoning played in economics, and it didn't take me long to see that this way of thinking about human behavior was congenial to me.

Figure 3.2   Louis Chan, Robert Lucas, and Chi-Wa Yuen at Victoria Peak in Hong Kong.

McCallum: How did you develop your outstanding mathematical tools?

Lucas: It is easy to forget how little math one needed to know to be at the technical end of economics, back in the early 1960s. I had had calculus and differential equations as an undergraduate, before I got into history. Samuelson's *Foundations* taught me (and the rest of my cohort) how people were using math in economics. In my summers as a graduate student, I took a linear algebra course and a rigorous calculus course. I also took the mathematical statistics sequence from Chicago's statistics department. With this background, I have kept learning on my own, and much of the math I use now I picked up since leaving graduate school.

McCallum: While you were a Ph.D. student at Chicago, which faculty members had major influences on your intellectual development? Describe these a bit, please.

Lucas: The biggest influence by far, on me and all my classmates, was Milton Friedman. His two graduate price theory courses were fabulously exciting and valuable: a life-changing experience. But I was a very receptive graduate student and learned a lot from many other people. Al Harberger was doing quantitative general equilibrium modeling then, in a way that still looks quite modern. Martin Bailey, Carl Christ, and Harry Johnson were our other macroeconomics teachers. Gregg Lewis went through his book on unions in an advanced seminar that I learned a lot from.

Among the younger faculty, Zvi Griliches taught econometrics, and encouraged technical types like me. Dale Jorgenson, a visitor in 1962–63, was inspiring to me. Don Bear taught a terrific course in mathematics for economists.

McCallum: Somehow I had the impression that Uzawa influenced you in some way. Is that just completely wrong?

Lucas: Uzawa joined the Chicago faculty the year after I left, so he was not one of my teachers. But I did attend two summer conferences on dynamic theory that Uzawa and David Cass organized, one at Chicago and another at Yale. These involved me in intense interactions with the best young theorists in economics. I liked the idealism and seriousness of the tone Uzawa and Cass set. I was flattered to be included, learned a lot, and gained a lot of confidence.

McCallum: Which workshops did you attend regularly?

Lucas: There were many fewer workshops then than we have now. Everything in econometrics and mathematical theory went on in the Econometrics Workshop. Zvi and Lester Telser ran it, and Merton Miller and Dan Orr from the business school were regulars. I was too. Al Harberger ran the Public Finance Workshop, which all the students working with him (as I was) attended. Gregg Lewis invited me to give a paper at the Labor Workshop, but I was not a regular there.

McCallum: So you did not attend the Money and Banking Workshop?

Lucas: Attendance in workshops then was by invitation, and I was never asked to attend the Money and Banking Workshop. But there was no reason why I should have been. Money and Banking was not one of my prelim fields (those were Econometrics and Public Finance) and I did not work with Friedman.

McCallum: I believe that you became an assistant professor at Carnegie Mellon—then Carnegie Tech—about 1963. Is that approximately correct?

Lucas: Yes. I came to the Graduate School of Industrial Administration —GSIA—in September 1963. Tren Dolbear, Mel Hinich, Mort Kamien, Lester Lave, and Tim McGuire came at the same time. I think we were the first cohort hired by Dick Cyert, then a new dean.

McCallum: How did you get started with rational expectations analysis? Did John Muth have much direct influence on your thinking?

Lucas: Before I left Chicago, Zvi Griliches told me to pay attention to Jack Muth, that he was someone I could learn a lot from. That turned out to be good advice! I learned a lot from Jack, but it was a few years before I appreciated the force of the idea of rational expectations. This happened when I was working on "Investment Under Uncertainty" with Ed Prescott.

McCallum: Do you have any thoughts about the intellectual processes that led Muth to his rational expectations hypothesis?

Lucas: The opening paragraphs of his "Rational Expectations and the Theory of Price Movements" are very informative and interesting. One can see the extent to which Muth was influenced by and was reacting to Herbert Simon's work on behavioral economics, and how this led him to such a radically nonbehavioral hypothesis as rational expectations. (I once tried to discuss this with Herb, thinking of it as an instance of the enormous, productive influence he had on all of us, but he took offense at the suggestion.)

Jack was the junior author in the Holt, Modigliani, Muth, and Simon monograph *Planning Production, Inventories, and Workforce*. This was a normative study—operations research—that dealt with the way managers should make decisions in light of their expectations of future variables, sales, for example. I'm sure it was this work that led Muth to think about expectations at a deeper level than just coming up with regression equations that fit data.

The power of thinking of allocative problems normatively, even when one's aim is explaining behavior and not improving it, was one of the main lessons I learned at Carnegie, from Muth and perhaps even more from Dave Cass. The atmosphere at Chicago when I was a student was so hostile to any kind of planning that we were not taught to think: How

Figure 3.3   Ed Prescott, Tom Sargent, Bob Lucas, and Buz Brock at a conference.

should resources be allocated in this situation? How *should* people use the information available to them to form expectations? But these *should* always be an economist's first questions. My Dad was wrong to think that socialism would deliver milk efficiently, but he was right to think about how milk *should* be delivered.

McCallum: Please describe other aspects of the intellectual atmosphere at GSIA that were important to your professional development.

Lucas: I guess I have already referred to the influences of Herb Simon, Dave Cass, and Ed Prescott in answering your question about Muth's influence. In general, GSIA offered me a nice mix of people whose point of view on economics was pretty close to mine, like Leonard Rapping and Allan Meltzer, and others like Simon, Muth, Cass, and Prescott, to name just a few, who could come at problems from angles I never would have hit on my own.

McCallum: Please describe aspects of the atmosphere at Chicago, after your return in 1974–75, that were important to your continued professional development.

Lucas: At Chicago, I began teaching graduate macroeconomics regularly for the first time in my career. (Allan Meltzer had done this at Carnegie.) This was a stimulus for me. My papers "Understanding Business Cycles" and "Problems and Methods in Business Cycle Theory" came out of the experience of organizing my thoughts on the entire field, the way teaching a graduate course in a top department forces one to do.

McCallum: Your Nobel Prize was awarded for work in reconstructing the fields of macro and monetary analysis so as to incorporate the hypothesis of rational expectations. Before we go on to other interests of yours, are there points regarding this topic that you would like to make? Has the macro profession evolved in a manner that you are pleased with?

Lucas: Like most scientists, I imagine, I tend to be pleased with developments that confirm my prejudices and make my conjectures look good. So I am happy about the successes of general equilibrium theory in macro and sad about the de-emphasis on money that those successes have brought about. Pleasure aside, though, I feel I have learned a huge amount from research in real business cycle theory. I think about the relation of theory to data and about the sources of fluctuations now at an entirely different level from the way I thought 15 years ago.

McCallum: How important quantitatively are technology shocks, in your opinion, in generating business cycles?

Lucas: The answer must depend on which cycles we are talking about. If we are discussing the U.S. Depression in the 1930s or the depression in Indonesia today or Mexico five years ago, I would say that technology shocks are a minor part of the picture. On the other hand, if we are talking about fluctuations in the postwar United States the relative importance of technology and other real shocks is *much* larger, something like 80% of the story.

McCallum: But "technology and other real shocks" would include shocks to preferences, government spending, terms of trade, and possibly other things. How about pure technology shocks—shocks to production functions—in the postwar U.S. context?

Lucas: I don't know how my 80% guess would break down among these and other real shocks. I'm not even sure there is such a thing as a "pure technology shock." I guess for me the central distinction is between shocks that competitive markets can deal with efficiently, without any intervention (all of those on your list, and more) and shocks that need to be offset by a monetary response.

McCallum: In your opinion, is price stickiness an important economic phenomenon?

Lucas: Yes. In practice it is much more painful to put a modern economy through a deflation than the monetary theory we have would lead us to expect. I take this to be what we mean by "price stickiness."

McCallum: There has been some disagreement among monetary economists concerning the most appropriate target variable for the European

Central Bank, with inflation and money growth targets being the leading contenders. What are your views on that issue?

Lucas: That's a classic question for any central bank. I like the policy you've studied of formulating a target for the path of nominal output and then using a slowly reacting feedback rule for the monetary base to keep the system moving toward that target. If you want to replace "nominal output" with "inflation rate," this policy still has a lot of appeal, though less. If you want to replace "monetary base" with "M1," it has even more appeal, to me.

If you replace "monetary base" with "short-term interest rate," you get a version that everyone seems to like nowadays, and I'm willing to get on board myself for pretty much anything that keeps the focus on price stability. But I don't understand how this particular feedback system works, and I am concerned about the kind of bad dynamics that Wicksell, and more recently Peter Howitt, worried about.

McCallum: Do you actually believe that the welfare costs of cyclical fluctuations are as small as indicated in your Jahnsson Lectures, or were these numbers presented mainly as a challenge to the profession to explain?

Lucas: I don't write things I don't believe in just to be provocative! Those estimates may be too small, but if so, it is an honest mistake. The estimates I reported there are the welfare cost of postwar U.S. consumption fluctuations, under the assumption that idiosyncratic risk is perfectly pooled. As I explained in the lectures, the costs of 1930s-level crashes were vastly higher, and were aggravated by the absence of unemployment insurance and other features of a modern welfare system.

The reason these costs came out so small is that they are proportional to the variance of consumption, which is very small in the postwar period in the United States. How can one get large costs from so little variability? No one else has, either, except by assuming enormous risk aversion. Of course, this reduced variability is due at least in part to the sensible monetary policy pursued over these years. My claim is not that monetary instability is incapable of causing great harm, but only that it has not done so over the past 50 years, in the United States.

McCallum: Could you make a few comments on your views regarding microeconomics over the past, say, 25 years?

Lucas: In the past 15 years, microeconomics has come to be synonymous with game theory in many places (not including Chicago!), and that is unfortunate. About 99% of all successful applied economics is still based on the idea of a competitive equilibrium. But game theory *has* given us a language for talking about resource allocation with private information and about issues of reputation that represents a huge advance over anything that you and I learned in graduate school.

McCallum: Some other major contributions of yours have concerned asset pricing theory, economic growth and development, and the role of economic theory in econometrics and policy analysis. Could you please tell us how you were led into each of them?

Lucas: The origin of my asset pricing paper makes the best story. I was interviewing Pentti Kouri, then a job-seeking new MIT Ph.D., in my office in Chicago. Kouri didn't want to waste our half hour talking about Chicago winters, so he asked me: "How would you price assets in the following economy?" and then went on to describe the model that is treated in my paper. I went to the blackboard and began writing Bellman equations and clearing markets, and the fact that you didn't need to know the value function to get a very tractable functional equation for prices fell right out in a few minutes. Kouri was not interested in collaborating, so I wrote up these results and others myself.

McCallum: What about your increased emphasis on growth and development? Did that stem partly from the Jahnsson Lecture numbers or had you been interested in this area all along?

Lucas: I taught an undergraduate elective in economic development at Carnegie Mellon, and have been interested in this area as long as I can remember. But my research is guided more by my hunches as to where I might be able to make some progress than anything else. I found myself slipping into the same old ruts in thinking about business cycles, and thought it would be good to think about something else.

McCallum: Your writing is regarded by many in the profession as quite elegant. Do you work hard at your writing?

Lucas: Thank you for the compliment. I revise a lot, though I think of that more as an effort to get the logic straight than as an attempt at style. I also read a lot of people who are *really* good writers, and I'm sure something rubs off.

McCallum: How did you manage to give up smoking?

Lucas: Well, I started smoking when I was 13 and quit when I was 56, so I'm not ready to set up as an adviser on this problem. I quit cold turkey, with the help of nicotine patches. Fear, nagging, and social stigma were all contributing factors.

McCallum: You and Paul Romer both made outstanding contributions to growth theory during the 1980s. Were you Paul's dissertation supervisor? Could you tell us a bit about your interactions on this topic?

Lucas: In teaching macroeconomics, I have been treating a many-country version of Solow's model as a (tentative) model of development for many years. Paul was certainly exposed to this set of problems in my class. But the increasing returns-externalities model that Paul developed in his thesis was entirely his, and new to me. Sherwin Rosen and Ted Schultz told Paul about Allyn Young's work, but I had never heard of that, either.

The model in Romer's thesis raises novel technical problems, since it does not converge to any steady state or balanced path. Jose Scheinkman helped him on this, and I believe chaired his thesis committee as well.

McCallum: Do you have any interest in working for a few years in an economic policy making position? Do you think that one or two years in such a position tends to improve or worsen an economist's subsequent academic work?

Lucas: Back in the late sixties, when George Schultz was Nixon's Secretary of Labor, Schultz asked me to work as an adviser to him. The job was then held by my friend Jack Gould, and it was an interesting position because Nixon was looking to Schultz for help on a much wider range of economic questions than just labor issues. Later Schultz moved to a more central job at OMB, and if I had taken the job I would have moved with him. Schultz called me in person, impressing my secretary at GSIA enormously, and for that matter (why be blasé?) impressing me too! But flattered or not, I was excited about my research at that time and didn't want to interrupt my work with a stay in Washington. I declined.

Do I regret this decision? When I turned the job down, Arthur Laffer accepted it. You never know about such things, but my guess would be that I, Art, and the U.S. economy were all better off as a result, and I can take some pleasure in my role in helping to locate a Pareto-dominant decision.

McCallum: How about writing a regular column on economics for a newspaper or popular magazine? Would you have any interest in such an undertaking?

Lucas: Maybe someday, but not now. I like the sense of discovery and intellectual progress that I can get from doing technical economics. In order to get this sense, one needs to spend a lot of time facing problems one doesn't understand and will probably never understand. This is hard to do, and as you get older and more famous you get more interesting and pleasant excuses to avoid doing it. The last thing I need is more such excuses.

4

An Interview with János Kornai

Interviewed by Olivier Blanchard
MASSACHUSETTS INSTITUTE OF TECHNOLOGY
June 10, 1998

Most of us are armchair economists. Whether our opinions are right or wrong, we can proffer them at little personal cost—the most we can lose is our reputation. Not so for János Kornai. For much of his life, speaking freely would have led him to land in jail, or worse. He faced a difficult choice. He could publish illegally, take the samizdat route, but reach a very small number of readers. He could instead respect a number of official taboos, publish legally, and reach a much wider readership. These difficulties have not prevented him from giving us the most informed and deepest critique of the socialist system to date. This interview is, I hope, successful in showing the degree to which Kornai's life and work have been intertwined, and how he came to believe what he believes today. Kornai is sharing his time between Harvard and Collegium Budapest. The interview took place in my office when I was visiting Harvard University in June 1998.

Blanchard: Your first book was *Overcentralization in Economic Administration* (1957), a book on the problems faced by central planning in practice. On the surface, it looks like a technical study of the problems of industry under central planning, but from the preface you have written for the second edition in 1989, it is clear that this was part of a larger analysis of the socialist system, much of which you did not want to put in print.

Reprinted from *Macroeconomic Dynamics*, 3, 1999, 427–450. Copyright © 1999 Cambridge University Press.

Figure 4.1   János Kornai, 1997.

How much of your later views had you already formed at the time? Did you see a reformed socialist system as a workable alternative? (You touch on this in your second preface.) How much of the analysis of the role and internal dynamics of the Communist Party (the main theme of the *Socialist System*, published in 1992) had you already worked out by then?

Kornai: There have been several stages in my life. When I was very young, I agreed with socialism. Then I became more and more critical of the Stalinist type of communism.

Blanchard: When did you start becoming disappointed with communism?

Kornai: My disappointment began in 1953. It was associated with the changes in the communist countries after the death of Stalin, when many facts, that had previously been hidden, became known. My reaction was cathartic and mainly concerned with ethical issues: the horrible crimes the system had committed—the imprisonment, torture, and murder of innocent people—made my most sincere beliefs seem naïve and shameful. Also, I began to recognize that the regime was economically dysfunctional and inefficient, created shortages, and suppressed initiative and spontaneity.

Overcentralization was my first draft of these critical views of the socialist economy. It got worldwide attention because it was the first critical book written by a citizen living inside the Bloc and not by an outside Sovietologist. I worked on it in 1955 and 1956; it was my graduate thesis.

Blanchard: Did you choose the topic yourself? Did you have a thesis adviser?

Kornai: I did choose the topic myself. I had a thesis adviser; Professor Tamás Nagy, who taught political economy at the Budapest Karl Marx University of Economic Sciences.

Blanchard: You were writing more or less coincidentally with the Revolution.

Kornai: Yes, yes. I finished it in September 1956, at the time when the atmosphere of the intellectual and political discourse began to change in Hungary, similarly to the changes in Prague 12 years later, in 1968. People in Hungary became more and more critical and more and more outspoken. . . . Just as a background story, we have public defenses of dissertations in Hungary and my thesis defense was held a few weeks before the Revolution of October 23. It became a public event: There were several hundred people there. . . .

Blanchard: How had they known about it? By word of mouth?

Kornai: Yes, absolutely. Drafts of it had been circulated, which also brought in a lot of people. In the days between the public defense and October 23, the discussion was reported in most dailies with highly appreciative comments.

But let me go back to my own personal history for a moment to answer your question if I could imagine a workable reformed socialism. Almost 30 years later, in the preface to the second edition of *Overcentralization*, I described the Kornai of 1954–56 as a "naïve reformer." The naïveté was honest: There and then, the need to change the political structure didn't even occur to me: I took it as a fact I didn't object to. State ownership was also something like an axiom: I was certainly not for privatization. I wanted to combine the existing system with a market, very similar to what happened 20 years later in Gorbachev's *perestroika*, so I might say that was the *perestroika* stage in my life. In this preface, I mentioned many others I thought to be akin: György Péter and Tibor Liska in Hungary, Włodzimierz Brus in Poland, Ota Sik in Czechoslovakia, and, of course, the towering figure, Gorbachev in Russia. Their reform ideas emerged at different points in time: Péter was an early pioneer who began the presentation of his thoughts as early as 1955, while Gorbachev became a reform-socialist in the late 1980s. The list contains academic scholars and active politicians. In spite of the differences, they share a common attribute. At a certain phase in their life, all these people—including me in the 1950s—thought that the fundament—the political structure which rested on the monopoly of the Communist Party and state ownership—could be maintained, and all that was needed to make the system work was to introduce market coordination instead of bureaucratic coordination.

However, this view of mine changed, as I discovered the reasons why market socialism could not work. So I became more and more critical of market socialism, including my earlier work. I discussed the ideas of naïve reform in several later writings, but at the time of writing the book, i.e., in 1955–56, I was still very naïve.

Blanchard: This book was very well received in the West, but it was, to say the least, not well received by the authorities in Hungary. How much surprised were you by the reception at home? How did it affect your life? How did it affect your research?

Figure 4.2 Calcutta, India, in 1975, during lecture tour of India.

Kornai: It was the dramatic and traumatic events of 1956 that changed my life, changed how I looked at the world, my *Weltanschauung*. Let's just recall a few events in my personal life. One of my close friends was not only arrested, but tried and executed. Many of my best friends were arrested, some others emigrated, and after having been celebrated for the book before the revolution, I was attacked as a "traitor" to socialism. I was fired, I lost my job.

Not only personal experience but, first of all, the great historical events of brief victory and the tragic defeat of the revolution made my naïveté collapse. The trauma of 1956 meant for me that I could no longer adhere to the leadership of the country by the Communist Party both for political and ethical reasons. I do not say that this happened overnight, since political understanding is a process, but it was a quick one with me.

The events of 1956 also derailed my research program. During the years of very severe repression, I had much more to say than what I actually put down on paper. I acted upon a kind of a self-censorship, which was based on my understanding of the limitations in publication. It influenced the choice of my research agenda and also how far I went in publishing my findings. In the extremely repressive era, following 1956, I decided to move to a politically less sensitive topic: mathematical planning, more closely the application of linear programming to planning, which brought me very close to neoclassical thinking.

Blanchard: On this topic, mathematical programming, were you self-taught, or did you have some mathematical background?

Kornai: No, I was self-taught. I attended some courses on mathematics, linear algebra, calculus, and so on, but practically I went through the literature on the subject by myself, and I worked together with mathematicians and computer scientists who were not economists. Later on, I got a job in the Computing Center of the Hungarian Academy of Sciences, where I worked full time on linear programming. The linear programming model has a very nice economic interpretation that I learned from the book of Dorfman, Samuelson, and Solow (1958). This book was one of my bibles at the time, so, in my own history of thinking, that was the period when I got the closest to neoclassical theory and for a while almost unreservedly accepted it.

Blanchard: Your next major book was *Anti-Equilibrium* (1971), a formal book on general equilibrium theory and its shortcomings. You have already talked a bit about the intellectual process that led from *Overcentralization* to *Anti-Equilibrium*. When did you become disillusioned with neoclassical thinking?

Kornai: I had two big waves of disillusionment in my life as an economist. The first one we have discussed briefly already: It was my losing faith in Marxian thinking. I started as a doctrinaire Marxian, then I became disillusioned with it, which made me reject it in the end. I still admire Marx as an intellectual genius; he had many ideas which are still useful. He was, however, absolutely wrong on many fundamental issues. Then came my almost unreserved admiration for neoclassical theory, a much less emotional feeling because of its pure rationality. However, the strong urge to understand the world around me in its complexity made me ask questions neoclassical theory failed to answer. This dissatisfaction prompted me to analyze the strengths and weaknesses of the theory. I tried to understand it carefully and give a critical appraisal. My rejection was free of political considerations; all I meant to do was to identify its shortcomings.

Ever since, I have never become a prisoner of any doctrine. I could probably call myself an eclectic economist who has learned from various schools. I have always protested if anyone tried to put me in a certain "box."

Blanchard: How much contact did you have with the people who were doing general equilibrium theory at that time?

Kornai: I wrote a paper with Tamás Lipták on two-level planning and submitted it to *Econometrica*. Malinvaud read it and invited me to a conference in 1963 at Cambridge, England. Before 1963, I had been denied a passport. I had a standing invitation to the London School of Economics for years, for instance, and I couldn't go.

Figure 4.3 Presenting the Presidential Address at the Econometric Society North American Meetings in Chicago, 1978. At his left is Tjalling Koopmans, who chaired the session.

In 1962–63, there was a general political amnesty. After that, the Kádár regime started to move step-by-step from brutal repression to what later became "goulash communism," the relatively soft and liberal version of communist regimes. From then on, more and more people were allowed to travel, and finally I too got permission to go to the Cambridge conference.

I met some really brilliant people there. With Edmund Malinvaud and Tjalling Koopmans, we became, so to say, friends; both of them were my mentors, they helped me in many ways. I also met Roy Radner, Lionel MacKenzie, and Robert Dorfman. They were my first personal contacts with the West. Then, on invitation from Kenneth Arrow, I went to Stanford in 1968. By then, I had the first draft of *Anti-Equilibrium* ready, and I showed it to Arrow and Koopmans. They read it and were very generous in their comments. They were not protective of general equilibrium theory or anything that I was criticizing; on the contrary. Both encouraged me, or rather urged me to publish the book.

Blanchard: They probably shared many of your views. . . .

Kornai: Yes, they shared many of them. Both of them would refer to the book later, in their Nobel Lectures.

Blanchard: In your book *Anti-Equilibrium*, you suggested several directions for future research. Twenty-seven years after publication, many of the puzzles have indeed been explored: asymmetric information; game theoretic characterizations of firms; bargaining in the labor market; the role of the government and the law; incomplete contracts, to mention just a few. Are you happy or happier with the state of economics today?

Kornai: That's an interesting formulation, but before reflecting on it, I would add one more item to your list: There is a serious interest in the non-Walrasian state of the economy nowadays, which was one of the issues raised in *Anti-Equilibrium*.

Well, yes, I am happier. When I wrote the book I thought that neo-classical thinking acted like a straitjacket, and no less than a revolution would be needed to wriggle out of it. But life has proved me wrong: Advance can be achieved in an evolutionary way more than I expected. Let me add a few subjective remarks to this. I want to be quite frank. As a member of the profession, I'm happy that progress has been made concerning the study of themes we've just listed. As the author of the book, I feel slightly bitter about its getting hardly any attention. The first, and nearly the last, people who gave it any credit were Arrow and Koopmans; then it somehow disappeared.

Blanchard: It was a very influential book. In France, where I come from, it was one of the books we all read. It became part of the common knowledge and as such, it is hardly ever mentioned. The same seems to have happened to many other ideas. Maybe it is a mark of success. . . .

Kornai: Maybe you are right, maybe not; I don't know. In any case, it seems to me that asking relevant questions doesn't give you much reputation, at least not in our profession. Yet, I still believe that asking the relevant question, even if one cannot give a constructive answer, forms a very important part of the research process.

Blanchard: A related question. How did you perceive yourself vis-à-vis the Western economics mainstream, then and now? Did your perceptions

Figure 4.4 On the "Yangtze Boat Conference" in China, 1985. The group also included James Tobin and Otmar Emminger, the former President of the Bundesbank.

change with proximity after you had accepted a position at Harvard in 1986?

Kornai: To put it into a nutshell, I would say that I am half in and half out of the mainstream. Social science, in my view is not a collection of true and exact statements about the world, but a cognitive process. I believe mainstream economics, and especially the rigorous, formalized neoclassical theories, play a significant yet limited role in this process. I would separate roughly three stages in the cognitive process: First, one perceives that there is a puzzle and sets out to solve it more or less by common sense and intuition. Then comes the middle stage, where the neoclassical theory enters to help to make the probably crude understanding more precise through exact assumptions, definitions, and propositions. The process is rounded off by the third stage, the interpretation of the results. I think what we call mainstream economics is very useful and instrumental in the middle stage, but it doesn't have much to do in the first and third stages. That is not simply a criticism of what mainstream economists write and publish but more or less a criticism of how we teach our young and future colleagues. We don't teach them about the first and third stages; instead, we put too much emphasis on the second stage and thus make them intellectually lopsided.

Blanchard: I would argue that the tradition in economics is that you take the first step in private and take the second in public, and I would also argue that the third step is now taken more and more systematically.

Kornai: I agree only partially with what you have just said. To formulate the right question and to make use of one's more or less good common sense is by no means a private affair. If in a premature state the researcher's mind is tied up by technicalities without leaving sufficient room for a free public discussion of the puzzle, his thinking is excessively constrained. We will perhaps discuss the problems of post-communist transition later on, but let me jump ahead here and use it as an example. There was a famous debate about gradualism versus the Big Bang as the most appropriate and successful way of transforming the economy. Now, reading through the literature, you will find splendid theoretical papers illustrating the theory of the Big Bang. But there also is a host of equally refined theoretical papers demonstrating that gradualism is just as fine. So, what?

After all, it is the context that defines how a certain phenomenon should be interpreted. Yet, we fail to teach our students to put theorems and propositions they learned at school into context. That was why many of the Western economists who went as advisers to Eastern Europe or Russia after the change of the system were forced to discover on the spot that everything depends on the context; in this sense they were unprepared

Figure 4.5   At Collegium Budapest, January 1998, receiving the *Festschrift* edited in his honor. From left to right are János Kornai, Professor Jenő Koltay, and Dr. János Gács.

for the job, although very well trained in the field of economics. The set of tools they brought with them did not include a deeper acquaintance with political science, sociology, psychology, history, et cetera. You can get a Ph.D. from Harvard or MIT without even getting close to these subjects. There's nothing wrong with neoclassical thinking in its place. It offers a workable research program. But as a way to train the mind, it's one-sided and too narrow.

Blanchard: Let us move further. In 1980, you published *Economics of Shortage*. After being burned for *Overcentralization*, and shifting to mathematical planning and *Anti-Equilibrium*, what made you, both intellectually and politically, return in print to the problems of the socialist system? Again, you've already referred to that, but would you mind saying more?

Kornai: Yes, there certainly was a shift in interest in my work over the years. However, on the one hand there was continuity because I had a lasting interest in the persistent phenomenon of the non-Walrasian state, especially in the socialist type of shortage economy or seller's market. I had treated these problems in *Anti-Equilibrium*: About a third of the book is devoted to seller's versus buyer's market issues. In 1972, I wrote a book criticizing the Stalinist growth pattern: *Rush versus Harmonic Growth*. In it I argue against unbalanced growth. On the other hand, you are certainly right: Over the years I did make a move toward politically more sensitive issues.

The reasons were varied: First of all, Hungary was slowly moving in a direction where limitations on the freedom of speech became less stringent. Another reason was my growing international reputation, due mainly to my work in mathematical economics and mathematical planning. All this allowed me more room for maneuvering at home. My principle was that if I felt I had certain constraints, I tried to exceed them by 20%. Due to the general trend in Hungary, the constraints slowly expanded, but I still tried to go beyond these limits. This strategy made it possible for me to write books that revealed the system's persistent troubles while still observing certain political taboos.

Blanchard: You mentioned earlier that you had been fired from your job in 1956 or 1957. Did you get that job back?

Kornai: Yes, I got the job back. The funny part of my story is that the same director who had celebrated me before October 1956, condemned me, and fired me after 1956, invited me back to the Institute of Economics, so I returned. Another typical thing was the following sequence of events: I had become a member of the American Academy and the British Academy before I was elected a member of the Hungarian Academy of Sciences. First I was a Visiting Professor at Stanford and Yale, and then I was invited to run a seminar at the Budapest University of Economics, which, in fact, did not offer me a regular professorship. But the regime in Hungary did follow what was happening to me, so they knew of my foreign acceptance and reputation, which widened my opportunities for writing.

Blanchard: The taboos you mentioned above were about the role of the Communist Party?

Kornai: There were four taboos in Hungary. (In Russia or in Czechoslovakia there were many more.) First, you couldn't question Hungary's belonging to the Warsaw Pact and its relationship to the Soviet Union; second, you couldn't question the Communist Party's monopoly of power; third, you could not reject the predominant role of state ownership; and fourth, you couldn't directly attack Marx, or even voice a serious critical view of him. An advantage of the Hungarian situation compared to that in Russia or Czechoslovakia was that you were not expected to make loyalty statements by actually telling the opposite of what you thought; you just had to leave these four issues alone.

Figure 4.6   At the Conference of the Scientific Advisory Board of the European Bank of Reconstruction and Development, Budapest, 1992. From left to right are Jean-Paul Fitoussi, Kenneth Arrow, János Kornai, and John Flemming.

You had to make a very difficult personal choice of life strategies. I mention this as it is by no means evident today. One choice was going, sort of, underground, write for "samizdat" and thus discarding taboos, which some of my friends did, and I admired the heroic risk-taking that involved. The price to be paid for this strategy was to give up the chances of reaching a wide readership. Another possibility was to defect. I followed a different route, similarly to some other Hungarian intellectuals: I published my views legally, but in a somewhat withdrawn manner. That was not without risks either, especially in case of deterioration in the general political situation; e.g., following a potential Stalinist restoration, it could have led to firing or even arrest. But it was certainly less risky under the prevailing political circumstances. The strategy I adopted involved a terribly difficult decision: It meant that I kept silent about some of my views and ideas. I never lied. I always wrote only the truth or what I thought the truth was, but I deliberately didn't write the full truth. I was hoping, which I think was quite reasonable, that many readers would read between the lines, or do some extrapolation. I even tried to give some hints, and I think I was successful in doing that.

I wrote the *Economics of Shortage* in Sweden, where I had long discussions with my wife during our walks in the woods about what chapters I should *not* include, how the book should end, et cetera. If you read the preface carefully, you'll find a list of subjects I omitted deliberately from the discussion, including the political monopoly of the Communist Party and state ownership. My message for the reader was "I know there are quite a few other things that would need discussing. Let it be your homework." I'm really proud of the fact that many readers including, for instance, people in China, Russia, and Poland told me after 1990 that they could follow me and understood what I was trying to say.

Blanchard: If you had to summarize the main contribution of the *Economics of Shortage* to economic thinking, would you single out "soft budget constraint"? Now that state socialism has practically disappeared as an economic system, what is the relevance of soft budget constraint? How would you characterize it as a general concept?

Kornai: Let me divide your question into two parts. You start by asking how I would summarize the main contribution, and immediately go on to the soft budget constraint. An East European or Russian or Chinese reader of the *Economics of Shortage* did not consider the theory of the soft budget constraint the main contribution at the time. For him or her the principal message of the book was this: The dysfunctional properties of socialism are systemic. I want to emphasize this appraisal in our conversation, because conveying this message I was rather isolated from the rest of the so-called reformers who were working on small changes to the communist system. In that sense, it's a revolutionary book, because the conclusion is that cosmetic changes and superficial reforms do not help. You have to change the system as a whole to get rid of the dysfunctional properties. That is the book's main contribution, and I think it had a great impact: The message got through. People in communist countries were much less interested in the soft budget constraint; they were interested in this central proposition. That was why it sold three editions in Hungary, 100,000 copies in China, and 80,000 in Russia. . . .

Blanchard: It sold more copies than some thrillers?

Kornai: Yes. There were certainly more royalties paid out for the thrillers. I did not get a penny for the 100,000 copies from the Chinese publisher, only a nice letter telling me that the book was awarded the title: "non-fiction bestseller of the year." I got a negligible royalty from Russia. What really matters in these cases is not the financial reward but the intellectual and political effect. I was happy that my ideas reached such a wide readership.

The concept of soft budget constraint had a much stronger impact on the profession in the West than in the East. It presents something that fits in with neoclassical thinking, but at the same time, steps out of it a bit, and brings some improvement on it. I think that's why it was and has remained influential. Perhaps there were other important findings in my work where I did not build a similar bridge between my results and the standard neoclassical thinking and therefore did not get a wider professional response.

My answer to the second part of your question is that soft budget constraint is not just a socialist phenomenon. It is very widespread and dominant under socialism, especially when market socialist reforms are introduced and the system is getting more profit-oriented and relaxed. It is sad, however, that the general validity of the concept is not sufficiently recognized. In my own understanding, there are many situations analogous to the soft-budget-constraint syndrome in a nonsocialist market economy. A former student of mine, Chenggang Xu at the London School of Economics, is now writing a paper analyzing the East Asian crisis using the same concept to explain the situation there. The relationship between the government, banks, and enterprises show signs of the soft-budget-constraint syndrome. The IMF bailouts of irresponsible borrowers in Japan, South Korea, and Indonesia—they are too big to let them fall—remind me again of soft budget constraint. In that sense, I find it a concept certainly valid in many cases: in the health sector, in industry and anywhere else where the state, the financial, and the production sectors are intertwined.

Blanchard: I think that the acceptance of the notion of soft budget constraint is now much wider than you state. It has indeed been used to describe the Asian crisis. But what was the impact of your work inside the socialist block, both on pretransition reforms and on transition?

Kornai: I think most leading reformers in the socialist countries read *Overcentralization*, and the book had some influence on their thinking. Later on, reformers also studied the Hungarian economic reforms of 1968. For instance, China adopted it as a model for its own reforms in the 1970s. So indirectly, I certainly had an influence on the reform process. As with every kind of intellectual effect, it is difficult to separate your own influence from that of others; therefore I cannot measure the strength of my impact.

In any case, this influence materialized only with a long time lag, 10 or 20 years after I published *Overcentralization*. By the time the market socialist reform first took momentum in Hungary, then in China, Poland, and the Soviet Union, I had already abandoned the idea of market socialism. I became highly critical of it, emphasizing the limitations of reforming socialism. That was the spirit of my articles on the Hungarian reform but, more importantly, that was the conclusion to be drawn by the reader of *Economics of Shortage*. A friend of mine called my and other's attitude to reforms "reform skepticism." In the 1970s and 1980s, this skeptical mentality was gradually gaining ground in Eastern Europe.

It became an ever-stronger conviction that partial reforms were not enough. I think my work contributed to that recognition.

Blanchard: Reading *The Socialist System*, published in 1992, it is not clear how much of the dynamics of collapse you had predicted before the event, and how much of it you explained after. Did you anticipate the type of transition that has actually taken place?

Kornai: Let me say a few words about the book before turning to the problem of right or wrong prognosis. *The Socialist System* is an attempt to describe the system as a whole. That is not a trivial objective, because most books only touch upon one or another aspect of a system. The great pioneer of this "system paradigm" was, of course, Karl Marx in *Das Kapital*.

Blanchard: How about Schumpeter?

Kornai: Schumpeter's work, his dynamic view of the entrepreneur and creative destruction has had a great impact on me. He indeed wrote a book, *Capitalism, Socialism and Democracy*, which intended to give a complex analysis of the two systems. But these two books, and a few others (e.g., some of Mises's and Hayek's works) are rather exceptional. A typical American textbook on economic systems is not written with the same ambition about capitalism with which I wrote about socialism. It doesn't give you a general model of capitalism, including the character-ization of the political, ideological, and social spheres.

Blanchard: It is not interdisciplinary.

Kornai: No, it's not. In writing the book, my intention was to grab the interaction and interdependence among the political structure, ideo-logy, ownership relations, the typical behavior of various actors—in short, the systemic properties. Also, to show the dynamics of the system.

Although I only started work on the book in 1986–87, the main ideas and structure of it had long been ready in my head. What my analysis of socialism predicted—in contrast to others'—was that patchwork-like reforms wouldn't strengthen the system; on the contrary, they would weaken it. The central idea of the book was to show that the classical, Stalinist system, however repressive and brutal it was, was coherent while the more relaxed, half-reformed Gorbachev-type of system was incoher-ent, and subject to erosion. I foresaw this erosion. What I did not foresee was the speed and exact timing of it. I have to admit that the events in 1989–90 were a real surprise for me. I hadn't expected the collapse of the Soviet system as early as that: It far exceeded all my expectations.

By the end of the 1980s, it was quite clear that the Hungarian version of the system was fast disintegrating. But for me the memory of 1956 in Budapest and of 1968 in Prague was still quite vivid, so I don't think my fear of the Russians interfering was ungrounded. Russian tanks would have probably been able to do the job again, as they did in 1956 and 1968. So the crucial puzzle was the extent of changes in the Soviet Union, not in Eastern Europe. Let me repeat: I didn't expect the erosion having started off by Gorbachev to work so fast.

Blanchard: Did you anticipate that Hungary would do no better than the Czech Republic or Poland? Do you now understand why? Were the previous reforms a help in Hungary after the change of the system?

Kornai: I don't think we can measure on a one-dimensional scale who is doing better. When doing a country-by-country analysis, the first thing to look at is the initial conditions, on which the appraisal of the changes should rest. I pointed out already in *The Socialist System* that the macro situation of the reforming countries was much worse than that of the nonreforming countries. The reason was simple: The Hungarian leadership wanted to maintain or regain the people's loyalty to the system with the help of popular measures. As soon as a country starts introducing market socialist reforms, there appear macro tensions, like a high inflation rate, a growing budget deficit, excess demand for credit, poor trade balance, and unbridled accumulation of debt. A comparison of Hungary and Czechoslovakia gives a tangible example. The relatively liberal, reforming Hungary had the largest per-capita debt in the communist region. It had made the most generous welfare commitments to its citizens, which shot up welfare spending and involved a lot of transfers. In a paper I wrote in 1992, I called Hungary a premature welfare state, as, in spite of being a poor country, it spent in percentage terms almost as much as Sweden on welfare, making the macroeconomic indicators even more unfavorable. At the same time the much more repressive Czechoslovak leader, Gustav Husak, was sufficiently tough to resist the temptation to reform.

So, in a way the balance was negative: The farther the reforms had gone the worse the macro state of the economy was in 1989–90. This means that Hungary had in some respect a much worse start than the Czech Republic.

On the other hand, the reforms had left a positive legacy as well. At the micro level they had exercised far-reaching, favorable influence: genuine property rights, a well-enforced legal infrastructure, a managerial elite and labor force that more or less understood how a market economy works, which greatly contributed to making Hungary an attractive place for foreign investment. All in all, one can say that the restructuring of the economy went better than elsewhere. So you have to be careful when assessing the changes.

Blanchard: Your point is important and very interesting, that the macro legacy may be worse while the micro legacy is better.

Kornai: Yes, but it only shows up if you look at several indicators, such as restructuring, technological change, the influx of foreign capital and foreign knowhow, et cetera, instead of concentrating on one single indicator.

Blanchard: Could it be that a softer budget constraint pre-transition also led to a softer budget constraint post-transition?

Kornai: Let's continue the comparison of Hungary and the Czech Republic: In hardening the budget constraint, Hungary was much tougher. It was the first country in the region to introduce a really rigorous bankruptcy act, along with Western-style accounting and banking acts, which led to a massive wave of liquidations. It surely improved Hungary's results in productivity, but also increased unemployment. One may ask whether that is a pro or a con. In any case, there was a spectacular celebration of the low unemployment rate in the Czech Republic. I'm not sure whether in a post-socialist economy low unemployment in itself is a virtue.

Blanchard: I'm not sure either. How do you view the economic research on transition? Did it get to the right issues right away?

Kornai: The questions raised by Western economists who became interested in the transition were right, but the list of issues they dealt with was incomplete. Anyway, the problem is not so much with the questions, but much more with the answers. The answers were sometimes oversimplified; they often remained outside the realm of the political and social context, although a careful contextual analysis could have helped recognizing which answer was right or wrong, timely or outdated.

Blanchard: Was there a very fast learning by doing? Did the analyses drastically improve, say, from 1990 to 1992 and 1993?

Kornai: There was no fast improvement, and there are many reasons for that. The first reason was that many people came just because they thought it was the thing to do: Let's go to some Eastern European country to give advice. They came and then left. Relatively few of them remained faithful to their initial interest and enthusiasm, and became experts in the field. I don't think there were many such people outside those working with the World Bank and the IMF, which, however, have problems of their own. First, they are subject to the strange practice of changing assignments, that is, if one becomes an expert in the field of post-communist transition, he is moved on to, say, Kenya or Colombia. This makes thorough learning really difficult. Second, they are in a delicate position politically. They are supposed to be nonpolitical, value-free technocrats, while most of the issues they are supposed to tackle are deeply political by definition: Every advice they give implies disguised or undisguised value judgments.

Blanchard: Have the people working on the socialist system, either from within or from outside, been able to use their knowledge to explain and help the transition?

Kornai: Most economists in the East were largely unprepared to deal with the problems thrown up by transition. I am talking about the whole region. Probably Hungary or Poland, where there had been some decent economic training for young people for a couple of years back, were in a better position. However, most of those filling certain positions are largely untrained for the job. While many of the Western economists don't understand the political and social context in the transition countries, many of their Eastern counterparts don't understand economics, which is probably worse. (And I'm not even sure if they understand politics or social issues.) Many of them are smart and have good intuition, good common sense, and a great routine in management gained in the socialist system or in the semimarket economy, but they were not trained as economists. Only a handful of them went through some serious training at Western universities. Others with a background in economics are now doing research; some are trying to get teaching positions somewhere in the West. Indeed, it will take many, many years to catch up with the West in that respect.

Altogether, I think, that the knowledge of economists both in the East and West is lopsided. However, what makes me really sad is that, instead of putting together their ideas, there is mutual distrust and a lack of discourse among them. It has been so far relatively rare for teams to be formed where the knowledge of the members could complement each other. This kind of cooperation must be forwarded by all means.

Blanchard: Do you think that, 10 years from now, Central Europe will look no different from Portugal or Italy, or that there will be important political and economic legacies of the socialist at work?

Kornai: I expect some convergence, so it will be less different, but I also expect to see traces in the same sense as you see traces of the Japanese past in today's Japan. Japan is still not the United States or Great Britain, and certainly a Latin American capitalist country is different from a Muslim capitalist country.

I expect two types of legacies or traces to survive, maybe diminishing over time: one in ideals, values, expectations, and social norms. These societies hold ideals of a far-reaching income-equalizing distribution. It's deeply embedded in the thinking of people, very much alive today. There is strong resistance against reforming, for instance, the welfare state; mind you, to some extent that applies to most Western European traditions, to the German or Austrian and even to the French or Swedish traditions. The second legacy is in the networks of people. When a country changes over from the rule of aristocracy to a bourgeois society, the aristocrats still have their own networks. I think people belonging to the elite of the former socialist regime have, with few exceptions, totally forgotten the Communist Manifesto but they have a network of friends from the old days. Right now these relations are extremely powerful in business, in politics, in cultural life. People who knew each other in the old system, know exactly who is a friend and who is an enemy; that won't cease overnight. However, 10 years is a relatively short time. You should ask the same question in about 20 or 30 years.

Blanchard: Many of these people seem to be quite competent in their new role.

Kornai: Yes, there is a natural selection; if you're incompetent, just to have a friend is not enough, so you retire or get a mediocre job. If you have the right friends plus you have certain gifts and talents, then you can make it. In any case, while these distinctive features and attitudes remain for a long time, post-communist countries will become "normal" capitalist economies.

REFERENCE

Dorfman, R., P.A. Samuelson & R.M. Solow (1958) *Linear Programming and Economic Analysis.* New York: McGraw–Hill.

5

An Interview with Franco Modigliani

Interviewed by William A. Barnett
UNIVERSITY OF KANSAS

and

Robert Solow
MASSACHUSETTS INSTITUTE OF TECHNOLOGY

November 5–6, 1999

Franco Modigliani's contributions in economics and finance have transformed both fields. Although many other major contributions in those fields have come and gone, Modigliani's contributions seem to grow in importance with time. His famous 1944 article on liquidity preference has not only remained required reading for generations of Keynesian economists but has become part of the vocabulary of all economists. The implications of the life-cycle hypothesis of consumption and saving provided the primary motivation for the incorporation of finite lifetime models into macroeconomics and had a seminal role in the growth in macroeconomics of the overlapping generations approach to modeling of Allais, Samuelson, and Diamond. Modigliani and Miller's work on the cost of capital transformed corporate finance and deeply influenced subsequent research on investment, capital asset pricing, and recent research on derivatives. Modigliani received the Nobel Memorial Prize for Economics in 1985.

Reprinted from *Macroeconomic Dynamics*, 4, 2000, 222–256. Copyright © 2000 Cambridge University Press. Barnett was on the faculty at Washington University in St. Louis when this article was written.

In macroeconomic policy, Modigliani has remained influential on two continents. In the United States, he played a central role in the creation of the Federal Reserve System's large-scale quarterly macroeconometric model, and he frequently participated in the semiannual meetings of academic consultants to the Board of Governors of the Federal Reserve System in Washington, D.C. His visibility in European policy matters is most evident in Italy, where nearly everyone seems to know him as a celebrity, from his frequent appearances in the media. In the rest of Europe, his visibility has been enhanced by his publication, with a group of distinguished European and American economists, of "An Economists' Manifesto on Unemployment in the European Union," which was signed by a number of famous economists and endorsed by several others.

This interview was conducted in two parts on different dates in two different locations, and later unified. The initial interview was conducted by Robert Solow at Modigliani's vacation home in Martha's Vineyard. Following the transcription of the tape from that interview, the rest of the interview was conducted by William A. Barnett in Modigliani's apartment on the top floor of a high-rise building overlooking the Charles River near Harvard University in Cambridge, Massachusetts. Those concluding parts of the interview in Cambridge continued for the two days of November 5–6, 1999, with breaks for lunch and for the excellent espresso coffee prepared by Modigliani in an elaborate machine that would be owned only by someone who takes fine coffee seriously. Although the impact that Modigliani has had on the economics and finance professions is clear to all members of those professions, only his students can understand the inspiration that he has provided to them. However, that may have been adequately reflected by Robert Shiller at Yale University in correspondence regarding this interview, when he referred to Modigliani as: "my hero."

Figure 5.1   Franco Modigliani (formal portrait photo, date unknown).

Barnett: In your discussion below with Solow, you mentioned that you were not learning much as a student in Italy and you moved to the United States. Would you tell us more about when it was that you left Italy, and why you did so?

Modigliani: After the Ethiopian war and the fascist intervention in the Spanish Civil War, I began to develop a strong antifascist sentiment and the intent to leave Italy, but the final step was the close alliance of Mussolini with Hitler, which resulted in anti-Semitic laws, which made it impossible to live in Italy in a dignified way. At that time I had already met my future wife, Serena, and we were engaged. Her father had long been antifascist and preparing to leave Italy. When those laws passed, we immediately packed and left Italy for France. We spent 1939 in France, where we made arrangements to leave for the United States. We left in August 1939 for the United States on the very day of the famous pact between Hitler and Stalin, which led to what was the later attack by Germany on Russia. I came to the United States with no prior arrangements with a university. I wanted very much to study economics, and I received a scholarship from the New School for Social Research, thanks in part to the fact that the school had many prominent intellectual antifascists, and one of them, the renowned antifascist refugee, Max Ascoli, helped me to get the scholarship.

Barnett: Franco, I understand that after you had left Italy you returned to Italy to defend your dissertation. Can you tell us whether there were any risks or dangers associated with your return to defend your dissertation?

Modigliani: Yes, it is true that when we left from Rome to Paris, I had finished all of my examinations to get my degree, but I had not yet defended my thesis. In July of 1939, before leaving Paris for the United States, I wanted to have all my records complete, and I decided to go back to Rome to defend my thesis. That operation was not without dangers, because by that time I could have been arrested. I had kept my contacts with antifascist groups in Paris, so there was the possibility of being harassed or being jailed. Fortunately nothing happened. My father-in-law was very worried, and we had made arrangements for him to warn us of any impending perils by a code. The code was all about Uncle Ben. If he was not feeling well, we should be ready to go. If he was dead, we should leave instantly. We never needed to use that code, but I felt relieved when I was able to complete my thesis, and then late in August we left for the United States.

Barnett: The famous painter and sculptor, Amedeo Modigliani, was born in Livorno, Italy, in 1884 and died in Paris in 1920. Was he related to your family?

Modigliani: There is no known relation.

Solow: Franco, the first thing I want to talk about is your 1944 *Econometrica* paper, "Liquidity Preference and the Theory of Interest and Money." When you were writing it, you were 25 years old?

Modigliani: Yes, about that. I hadn't studied very much in Italy of any use. There was no useful teaching of economics. What was taught there was something about the corporate state. So all I picked up was at the New School of Social Research in New York with the guidance of Jacob Marschak.

Solow: When was that?

Modigliani: That was 1939 through 1941–42.

Solow: So your main guide was Jascha Marschak.

Modigliani: Jascha Marschak was my mentor. We studied Keynes and the *General Theory* in classes with Marschak. I attended two different seminars, but in addition received a lot of advice and support from him. He suggested readings and persuaded me of the importance of mathematical tools, acquired by studying some calculus and understanding thoroughly the great book of the day by R.G.D. Allen, *Mathematical Analysis for Economists*, and studying some serious statistics (attending Abraham Wald lectures at Columbia); and last but not least he sponsored my participation in a wonderful informal seminar, which included besides Marschak people like Tjalling Koopmans and Oskar Lange. But unfortunately, to my great sorrow, Marschak in 1942 left New York for Chicago. He was replaced by another notable mind, Abba Lerner. I had a lot of discussions with him about Keynes. At that time, Abba Lerner was pushing so-called functional finance.

Solow: Yes, the famous "steering wheel."

Modigliani: Functional finance led me to the 1944 article. In functional finance, only fiscal policy could have an impact on aggregate demand. Therefore, it was an economy that belonged to what I later called the Keynesian case. I tried to argue with Lerner and to have him understand that Keynes did not say that. That was the origin of the 1944 article, trying to put Keynes in perspective.

Solow: Now, with Marschak or Lerner, had you read any of the earlier mathematical models of Keynesian economics, such as Hicks's, of course, or Oscar Lange's articles?

Modigliani: Well, I was familiar with the literature, and of course it had hit me, as is visible in my articles. Hicks's article on Keynes and the classics was a great article, and it was the starting point of my article, except that in Hicks the rigidity of wages was just taken as a datum, and no consideration was given to alternatives. It was just the one system, and fixed forever.

Solow: What he later called "a fixed-price model."

Figure 5.2 In Stockholm in December 1991, at a reunion of the Nobel Prize winners. From left to right are Kenneth Arrow, Franco Modigliani, Paul Samuelson, and Robert Solow.

Modigliani: Fixed price so that he could deal in nominal terms as though they were real. Money supply is both nominal and real.

Barnett: Prior to your arrival at MIT, you were at a number of American universities, including the New School for Social Research, the New Jersey College for Women (now Douglas College), Bard College of Columbia University, the University of Chicago, the University of Illinois, Carnegie Institute of Technology (now Carnegie Mellon University), and Northwestern University. Prior to MIT, what were the most productive periods for you in the United States?

Modigliani: The most productive period was unquestionably the eight years or so (1952–60) spent at Carnegie Tech, with an exceptionally stimulating group of faculty and students, led by two brilliant personalities, the dean, G.L. Bach, and Herbert Simon, working on the exciting task of redesigning the curriculum of modern business schools, and writing exciting papers, some of which were to be cited many years later in the Nobel award: the papers on the life-cycle hypothesis and the Modigliani and Miller papers.

Barnett: I've heard that while you were teaching at the New School, you had an offer from the Economics Department at Harvard University, which at that time was by far the best economics department in the United States. But to the surprise of the faculty, you turned down the offer. Why did you do that?

Modigliani: Because the head of the department, Professor Burbank, whom I later found out had a reputation of being xenophobic and anti-Semitic, worked very hard and successfully to persuade me to turn down the offer, which the faculty had instructed him to make me. He explained that I could not possibly hold up against the competition of bright young people like Alexander, Duesenberry, and Goodwin. "Be satisfied with being a big fish in a small pond." Actually it did not take me too long to be persuaded. Then, after my meeting with Burbank, I had scheduled a lunch with Schumpeter, Haberler, and Leontief, who had expected to congratulate me on joining them. But they literally gave me hell for letting Burbank push me over. Nevertheless, in reality I have never regretted my decision. Harvard's pay at that time was pretty miserable, and my career progressed much faster than it would have, if I had accepted the offer.

Barnett: I understand that the great football player Red Grange (the Galloping Ghost) had something to do with your decision to leave the University of Illinois. What happened at the University of Illinois that caused you to leave?

Modigliani: In short it was the "Bowen Wars," as the episode came to be known in the profession. The president of the university brought in a new wonderful dean, Howard H. Bowen, to head the College of Commerce, which included the Department of Economics. But the old and incompetent faculty could not stand the fact that Bowen brought in some first-rate people like Leo Hurwicz, Margaret Reid, and Dorothy Brady. The old faculty was able to force Bowen out, as part of the witch hunt that was going on under the leadership of the infamous Senator Joseph McCarthy. The leader of the McCarthyite wing of the elected trustees was the famous Red Grange. I then quit in disgust with a blast that in the local press is still remembered: "There is finally peace in the College of Commerce, but it is the peace of death." My departure was greeted with joy by the old staff, proportional to their incompetence. But 40 years later, the university saw fit to give me an honorary degree!

Solow: Well, how do you look at the 1944 paper now? Would you change it drastically if you were rewriting it?

Modigliani: Yes! Not really in content, but in presentation. That is what I have been doing in my autobiography. I am revising that paper completely and starting from an approach which I think is much more useful. I am starting from the notion that both the classics and Keynes take their departure from the classical demand for money model, which is one of the oldest and best-established paradigms in economics. The demand for money is proportional to the value of transactions, which at any point can be approximated as proportional to nominal income (real income multiplied by the price level). The nominal money supply is exogenous. Therefore, the money market must reach an equilibrium through changes *in nominal income*. Nominal income is the variable that clears the money market.

Where then is the difference between classical and Keynesian economics? Simple: The classics assumed that wages were highly flexible and output fixed by full employment (clearing of the labor market). Thus the quantity of money had *no effect on output but merely determined the price level, which was proportional to the nominal money supply* (the *quantity theory of money*). On the other hand, Keynes relied on the *realistic assumption* that wages are rigid (downward). That is, they do not promptly decline in response to an excess supply of labor. Workers do not slash their nominal wage demands, and firms do not slash their wage offers, when unemployment exceeds the frictional level. What, then, clears the money market? Again, it is a decline in nominal income. But since prices are basically fixed, the decline must occur in real income and particularly in employment. When there is insufficient nominal money supply to satisfy the full employment demand for money, the market is cleared through a decline in output and employment. As Keynes said, the fundamental issue is that prices are not flexible.

Solow: Not instantly flexible.

Modigliani: That's right. They may very slowly respond, but a very slow adjustment of the real money supply can't produce the expansion of the real money supply needed to produce a rapid reestablishment of equilibrium. What, then, reestablishes equilibrium? Since wages and prices are fixed, the decline in nominal income can only occur through a decline in real income and employment. There will be a unique level of real income that clears the money market, making the money demand equal to the money supply.

Solow: No mention of the interest rate?

Modigliani: The interest rate comes next, as a link in the equilibrating mechanism. In fact, Keynes's unique achievement consisted not only in showing that unemployment is the variable that clears the money market; he also elaborated the mechanism by which an excess demand for money causes a decline of output and thus in the demand for money, until the demand matches the given nominal money supply. In the process of developing this mechanism, unknown to the classics, he created a new branch of economics: *macroeconomics.*

Macroeconomics, or the mechanisms through which money supply determines output (employment), stands on four basic pillars, with which, by now, most economists are familiar: (1) liquidity preference, (2) the investment function, (3) the consumption or saving function, and (4) the equality of saving and investment (properly generalized for the role of government and the rest of the world).

Liquidity preference is not just the fact that the demand for money depends on the interest rate; it brings to light the profound error of classical monetary theory in assuming that the price of money is its purchasing power over commodities (baskets per dollar) and that, therefore, a shortage of money must result in a prompt rise in its purchasing power (a fall in the price level). In reality, of course, money has many prices, one in terms of every commodity or instrument for which it can be exchanged. Among these instruments, by far the most important one is *"money in the future,"* *and its price is money tomorrow per unit of money today*, which is simply $(1 + r)$, where r is the relevant interest rate.

Furthermore, experience shows that financial markets are very responsive to market conditions: Interest rates (especially in the short run) are highly flexible. So, if money demand is short of supply, the prompt reaction is not to liquidate the warehouse or skimp on dinner, forcing down commodity prices, but a liquidation in the portfolio of claims to future money (or a rise in borrowing spot for future money), leading to a rise in the terms of trade between money today and tomorrow—that is, a rise in interest rates. And this starts the chain leading to lower output through a fall in investment, a fall in saving, and thus in income and employment. It is this fall, together with the rise in interest rates, that reduces the demand for money till it matches the supply.

Solow: Yes, so the interest rate is a key price.

Modigliani: Actually it's one plus the interest rate. If you are short of money, and the system does not have enough money, the first thing it attempts is to get more spot money by either liquidating assets or by borrowing, which is borrowing money today against money tomorrow. Interest rates rise, reducing investment, and then comes the great equation: investment equals savings—an identity that is so far from the classical view that in the beginning they would not even believe it.

Solow: Right.

Modigliani: And income then adjusts so that the demand for money is finally equated to its supply. This will result in both a higher interest rate and a lower income. The two together will serve to equate the money demanded with the given supplied. And how much must interest rates rise or income decline? That depends upon the parameters of the system (demand elasticities).

Solow: But exactly! And Keynes's fundamental contribution then was to say that it's not the interest rate and the price level, but interest and real output.

Modigliani: Yes, precisely. I think this is the way to look at it. It is the output that adjusts demand and supply.

Solow: What you just described is maybe a different way of telling a story and saying what's important, but it's not fundamentally different from what's in the 1944 paper or in the IS–LM apparatus.

Modigliani: Absolutely. But I suggest that to think of unemployment not as a transitory disease, but as a variable that clears the money market, is a useful and significant innovation. Unemployment is an equilibrating mechanism. It seems like a dysfunction, since we think that full employment is what an economy should produce. But unemployment is a systematic feature of an economy relying on money to carry out transactions. To avoid unemployment, it takes continuous care by either setting the right money supply or fixing the right interest rate. There is no other way to get full employment. There is nothing automatic about it.

Barnett: Some work on monetary policy has emphasized the possibility that the monetary transmission mechanism works through a credit channel. The implication of this research is that monetary policy may affect consumer and business spending, because it affects the quantity of credit available to agents, rather than the interest rate. This work is often motivated by the observation that the interest elasticity of spending is too low to explain the large impact monetary policy appears to have on real economic activity. Do you think there is an important credit channel for monetary policy?

Modigliani: My attitude toward this question, about which I have done much thinking and some writing, is that in the end it is an empirical question, not an a priori question. It is entirely credible that monetary policy may work, in part, through changing the volume of credit supplied by banks in the form of commercial loans, as well as its cost. That way it may have the same effects as acting through market interest rates, but without necessarily producing large movements in interest rates. I think that future research will help in sorting this out. But the answer will not be perpetual, since the answer depends upon the structure of financial intermediaries and the laws regulating them.

Solow: Now one of the questions I've wanted to ask you, which I think you've already now answered, is what does it mean to be a Keynesian today? But I take it that what you just said is the essence of Keynesian economics, and by that definition you would describe yourself as a Keynesian.

Modigliani: Absolutely. I consider myself a Keynesian. Now as I think it over in this light, I consider Keynesian economics to be a great revolution, having a really tremendous impact, with tremendously novel ideas. Again I consider myself a Keynesian in the very fundamental sense that I know the system does not automatically tend to full employment without appropriate policies. Price flexibility will not produce full employment, and therefore unemployment is always due to an insufficiency of real money. But it must be recognized that there are certain circumstances under which the Central Bank may not be able to produce the right real money supply. For instance, the case of Italy was interesting. Unemployment there was due to the fact that real wages were too high, in the sense that they resulted in substantially negative net exports at full employment. Under those circumstances, if the Central Bank expanded the money supply to create more aggregate demand and employment, the balance of trade would run into nonfinancable deficits, and the Central Bank would be forced to contract. So, you're not always able to increase the real money supply. But that's not the case in Europe, where the money supply could be easily increased and the unemployment is largely due to insufficient real money supply.

Solow: You know I rather agree with you about that.

Modigliani: Interest rates are too high. There is not enough real money being supplied. This is not being understood. Keynes is not being understood. That's the main source of European unemployment. Some improvements in the labor market, such as more wage flexibility, could help, but would not get very far without a significant rise in aggregate demand (which at present would not significantly increase the danger of inflation).

Solow: Right, but you cannot get European central bankers to see that.

Modigliani: In Europe they accept the view that long-lasting unemployment contributes to the current high level because it reduces search by the unemployed, *causing long-term unemployment.* No, sir. That's a consequence of the too restrictive policy.

Barnett: You have argued that stock market bubbles sometimes are produced by misinterpreting capital gains as a maintainable component of current returns (a permanent addition to current profits). Do you believe that that phenomenon is going on now, or do you believe that current stock market valuations are consistent with the fundamentals?

Modigliani: I am very much interested and concerned about bubbles, and I believe that bubbles do exist. They are one of the sources of malfunctioning of the market mechanism. The essence of these bubbles is that indeed capital gains get confused with profits, and this results in the stock becoming more attractive, so people bid up the price, which produces more capital gains, and so on. I believe that indeed the stock market in the United States is in the grips of a serious bubble. I think the overvaluation of stocks is probably on the order of 25% or so, but, by the nature of the process, it is not possible to predict just when the whole thing will collapse. In my view, there will be a collapse because if there is a marked overvaluation, as I hold, it cannot disappear slowly.

Barnett: How does your research help us understand what has occurred over the past few years in the volatile economies of East Asia?

Modigliani: My view is that what has happened in East Asia is very much in the nature of a bubble, where expected high returns have attracted capital. The attraction of capital has held up exchange rates, permitting large deficits in the balance of trade; the influx of capital has supported the exchange rate making capital investment more attractive. So, you have a spiral until people realize that those returns are really not maintainable. I think it is important for the future of the international situation to set up systems under which bubbles cannot develop or are hard to develop, such as requiring reserves against short-term capital movements.

Solow: Now, I want to ask what's your current belief about wage behavior? How would you today model the behavior of nominal or real wages?

Modigliani: This, I think, is one of the fundamental issues that we face today, because in my model the wage and the price level are exogenous. Why is the price level exogenous? Because prices fundamentally depend upon wages, and wages are not flexible. Wages are certainly not responding mechanically to unemployment. So what do we do about wages? Well, I do think that some of this rigidity of wages is historical. It's very likely that in the nineteenth century the situation was different. In that century there was a greater role for competitive industries such as agriculture. In any event, the wage is *the* fundamental component of the price level. What's going to determine wages? Well, we've come to a difficult period, mostly since unions in Europe have been very powerful. They've become unreasonable and pushed for higher and higher wages, nominal wages. But my view is that in the long run we'll have to reach the point at which the wage, the nominal wage, is negotiated in a general simultaneous settlement of wages and prices. Now that's what's happened in Italy.

Solow: Say some more about that.

Modigliani: What saved Italy from the tremendously disastrous situation that existed just before devaluation was the fact that workers agreed to fix nominal wages for three years together with a price program, so that real as well as nominal wages were set. To me, that is the future because I do not know what else to say about the price picture.

Solow: What you're saying is that Keynes's remark that labor cannot determine the real wage may turn out to be false because institutions change and permit bargaining over the real wage.

Figure 5.3   In Stockholm in 1985, after receiving the Nobel Prize.

Modigliani: That's right. Yes, yes.

Solow: What's your current feeling about NAIRU, the nonaccelerating-inflation rate of unemployment?

Modigliani: I think it is true that if unemployment gets too low, then you will have accelerating inflation, not just higher inflation but higher rate of change of inflation. But I do not believe that if unemployment gets very high, you'll ever get to falling nominal wages. You may get very low acceleration of wages, or you may get to the point at which wages don't move. But I don't believe that high unemployment will give us negative wage changes.

Solow: We might even get falling wages for a while, but you would surely not get accelerating reductions in wages. No believer in the NAIRU ever wants to speak about that side of the equation.

Modigliani: That's right. So I think that these views are consistent, in the sense that left alone there may be a tendency for the system to be always in inflation. The Central Bank can pursue full employment policy without simultaneously being concerned that it must keep the inflation rate at zero. What I regard as a real tragedy today is the fact that all of a sudden the European banks and many other banks have shifted to the single-minded target of price stability. I think that is one of the sources of the European tragedy, in contrast with the shining performance of the United States. No concern whatever about employment.

Solow: Well, they argue that there is nothing they can do about it, but you and I think that's fundamentally wrong and simply a way of avoiding responsibility.

Modigliani: Exactly. And on the contrary, I think they should say the priority target should be "first unemployment," though price stability is also very important. There are situations in which indeed you may either have to accommodate inflation or stop it at the cost of temporary unemployment. I think *then* I would accept unemployment as a temporary state to stop an inflationary spiral. But to say that price stability is *the* only target, I think is wrong.

Solow: So, you don't believe that the NAIRU in France is 13% today?

Modigliani: Absolutely not, absolutely not. Nor do I believe that here in this country it is as low as 4%. I have great doubts about the stability of NAIRU but even more about the appropriate way to estimate it.

Barnett: While I was an undergraduate student at MIT, I was permitted to take your graduate course in corporate finance. I shared with the graduate students in the class the view that the Modigliani–Miller work on the cost of capital was dramatically raising the level of sophistication of the field of corporate finance. What motivated you to enter that area of research, and what earlier research inspired you?

Modigliani: Ever since my 1944 article on Keynes, I have become interested in empirical tests of the Keynesian structure. As everybody knows, one of the key components of that structure is the investment function, which explains investment in terms of the interest rate, seen as the cost of capital, the cost of funds invested. I was then under the influence of the views of the corporate finance specialists that the cost of funds depended upon the way in which the firm was financed. If you issued stock, then the cost of that would be the return on equity, which might be 10%, but if you used bonds, the cost would be their interest rate, which might be only 5%. That sort of answer didn't seem to me to be very convincing. In the end, what was the cost of capital: 5% or 10%? To an economist it could not be rational to say that the required return was 5% if you chose to finance the project by debt and 10% if you chose equity. After listening to a paper by David Durand suggesting (and then rejecting) the so-called "entity theory" of valuation, I gradually became convinced of the hypothesis that market value should be independent of the structure of financing, and was able to sketch out a proof of the possibility of arbitraging differences in valuation that are due only to differences in the liability structure. This result later became part of the proof of the Modigliani–Miller theorem. In essence, the market value of liabilities could not depend on its structure, because the investor could readily reproduce any leverage structure through personal lending or borrowing (as long as there was no tax impediment). As a consequence, there was no difference between the use of equity and debt funds. Even though debt had a lower apparent cost, it increased the required return on equity, and the weighted average of the two would be unaffected by the composition. I unveiled my proof in a class in which Miller happened to be an auditor. He was convinced instantly and decided to join me in the crusade to bring the truth to the heathens.

The theorem, which by now is well known, was proven very laboriously in about 30 pages. The reason for the laboriousness was in part because the theorem was so much against the grain of the teachings of corporate finance—the art and science of designing the "optimal capital structure." We were threatening to take the bread away, and so, we felt that we had to give a "laborious" proof to persuade them. Unfortunately, the price was paid by generations of students that had to read the paper; I have met many MBA students that remember that paper as a torture, the most difficult reading in the course. It's too bad because, nowadays, the theorem seems to me to be so obvious that I wonder whether it deserves two Nobel Prizes. All that it really says is that (with well-working markets, rational-return-maximizing behavior for any given risk, and no distorting taxes) the value of a firm—its market capitalization of all liabilities—must be the value of its assets. The composition of the claims can change (equity, debt, preferred, convertible preferred, derivatives, and what not), but the aggregate value of the claims cannot change. It is the value of the assets. Of course, it is true that this conclusion implies that the way that you finance investment is immaterial. It follows that in estimating the required return, the cost of capital, we do not have to bother with the details of the composition of the financing. In that sense, Jorgenson is right.

In later years, the Modigliani–Miller theorem has provided the foundation for the work on derivatives—such as options. All of that work assumes that the underlying value of the firm is independent of its current liability structure. But let me remind you of the assumptions needed to establish the theorem and, in particular, the assumption of no distorting effects of taxation on the net-of-tax amount received by an individual from one dollar of before-interest corporate earnings. If there are such effects, then the situation is more complicated, and in fact in this area there is a disagreement between Miller and me. I believe that taxes can introduce a differential advantage between different kinds of instruments, while Miller thinks not. But I should add that even though, in principle, taxation could affect the comparative advantage of different instruments, Miller and I agree that, with the current system of taxation, the differences are unlikely to be appreciable.

Solow: Now I want to make room here for you to make a brief comment about real business-cycle theory. If you look at macroeconomic theory today, what has replaced the Keynesian economics that you and I both accept is, in the minds of young people, real business-cycle theory.

Modigliani: I have no difficulty in believing that business cycles can exist in the real economy. You don't need money, and I myself built models of that kind, when it was fashionable. There was Hicks's article on the business cycle, and then Sidney Alexander had a very interesting article on the introduction of a bound that can permit you to get a cycle without money. But I think that has little to do with Keynesian unemployment. In the thirties, for instance, there was a tremendous depression that I think was caused by an insufficiency of real money. That was a horrible error made by the Federal Reserve, a point on which Milton Friedman and I agree. There was a serious shortage of real money and irresponsible behavior in letting the money supply shrink. I think that unemployment is mostly due to the rigidity of wages and to the shifting conditions. Therefore, there is the need for adjustment by the Central Bank, and the adjustment must be fast enough.

Solow: What's distinctive about real business-cycle theory is not just that it says that the monetary mechanism has nothing to do with cycles, but that business cycles, as we observe them, are optimal reactions of the economy to unexpected shocks to technology and tastes and things like that.

Modigliani: Yes, yes. Well, of course, much of this goes back to rational expectations, and my attitude toward rational expectations is that it is a wonderful theory. It is indeed the crowning of the classical theory. The classical theory spoke of optimal response to expectations. Lucas and company add optimal formation of expectations. From that point of view, I am satisfied that that is what economic theory would say; and I am proud because I contributed an important concept, which is, I think, at the essence of rational expectations, namely, the existence of expectations that map into themselves.

Solow: Self-validating.

Modigliani: Self-validating. No, not "self-validating"—"internally consistent."

Solow: That's what I meant by self-validating. There is one set of expectations that is self-validating, not that every set is self-validating.

Modigliani: That's right, because usually self-validating means that it happens because you expect it. This is not the case. In addition, I believe that it is *not* a description of the world. I don't believe that the world is behaving rationally in that extreme sense, and there are many circumstances under which the model will not apply. In particular, I do not believe that that model justifies the conclusion that anything the government does is bad.

Solow: It adds variance and the mean is already right, so discretionary policy is bad.

Modigliani: It creates noise, so therefore whatever government does is bad. Wage rigidity to me is a perfect example contradicting the above conclusion. Nor can you dispose of wage rigidity with the hypothesis of staggered contract. If that contract is rational, then wages *are* rigid and one better take this into account in theory and policy; or the staggered contract is not rational and in a Chicago world, it should have long ago disappeared.

Barnett: Robert Barro, who I understood was a student in some of your classes, advocates a version of Ricardian equivalence that appears to be analogous in governmental finance to the Modigliani–Miller theorem in corporate finance and in some ways to your life-cycle theory of savings with bequests. In fact, he sometimes speaks of one of your classes at MIT that he attended in 1969 as being relevant to his views. But I understand that you do not agree with Barro's views of government finance. Why is that?

Modigliani: Barro's Ricardian equivalence theorem has nothing in common with the Modigliani–Miller proposition, *except the trivial relation that something doesn't matter*. In the Modigliani–Miller theorem, it is capital structure, and in the Barro theorem it is government deficit. In my view, Barro's theorem, despite its elegance, has *no* substance. I don't understand why so many seem to be persuaded by a proposition whose proof rests on the incredible assumption that everybody cares about his heirs as if they were himself. If you drop that assumption, there is no proof based on rational behavior, and the theorem is untenable. But that kind of behavior is very rare and can't be universal. Just ask yourself what would happen with two families, when one family has no children and another family has 10. Under Ricardian equivalence, both families would be indifferent between using taxes or deficit financing. But it is obvious that the no-children family would prefer the deficit, and the other would presumably prefer taxation. Indeed, why should the no-children family save more, when the government runs a deficit? I am just sorry that any parallel is made between Modigliani–Miller and Ricardian equivalence.

I have in fact offered concrete empirical evidence, and plenty of it, that government debt displaces capital in the portfolio of households and hence in the economy. My paper is a bit old, though it has been replicated in unpublished research. But there is an episode in recent history that provides an excellent opportunity to test Barro's model of no burden against the life-cycle hypothesis measure of burden—the displacement effect. I am referring to the great experiment unwittingly performed by Reagan cutting taxes and increasing expenditure between 1981 (the first Reagan budget) and 1992. The federal debt increased $3\frac{1}{4}$ times or from 7% of initial private net worth to about 30%. In the same interval, disposable (nominal) personal income grew 117% [all data from the

Economic Report of the President, 1994, Table B-112 and B-28]. According to my model, private wealth is roughly proportional to net-of-tax income, and hence it should also have increased by 117%, relative to the initial net worth. But net national wealth (net worth less government debt, which represents essentially the stock of productive private capital) should have increased 117% minus the growth of debt, or 117 − 23 = 94% (of initial net worth). The 23% is the crowding-out effect of government debt, according to the life-cycle hypothesis. The actual growth of national wealth turns out to be 88%, pretty close to my prediction of 94%. On the other hand, if the government debt does not crowd out national wealth, as Barro firmly holds, then the increase in the latter should have been the same as that of income, or 117% compared with 88%. Similarly for Barro the growth of private net worth should be the growth of income of 117% *plus* the 23% growth of debt, or 140%. The actual growth is 111%, very close to my prediction of 117% and far from his, and the small deviation is in the direction opposite to that predicted by Barro.

Figure 5.4   In Stockholm in 1985, after receiving the Nobel Prize. Left to right are Sergio Modigliani (son), Leah Modigliani (granddaughter), Franco Modigliani, Queen Silvia of Sweden, King Gustav Adolph of Sweden, Serena Modigliani (wife), Suzanne Modigliani (wife of Sergio), Andre Modigliani (son), and Julia Modigliani (granddaughter).

Why do so many economists continue to pay so much attention to Barro's model over the life-cycle hypothesis?

Solow: Okay, let's move on. I think the next thing we ought to discuss is your Presidential Address to the American Economic Association and how, in your mind, it relates both to the 1944 paper that you've been talking about and your later work.

Modigliani: As I said before about Keynes, I stick completely to my view that to maintain a stable economy you need stabilization policy. Fiscal policy should, first of all, come in as an automatic stabilizer. Secondly, fiscal policy might enter in support of monetary policy in extreme conditions. But normally we should try to maintain full employment with savings used to finance investment, not to finance deficits. We should rely on monetary policy to ensure full employment with a balanced budget. But one thing I'd like to add is that it seems to me that in the battle between my recommendation to make use of discretion (or common sense) and Friedman's recommendation to renounce discretion in favor of blind rules (like 3% money growth per year), my prescription has won hands down. There is not a country in the world today that uses a mechanical rule.

Solow: It's hard to imagine in a democratic country.

Modigliani: There is not a country that doesn't use discretion.

Solow: You know, I agree with you there. How would you relate the view of your Presidential Address to monetarism? It was stimulated by monetarism, in a way. How do you look at old monetarism, Milton Friedman's monetarism, now?

Modigliani: If by monetarism one means money matters, I am in agreement. In fact, my present view is that *real* money is the most important variable. But I think that a rigid monetary rule is a mistake. It is quite possible that in a very stable period, that might be a good starting point, but I would certainly not accept the idea that that's the way to conduct an economic policy in general.

Solow: And hasn't Milton sometimes, but not always, floated the idea that he can find no interest elasticity in the demand for money.

Modigliani: I've done several papers on that subject and rejected that claim all over the place. Anybody who wants to find it, finds it strikingly—absolutely no problem.

Solow: You had a major involvement in the development of the Federal Reserve's MPS quarterly macroeconometric model, but not lately. How do you feel about large econometric models now? There was a time when someone like Bob Hall might have thought that that's the future of macroeconomics. There is no room for other approaches. All research will be conducted in the context of his model.

Modigliani: Right. Well, I don't know. I imagine that, first of all, the notion of parsimoniousness is a useful notion, the notion that one should try to construct models that are not too big, models that are more compact in size. I think that at the present time these models are still useful. They still give useful forecasts and especially ways of gauging responses to alternative policies, which is most important. But under some international circumstances, there is no room for domestic monetary policy in some countries. In such a country, an econometric model may not be very helpful. But an econometric model would be somewhat useful in considering different fiscal policies.

Barnett: Has mentoring younger economists been important to you as your fame grew within the profession?

Modigliani: My relation with my students, which by now are legion, has been the best aspect of my life. I like teaching but I especially like working with students and associating them with my work. Paul Samuelson makes jokes about the fact that so many of my articles are coauthored with so many people that he says are unknown—such as Paul Samuelson himself. The reason is that whenever any of my research assistants has developed an interesting idea, I want their names to appear as coauthors. Many of my "children" now occupy very high positions, including Fazio, the Governor of the Bank of Italy, Draghi, the Director General of the Treasury of Italy, Padoa Schioppa, a member of the Directorate of the European Central Bank, and Stan Fischer, Joe Stiglitz, and several past and current members of the Federal Reserve Board. All have been very warm to me, and I have the warmest feeling for them.

Solow: Now if you were giving advice to a young macroeconomist just getting a Ph.D., what would you say is the most fertile soil to cultivate in macroeconomics these days?

Modigliani: I think that these days, in terms of my own shifts of interest, I've been moving toward open-economy macroeconomics and especially international finance. It's a very interesting area, and it's an area where wage rigidity is very important. Now the distinction becomes very sharp between nominal wage rigidity and real wage rigidity.

Solow: Explain that.

Modigliani: With nominal wage rigidity, you will want floating exchange rates. With real rigidity, there's nothing you can do about unemployment. I've been looking at the experiences of countries that tried fixing exchange rates and countries that tried floating exchange rates, and I am finding that both experiences have not been good. Europe has been doing miserably.

Barnett: You have been an important observer of the international monetary system and the role of the United States and Europe in it, and I believe that you have supported the European Monetary Union. Would you comment on the EMS and the future of the international monetary system, in relation to what you think about the recent financial crises and the role that exchange rates have played in them?

Modigliani: Yes, I have been a supporter of the euro, but to a large extent for its political implications, peace in Europe, over the purely economic ones. However, I have also pointed out the difficulties in a system which will have fixed exchange rates and how, for that to work, it will require a great deal of flexibility in the behavior of wages of individual countries having differential productivity growth and facing external shocks. I have also pointed out that the union was born under unfavorable conditions, as the role of the central bank has been played, not legally but *de facto*, by the Bundesbank, which has pursued consistently a wrong overtight monetary policy resulting in high European unemployment. It has reached 12% and sometimes even higher, and that policy is now being pursued to a considerable extent by the European Central Bank, which is making essentially the same errors as the Bundesbank. This does not promise too much for the near future.

Solow: What we're going to do now is switch over to talking about the life-cycle theory of savings, and what I'd like you to do is comment on the simplest life-cycle model, the one that you and Albert Ando used for practical purposes, with no bequests, et cetera.

Modigliani: Well, let me say that bequests are not to be regarded as an exception. Bequests are part of the life-cycle model. But it is true that you can go very far with assuming no bequests, and therefore it's very interesting to follow that direction. The model in which bequests are unimportant does produce a whole series of consequences which were completely unrecognized before the Modigliani–Brumberg articles. There were revolutionary changes in paradigm stemming from the life-cycle hypothesis. Fundamentally, the traditional theory of saving reduced to: the proportion of income saved rises with income, so rich people (and countries) save; poor people dissave. Why do rich people save? God knows. Maybe to leave bequests. That was the whole story, from which you would get very few implications and, in particular, you got the implication that rich countries save and poor countries dissave, an absurd concept since poor countries cannot dissave forever. No one can. But from the life-cycle hypothesis, you have a rich set of consequences. At the *micro* level, you have all the consequences of "Permanent Income," including the fact that consumption depends upon (is proportional to) *permanent* income, while saving depends basically on transitory income: The high savers are not the rich, but the temporarily rich (i.e., rich relative to their own normal income).

The difference between life-cycle and permanent income is that the latter treats the life span as infinite, while in the life-cycle model, lifetime is finite. For the purpose of analyzing short-term behavior, it makes no difference whether life lasts 50 years or forever. So you do have fundamentally the same story about the great bias that comes from the standard way of relating saving to current family income. But, in fact, in reality it does make a difference what the variability of income is in terms of short term versus long term. The marginal propensity to save of farmers is much higher than that of government employees, not because farmers are great savers, but because their income is very unstable. Other consequences that are very interesting include the fact, found from many famous surveys, that successive generations seem to be less and less thrifty, that is, save less and less at any given level of income. These conclusions all are consequences of the association between current and transitory income.

Then you have consequences in terms of the behavior of saving and wealth over the lifetime, and here is where the difference between life cycle and permanent income become important. With the life-cycle hypothesis, saving behavior varies over the person's finite lifetime, because with finite life comes a life cycle of income and consumption: youth, middle age, children, old age, death, and bequests. That's why there is little saving when you are very young. You have more saving in middle age, and dissaving when you are old. With infinite life, there is no life cycle. Aggregate saving reflects that life cycle and its interaction with demography and productivity growth, causing aggregate saving to rise with growth, as has been shown with overlapping generations models. All that has been shown to receive empirical support.

Solow: Dissaving and old age, as well?

Modigliani: Right. Now let me comment on that. Some people have spent a lot of time trying to show that the life-cycle model is wrong because people don't dissave in old age. That is because the poor guys have just done the thing wrong. They have treated Social Security contribution as if it were a sort of income tax, instead of mandatory saving, and they have treated pension as a handout, rather than a drawing down of accumulated pension claims. If you treat Social Security properly, measuring saving as income earned (net of personal taxes) minus consumption, you will find that people dissave tremendous amounts when they are old; they largely consume their pensions, while having no income.

Solow: They are running down their Social Security assets.

Modigliani: In addition to running down their Social Security assets, they also are running down their own assets, but not very much. Somewhat. But, if you include Social Security, wealth has a tremendous hump. It gets to a peak at the age of around 55–60 and then comes down quickly. All of these things have been completely supported by the evidence. Now, next, you do not need bequests to explain the existence of wealth, and that's another very important concept. Even without bequests, you can explain a large portion of the wealth we have. Now that does not mean there are no bequests. There are. In all my papers on the life-cycle hypothesis, there is always a long footnote that explains how to include bequests.

Solow: How you would include it, yes.

Modigliani: In such a way that it remains true that saving does not depend upon current income, but on life-cycle income. That ensures that the ratio of bequeathed wealth to income tends to remain stable, no matter how much income might rise. It is also important to recognize the macro implications of the life cycle, which are totally absent in the permanent-income hypothesis, namely, that the saving rate depends not on income, but on income growth. The permanent income hypothesis has nothing really to say; in fact, it has led Friedman to advance the wrong conclusion, namely that growth *reduces saving*. Why? Because growth results in expectations that future income will exceed current income. But with finite lifetime, terminating with retirement and dissaving, growth generates saving.

Consider again the simplified case of no bequests. Then each individual saves zero over its life cycle. If there is no growth, the path of saving by age is the same as the path of saving over life: it aggregates to zero. But if, say, population is growing, then there are more young in their saving phase than old in the dissaving mode, and so, the aggregate saving ratio is positive and increasing with growth. The same turns out with productivity growth, because the young enjoy a higher life income than the retired. Quite generally, the life-cycle model implies that aggregate wealth is proportional to aggregate income: hence the rate of growth of wealth, which is saving, tends to be proportional to the rate of growth of income. This in essence is the causal link between growth rate and saving ratio, which is one of the most significant and innovative implications of the life-cycle hypothesis.

Barnett: There has been much research and discussion about possible reforms or changes to the Social Security System. What are your views on that subject?

Modigliani: The problems of the Social Security System are my current highest interest and priority, because I think its importance is enormous; and I think there is a tragedy ahead, although in my view we can solve the problem in a way that is to everyone's advantage. In a word, we need to abandon the pay-as-you-go system, which is a wasteful and inefficient system, and replace it with a fully funded system. If we do, we should be able to reduce the Social Security contribution from the 18% that it would have to be by the middle of the next century, to below 6% using my approach, and I have worked out the transition. It is possible to go from here to there without any significant sacrifices. In fact, it can be done with no sacrifice, except using the purported surplus to increase national saving rather than consumption. And given the current low private saving rate and huge (unsustainable) capital imports, increasing national saving must be considered as a high priority.

Barnett: Are there any other areas to which you feel you made a relevant contribution that we have left out?

Modigliani: Perhaps that dealing with the effects of inflation. At a time when, under the influence of rational expectations, it was fashionable to claim that inflation had no *real* effects worth mentioning, I have delighted in showing that, in reality, it has extensive and massive real effects; and they are not very transitory. This work includes the paper with Stan Fisher on the effects of inflation, and the paper with Rich Cohen showing that investors are incapable of responding rationally to inflation, basically because of the (understandable) inability to distinguish between nominal and Fisherian real interest rates. For this reason, inflation systematically depresses the value of equities.

I have also shown that inflation reduces saving for the same reason. Both propositions have been supported by many replications. In public finance, the calculation of the debt service using the nominal instead of the real rate leads to grievous overstatement of the deficit-to-income ratio during periods of high inflation, such as the mid-seventies to early eighties in the presence of high debt-to-income ratios. In corporate finance, it understates the profits of highly levered firms.

Figure 5.5   At the Kennedy Library in Boston in the spring of 1998, talking with the King of Spain.

Barnett: Your public life has been very intense, at least starting at some point in your life. I presume that you do not agree with Walras, who believed that economists should be technical experts only, and should not be active in the formation of policy. Would you comment on the role of economists as "public servants"?

Modigliani: I believe that economists should recognize that economics has two parts. One is economic theory. One is economic policy. The principles of economic theory are universal, and we all should agree on them, as I think we largely do as economists. On economic policy, we do not necessarily agree, and we should not, because economic policy has to do with value judgments, not about what is true, but about what we like. It has to do with the distribution of income, not just total income. So long as they are careful not to mix the two, economists should be ready to participate in policy, but they should be careful to distinguish what part has to do with their value judgment and what part with knowledge of the working of an economy.

Barnett: You have been repeatedly involved in advocating specific economic policies. Were there instances in which, in your view, your advice had a tangible impact on governments and people.

Modigliani: Yes, I can think of several cases. The first relates to Italy and is a funny one. Through the sixties and seventies, Italian wage contracts had an escalator clause with very high coverage. But in 1975, in the middle of the oil crisis, the unions had the brilliant idea of demanding a new type of escalator clause in which an $x\%$ increase in prices would entitle a worker to an increase in wages not of $x\%$ of *his* wage but of $x\%$ of the *average* wage—the same number of liras for everyone! And the high-wage employers went along with glee! I wrote a couple of indignant articles trying to explain the folly and announcing doomsday. To my surprise, it took quite a while before my Italian colleagues came to my support. In fact, one of those colleagues contributed a "brilliant" article suggesting that the measure had economic justification, for, with the high rate of inflation of the time, all real salaries would soon be roughly the same, at which time it was justified to give everyone the same cost-of-living adjustment! It took several years of economic turmoil before the uniform cost-of-living adjustment was finally abolished and its promoters admitted their mistake. It took until 1993 before the cost-of-living adjustment was abolished all together.

A second example is the recommendations in the 1996 book by two coauthors and me, *Il Miracolo Possibile* [The Achievable Miracle], which helped Italy to satisfy the requirement to enter the euro. This, at the time, was generally understood to be impossible, because of the huge deficit, way above the permissible 3%. We argued that the deficit was a fake, due to the use of inflation-swollen nominal interest rates in the presence of an outlandish debt-to-income ratio ($1\frac{1}{4}$), but the target was achievable through a drastic reduction of inflation and corresponding decline in nominal rates. This could be achieved without significant real costs by programming a minimal wage and price inflation through collaboration of labor, employer, and government. It worked, even beyond the results of the simulations reported in the book! And Italy entered the euro from the beginning.

A third example is my campaign against European unemployment and the role played by a mistaken monetary policy. "An Economists' Manifesto on Unemployment in the European Union," issued by me and a group of distinguished European and American economists, was published a little over a year ago. Although it is not proving as effective as we had hoped, it is making some progress.

Finally, I hope that our proposed Social Security reform will have a significant impact. Here the stakes are truly enormous for most of the world, but the payoff remains to be seen.

6

An Interview with Milton Friedman

Interviewed by John B. Taylor
STANFORD UNIVERSITY
May 2, 2000

"His views have had as much, if not more, impact on the way we think about monetary policy and many other important economic issues as those of any person in the last half of the twentieth century." These words in praise of Milton Friedman are from economist and Federal Reserve Chair Alan Greenspan. They are spoken from a vantage point of experience and knowledge of what really matters for policy decisions in the real world. And they are no exaggeration. Many would say they do not go far enough.

It is a rare monetary policy conference today in which Milton Friedman's ideas do not come up. It is a rare paper in macroeconomics in which some economic, mathematical, or statistical idea cannot be traced to Milton Friedman's early work. It is a rare student of macroeconomics who has not been impressed by reading Milton Friedman's crystal-clear expositions. It is a rare democrat from a formerly communist country who was not inspired by Milton Friedman's defense of a market economy written in the heydays of central planning. And it is a rare day that some popular newspaper or magazine around the world does not mention Milton Friedman as the originator of a seminal idea or point of view.

Any one of his many contributions to macroeconomics (or rather to monetary theory, for he detests the term macroeconomics) would be an extraordinary achievement. Taken together, they are daunting:

Reprinted from *Macroeconomic Dynamics*, 5, 2001, 101–131. Copyright © 2001 Cambridge University Press.

- permanent income theory;
- natural rate theory;
- the case for floating exchange rates;
- money growth rules;
- the optimal quantity of money;
- the monetary history of the United States, especially the Fed in the Great Depression, not to mention contributions to mathematical statistics on rank-order tests, sequential sampling, and risk aversion, and a host of novel government reform proposals from the negative income tax, to school vouchers, to the flat-rate tax, to the legalization of drugs.

Milton Friedman is an economist's economist who laid out a specific methodology of positive economic research. Economic experts know that many current ideas and policies—from monetary policy rules to the earned-income tax credit—can be traced to his original proposals. He won the Nobel Prize in Economics in 1976 for "his achievements in the field of consumption analysis, monetary history and theory and for his demonstration of the complexity of stabilization policy." Preferring to stay away from formal policymaking jobs, he has been asked for his advice by presidents, prime ministers, and top economic officials for many years. It is in the nature of Milton Friedman's unequivocally stated views that many disagree with at least some of them, and he has engaged in heated debates since graduate school days at the University of Chicago. He is an awesome debater. He is also gracious and friendly.

Born in 1912, he grew up in Rahway, New Jersey, where he attended local public schools. He graduated from Rutgers University in the midst of the Great Depression in 1932. He then went to study economics at the University of Chicago, where he met fellow graduate student Rose Director whom he later married. For nearly 10 years after he left Chicago, he worked at government agencies and research institutes (with one year visiting at the University of Wisconsin and one year at the University of Minnesota) before taking a faculty position at the University of Chicago in 1946. He remained at Chicago until he retired in 1977 at the age of 65, and he then moved to the Hoover Institution at Stanford University. I have always found Milton and Rose to be gregarious, energetic people, who genuinely enjoy interacting with others, and who enjoy life in all its dimensions, from walks near the Pacific Ocean to surfs on the World Wide Web. The day of this interview was no exception. It took place on May 2, 2000, in Milton's office in their San Francisco apartment. The interview lasted for two and a half hours. A tape recorder and some economic charts were on the desk between us. Behind Milton was a floor-to-ceiling picture window with beautiful panoramic views of the San Francisco hills and skyline. Behind me were his bookcases stuffed with his books, papers, and mementos.

The interview began in a rather unplanned way. When we walked into his office Milton started talking enthusiastically about the charts that were on his desk. The charts—which he had recently prepared from data he had downloaded from the Internet—raised questions about some remarks that I had given at a conference several weeks before—which he had read about on the Internet. As we began talking about the charts, I asked if I could turn on the tape recorder, since one of the topics for the interview was to be about how he formulated his ideas—and a conversation about the ideas he was formulating right then and there seemed like an excellent way to begin the interview. So I turned on the tape recorder, and the interview began. Soon we segued into the series of questions that I had planned in advance (but had not shown Milton in advance). We took one break for a very pleasant lunch and (unrecorded) conversation with his wife Rose before going back to "work." After the interview, the tapes were transcribed and the transcript was edited by me and Milton. The questions and answers were rearranged slightly to fit into the following broad topic areas:

- money growth, thermostats, and Alan Greenspan;
- causes of the great inflation and its end;
- early interest in economics;
- graduate school and early "on-the-job" training;
- permanent income theory;
- the return of monetary economics;
- fiscal and monetary policy rules;
- the use of models in monetary economics;
- the use of time-series methods;
- real business-cycle models, calibration, and detrending;
- the natural rate hypothesis;
- rational expectations;
- the role of debates in monetary economics;
- capitalism and freedom today;
- monetary unions and flexible exchange rates.

Money Growth, Thermostats, and Alan Greenspan

Friedman: [*Referring to the charts in Figures 6.1 and 6.2*] I thought that you'd be interested in these charts. Don't you think it's as if the Fed has installed a new and improved thermostatic controller in the 1990s![1]

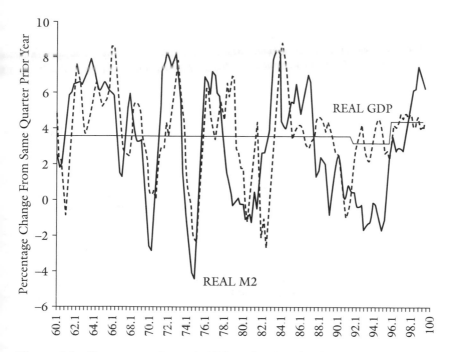

Figure 6.1 Year-to-year change in U.S. real M2 and real GDP, 1960.1–1999.3.
Source: Milton Friedman, February 20, 2000.

Taylor: I can see that there is a change in the relationship between money growth and real GDP and that the size of fluctuations in the economy has diminished greatly. There is much greater stability starting in the early 1980s.

Friedman: The change in stability really comes in 1992.

Taylor: Isn't 1982 the best break point?

Friedman: I think 1992 is the break. [*Referring to the charts in Figure 6.2*] Here are the charts that show the velocity of M1, M2, and M3 against the logarithmic trend.

Taylor: One reason to focus on 1982 is that it was the beginning of an expansion. There are also statistical tests that several people have done to test when the size of the fluctuations changed. Most say that it is in the early 1980s. Since then, the fluctuations in real GDP seem smaller. There is only one recession in 1991 and that is pretty small.

Friedman: [*Pointing to the dip in real GDP growth in 1990–91*] But this looks like a pretty big recession.

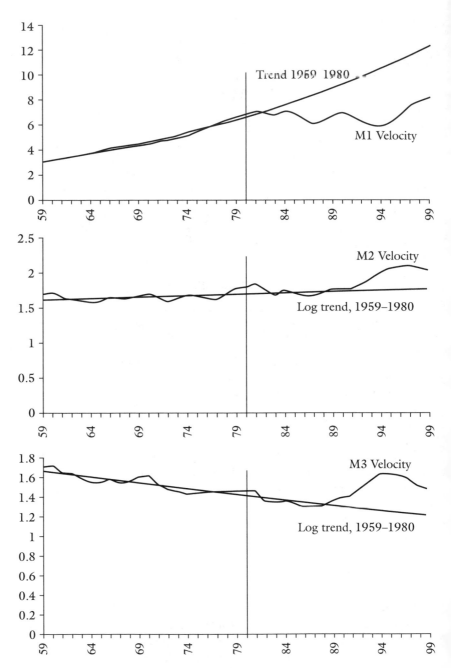

Figure 6.2 Velocity of M1, M2, M3, and log trends based on data from 1959 to 1980, annual data, 1959–99.
Source: Milton Friedman, April 30, 2000.

Taylor: Well, whatever the break point is, why do you think things have changed? Why, as you put it, does the Fed seem to be operating the monetary-policy thermostatic regulator so much better now? What do you think the reason is?

Friedman: I'm baffled. I find it hard to believe. They haven't learned anything they didn't know before. There's no additional knowledge. Literally, I'm baffled.

Taylor: What about the idea that they have learned that inflation was really much worse than they thought in the late 1970s, and they therefore put in place an interest-rate policy that kept inflation in check and reduced the boom/bust cycle?

Friedman: I believe that there are two different changes. One is a change in the relative value put on inflation control and economic stability and that did come in the eighties. The other is the breakdown in the relation between money and GDP. That came in the early nineties, when there was a dramatic reduction in the variability of GDP. What I'm puzzled about is whether, and if so how, they suddenly learned how to regulate the economy. Does Alan Greenspan have an insight into the movements in the economy and the shocks that other people don't have?

Taylor: Well, it's possible.

Friedman: Another explanation is that the information revolution has enabled enterprises to manage inventories so much better, as you pointed out in your recent discussion. But inventories can't be the answer because the same thing has happened to noninventories.

Taylor: I agree with that. If you look at final sales, you see the same change in stability, unless you really want to focus on very-short-term wiggles, such as the quarterly rates of change in real GDP during an expansion.

Friedman: And it may get big again. It may be a statistical artifact. They may have somehow changed their methods. There have been significant changes in estimation.

Taylor: Yes, but going back to the possibility that the Fed has more knowledge, do you think that they have learned more about controlling liquidity or money while at the same time recognizing the fact that there are these shifts in velocity?

Friedman: But then again, if you look at these shifts in velocity, they don't come until 1992.

Taylor: Well, what about this one?

Friedman: That's M1, but, all along, M2 has been the preferred aggregate exactly because of this change, which was the result of eliminating the prohibition on paying interest on demand deposits. So I don't think you can explain it through velocity. It looks as if somehow in

1992—1991–92—they were able to install a good thermostat instead of a bad one. Now, is Alan Greenspan a good thermostat compared to other Fed chairmen? That's hard to believe.

Causes of the Great Inflation and its End

Taylor: Hard to believe, yeah. Well, let's go back to an earlier period when things did not look so good. In recent years, there has been a lot of interest in what caused the Great Inflation of the 1970s and what caused its end. Why did inflation start to rise in the late 1960s and 1970s in the United States?

Friedman: Yes, the Great Inflation. The explanation for that is fundamentally political, not economic. It really had its origin in Kennedy's election in 1960. He was able to take advantage of the noninflationary economic conditions he inherited to "get the economy moving again." With zero inflationary expectations, monetary and fiscal expansions affected primarily output. The delayed effect on prices came only in the mid-sixties and built up gradually. Already by then, Darryl Francis of the St. Louis Fed was complaining about excessive monetary growth. Inflation was slowed by a mini-recession but then took off again when the Fed overreacted to the mini-recession. In the seventies, though I hate to say this, I believe that Arthur Burns deserves a lot of blame, and he deserves the blame because he knew better. He testified before Congress that, if the money supply grew by more than 6 or 7% per year, we'd have inflation, and during his regime it grew by more than that. He believed in the quantity theory of money but he wasn't a strict monetarist at any time. He trusted his own political instincts to a great degree, and he trusted his own judgment. In 1960, when he was advising Nixon, he argued that we were heading for a recession and that it was going to hurt Nixon very badly in the election, which is what did happen. And Nixon as a result had a great deal of confidence in him.

From the moment Burns got into the Fed, I think politics played a great role in what happened. So far as Nixon was concerned, there is no doubt, as I know from personal experience. I had a session with Nixon sometime in 1970—I think it was 1970, might have been 1971—in which he wanted me to urge Arthur to increase the money supply more rapidly [*laughter*] and I said to the President, "Do you really want to do that? The only effect of that will be to leave you with a larger inflation if you do get reelected." And he said, "Well, we'll worry about that after we get reelected." Typical. So there's no doubt what Nixon's pleasure was.

Taylor: Do you think Burns was part of the culture of the times in that he put less emphasis on inflation, or that he was willing to risk some inflation to keep unemployment low, based on the Philips curve?

Friedman: Not at all. You read all of Arthur's writings up to that point and one of his strongest points was the avoidance of inflation. He was not part of that Keynesian group at all. In fact, he wrote against the Keynesian view. However, it did affect the climate of opinion in Washington, it did affect what activities of the Fed were viewed favorably and unfavorably, and therefore it did affect it that way, but not through his own beliefs of the desirability of inflation.

Taylor: Another thing that people say now is that Burns was as confused as other people were about potential GDP, and that he thought the economy was either below capacity or that it was capable of growing more rapidly than it was. Do you think that was much of a factor?

Friedman: I don't think that was a major factor. I think it may have been a factor.

Taylor: Mainly political?

Friedman: Yeah.

Taylor: What about the end of the Great Inflation? It lasted beyond Burns's time. We had G. William Miller and then Paul Volcker.

Friedman: Well, there's no doubt what ended it. What ended it was Ronald Reagan. If you recall the details, the election was in 1980. In October of 1979, Paul Volcker came back from a meeting in Belgrade, in which the United States had been criticized, and he announced that the Fed would shift from using interest rates as its operating instrument to using bank reserves or base money. Nonetheless, the period following that was one of very extreme fluctuations in the quantity of money. The purpose of the announcement about paying attention to the monetary aggregates was to give Volcker a shield behind which he could let interest rates go.

[*Pointing to Figure 6.1*] That's the period, here . . . ups and downs. (The picture of the nominal money supply is very much the same as for the real money supply.) They did step on the brake, and in addition, sometime in February 1980, Carter imposed controls on consumer credit. When the economy went into a stall as we were approaching the election, the Fed stepped on the gas. In the five months before the election, the money supply went up very rapidly. Paul Volcker was political, too. The month after the election, the money supply slowed down. If Carter had been elected, I don't know what would have happened. However, Reagan was elected, and Reagan was determined to stop the inflation and willing to take risks. In 1981, we got into a severe recession. Reagan's public-opinion ratings went down, way down. I believe no other president in the postwar period would have accepted that without bringing pressure on the Fed to reverse course. That's the one key step: Reagan did not. The recession went on in 1981 and 1982. In 1982, finally Volcker turned around and started to raise the money supply and at that point the recession came to an end and the economy started expanding.

Taylor: Your explanations of both the start and end of the Great Inflation are very much related to changes in people in leadership positions, as distinct from changes in ideas. What you seem to be saying is that it was mostly Burns, Nixon, Reagan. Could you comment on that a little bit?

Friedman: I may be overemphasizing Burns's role. I certainly am not overemphasizing Reagan's. And again, in both cases I feel I have personal evidence. I was one of the people who talked to Reagan and there's no question that Reagan understood the relation between the quantity of money and inflation. It was very clear, and he was willing to take the heat. He understood on his own accord, but he also had been told so, that you could not slow down the inflation without having a recession.

Taylor: In the first case, a president didn't take your advice, and in the second case, a president did take your advice.

Friedman: Correlation without causation. They were different characters and persons. Nixon had a higher IQ than Reagan, but he was far less principled; he was political to an extreme degree. Reagan had a respectable IQ, though he wasn't in Nixon's class. But he had solid principles and he was willing to stick up for them and to pay a price for them. Both of them would have acted as they did if they had never seen me or heard from me.

Early Interest in Economics

Taylor: I'd like to change the topic from politics to your work in economics. I hope you can share some personal recollections about your remarkable contributions to economics, especially to macroeconomics. How did you get the ideas? Who influenced you? Which parts of your background, education, or work experience were most important? I know it's a long time ago . . .

Friedman: It is a long time ago! But sure, you go right ahead, but I don't trust my memory that far back.

Taylor: Just to get started, let's go back to when you went to college at Rutgers. At first you were interested in mathematics, but then you got interested in economics. Is that correct?

Friedman: I graduated with essentially a double major of mathematics and economics.

Taylor: You got interested in economics in college though?

Figure 6.3 In own living room.

Friedman: Yeah.

Taylor: And the two people who you say influenced you early on were two economists: Arthur Burns and Homer Jones. Could you share a little bit about how that occurred? Was Burns teaching you microeconomics, or was he more influential on the macroeconomic side of things?

Friedman: It was much more micro than macro. We had a seminar with Burns in which we went over the draft he had written of his book on production trends in the United States. As we went over his manuscript with him, it was one of the best educational experiences I've ever had, because it gave me a feeling for how to do research. It demonstrated a willingness on his part to accept criticism from people who were not in a way his peers, and so it was a very educational experience.

So far as Homer was concerned, Homer taught a course on statistics and one on insurance. He was a novice himself; he was just keeping one lesson ahead of his students. He clearly was a disciple of Frank Knight of Chicago. He was a member of the Chicago school of economics as it was then. And Homer had a very great influence on me both through his teaching and by getting me to Chicago!

Taylor: He taught you statistics mainly?

Friedman: That, plus the course on insurance, which dealt with economic issues.

Taylor: So you didn't really study macroeconomics or monetary theory much then?

Friedman: I'm sure I had a course in money and banking. It was a standard undergraduate course, no real macro. I didn't get any real training in economics until I went for graduate work in Chicago.

Taylor: It is remarkable that Burns would be working with undergraduates at that level on his own research, that level of detail.

Friedman: Burns at that time was finishing his Ph.D. dissertation. He was a young man; he was not what you think of usually. He had just gotten married and was living in Greenwich Village. He had long hair, long fingernails. You know, he was a different character than he was later on. But he was always an enormously able person intellectually and very dedicated to the research he was doing, to getting it right. And somehow, I'm not sure where, Marshall came in. He was a great student of Marshall and a great admirer of Marshall.

Taylor: So he introduced you to Marshall?

Friedman: Yeah.

Taylor: What about the idea that the free-market system is a good way to organize a society? Was that part of the microeconomics you were learning?

Friedman: Remember, I'm talking about 1928–32; that was before the real change in public opinion, and that really wasn't the kind of issue then that it was scheduled to become. There was, of course, discussion about the breakdown of the economic system, but I graduated in June of 1932 and most of my years there, 1928, 1929, people didn't teach "if markets work well"; they just taught markets. You took it for granted in a sense. Of course, there was a strong intellectual movement toward socialism but it wasn't of the kind that later developed. Norman Thomas was at that time the leading socialist; he was enormously respected, and he got more votes as candidate for president in 1928 than any socialist ever did before or since. The intellectual community in general was socialist, but so far as the department of economics was concerned, I don't think there was much of that.

Taylor: So you wouldn't even have given it a thought?

Friedman: No, I never got involved in politics. I probably would have described myself as a socialist, who knows. When I graduated from college, I wrote myself an essay about what I believed at the time, and I left it in my mother's apartment where I grew up; my father had died when I was in high school. When I went back years later and tried to find it, I never could find it, and I've regretted that very much. That would be a nice document for this purpose.

Taylor: You can't even guess what you wrote?

Friedman: I'm pretty sure I did not have the views I later developed. I probably had the standard views that we needed to do something, but I have no idea what they were.

Taylor: So economics was more technical—supply-and-demand curves, this is how a market works—rather than philosophical?

Friedman: My impression is that it was much less philosophical.

Taylor: So how did Homer Jones encourage you to go to Chicago?

Friedman: He not only encouraged me to go, he made it possible for me to go. People now don't recognize what the situation was then. There were very few scholarships, almost no fellowships of the sort we now take for granted. When I graduated from Rutgers, I applied for graduate work to a number of places, and I received two offers, one from Brown University in applied mathematics, and one from Chicago, thanks to Homer, in economics. Both of them were tuition scholarships, no money beyond free tuition. That was the standard practice at that time. Graduate students mostly paid their own way.

Taylor: Did you have an idea of what you wanted to work on as an economist then?

Friedman: None whatsoever. When I originally entered college, I thought I was going to be an actuary and I took actuarial exams because that was the only way that I knew of that a person could make a living using mathematics. And it is, it's a very skilled job. Only after I got into college and started taking economics courses as well as mathematics courses did I discover that there were alternatives. Of course, the fact that we were in a depression at that time made economics a very important subject.

Graduate School and Early "On-the-Job" Training

Taylor: You were at Chicago for graduate school for a year and then you went to Columbia for a year, and then you went back to Chicago. My understanding is that during this time you developed an interest in mathematical statistics and working with data, with Henry Schultz at Chicago and with Harold Hotelling and Wesley Mitchell at Columbia. And right after graduate school you took a job in Washington working on a new consumer spending survey, and then you moved to New York to work on income survey data with Simon Kuznets. Did working with data and using mathematical statistics interest you a lot?

Friedman: Yes, it did. First of all at Chicago I took Schultz's course in statistics, and when I came back to Chicago after a year at Columbia, I came back as a research assistant to Schultz. Let me go back, and really trace this to Rutgers, to Arthur Burns, because the book that we reviewed, *Production Trends in the United States*, which was his doctoral dissertation, was essentially data analysis. The thesis of the book is that retardation in the growth of each industry separately does not imply retardation in the economy as a whole.

Taylor: My impression is that, at least in your early work with survey data, you put less emphasis on economic models, or formal theories, and more on describing the facts and using mathematical statistics?

Friedman: No, I don't think so. I was trying to explain the data, but not through models, not through multi-equation models, but through more informal stories—basically trying to appeal to microeconomic interactions.

My first year in Chicago really gave me an understanding of economics as a theoretical discipline. In my first year at Chicago, Jacob Viner, Frank Knight, and Lloyd Mints were my main teachers. Both of what's now called micro and macro. I hate those words, I think it's price theory and it's monetary theory. Why the hell do we have to use these Greek words?

Anyway, it seemed to me at that time, spending a year at Chicago first and then a year at Columbia was the ideal combination. Chicago gave you the theoretical basis with which you can interpret the data. Also, there was an empirical slant at Chicago compared with an institutional slant at Columbia. When I went to Washington to work at the National Resources Council in 1935, my work was almost entirely statistical, very little economic theory.

Taylor: Before you went to Washington, you wrote your first published paper, an article criticizing a method proposed by the famous Professor Pigou of Cambridge University. It was published in 1935 in the *Quarterly Journal of Economics*; it must have been written in your first or second year in graduate school. What motivated you to write and publish such an article?

Friedman: Schultz's book that I was working on was on the theory and measurement of demand, the Pigou article was on the elasticity of demand, so it came right out of what I was doing with Schultz. He probably suggested that I publish it, I don't remember.

Taylor: Pigou took the article as a very strong criticism and there was a debate. Did you enjoy that aspect of it?

Friedman: What really happened is this: I sent the article to the *Economic Journal*, where the editor was John Maynard Keynes. Keynes rejected the article on the grounds that Pigou didn't think it was right. I then sent the article to the *Quarterly Journal of Economics*, where Taussig was editor. Fortunately, in submitting it to the *Quarterly Journal of Economics*, I said that I had earlier submitted it to the *Economic Journal* and gave the reason why it was rejected and why I didn't think that was right. I guess it was published in the *Quarterly Journal of Economics* because it was refereed by Leontief. Then Pigou submitted a criticism of it to the *Quarterly Journal of Economics* and Taussig wrote to me and sent me a copy of the criticism. The *Quarterly Journal of Economics* then published both Pigou's criticism and my response.

Taylor: Did that experience whet your appetite for controversy?

Friedman: I really can't say. That's now what, 1935; it's 65 years ago.

Taylor: That story reminds me of referee work you once did for me when I was an editor at the *American Economic Review*. You signed your "anonymous" referee report!

Friedman: I always believed I should be responsible for what I write. I didn't want to go under an anonymous name. And I've never been willing to publish something under my name written by somebody else. You know, I've frequently been asked to, somebody wants propaganda for something or other, but I don't believe that's the appropriate thing to do.

Taylor: I want to ask you about your work at the Statistical Research Group at Columbia University during World War II, but what other experiences were important around that time in your career?

Friedman: So far as your questions about economics versus statistics is concerned, you should note that, for the two years before I went to the Statistical Research Group, I was at the U.S. Treasury Department where it was entirely economics and negligible statistics. We were designing the wartime tax program. Unfortunately, a large part of the income tax today derives from what happened during the war. That was when withholding was introduced, that was when rates were really hiked way up and they were made more progressive, so everyone of the present disputes existed then, even the marriage penalty. In the proposal we made at the Treasury, we eliminated the marriage penalty but our solution wasn't politically feasible. There was a very good group of economists at the Treasury, including Lowell Harris and Bill Vickrey.

Taylor: So that was also part of the war effort?

Friedman: Sure. I went there in 1941 just before we got into the war and the big issue during that period was the argument between the price control people and the people who wanted to hold down inflation through taxation. In the summer of 1941, I participated in a research project with Carl Shoup and we wrote a book, *Taxing to Prevent Inflation*. It's not something I'm very proud of now. It was in the style of a model and it had to do with how much taxation was required to prevent inflation, which I now believe was the wrong issue.

Taylor: You published a paper in the *American Economic Review* in 1942 on the inflationary gap. I want to come back to that, but was it also part of your work at Treasury?

Friedman: Oh yes, it was while I was at the Treasury.

Taylor: Let's discuss your work at the Statistical Research Group in New York during the war. It was heavily statistically oriented, but was there much economics?

Friedman: Oh, entirely statistically oriented; no economics at all. I shouldn't say no economics at all. One of the things that was found out during the war was that social scientists are more effective than natural scientists in dealing with many wartime data problems because social scientists are accustomed to dealing with bad data and natural scientists are accustomed to dealing with good data. And here you have all sorts of problems that arose involving the analysis of data.

Taylor: Do you think that social scientists have a better sense of approximation? What is their advantage?

Friedman: Social scientists have ways of trying to judge the quality of data, to find proxies, to find substitutes, to find ways of evaluating it. Now, in what we did at the statistical research group, that wasn't so evident most of the time.

Taylor: What kind of problems did you work on?

Friedman: We were primarily concerned with such problems as: You've got an antiaircraft missile. It's possible to produce it in such a way that you can control how many pieces it breaks into when it explodes. Should you have a lot of little pieces, so there's a high probability of hitting, but it won't be as harmful to the object hit? Or, should you have a few big pieces, each of which will destroy the plane you're shooting at if it hits it, but the probability of hitting it is less? One of the jobs I worked on was to write a paper on the optimum number of pieces into which to break up a shell. We had data from various test firings on what would be the effect if a fragment of a certain size hit a certain place on a plane, and so on. It was that kind of a problem. Now that's an economic problem.

Taylor: Could you elaborate on that? Why is it an economic problem?

Friedman: I mean it in a broader sense. What we discovered on that project is what you always discover in economics. If you ask people what are the biggest industries in the United States, they'll give you the wrong answer every time. They'll say steel or automobiles. More people are employed in domestic service than in either steel or automobiles and many more still in wholesale or retail trade. That is because those industries consist of a large number of small enterprises. So in this shell project, the naval experts and the military people all came down for a fairly small number of large fragments, so if you hit, you really do damage. Our calculation came out with something different. We showed that there should be a large number of small fragments because the probability of hitting is so much higher than with the large pieces. And that's why I say that's an economic problem—maximization subject to restraints. Again, it always comes down to, should you have one big aircraft carrier or two small ones?

Taylor: Maybe you could say a little about your work on sequential testing. How did you get the idea?

Friedman: Well, Allen Wallis tells the story in an article in the *Journal of the American Statistical Association*. Allen came back to the office one day saying that he had just been with a navy captain who had been observing tests of artillery. The captain said, "You know these statisticians always have to make so many shots, but I know long before the test is done which is the right one." And so Allen came back and said, "You know, there's some sense in that." We agreed and we thought about it and I fixed up an example in which I was able to demonstrate that by having a good stopping rule, you could achieve the same probability of error with a much smaller sample on average.

We knew we didn't have the mathematical competence and could not afford the time to do this ourselves, so we shopped around. But we stated the problem in such a way that statisticians found it difficult to accept. We said, "We know how to construct a test that's more powerful than the uniformly most powerful test." They said, "That's mathematically impossible, you can't do that—we've proved that this is the most powerful test." And so statisticians wouldn't have anything to do with it. Then, we talked to Abraham Wald, and he initially had the same reaction. But then he went home and a day later he called and said, "You are right and I know how to do it and I know what the answer is."

Taylor: A lot of things followed from that important discovery. And you had worked out a little numerical example to show that it would work, at least in some cases?

Friedman: A very simple case, I've forgotten what it was. And then later, one of the jobs we had was to advise the Navy on sampling inspection. So we got up a whole series of sampling inspection programs including sequential analysis using those findings.

One of the other problems, probably the most important one I worked on, had to do with proximity fuses, which are used when firing an antiaircraft gun at an incoming bomber or fighter. A proximity fuse is designed to eliminate the error in timing by being so adjusted that it would go off when it was near the target. The fuse sends out a radio signal that would bounce back from the target; if the target was close enough, the fuse would go off. The radio signal sent out could be adjusted to different angles and different intensities. What was the optimum design of the proximity fuse to maximize the chance of hitting the object? A very interesting problem, and one that we spent a lot of effort on.

Taylor: That sounds like an amazingly complex problem to be working on. Did you write up papers or reports?

Friedman: Oh, sure. I have those reports somewhere.

Taylor: How did you feel about writing important papers that you wouldn't be able to publish, to show to the world?

Friedman: You can't conceive of what the situation was at the time. The war was the most important thing going on and everybody, not me particularly, but everybody was putting aside almost all other considerations to contribute what they could to help in the war. I don't think there was any feeling on the part of any of us that we were concerned about what would happen to our research. In any event, this was in an area that was not of much long-term interest for me.

Taylor: What about the methodology of optimization that you used at the Statistical Research Group. Is that something that you have used later in economic research, perhaps in your research on monetary policy rules?

Friedman: I think it comes the other way. The economic view of seeking an optimum subject to constraints was a way to approach these military problems, rather than the other way around. But I will say that that was very interesting because it was so different from anything we had been exposed to before.

Taylor: Is there anything else that you would like to add?

Friedman: No, I really don't think there is. The Statistical Research Group got me involved with a group of people that I wouldn't otherwise have been involved with. For example, it was the way I got to know Jimmy Savage. He and I wrote a number of papers later together.

Taylor: Do you remember how you happened to write the paper with Savage on utility functions, which gave risk preference at low incomes?

Friedman: I don't know. I honestly don't know. Somehow Jimmy and I must have been talking about it, but I cannot reproduce it. Jimmy Savage was a real genius, there's no question that he was a remarkable character.

Taylor: How did you come to collaborate with him?

Friedman: We got to know one another at the Statistical Research Group. What happened was that at the time he didn't know how to write and I was forced to rewrite some of his papers. He later developed into an excellent writer. You know, he was almost blind, he could only see out of one corner of his eye. He was trained as a mathematician, he had a Ph.D. in mathematics, and then he went on to statistics and really revolutionized statistics. How we got into the risk paper, I no longer have the slightest recollection.

Permanent Income Theory

Taylor: Now let's go on to your research. Let's start with your research on the consumption function. I understand that you think that this is your best purely scientific contribution.

Friedman: I think it is.

Taylor: Could you say a little more about it? Relating to our earlier discussion, did your early work with data and mathematical statistics help you develop the idea?

Friedman: Aside from the work I did on the consumer spending survey in Washington during the 1930s, I also spent several years at the National Bureau of Economic Research working with Simon Kuznets. That ended up in the book, *Income from Independent Professional Practice*. It served as my Ph.D. dissertation. It was largely statistical and empirical, dealing with a whole bunch of questionnaires Kuznets had sent out while he was working at the Department of Commerce. But it also involved the application of economic theory dealing with the explanation for differences of income in different professions. An early venture in the analysis of human capital.

The book on the consumption function was a combination of ideas from the professional income study, from the consumers' spending study, and the work I was doing on methodology (which ultimately appeared in the article I wrote on methodology). What I like about the consumption function book is that it is the best example I know, in my own work, of the methodological principles that are laid out in my essay on methodology. You start with a hypothesis. It has implications. You test whether those implications are correct or not. If the implications are not correct, you try to adjust your hypothesis and readjust.

In this case I started out with a hypothesis that is similar to that which underlies the distinction between real and nominal interest rates. How do people adjust their expectations? How do they decide what fraction of their income to spend? I developed the hypothesis along these lines. I put it in a form in which it could be tested and I derived its implications. I tested those implications and, on the whole, they tended to confirm the hypothesis. I suggested additional tests that should be made to test the hypothesis. So it was, in this way, methodologically pure.

In addition, it produced a hypothesis that seemed to explain the data. As you know, the original pressure for the analysis was the apparent inconsistency between two bodies of data: long time-series data and cross-sectional budget data on consumption and income. The question was: "How could you reconcile those two apparently contradictory bodies of data?" A lot of hypotheses had been offered to reconcile them. The hypothesis I offered, the permanent income hypothesis, seemed to me a much more elegant way to rationalize that difference. And it had, as special cases, almost all of the alternative hypotheses, so it was a consolidation of a lot of empirical evidence as well as theoretical analysis.

Taylor: It seems to me that your signal extraction characterization of the problem, as we call it these days, was quite revolutionary at the time.

Figure 6.4   Milton Friedman, March 1992.

Friedman: That really came out of the work with Kuznets's data on incomes from professional practice. In that earlier work, I introduced the concepts of permanent income and transitory income in a simplified form, and I just carried that right over. In the professional income data research, I had three categories: permanent, quasi permanent (that's what I called the intermediate one), and transitory. Later I got it down to two.

Taylor: Where did you get the idea to use such statistical decomposition theories in economics?

Friedman: Just from the fact that I was simultaneously becoming an expert in statistical analysis.

Taylor: I guess it is an example of the benefits of a little crossfertilization. Your work on the consumption function got characterized sometimes as kind of an attack on the Keynesian consumption function. Did that motivate you at all?

Friedman: I don't think so, and it isn't an attack, it's just a demonstration that the Keynesian consumption function is not a long-run function; it's a transitory function as he defined it.

Taylor: Did you argue that your theory would imply that a Keynesian model wouldn't be very stable?

Friedman: I think I did argue that in the conclusion.

The Return of Monetary Economics

Taylor: When did your interests in monetary economics begin, exactly?

Friedman: It really began I guess when I was serving in the Treasury Department from 1941 to 1943, because the crucial question was, "What are we going to do to keep down inflation?" Everybody was aware that, during the First World War, taxes had paid for a very small fraction of the war and, during the Second World War, they were determined to raise the fraction paid for by taxes. At the same time, they also had the problem of predicting inflation and that's how I got involved. I was at the Treasury, Division of Tax Research, and our job was to prepare tax proposals for Congress.

The problem—it was interesting from a political point of view and from a scientific point of view—was that a group in the administration who were trying to get a price control statute didn't want us to come up with a tax proposal because they were afraid we would say, "we can stop inflation through taxes, we don't need price controls." They wanted price controls.

We were making estimates of the amount of taxes you would need to stop inflation. Our estimates of how much taxes you would need were much higher than comparable estimates made by those favoring price controls. A month after the price control law was passed, their estimates were much higher than ours. *Now* they wanted all the help they could get from the tax system.

Taylor: Why didn't people mention money through all of this talk about inflation? Was it discussed at all?

Friedman: Hardly. As a result of the Keynesian revolution, money had almost dropped out of the picture. I look back at that and say, how the hell could I have done that? I had good training in monetary theory at Chicago and yet, once the Keynesian revolution came along, everything was on taxes and spending, everything was on fiscal policy, and that's why I was trying to answer the question about the level of taxation needed to stem inflation. With a sufficiently expansive monetary policy, no amount of taxes could do it. It was the wrong question. The right question was, "What monetary policy do we need?" That was the result of the mindset we had.

Taylor: So that's when your 1942 *American Economic Review* article on the inflationary gap was written. When did you go back to basic monetary theory you had learned at Chicago?

Friedman: All I know is from the record. When I republished that article in *Essays in Positive Economics* [published in 1953], I added sections about money and I had a footnote saying that the original article was deficient in this respect. It must have been only a few years before, somewhere in between, that I suddenly realized, or somebody made me realize that money mattered. I no longer remember now.

Fiscal and Monetary Policy Rules

Taylor: Of your two early articles on stabilization policy, the first one is on fiscal policy rules, which had implications for money, of course, and the second one focused more on money growth rules. Could you talk a little about that?

Friedman: Sure. In the earlier paper, I was at the point where I would say money is important but the quantity of money should vary counter-cyclically—increase when there was a recession and, the opposite, decrease when there was an expansion. Rules for taxes and spending that would give budget balance on average but have deficits and surpluses over the cycle could automatically impart the right movement to the quantity of money.

Then I got involved in the statistical analysis of the role of money, and the relation between money and money income. I came to the conclusion that this policy rule was more complicated than necessary and that you really didn't need to worry too much about what was happening on the fiscal end, that you should concentrate on just keeping the money supply rising at a constant rate. That conclusion was, I'm sure, the result of the empirical evidence.

Taylor: Was part of the reason for the change that the link from deficits and surpluses to changes in money growth were not so tight with changes in the money multiplier?

Friedman: Partly it was that, and partly it was that the link from fiscal policy to the economy was of no use.

Taylor: I remember Bob Lucas saying, in reference to your constant money growth proposals, that they were designed to work in the long run, but that, when you thought about it, they worked well in the short run too. Were you thinking more of the long run? How did you think about the short run?

Friedman: I'm sure I was thinking more of the long run. I've always had the view that you ought to try to design policies for the long run. Given the view that you want the role of government to be stable, that immediately imposes on you a long-run point of view.

Taylor: Did you have a sense that they would work well in the short run?

Friedman: I don't think so.

Taylor: But didn't your first proposal have some of that? If you increase money growth in a recession because of the deficit, and if you retract money growth in a boom because of the surplus, that seems to me to be a short-run consideration.

Friedman: That was short run. That was still the relic of the Keynesian thinking. It was really a waste, I think, trying to reconcile the Keynesian thinking with the monetarist thinking.

Taylor: Was there any relationship between your thinking about these monetary control issues, and your work in statistical analysis? Did you think about these policy problems as regulator problems, thermostats, in any way?

Friedman: Oh yes, I'm sure I did. Thermostatic analysis goes back decades. There were several articles by Levis Kochin, at the University of Washington, on thermostatic analysis of the relation between the quantity of money and the economy.

Taylor: Continuing on the issues of money and monetary policy, in the early 1950s you were one of the very few people who were talking about money, but real controversy developed later, perhaps not until the 1960s.

Friedman: There was no controversy in the sense that I was simply way out in left field. In the 1950s, Chicago and UCLA, maybe, were the only places where anybody was talking about money.

Taylor: Did you think your proposal for a fixed money growth rule or your empirical work on the importance of money in the economy was more responsible for setting off the debate?

Friedman: I'm not sure what you're asking. For the fixed-growth rule to make sense you had to have an empirically supported theory with money in the model. The fixed-growth rule was not original with me; it's a rule that was recommended repeatedly decades ago by different economists.

Taylor: You certainly get the credit for most of it and you deserve it.

Friedman: Perhaps I was a better publicist.

Taylor: But if you explain things more clearly and explicitly than others, you put yourself out further on a limb and therefore you deserve more of the credit when you are right.

Friedman: Certainly the argument that money plays an important role in the economy has been settled. That was the result of the so-called radio AM/FM debates [Ando and Modigliani versus Friedman and Meiselman].

Taylor: Yes, that debate is not going on much anymore.

Friedman: It's over, everybody agrees fundamentally.

Taylor: Agrees with you?

Friedman: In large part, but not wholly. I still have more extreme views about the unimportance of fiscal policy for the aggregate economy than the profession does.

The Use of Models in Monetary Economics

Taylor: In looking back at these monetary versus fiscal debates, it seems that most of your articles are empirical rather than theoretical. Macroeconomic models appear sometimes, but they are not the main focus. Would you agree with that?

Friedman: I believe that one reason the work had whatever effect it has had is because it did have an empirical base. I believe that I can honestly say that I never reached a judgment about monetary or fiscal policy because of my beliefs in free markets. I believe that the empirical work is independent and honest in that sense. If fiscal policy had deserved to play a much larger role, that would have shown up in the data.

Taylor: In your work in consumption theory, for example, there is a more explicit model than in your work in the money area. Is that because you feel it's just too difficult to use models in the latter. Is macro a much more difficult area? Why do you think there is that difference?

Friedman: I really don't know. I think it's partly to do with the use of mathematics in economics in general, and I go back to what Alfred Marshall said about economics: Translate your results into English and then burn the mathematics. I think there's too much emphasis on mathematics as such and not on mathematics as a tool in understanding economic relationships. I don't believe anybody can really understand a 40-equation model. Nobody knows what's going on and I don't believe it's a very reliable way to get results.

Taylor: Didn't the work you did during the war involve complex mathematical models?

Friedman: They very seldom had models of that kind. The one place where you seem to be having that kind of modeling now is in the debate about global warming. And those models seem to be very unreliable and inaccurate. But if you think of physics, they usually have models with only a few equations. In any event, if you have a lot of equations, you ought to be able to draw implications from them that are capable of being understood. You should not present the model and say, now its up to you to test. I think the person who produces the model has some obligation to state what evidence would contradict it.

Taylor: I know that many people who follow the overall economy worry about using models for the reasons you're saying. But do you think the models can be helpful just to keep track of the many relationships?

Friedman: I don't want to say you shouldn't use models. Somebody will come up with one that will prove me wrong. People should do what they want to do. But I think, on the record, you've got to ask yourself whether large-scale modeling is going to continue to exist. You can't do without models—don't misunderstand me. You always have to have some kind of theoretical construct in your mind and that's a model. I think the large models are conceptually different from those with a few equations.

The Use of Time-Series Methods

Taylor: In recent years, you have had some debates with David Hendry about statistical issues relating to your empirical work on money. And that's related to the use of modern methods of statistics and time series. Could you describe your views about various approaches to time-series analysis? Where do you see some advantages and disadvantages?

Friedman: I think the major issue is how broad the evidence is on which you rest your case. Some of the modern approaches involve mining and exploring a single body of evidence all within itself. When you try to apply statistical tests of significance, you never know how many degrees of freedom you have because you're taking the best out of many tries. I believe that you have a more secure basis if, instead of relying on extremely sophisticated analysis of a small fixed body of data, you rely on cruder analysis of a much broader and wider body of data, which will include widely different circumstances. The natural experiments that come up over a wide range provide a source of evidence that is stronger and more reliable than any single very limited body of data.

Let me put it another way. I don't believe that we can possibly understand enough about the economy as a whole to be able to predict or interpret small changes. The best we can hope for is to be able to understand significant larger changes. And, for that, you want a wide body of data and not a narrow body of data. If you have a complex model and then try to extrapolate outside of that model, it will not be very reliable.

I learned that lesson very well while I was at the Statistical Research Group, going back to that. One of the problems I worked on was a metallurgy problem with an application to jet engines. There was a big project during the war of trying to determine the alloy that would have the greatest strength under high temperatures. We were called in as statistical consultants to the various groups working on the problem. I had a lot of data from all their experiments. I computed a multiple regression using these data—data that had been derived by hanging a weight on an experimental turbine blade to see how long it took for the blade to rupture at a given temperature. I regressed the length of time to rupture on the chemical composition and various other variables based on the best metallurgical theory I could find. I got an excellent correlation. So I used my regression to predict what new alloys would have a longer time before rupture. I got wonderful results even though I insisted on restricting every variable separately to the range of values that had been used in the experiment. My equation predicted something like 200 hours until rupture for my constructed alloy. That would have been an enormous success compared to the existing alloys.

Unlike in economics, we could put the prediction to a test. I called some people up at MIT and they constructed this alloy and tested it. And it took an hour, or maybe two hours, to break. It was an utter failure! That taught me that you could not depend on a narrow range of evidence using a lot of variables. I think I had a half-dozen or more variables.

By the way, at that time we did not have our present high-speed computers. So on that occasion I had to use the Mark I or some big machine up at Harvard, which was a collection of IBM sorting equipment. With the desk calculators we had, it would have taken three months to compute the regression. It took 40 hours up at Harvard. That was an enormous achievement. Now it would take five seconds on my Mac.

Taylor: So, did you have to have more discipline in trying out different regressions then?

Friedman: Boy, you sure did! Improvements in computing capacity have made this problem much more serious. It is so easy to fish around for high correlations. I don't have any confidence in a correlation obtained that way. People today pay all too little attention to the quality of data they're analyzing as opposed to the sophistication of the methods they use.

Taylor: As you described earlier, your first few jobs were very data-intensive. Do you think that kind of work is rewarded very much today?

Friedman: No, it isn't rewarded today.

Taylor: And many young economists do not seem to find it as enjoyable as more theoretical work. Did you find it enjoyable?

Friedman: Well, yes. I did and I do. It's kind of fun trying to figure out what's wrong with the data, like these charts we were looking at. Why is this damn thing happening? Is this is a pure data issue? Then we can think of all these great theories we love to try to explain the data, and that's where the fun comes in.

Real-Business-Cycle Models, Calibration, and Detrending

Taylor: A related question on statistical analysis, and on time series in particular, concerns the trend in the economy, whether you come back to a deterministic trend or not. Some real-business-cycle work was generated by the notion that real GDP does not come back to trend. What do you think about the real-business-cycle view?

Friedman: Well, I've always been rather skeptical about the real business cycle, primarily on the grounds of its empirical methodology, which is not to try to fit the data, but rather to calibrate. I think that's not a reliable way to get good results. I think Slutsky proved that years and years ago.

Taylor: Can you elaborate a little bit on that? Why don't you think that's a legitimate way to proceed?

Friedman: It's a perfectly legitimate way to derive hypotheses, but it doesn't test them. If I show you that with this calibration I get results that look like the observed data, okay, that's interesting. But why don't you go test it and use your analysis to see if you can reproduce real data that way and predict it for a period for which you did not have the data when you formulated your hypothesis. Either backward, or for another country, or something.

Taylor: So, just the fact that it looks like a business cycle is not enough?

Friedman: That's what I say. Slutsky proves that with an accumulation of random shocks. Maybe Slutsky's series are right there [*pointing to Figure 6.1*], I do believe that short-run fluctuations in the economy are simply the accumulation of random shocks. I don't believe there is such a thing as a business cycle. I think there are fluctuations and there are reaction mechanisms. Various parts of the economy react systematically to shocks to the system, but in the sense of regularly recurring cycles, the kind of thing that Mitchell was trying to describe, I don't think they exist.

Taylor: What about the notion that the economy returns to a trend after a recession?

Friedman: Well, I don't know what the opposite view is.

Taylor: The opposite view is that if you are at the bottom of a recession, then your best guess is that you're going to have only trend growth from that point onward.

Friedman: Oh, I see what you're saying. Oh, no, no, I think that there is a basic equilibrium position and the economy as a whole will tend to return to it. But that trend may change sometimes. Surely if something has been going on for 100 years, you've got to be a little skeptical in saying it's not going to go on again!

The Natural Rate Hypothesis

Taylor: Let's talk about a concept of equilibrium that you have made famous—the natural rate of unemployment. Your Presidential Address to the American Economic Association in December 1967 was on the Phillips curve and the natural rate hypothesis. It must have been quite an event. Could you talk a little about how that happened?

Friedman: The basic ideas in my Presidential Address were already present in a comment that I made at a conference on guidelines, the proceedings of which were published in a 1966 book edited by George Shultz and Robert Aliber [Solow (1966)].

I'm sure the basic idea grew out of the discussions about guidelines and, in particular, out of the Samuelson and Solow paper on the Phillips curve. I can't say exactly where my ideas originated; all I know is by the time I gave the Presidential Address in 1967, there was nothing new in that compared to what I had earlier published. Arthur Burns was in the chair when I gave the Presidential Address, and he had gone over the Address earlier. Arthur always went over my papers.

Taylor: You're kidding. He would read all your papers?

Friedman: Sure, and I went over his. Despite what I said about his chairmanship of the Fed, Arthur was a first-rate economist. He had a feeling for the English language and an ability to use it, which was unusual. He was always one of the most valuable critics of anything I wrote. He didn't always agree with what I wrote, don't misunderstand me, and I'm not sure on this occasion that he agreed with me, but he was one of the people who had commented on early drafts of the paper. At the time, I never had any expectation that it would have the impact it did. It only had that impact because of the accidental factor that you had a test right after.

Taylor: Yes, very impressive.

Friedman: This was one of the few occasions when something was predicted in advance and confirmed later.

Taylor: Did you think much in advance about whether this would be a good topic for the Presidential Address?

Friedman: You want to talk on what you are working on, and the major focus of my work at that time was monetary policy, so I talked about the role of monetary policy.

Taylor: That work has, of course, generated much work by others. One could argue that the whole rational expectations revolution came out of that research because you focused on expectations.

Friedman: I think the focus on expectations was important. But as for rational expectations, I think you have to give Bob Lucas a lot of credit for that.

Rational Expectations

Taylor: That brings me to the question about what causes the short-run impact of money. Do you feel that it's mainly unfulfilled expectations or do you think that sticky prices and wages play a role?

Figure 6.5 At 80th birthday party in 1992, given by the Frazer Institute in Vancouver.

Friedman: You've mentioned both the things that are no doubt the legitimate causes. After all, a wage agreement is not for a day, it's for a year, two years, three years. It's costly to change prices and so on, but I think the most important single thing is the tendency for expectations to be backward looking and to be adjusted slowly so that it takes time before any expectation is altered by the impact of an event.

Taylor: Does that mean you disagree with rational expectations?

Friedman: I have no basic disagreement with rational expectations. The question is, "how do you form your rational expectations." Let me start over. You are talking about what's going to happen tomorrow. The price is either going to go up or it isn't. If it goes up, the probability that it went up is one; the probability that it went down is zero.

What you are doing with rational expectations is to ask yourself, what is the probability that the movement tomorrow will be up or the movement tomorrow will be down. And now the thing that you have to ask yourself is, "I have an expectation. How do I know after the event whether that expectation was fulfilled or not? I said the probability that the price was going to go up was 60%; now, it actually went up. Does that confirm it? I can't tell. I have to have a lot of similar cases." And so, the notion of "correct rational expectations" is a notion I find very hard to give much content to.

If the idea is that people try to predict what is going to happen tomorrow, then rational expectations, in that sense, certainly makes sense, but on what do they base their rational expectations? They base it on past experiences; there is always going to be a lag in expectations catching up.

The Role of Debates in Monetary Economics

Taylor: In my view the debates in macroeconomics have helped get people interested, and this has motivated more research. Was there some strategy behind your role in generating debate?

Friedman: I don't think so. It just happened. I think most of the things that just happen are likely to be more valuable and interesting than those you plan!

Taylor: How did you get to be such a good debater? Did that just happen too?

Friedman: That just happened, too.

Taylor: You weren't a debater in college?

Friedman: I may have been involved, but that was not a major activity of mine. I just like to talk, that's all! And I like to argue. I enjoy the stimulus of arguments back and forth, but I never did anything special to improve my skill as a debater.

Taylor: Well, I do think it's an effective way to get people interested.

Friedman: It is, I agree with you. What people like is that a person is willing to take positions. He's not hedging all the time. The idea of the one-armed economist, one-handed, I guess.

Taylor: I always have to watch when I say "on the other hand."

Friedman: Right!

Taylor: Is hedging your views something that you strive not to do?

Friedman: No. It's the way I am. You know, somehow or other, people have a tendency to attribute to me a long-term plan; they think I must have planned this campaign. I did no planning whatsoever. These things just happened in the order in which they happened to happen. And luck plays a very large role, a very large role indeed. Take the effect of presidential elections.

Capitalism and Freedom Today

Taylor: Let me ask about your work on capitalism and freedom. *Capitalism and Freedom* was published in 1962 and has influenced people all over the world, but you did not do a second edition. Is there a reason?

Friedman: I think *Free to Choose* is, in a sense, another edition, from a different perspective. But since my main activity was science and economics, this is essentially a secondary activity.

Taylor: You mean to say that *Capitalism and Freedom* was secondary?

Friedman: Oh, sure. It was a series of lectures I gave at Wabash College in 1956 at a summer conference for assistant professors. The organizers wanted me to talk about free markets and those lectures were really the basis for *Capitalism and Freedom*. It was not a book that was conceived from the outset as a book.

Taylor: Did you take much time to write them?

Friedman: I had to spend time preparing the initial lectures and I also spent a lot of time editing the volume, but it was an avocation rather than a vocation. My wife did most of the work of turning the transcripts of the lectures into publishable prose.

Taylor: As your public policy work is in general?

Friedman: It's always been an avocation. I've often had students come up to me and say that they want to promote free markets or they want to get involved in politics and the advice I uniformly gave is, don't do that as a profession. Get yourself established in something you believe in and can work in and which has no necessary ideological component, so you have a little nest. Then go on and get involved in public policy; otherwise the public policy will impose itself on you and will affect what you believe rather than your beliefs affecting it. That's why I think that people stay in Washington too long.

Taylor: I remember one time when I was working in Washington, as a member of the Council of Economic Advisers, you said as much to me. I called to get your support on an important policy issue, and your first answer was, "Why don't you just come back to Stanford. You have been there too long." But how did you manage to have so much impact?

Friedman: I stayed away from Washington.

Taylor: Would you like to see a new *Capitalism and Freedom*, one that would be oriented to where we are now? In many respects the world has moved in the direction that you advocated. Do we need another book? Do you think we have moved?

Friedman: We need another one, but I can't write it. In many ways we are worse off. Government spending as a fraction of income is higher now than when *Capitalism and Freedom* was published. A good deal higher. Unless I'm mistaken, I think it was 30% then and 40% now.

Taylor: That is for the United States?

Friedman: Yeah, just for the United States. And also worldwide; I once got together a list of 10–12 countries and how much they were spending as a fraction of income, and in every single country the fraction of income spent by government had gone up. We're much better off in the realm of ideas. The intellectual climate of opinion is more favorable to a free-market society, but the practical world is less favorable. Just look at the regulations we've got now that we didn't have then.

Taylor: That's true, there is more social regulation, but millions of people around the world have been freed from communism.

Friedman: That's true. In the former communist countries, there's no doubt. In a country like Britain, France, or Germany, I'm sure there are more regulations now than there were 30–40 years ago, so that, far from having moved in the right direction, in practice it's moved in the wrong direction. And that's why, going back to your comment, that's why we need another *Capitalism and Freedom* to start from where we are now.

Monetary Unions and Flexible Exchange Rates

Taylor: Let me ask a question about monetary issues that relates to the global economy. You have Europe's new single currency, and you have Bob Mundell arguing that we should have one world currency. You also have talk about dollarization in Argentina and a greater commitment to floating in Brazil. Where is this all going?

Friedman: From the scientific point of view, the euro is the most interesting thing. I think it will be a miracle—well, a miracle is a little strong. I think it's highly unlikely that it's going to be a great success. It would be very desirable and I would like to see it a success from a policy point of view, but as an economist, I think there are real problems, arising in a small way now when you see the difference between Ireland and Italy. You need different monetary policies for those two countries, but you can't have it with a single currency. Yet they are independent countries; you are not going to have many Italians moving to Ireland or vice versa. So I do not share Bob Mundell's unlimited enthusiasm for the euro. But it's going to be very interesting to see how it works. For example, I saw a study in which somebody tried to ask the question, "What is the effect of having a common currency on the volume of intercountry trade?" And the result was surprising. It was that having a common currency had a surprisingly large effect, about four times the effect of geographical proximity or of flexible exchange rates. Now that was just a small sample.

Taylor: And beware of multiple regressions!

Friedman: Right! At any rate, one thing that I could be leaving out in my evaluation of the dangers of the euro is the effect of a common currency on the volume of trade between the countries. If it has a major effect on trade, it may enable trade to substitute for the mobility of people.

Taylor: Do you think that the depreciation of the euro is bad sign? [It was about $0.90 at that time.]

Friedman: No, not for a second. At the moment the situation is very clear. The euro is undervalued; the U.S. dollar is overvalued. As a result of the undervaluation of the euro, the producing enterprises in Europe are doing very well, the consumers in Europe are suffering, the consumers in the United States are getting a good deal, and the opposite is true for the producers in the United States. And there's very little doubt that within the next few years that's going to come together. Relative to the dollar, the euro will appreciate and the dollar will depreciate.

Taylor: One of your most famous articles is the one advocating flexible exchange rates, though you stressed microeconomic speculation more than macroeconomic issues in that article. Do you want to say something about how that article came about?

Friedman: That article originated from three months I spent in France as a consultant to the Marshall Plan agency in 1950. At the time, the German mark was having balance-of-payments problems and I was asked to analyze proposed solutions. I concluded that the best solution would be to float the exchange rate, but that was so far out of sync with the attitudes of the time that it was summarily rejected.

Taylor: That article, like many others of yours, has been tremendously influential.

Friedman: Yes, I think it has been very influential.

Taylor: Does it surprise you sometimes, the things that are more influential than others?

Friedman: I think it's almost impossible to predict what will be influential. You know that from your own work. You never dreamed when you presented the Taylor Rule that it was going to become worldwide conventional wisdom.

Taylor: I think that's true.

Friedman: It's an accident what happens to get picked up and what doesn't. It depends on the circumstances that develop afterward.

Taylor: Well, that's sounds like a good place to end, but maybe I should just ask one more question: Is there anything else you want to say?

Friedman: I don't want to say anything else. I've already said too much.

Taylor: Thank you. I have enjoyed this interview greatly.

NOTE

1. On editing the transcript of our conversations, Milton Friedman added the following explanation of his reference to "thermostatic control":

> The temperature in a room without a thermostat but with a heating system will be positively correlated with the amount of fuel fed into the heating system and may vary widely. With a thermostat set at a fixed temperature, there will be zero correlation between the intake of fuel and the room temperature, a negative correlation between the intake of fuel and external temperature. Also, the room temperature will vary little.

> By analogy, without a successful monetary policy to stabilize the economy (thermostat), there will tend to be a positive correlation between the quantity of money (the fuel) and GDP (the temperature), as there is in Figure 6.1 before 1992, and both may vary widely. With a successful monetary policy, there will be a zero correlation between the quantity of money and GDP, as there is in Figure 6.1 after 1992.

Money may still vary widely, but GDP will vary little, as in Figure 6.1 after 1992.

REFERENCE

Solow, R.M. (1966) Comments on "The case against the case against the guide-posts." In G.P. Shultz & R.Z. Aliber (eds.), *Guidelines, Informal Controls, and the Market Place*, pp. 55–61. Chicago: University of Chicago Press.

7

An Interview with Paul A. Samuelson

Interviewed by William A. Barnett
UNIVERSITY OF KANSAS
December 23, 2003

It is customary for the interviewer to begin with an introduction describing the circumstances of the interview and providing an overview of the nature and importance of the work of the interviewee. However, in this case, as Editor of this journal, I feel it would be presumptuous of me to provide my own overview and evaluation of the work of this great man, Paul Samuelson. The scope of his contributions has been so vast (averaging almost one technical paper per month for over 50 years) that it could be particularly difficult to identify those areas of modern economic theory to which he has *not* made seminal contributions.[1] In addition to his over 550 published papers, his books are legendary. He once said: "Let those who will—write the nation's laws—if I can write its textbooks."

Instead of attempting to provide my own overview, I am limiting this introduction to the following direct (slightly edited) quotation of a few paragraphs from the Web site, *The History of Economic Thought*, which is maintained online by the New School University in New York[2]:

> Perhaps more than anyone else, Paul A. Samuelson has personified mainstream economics in the second half of the twentieth century. The writer of the most successful principles textbook ever (1948), Paul Samuelson has been not unjustly considered *the* incarnation of the economics "establishment"—and as a result, has been both lauded and vilified for virtually everything right and wrong about it.

Reprinted from *Macroeconomic Dynamics*, 8, 2004, 519–542. Copyright © 2004 Cambridge University Press.

Figure 7.1   Paul A. Samuelson.

Samuelson's most famous piece of work, *Foundations of Economic Analysis* (1947), is one of the grandest tomes that helped revive Neoclassical economics and launched the era of the mathematization of economics. Samuelson was one of the progenitors of the Paretian revival in microeconomics and the Neo-Keynesian Synthesis in macroeconomics during the post-war period.

The *wunderkind* of the Harvard generation of 1930s, where he studied under Schumpeter and Leontief, Samuelson had a prodigious grasp of economic theory, which has since become legendary. An unconfirmed anecdote has it that at the end of Samuelson's dissertation defense, Schumpeter turned to Leontief and asked, "Well, Wassily, have we passed?" Paul Samuelson moved on to M.I.T. where he built one of the century's most powerful economics departments around himself. He was soon joined by R.M. Solow, who was to become Samuelson's sometime co-writer and partner-in-crime.

Samuelson's specific contributions to economics have been far too many to be listed here—being among the most prolific writers in economics. Samuelson's signature method of economic theory, illustrated in his *Foundations* (1947), seems to follow two rules which can also be said to characterize much of Neoclassical economics since then: With every economic problem, (1) reduce the number of variables and keep only a minimum set of simple economic relations; and (2) if possible, rewrite it as a constrained optimization problem.

In microeconomics, he is responsible for the theory of revealed preference (1938, 1947). This and his related efforts on the question of utility measurement and integrability (1937, 1950) opened the way for future developments by Debreu, Georgescu-Roegen, and Uzawa. He also introduced the use of comparative statics and dynamics through his "correspondence principle" (1947), which was applied fruitfully in his contributions to the dynamic stability of general equilibrium (1941, 1944). He also developed what are now called "Bergson–Samuelson social welfare functions" (1947, 1950, 1956); and, no less famously, Samuelson is responsible for the harnessing of "public goods" into Neoclassical theory (1954, 1955, 1958).

Samuelson was also instrumental in establishing the modern theory of production. His *Foundations* (1947) are responsible for the envelope theorem and the full characterization of the cost function. He made important contributions to the theory of technical progress (1972). His work on the theory of capital is well known, if contentious. He demonstrated one of the first remarkable "Non-Substitution" theorems (1951) and, in his famous paper with Solow (1953), initiated the analysis of dynamic Leontief systems. This work was reiterated in his famous 1958 volume on linear programming with Robert Dorfman and Robert Solow, wherein we also find a clear introduction to the "turnpike" conjecture of linear von Neumann systems. Samuelson was also Joan Robinson's main adversary in the Cambridge Capital Controversy—introducing the "surrogate" production function (1962), and then subsequently (and graciously) relenting (1966).

In international trade theory, he is responsible for the Stolper–Samuelson Theorem and, independently of Lerner, the Factor Price Equalization theorem (1948, 1949, 1953), as well as (finally) resolving the age-old "transfer problem" relating terms of trade and capital flows, as well as the Marxian transformation problem (1971), and other issues in Classical economics (1957, 1978).

In macroeconomics, Samuelson's multiplier–accelerator macrodynamic model (1939) is justly famous, as is the Solow–Samuelson presentation of the Phillips Curve (1960) to the world. He is also famous for popularizing, along with Allais, the "overlapping generations" model which has since found many applications in macroeconomics and monetary theory. In many ways, his work on speculative prices (1965) effectively anticipates the efficient markets hypothesis in finance theory. His work on diversification (1967) and the "lifetime portfolio" (1969) is also well known.

Paul Samuelson's many contributions to Neoclassical economic theory were recognized with a Nobel Memorial prize in 1970.

Barnett: As an overture to this interview, can you give us a telescopic summary of 1929 to 2003 trends in macroeconomics?

Samuelson: Yes, but with the understanding that my sweeping simplifications do need, and can be given, documentation.

As the 1920s came to an end, the term macroeconomics had no need to be invented. In America, as in Europe, money and banking books preached levels and trends in price levels in terms of the Fisher–Marshall $MV = PQ$. Additionally, particularly in America, business-cycles courses eclectically nominated causes for fluctuations that were as diverse as "sunspots," "psychological confidence," "over- and underinvestment" pathologies, and so forth. In college on the Chicago Midway and before 1935 at Harvard, I was drilled in the Wesley Mitchell statistical descriptions and in Gottfried Haberler's pre-*General Theory* review of the troops.

Read the puerile Harvard book on *The Economics of the Recovery Program*, written by such stars as Schumpeter, Leontief, and Chamberlin, and you will agree with a reviewer's headline: Harvard's first team strikes out.

Keynes's 1936 *General Theory*—paralleled by such precursors as Kahn, Kalecki, and J.M. Clark—gradually filled in the vacuum. Also, pillars of the $MV = PQ$ paradigm, such as all of Fisher, Wicksell, and Pigou, died better macroeconomists than they had earlier been—this for varied reasons of economic history.

Wicksell was nonplussed in the early 1920s when postwar unemployment arose from his nominated policy of returning after 1920 back to pre-1914 currency parities. His long tolerance for Say's Law and neutrality of money (even during the 1865–1900 deflation) eroded away in his last years. For Fisher, his personal financial losses in the 1929–34 Depression modified his beliefs that V and Q/V were quasi constants in the $MV = PQ$ tautology. Debt deflation all around him belied that. Pigou, after a hostile 1936 review of *The General Theory* (occasioned much by Keynes's flippancies about Marshall and "the classics"), handsomely acknowledged wisdoms in *The General Theory*'s approaches in his 1950 *Keynes's General Theory: A Retrospective View*.

I belabor this ancient history because what those gods were modifying was much that Milton Friedman was renominating about money around 1950 in encyclopedia articles and empirical history. It is paradoxical that a keen intellect jumped on that old bandwagon just when technical changes in money and money substitutes—liquid markets connected by wire and telephonic liquid "safe money market funds," which paid interest rates on fixed-price liquid balances that varied between 15% per annum and 1%, depending on price level trends—were realistically replacing the scalar M by a vector of $(M_0, M_1, M_2, \ldots, M_{17}$, a myriad of bonds with tight bid-asked prices, . . .). We all pity warm-hearted scholars who get stuck on the wrong paths of socialistic hope. That same kind of regrettable choice characterizes anyone who bets doggedly on ESP, or creationism, or. . . . The pity of it increases for one who adopts a simple theory of positivism that exonerates a nominated theory, even if its premises are unrealistic, so long only as it seems to describe with approximate accuracy some facts. Particularly vulnerable is a scholar who tries to *test* competing theories by submitting them to *simplistic* linear regressions with no sophisticated calculations of Granger causality, cointegration, collinearities and ill-conditioning, or a dozen other safeguard econometric methodologies. To give one specific example, when Christopher Sims introduces both *M and an interest rate* in a multiple regression testing whether M drives P, Q/V, or Q in some systematic manner congenial to making a constant rate of growth of money supply, M_1, an optimal guide for

Figure 7.2   New York, February 19, 1961. Seated left to right, participating guests who appeared on the first of The Great Challenge symposia of 1961: Professor Henry A. Kissinger, Director of the Harvard International Seminar; Dr. Paul A. Samuelson, Professor of Economics at MIT and President of the American Economic Association; Professor Arnold J. Toynbee, world historian; Admiral Lewis L. Strauss, former Chairman of the Atomic Energy Commission and former Secretary of Commerce; Adlai E. Stevenson, U.S. Ambassador to the United Nations; and Howard K. Smith, CBS news correspondent in Washington, moderator of the program. The topic: "The World Strategy of the United States as a Great Power."

policy, then in varied samples the interest rate alone works better without M than M works alone or without the interest rate.

The proof of the pudding is in the eating. There was a widespread myth of the 1970s, a myth along Tom Kuhn's (1962) *Structure of Scientific Revolutions* lines. The Keynesianism, which worked so well in Camelot and brought forth a long epoch of price-level stability with good Q growth and nearly full employment, gave way to a new and quite different macro view after 1966. A new paradigm, monistic monetarism, so the tale narrates, gave a better fit. And therefore King Keynes lost self-esteem and public esteem. The King is dead. Long live King Milton!

Contemplate the true facts. Examine 10 prominent best forecasting models 1950 to 1980: Wharton, Townsend–Greenspan, Michigan Model, St. Louis Reserve Bank, Citibank Economic Department under Walter Wriston's choice of Lief Olson, et cetera. When a specialist in the Federal Reserve system graded models in terms of their accuracy for *out-of-sample* future performance for a whole vector of target macro variables, never did post-1950 monetarism score well! For a few quarters in the early 1970s, Shirley Almon distributed lags, involving [$M_i(-1)$, $M_i(-2)$, ..., $M_i(n)$], wandered into some temporary alignment with reality. But then, outfits like that at Citibank, even when they added on Ptolemaic epicycle to epicycle, generated monetarism forecasts that diverged systematically from reality. Data mining by dropping the M_i's that worked worst still did not attain statistical significance. Overnight, Citibank wiped out its economist section as superfluous. Meantime, inside the Fed, the ancient Federal Reserve Board–MIT–Penn model of Modigliani, Ando, et al. kept being tweaked at the Bank of Italy and at home. For it, M did matter as for almost everyone. But *never did M alone matter systemically, as post-1950 Friedman monetarism professed.*

It was the 1970s supply shocks (OPEC oil, worldwide crop failures, ...) that worsened forecasts and generated stagflation incurable by either fiscal or central bank policies. That's what undermined Camelot cockiness— not better monetarism that gave better policy forecasts. No Tom Kuhn case study here at all.

Barnett: Let's get back to your own post-1936 macro hits and misses, beliefs, and evolutions.

Samuelson: As in some other answers to this interview's questions, after a struggle with myself and with my 1932–36 macro education, I opportunistically began to use *The General Theory*'s main paradigms: the fact that millions of people without jobs envied those like themselves who had jobs, while those in jobs felt sorry for those without them, while all the time being fearful of losing the job they did have. These I took to be established facts and to serve as effective evidence that prices were not being *un*sticky, in the way that an auction market needs them to be, *if full employment clearing were to be assured.* Pragmatically and opportunistically, I accepted this as tolerable "micro foundations" for the new 1936 paradigm.

A later writer, such as Leijonhufvud, I knew to have it wrong, when he later argued the merits of Keynes's subtle intuitions and downplayed the various (identical!) mathematical versions of *The General Theory*. The so-called 1937 Hicks or later Hicks–Hansen IS–LM diagram will do as an example for the debate. Hansen never pretended that *it* was something original. Actually, one could more legitimately call it the Harrod–Keynes system. In any case, it was isomorphic with an early Reddaway set of equations and similar sets independently exposited by Meade and by Lange. Early on, as a second-year Harvard graduate student, I had translated Keynes's own words into the system that Leijonhufvud chose to belittle as unrepresentative of Keynes's central message.

Just as Darwinism is not a religion in the sense that Marxism usually is, my Keynesianism has always been an evolving development, away from the Neanderthal Model T Keynesianism of liquidity traps and inadequate inclusion of stocks of wealth and stocks of invested goods, and, as needed, included independent variables in the mathematical functions determinative of equilibria and their trends.

By 1939, Tobin's Harvard Honors thesis had properly added Wealth to the Consumption Function. Modigliani's brilliant 1944 piece improved on 1936 Keynes. Increasingly, we American Keynesians in the Hansen School—Tobin, Metzler, Samuelson, Modigliani, Solow, . . . —became impatient with the foot-dragging English—such as Kahn and Robinson—whose lack of wisdoms became manifest in the 1959 Radcliffe Committee Report. The 1931 Kahn that I admired was not the later Kahn, who would assert that the $MV = PQ$ definition contained bogus variables. Indeed, had Friedman explicitly played up, instead of playing down, the key fact that a rash Reagan fiscal deficit could raise V systematically by its inducing higher interest rates, Friedman's would have been less of an eccentric macro model.

I would guess that most MIT Ph.D.'s since 1980 might deem themselves *not* to be "Keynesians." But they, and modern economists everywhere, do use models like those of Samuelson, Modigliani, Solow, and Tobin. Professor Martin Feldstein, my Harvard neighbor, complained at the 350th Anniversary of Harvard that Keynesians had tried to poison his sophomore mind *against saving*. Tobin and I on the same panel took this amiss, since both of us since 1955 had been favoring a "neo-classical synthesis," in which full employment with an austere fiscal budget would *add to capital formation* in preparation for a coming demographic turnaround. I find in Feldstein's macro columns much the same paradigms that my kind of Keynesians use today.

On the other hand, within any "school," schisms do tend to arise. Tobins and Modiglianis never approved of Robert Eisner or Sidney Weintraub as "neo-Keynesians," who denied that lowering of real interest rates might augment capital formation at the expense of current consumption. Nor do I regard as optimal Lerner's Functional Finance that would sanction any sized fiscal deficit so long as it did not generate inflation.

In 1990, I thought it unlikely ever again to encounter in the real world liquidity traps, or that Paradox of Thrift, which so realistically did apply in the Great Depression and which also did help shape our pay-as-you-go nonactuarial funding of our New Deal social security system. In economics what goes around may well come around. During the past 13 years, Japan has tasted a liquidity trap. When 2003 U.S. Fed rates are down to 1%, that's a lot closer to 0% than it is to a more "normal" real

Figure 7.3   From left to right at back: James Tobin and Franco Modigliani. From left to right in front: Milton Friedman and Paul A. Samuelson. All four are Nobel Laureates in Economics.

interest rate of 4% or 5%. Both in micro- and macroeconomics, master economists know they must face up to *nonstationary time series* and the difficulties these confront us with.

If time permits, I'll discuss later my qualified view about "rational expectations" and about "the New Classicism of Say's Law" and neutrality of money in effectuating systemic real-variable changes.

Barnett: What is your take on Friedman's controversial view that his 1950 monetarism was an outgrowth of a forgotten subtle "oral tradition" at Chicago?

Samuelson: Briefly, I was there, knew all the players well, and kept class notes. And beyond Fisher–Marshall $MV = PQ$, there was little else in Cook County macro.

A related and somewhat contradictory allegation by David Laidler proclaimed that Ralph Hawtrey—through Harvard channels of Allyn Young, Lauchlin Currie, and John H. Williams—had an important (long-neglected) influence on Chicago's macro paradigms of that same 1930–36 period. Again, my informed view is in the negative. A majority of the Big Ten courses did cite Hawtrey, but in no depth.

Before comparing views with me on Friedman's disputed topic (and after having done so), Don Patinkin denied that in his Chicago period of the 1940s any trace of such a specified oral tradition could be found in his class notes (on Mints, Knight, Viner), or could be found in his distinct memory. My Chicago years predated Friedman's autumn 1932 arrival and postdated his departure for Columbia and the government's survey of incomes and expenditures. I took all the macroeconomic courses on offer by Chicago teachers: Mints, Simons, Director, and Douglas. Also in that period, I attended lectures and discussions on the Great Depression, involving Knight, Viner, Yntema, Mints, and Gideonse. Nothing beyond the sophisticated account by Dennis Robertson, in his famous *Cambridge Handbook on Money*, of the Fisher–Marshall–Pigou $MV = PQ$ paradigm can be found in my class notes and memories.

More importantly, as a star upper-class undergraduate, I talked a lot with the hotshot graduate students—Stigler, Wallis, Bronfenbrenner, Hart —and rubbed elbows with Friedman and Homer Jones. Since no whisper reached my ears, and no cogent publications have ever been cited, I believe that this nominated myth should not be elevated to the rank of plausible history of ideas. Taylor Ostrander, then unknown to me, did graduate work on the Midway in my time and has kept copious notes. I have asked him and Warren Samuels to comb this important database to confirm or deny these strong contentions of mine.

Having killed off one 1930s Chicago myth, I do need to report on another too-little-noticed genuine macro oral tradition from the mid-1930s Chicago. It is not at all confirmatory of the Friedman hypothesis, and is indeed 180 degrees opposed to that in its eclectic doubts about simplistic monetarism. Nor can I cogently connect it with a Young–Hawtrey influence.

You did not have to be a *wunderkind* to notice in the early 1930s that traditional orthodox notions about Say's Law and neutral money were sterile in casting light on contemporary U.S. and global slumps. Intelligently creative scholars such as Simons and Viner had by the mid-1930s learned something from current economic history about inadequacies of the simple $MV = PQ$ paradigm and its "M alone drives PQ" nonsequitur.

Keynes, of course, in shedding the skin of the author of the *Treatise*, accomplished a virtual revolution by his liquidity preference paradigm, which realistically recognized the *systematic* variabilities in V. Pigou, when recanting in 1950 from his earlier bitter 1936 review of *The General Theory*, in effect abandoned what was to become 1950-like monistic Friedmanisms.

Henry Simons, to his credit, already in my pre-1935 undergraduate days, sensed the "liquidity trap" phenomenon. I was impressed by his reasonable dictum: When open-market operations add to the money supply and at the same time *subtract equivalently* from outstanding quasi-zero-yielding

Treasury bills that are *strong money substitutes*, little increase can be expected as far as spending and employment are concerned. Note that this was some years before the 1938 period, when Treasury bills came to have only a derisory yield (sometimes negative).

Experts, but too few policymakers, were impressed by some famous Viner and Hardy researches for the 1935 Chicago Federal Reserve Bank. These authors interpreted experience of borrowers who could not find lenders as a sign that during (what we subsequently came to call) "liquidity trap times" money is *tight* rather than loose: Safe Treasury bills are cheap as dirt just because effective tightness of credit chokes off business activity and thereby lowers the market-clearing short interest rate down toward the zero level. Hoarding of money, which entailed slowing down of depression V, is then not a psychological aberration; rather, it is a cool and sensible adjustment to a world where potential plenty is aborted by failures in both investment and consumer spending out of expectable incomes (multiplier and accelerator, rigidity of prices and wages, et cetera).

Go back now to read Friedman's article for the 1950 *International Encyclopedia of the Social Sciences*, where as an extremist he plays down (outside of hyperinflation) the effects of i (the interest rate) and fiscal deficits on V, to confirm that this Simons–Viner–Hardy Chicago oral tradition is not at all the one he has for a long time claimed to be the early Chicago tradition. (In his defense, I ought to mention that Friedman had left Chicago for Columbia by the time of the Viner–Hardy publications.) The commendable 1932 Chicago proclamation in favor of expanded deficit fiscal spending was itself a recognition of the limited potency of $\partial(PQ)/\partial M$. In terms of latter-day logic, a consistent Friedman groupie ought to have refused to sign that 1932 Chicago proclamation. Meantime, in London, Hayek's 1931 *Prices and Production* had converted the usually sensible Lionel Robbins into the eccentric belief that anything that expanded MV or PQ would only make the Depression worse!

Barnett: You first surfaced as a comer at the University of Chicago. What is your final take on your Midway days?

Samuelson: I was reborn when at age 16 on January 2, 1932, 8:30 a.m., I walked into a Midway lecture hall to be told about Malthusian population. At the zenith of Hutchins's New Chicago Plan, I got a great education in width: physical, biological, and social sciences topped off by humanities.

January 2, 1932, was an auspicious time to begin economic study for two unrelated reasons. The Great Depression was then at its nadir—which attracted good minds into economics and which presented exciting puzzles needing new solutions. The Chicago Midway was a leading center (maybe *the* leading center) for neoclassical economics, and I

Figure 7.4   From left to right, at the University of Chicago Centennial, 1991: Rose Director Friedman, Milton Friedman, Paul A. Samuelson, and George Stigler.

found exciting Frank Knight, Henry Simons, Jacob Viner, and Paul Douglas. My very first teacher, Aaron Director (now around 100), I liked as an iconoclastic teacher. He was the only man alive who could (later) speak of "my radical brother-in-law Milton Friedman." Long without Chicago tenure, his bibliography was epsilon. But without any database, he was a primary creator both of the second Chicago School—of Friedman, Stigler, Becker after Knight, Viner, Douglas, Schultz, Nef, and Simons—and present-day antitrust inactivism.

What incredible luck, while still adolescent, to stumble onto the subject that was of perfect interest to me and for which I had special aptitudes! What work I have done has been for me more like play. And always I have been overpaid to do it.

Director's published works are nearly nil, but his was later a major influence on (or against?) antitrust policy, and his stubborn iconoclasm had a significant role in creating the Second Chicago School of Friedman, Stigler, Coase, and Becker. (See the Stigler autobiography.) Since I entered college before graduating from high school, I missed the 1931 autumn quarter during which the Social Science Survey 1 curriculum surveyed economics popularly. As a makeshift, I was put into an old-fashioned, beginners' course that was being phased out. Slichter's *Modern Economic Society* was Director's assigned text, even though he did not speak well of it. (The following quarter, Lloyd Mints carried on with Richard Ely's best-selling *Outline of Economics*, with micro theory largely by Allyn Young.) Director's best gift to me was his unorthodox assignment of Gustav Cassel's *Theory of Social Economy* chapter on "the arithmetic of pricing," as stolen by Cassel from Walras. Few knew in those Model T days about the mathematics of general equilibrium in economics.

But it was Henry Simons, Frank Knight, and Jacob Viner who most influenced my mind. I may have taken more different economics courses at Chicago than anyone before 1935. Certainly, I was overprepared when entering the Harvard Graduate School in 1935. I also carried the baggage of excessive admiration of Frank Knight until time eroded that away.

The best that Knight told us in those days was that in rare depression times, inexplicably Say's Law and market clearing somehow didn't obtain temporarily. Most of the time, normalcy would serendipitously return and maybe then we could live happily ever after. Maybe. Meantime the only present choice was between communism and fascism. And for himself, Knight would not choose the latter. Later, understandably, he recovered from that failure of nerve and reneged on his circulated text. Somewhere in my files will be found a copy of his doomsday text.

This explains the second reason why 1932 was a great time for an eager teenager to enter economic study. Our subject had myriads of challenging open problems—problems that mathematical techniques could throw light on, and also close out. I once described this as being like fishing in a virgin Canadian lake. You threw in your hook and out came theorem after theorem. Viner is a useful example. He was a great economist, and perhaps the most learned one on the 1931 globe. He was also a subtle theorist. With suitable training at McGill and Harvard, Viner could have been a leading mathematical economist. However, Stephen Leacock and Frank Taussig taught him no mathematics at all. This made him fearful of acne-age students like me and our generations, who seemed to provide him with painful competition. (To do Viner justice, let me state that the 1930s graphics of trade theory by Lerner, Leontief, me, and Meade was in its essence already in a 1931 LSE Viner lecture, that the young Lerner would probably have attended.)

I carried a stout staff in the fight to lift the level of mathematical techniques during the second third of the twentieth century. But an evolving science does not wait for any one indispensable genius to arrive.

Others in plenty would have come along, trained by Hotellings, Evanses, and Frisches to accomplish that overdue task.

Although I've had an acquaintanceship with scores of leading world mathematicians and physicists, I've been surprised at how little help I've been able to garner from presenting orally some unsolved puzzles to them. I should not have been surprised. It is not that a Birkhoff, or Quine, or Ulam, or Levinson, or Kac, or Gleason was incapable of clearing up my open questions. Rather, it is the case that a busy mathematician has no motivation to waste his (or her) time getting intuitively briefed on someone else's models in the idiosyncratic field of mathematical economics. Fortunately, access to the good Harvard and MIT libraries enabled one to ferret out needed book expositions. And it was my good luck that Harvard's E.B. Wilson, only protegé of thermodynamicist Willard Gibbs, provided essential hints that helped in the development of revealed preference and the anticipation of the inequalities techniques in post-1945 economics programming.

Barnett: For some months in 1936 at Harvard, legend reports, you resisted conversion to Keynes's *General Theory*. Any truth in that?

Samuelson: After 1936 February, when copies of *The General Theory* arrived in Cambridge, I did struggle with my own initial criticisms of the book; and I suspect my begrudging acceptance of the Keynesian revolution in paradigm was importantly the result of Henry Simon's remark about short-term bonds as a substitute for *M*, when the interest rates are low. I was influenced by that, plus my earlier recognition that prices and price levels are sticky, and therefore neutral money and Say's Law lose realism. I knew 100 people without jobs in 1931–34 and 100 with jobs. The groups would never voluntarily change places: the latter felt very lucky. The former, about equal in ability, felt unlucky. That's not what happens when auction markets equate supply and demand.

Timing is everything. My Society of Fellows 1937–40 prewar leisure enabled the publication in 1948 of *Foundations of Economic Analysis.* Groups of youngsters all over the world joined to master its fundamentals. Not until 1983 did I prepare an enlarged edition with terse exposition of post-1947 developments. Why did this better book sell so poorly in comparison with its predecessor? It was because practitioners everywhere had become so much more sophisticated by the end of the century. Schumpeter would say: Monopoly profits are bound to erode away, as knowledge spreads, which is a good thing.

Barnett: So why did you leave Chicago for Harvard?

Samuelson: Given my volition, I would never have left Chicago, but a new Social Science Research Council Fellowship, awarded to the eight most promising economics graduates, bribed me to go to a different university. The effective choice was between Harvard and Columbia. Without exception, my Chicago mentors advised Columbia. By miscalculation, I opted for Harvard, not even knowing that it was about to move out of lean seasons, thanks primarily to the European immigrants Schumpeter, Leontief, Haberler, and also later Alvin Hansen.

Three years later, at Harvard, I did thank providence for my hegira *away from* the Midway—where I would have missed out on three great twentieth-century revolutions in economics: the mathematics revolution, the imperfect competition revolution, and the Keynesian effective-demand revolution. I deplore adversary procedures in the healthy evolution of a scientific discipline. Remaining at dogmatically conservative Chicago or accepting its lucrative 1947 professorship would have made me more radical than I wanted to be. For my temperament, serenity would be much more fruitful than the stimulus of polemical debate. I speak only for myself.

Barnett: Franco Modigliani, in his interview in *Macroeconomic Dynamics* [see Chapter 5], stated that he was discouraged from pursuing an offer early in his career from Harvard University by its Economics Department chair, whom Modigliani characterized as anti-Semitic and xenophobic. When you acquired your Ph.D. from Harvard as an A+ student, having produced one of the most extraordinary dissertations of all times, you were offered a position by MIT, but not by Harvard. Do you believe that the prejudices of the Harvard department chair at that time had a role in Harvard's enormous mistake in that regard? If not, why did they fail to hire you immediately upon receipt of your Ph.D.?

Samuelson: Anti-Semitism was omnipresent in pre-World War II academic life, here and abroad. So, of course, my WASP wife and I knew that would be a relevant factor in my career at Harvard. But by 1940, times were changing. Perhaps I had too much of William Tell's hauteur in my personality to ingratiate myself with the circles who gave limited weight to merit in according tenure. When MIT made a good offer, we thought this could test whether there was great enthusiasm for my staying at Harvard. When Harvard's revealed preference consisted of no majority insistence that I stay, we moved three miles down the Charles River. (My Mark Perlman *Festschrift* piece provides a memoir of an earlier "politically incorrect" age.)

In retrospect, that was the luckiest decision I ever made. In less than a decade, postwar MIT developed into a powerhouse in frontier economics. The Ivy League snared future Rhodes scholars. Our magnet attracted most of the NSF Fellows in economics.

Barnett: Tell us about Harvard in the 1930s.

Samuelson: Hitler (and Lenin) did much for American science. Leontief, Schumpeter, and Haberler brought Harvard to life after a lean period. Alvin Hansen was for me an important influence. Outside of economics, both in the physical sciences and the medical–biological sciences, the U.S. dominates. Actually, toward the end of World War II, when victory was no longer in doubt, I was lent by the Radiation Laboratory to help the Vanevar Bush Secretariat draft *Science, the Endless Frontier*. Biochemist John Edsall (Harvard), Robert Morison (physiologist at the Rockefeller Foundation), and I did a lot of the drafting—of course under the instruction of I.I. Rabi, Edwin Land, Olivier Buckley (head of Bell Lab), and other members of Bush's appointed committee. Against some resistance, what emerged was beyond my fondest hopes: an NSF (inclusive of the social sciences), a vastly expanded NIH, rather than a nominated plan to give every U.S. county its population quota of dollar subsidies for research.

Barnett: As you have mentioned, Hitler was responsible for an extraordinary migration of many of Europe's greatest economists to the United States, including Koopmans, Leontief, Schumpeter, Marschak, Haberler, and Kuznets, along with most of the Austrian School of Economics. They in turn helped to attract to this country other major European economists, such as Hurwicz, Debreu, Theil, Bhagwati, Coase, and Fischer. But it is widely believed in much of the world that the United States no longer has the clear political advantage for scholars over Europe that existed at that time, and in fact there is now an increase in the number of American students deciding to study in Canada. Is America in danger of losing its intellectual comparative advantages for economists to other countries?

Samuelson: I do not discern any trend toward foreign out-competition of U.S. science. Sole reason: our predominant real GDP, and the brain drain *to us* it has induced.

Barnett: Your research from the beginning has shown exceptional influence from the physical sciences, and you mention the work of physical scientists extensively throughout your research, as you did in your famous *Foundations*. How did you become so heavily influenced by physical scientists? Did you study their work at some point in your education?

Samuelson: I would be rash to ignore analytical sciences outside of the social sciences. But I would be stupid, if out of "physics envy" or snake oil salesmanship, I would inject into economic theory analytical mathematics that fit only gases and liquids. In my writings, I have criticized wrong analogies to physics by Irving Fisher (whom I admire as a superlative American theorist). Even the genius of von Neumann has not escaped my critical auditings. I have given only qualified approval to

Marshall's hope for a more *biological* and less *physical* approach to future economics. But that has not aborted my writings in demographical genetics, not all unqualifiably admiring of R.A. Fisher's genetical writings. Maybe someday, future Philip Morowskis or Roy Weintraubs will better fine-tune their nuances.

Barnett: Throughout your career, you have tended to have your "finger in every pie" within the field of economics. But at the present time, it is difficult to think of any economists who are "generalists" in such a total sense. To be influential in any area of economics requires a degree of specialization that virtually rules out broad influence throughout the field. Is that because of the dramatic expansion of the field and its growth in both breadth and depth, or is it because we don't yet have another young Samuelson on the scene?

Samuelson: If only because of the explosion of total numbers of academic and nonacademic economists, no young Samuelson today could hope to be the kind of generalist that I used to be. Remember I got a young start. I was a fast and voracious reader who turned the pages of *all* the newly current exchange journals at Harvard's *Quarterly Journal of Economics* office. The micro tools that worked in general theory also worked in trade theory. With some help from me, post-Keynesian macroeconomics lent itself to complete general equilibrium techniques. Post-Fisher pure finance theory was poised to explode. Since probability was a passion with me, the banal statistics taught at Harvard naturally spurred me on to Fisher, Neyman–Pearson, and Wald–Savage further developments.

Having a facile pen helped. Before MIT Chairman Ralph Freeman drafted me to author an elementary text, I wrote for *New Republic* and other publications. Hansen brought me into Washington New Deal circles.

Barnett: The economics profession widely was in error about the consequences of the Second World War. It is well known that a large percentage of the economics profession, including you in an article in the *New Republic*, expected an economic collapse at the end of the war. There were a few exceptions, such as Alvin Hansen and Sumner Slichter. Why did so many economists expect the economy to perform badly at the end of the war? In retrospect, it is difficult to understand why that would have been believed, especially in the United States.

Samuelson: Often I've stated how I hate to be wrong. That has aborted many a tempting error, but not all of them. But I hate much more to *stay* wrong. Early on, I've learned to check back on earlier proclamations. One can learn much from one's own errors and precious little from one's triumphs. By September of 1945, it was becoming obvious that oversaving was not going to cause a deep and lasting postwar recession. So then and there, I cut my losses on that bad earlier estimate. Although Hansen was wise enough to expect a postwar restocking boom, it was his and Keynes's teachings about declining investment opportunities that predisposed my activist contemporaries to fear a post-peace depression. Aside from Hansen and Slichter, Willy Fellner and W.W. Woytinski taped things right: Accumulated saving from the way we financed the war and rationed resources, plus lust for long-delayed comforts and luxuries, were the gasoline that shifted resources from war to full-employment peacetime uses. I knew that argument but did not know what weight to give to it. (Scores of older economists were optimists about 1946 full employment. But if their only support for this view was a dogmatic belief in Say's Law, they [Knight is an example] carried little weight with me.)

Mention should be made of another mid-1940s Samuelson error. I judged that the market-clearing real interest rate level would be 3% or less. That big mistake of course correlated with the earlier unemployment error. I was too stubbornly slow in cutting my losses on that hunch.

Barnett: You were an important adviser to President John Kennedy. To this day, politicians of both major political parties tend to point to Kennedy's economic policy for support of their agendas. To what degree were those policies influenced by you, and who else played a role in those economic policies?

Samuelson: With great reluctance, I let Senator John F. Kennedy recruit me to his think tank. From nomination date to inaugural day I became his chief economic advisor. Our styles and chemistries clicked. I've never regretted staying out of Washington for two reasons: (1) Research is my true love. (2) The CEA team of Heller, Tobin, and Gordon was the greatest ever. (I did help pick them.) Only when they needed my extra heavy lifting from Cambridge did I weigh in.

Barnett: How did you become a mathematical economist? Legends proliferate that you began in physics, or mathematics, and then levitated down to economics.

Samuelson: The truth is that, although I did have aptitude for school math, it was only early in my economic studies that I realized how useful more, and still more, math would be for the puzzles my generation would have to face.

Beulah Shoesmith, spinster, was a famous mathematics teacher at Hyde Park High School near the University of Chicago. A number of scientists came from her workshop. Two of the eight recipients of the 1996 Medal of Science had been her pupils, as were Roy Radner and my brother Bob Summers. I took the many courses offered: advanced algebra, solid geometry, and (boring, surveyor-like) trigonometry. However, in the old-fashioned curriculum, neither calculus nor analytic geometry was considered to be a precollege subject—a terrible mistake. So, after my freshman college year, I hurried to make up for lost time.

Aside from mathematics coursework, I was to a considerable degree self-taught. (When I thought determinants were boring, graduate student George Stigler showed me the big ones Henry Schultz assigned. That wised me up.) Before I knew about Lagrange multipliers, I had worked out the Stackelberg improvements on the Cournot–Nash solution to duopoly. In working out a theory of the circulation of the elite, I discovered matrix multiplication before I knew about matrices—Markov, Frobenius, or Minkowski. I took or audited, at Chicago or Harvard, useful courses from Barnard, Graves, George Birkhoff, Hassler Whitney, Marshall Stone, and especially Edwin Bidwell Wilson. E.B. had been the only protegé at Yale of Willard Gibbs. Since I was Wilson's main protegé, that makes me kind of a grandson to Gibbs.

Fortunately, I was enough ahead of my contemporaries in economics that I had all the time in the world to spend in the library stacks on mathematics. Never did I reach a limit to usefulness of more elaborate mathematics. My economic problems dictated where my math preoccupations should go—not vice versa. Of course, it was Edgeworth, Walras, Pareto, Gibbs, E.B. Wilson, Griffith Evans, Frank Ramsey, Bowley, R.D.G. Allen, Hicks, Frisch, Lotka, Leontief, and von Neumann who were my masters. I'm afraid that I was a captious pupil, often stubbornly critical of my betters. (Example: von Neumann's foundations for cardinal utility in stochastic Laplacian choice begged the issue of the Ramsey–Marschak–Savage–Debreu independence axiom by burying that in his zeroth axiom. Worse, he stubbornly ignored all of his critics.)

At Harvard [1935–40], economists learned little statistics, except in E.B. Wilson's small seminar. Outside Schultz's specialized graduate course, the Chicago economics curriculum had been little

Figure 7.5 Paul Samuelson with Bill Clinton in the White House.

Figure 7.6   Paul Samuelson (front left) with Jerome Friedman (Nobel Prize in Physics), Theodore Schultz (Nobel Prize in Economics), James Watson (Nobel Prize in Biology), and George Stigler (Nobel Prize in Economics) at the University of Chicago Centennial, 1991.

better. In the early 1930s, I had to read, on my own, Thurstone's little potboiler to learn about the rudiments of statistics. Only at Columbia was Hotelling teaching 1920–30 R.A. Fisher. Of course, all this changed rapidly once Wald, Feller, Tukey, and Savage entered the scene.

Barnett: How can we relate your Stolper–Samuelson work, and your later Heckscher–Ohlin–Samuelson research to the present revolts against globalization? Can this trend among some of the world's youth be viewed as opposition by the political left to the implications of your work on trade?

Samuelson: Trade is confirmed to be a substitute for massive immigration from poor to rich countries. U.S. labor has lost its old monopoly on American advanced know-how and capital. U.S. total real GDP has net gained [1950–2003] from foreign export-led growth in Pacific Asia and the EU. However, free trade can also systematically affect U.S. wages/ GDP share and overall inequality. My little Nobel Lecture ["International Trade for a Rich Country," lecture before the Swedish–American Chamber of Commerce, New York City, May 10, 1972: Stockholm: Federation of Swedish Industries pamphlet, 1972] pointed out that a rich place *can lose net* when a poor one newly gains *comparative* advantage in activities in which previously the rich county had enjoyed comparative advantage. Free trade need not help *every*body *every*where.

Barnett: Do you have views and reactions to the "rational expectations" approach and real-business-cycle theory? In the dialogue between James Tobin and Robert Shiller in *Macroeconomic Dynamics* [moderated by David Colander; see Chapter 16], Tobin stated that real-business-cycle theory is "the enemy." In contrast, as is seen in much of the published research appearing in this journal, the use of rational expectations theory (sometimes weakened to include learning) and stochastic dynamic general equilibrium theory is common within the profession among macroeconomists of many political views.

Samuelson: Yes, but a lot of different things are loosely related to the words "rational expectations." One extreme meaning relates to "the New Classical doctrine," which alleges in effect that Say's Law does obtain even in the short run. I do happen to believe that the U.S. economy 1980–2003 behaves nearer to Say's Law's quasi full-employment than did the 1929–60 U.S. economy, or than do say the modern French and German economies. But this belief of mine do not necessarily require a new Lucas–Sargent methodology. Sufficient for it is two things:

(1)   The new 1950–2003 freer global trade has effectively intensified competition with U.S. labor from newly trainable, low-wage Pacific Rim labor—competition strong enough effectively to emasculate the powers of American trade unions (except in public service and some untradeable goods industries). Nowadays every short-term victory by a union only speeds up the day that its industry moves abroad.

(2)   There has been a 1980–2003 swing to the right among voters, whose swing away from "altruism" is somewhat proportional to the *time elapsed* since the Great Depression and since the U.S. government's effective organization for World War II's "good" war. As a result, trade unions no longer benefit from government's help.

A "cowed" labor force runs scared under the newly evolved form of ruthless corporate governance. In contrast to Japan, when a U.S. CEO fires redundant workers quickly, Wall Street bids up the price of the firm's shares.

Another weak form of "rational expectations" I agree with. "Fool me once. Shame on you. Fool me twice. Shame on me." Economic historian Earl Hamilton used to agree with the view that, when New World gold raised 1500–1900 price levels, nominal wages tended systematically to lag behind. Kessel and Alchian had a point in suspecting that people would at least in part learn to anticipate what has long been going on. I concur to a considerable but limited degree.

Some rational expectationists overshoot, in my judgment, when they exaggerate the "neutrality of money" and the "impotence of government to alter *real* variables." Friedman's overly simple monetarism à la 1950, was criticized from his left for its gross empirical errors. What must have cut him more personally would come from any Lucas follower who accused Friedman of *fallaciously* predicting that mismanagement of M in $MV = PQ$ was capable of deep real damage rather than of mere nominal price-level gyration.

Modern statistical methodology, I think, benefits much from Lucas, Sargent, Hansen, Brock, Prescott, Sims, Granger, Engle, and Stock–Watson explorations and innovations. But still much more needs to be analyzed. Strangely, theory-free vectoral autoregressions do almost as well. Also, variables that pass Granger causality tests can seem to perform as badly in future samples as those that fail Granger tests. And, still the nonstationariness of economic history confounds actual behavior and necessarily weakens our confidence in inferences from past samples.

This does not lead me to *nihilism*; but hopefully, only to *realism*, and, à la Oliver Twist, to urge for *more* research.

At many a Federal Reserve meeting with academic consultants, there used to be about one rational expectationist. So unuseful seemed their contributions and judgments that the next meeting entailed a new rational expectationist. And each year's mail would bring to my desk a few dozen yellow-jacket manuscripts from the National Bureau, purporting to test some version of rational expectationism. Many were nominated for testing; few passed with flying colors the proposed tests. I continue to live in both hope and doubt.

In some quarters, it is a popular belief that macroeconomics is less scientific than micro and less to be admired. That is not my view. I think macroeconomics is very challenging, and at this stage of the game it calls for wiser judgments. A lively science thrives on challenges, and that is why I transfer a good deal of my time and energy from micro to macro research. Probably as a syndicated columnist, I have published at monthly intervals a couple of thousand different journalistic articles. Maybe more. My aim is not to be interesting but rather, as best as I can, not to be wrong. When my conjecture is still a conjecture, I try to mark it as such. My notion of a fruitful economic science would be that it can help us explain and understand the course of actual economic history. A scholar who seriously addresses commentary on contemporary monthly and yearly events is, in this view, practicing the study of history—history in its most contemporary time phasing.

NOTES

1. Perhaps those rare exceptions might include game-theoretic and topological models and maybe the recent literatures on complex unstable nonlinear dynamics, sunspots, and incomplete markets. But I would not be surprised, if he were to correct those speculations as misperceptions, if I were to ask.
2. The current URL of that Web site is http://cepa.newschool.edu/het/home.htm

8

An Interview with Paul A. Volcker

Interviewed by Perry Mehrling

BARNARD COLLEGE, COLUMBIA UNIVERSITY

April 18, 2000

Paul A. Volcker has spent most of his life in public service, at the Treasury under President Kennedy (1962–65) and then as Undersecretary for Monetary Affairs under President Nixon (1969–74), as President of the Federal Reserve Bank of New York (1975–79), and finally as Chairman of the Board of Governors of the Federal Reserve System under both President Carter and President Reagan (1979–87) (see Neikirk, 1987). Born in 1927, his worldview was formed by childhood experience of the Great Depression and World War II, times of great national trial that led ultimately to recommitment and reconstruction. He went into public service in order to be a part of the rebuilding effort, but it was his fate instead to be involved mainly in managing pressures that would ultimately lead to the breakdown of the Bretton Woods system internationally and the Glass–Steagall banking system domestically. Consequently, there is some sadness today when he looks back on his career, but there is also a sense of accomplishment. In spite of everything, there was no depression and there was no world war. The possibility and hope for progress in years to come remains alive.

The interview took place in Volcker's office at Rockefeller Center in New York City. His fourth-floor windows look out over the sunken plaza to the gold-leafed statue of Prometheus stealing fire from the gods, and then on farther to the elegant GE building, which is familiar to anyone

Reprinted from *Macroeconomic Dynamics*, 5, 2001, 434–460. Copyright © 2001 Cambridge University Press.

Figure 8.1   Paul A. Volcker.

who has visited New York. Over the front entrance it is just possible to see the inscription adapted from Isaiah 33:6, "Wisdom and Knowledge shall be the stability of thy times." It strikes me as an appropriate inscription for the building, reminding one that this most beautiful complex was built in the years of the Great Depression. Today, with the forthcoming interview in mind, it reminds me also of the stakes involved in the conduct of monetary policy.

Mehrling: I take it that you've always been interested in public service, given your childhood in the Depression and the example of your father who served as city manager of Teaneck. What's less clear is, why money? How did you get interested in devoting public service to the problems of the monetary side of the economy?

Volcker: Partly, these things happen by accident. My first introduction in an academic sense was a course in money and banking I took from Friedrich Lutz at Princeton. He was a fairly well-known professor at that time, a very good lecturer, always very logical and straightforward. His course somehow intrigued me because it seemed less flaky than a lot of economics. At that time, I had the illusion that balance sheets balance, that a number for loans, or a number for something else, really was an accurate number. It just somehow—I can't say it seemed more logical—it intrigued me.

And then I wrote my thesis on the Federal Reserve, again sort of by accident. I'm a great procrastinator. I was a half-year out of cycle because when I first went to Princeton it was three terms a year—this was what they did during the war. I had to write a senior thesis, and in my procrastinating way during the spring semester, which was the first semester of my senior year, I sat around, floundering around, not knowing quite what to write about, and I didn't do anything for that whole semester. I don't know where I got this idea of the Federal Reserve, but it seemed simpler and more straightforward to some degree than other things and, as I say, I was intrigued by money and banking. Anyway, somehow Frank Graham was assigned to me as a supervisor.

I was never close to professors. I thought they never had time for me, and I didn't have much interaction, but then I got assigned one of the leading professors in the economics department! I remember visiting him when I was first assigned, probably late in September, and I said that I was a little bit worried about getting this done, and he said, "You've got plenty of time." "I'm worried," I said, "because I graduate in January!"

After that, I'll never forget how helpful he was. When I got done reading and organizing, I began writing, probably in December. I would sit away in my little carrel scribbling out chapters, and I would give them to him, long chapters written in longhand. He would read them, make some comments, and give them back to me very promptly. You can't imagine a professor doing that now! He would insist upon having it typed, not having to give it back in a few days, much less the next day.

Mehrling: The thesis was about the origin of the Fed, the history of the Fed?

Volcker: Well, it goes back through the history, but it was more on current policy. Two or three chapters on history, monetary doctrine I suppose, real-bills doctrine, all that stuff. Years later, I went back to Princeton to give a lecture, and some student said, "Well, I read your thesis and you say we ought to abolish the independent Federal Reserve. What do you have to say about that?" All I thought to say at the time was that one's education continues after college! Later, when I went back and looked at what I had written, in fact what I said was, if they're not going to do a better job than they are doing now, and they are acting under the thumb of the Treasury, which they were in those days, there is no point in being independent. You might as well be part of the Treasury.

Mehrling: Then you went off from there to Harvard, to the Littauer School of Public Policy. You did that right away?

Volcker: Well, I graduated in January or February, so I had six months or whatever it was. I was interested in public service, so I went down to Washington just cold, wandering around to a few agencies asking whether they had a job, including the Federal Reserve. They told me they didn't. I used to tell a joke about it, that I was turned down for a job at the Federal Reserve! I just wandered in cold, and actually I did get interviews with a few very senior men, but you know they didn't want to hire somebody who was just going to be there a few months. I eventually ended up at the Federal Reserve Bank of New York, so that was fine, my first real job. After that I went on to graduate school.

Mehrling: When you were at the Littauer School, that was when you met Alvin Hansen? Did you take classes with him? Did you take that famous seminar with John Williams?

Volcker: Well, Hansen had a one-semester course. I think it was called Money and Banking. It was a very clear logical didactic dissertation of Keynesian theory. It was straight out of the *General Theory*. We read the *General Theory* comprehensively. Hansen was a very powerful teacher because it was all so clear in his mind.

Williams had the second half of the course, and everything was cloudy, always questioning; he didn't put numbers around everything. It was a great contrast. They also had this fiscal policy seminar. It was very well known, but I didn't normally attend it. I don't know why. Maybe I considered it more advanced.

Mehrling: So you learned Keynes from Hansen, and fuzzy from Williams. Which style did you like better?

Volcker: I remember very well Hansen laying this all out very logically and straightforwardly. One of the books we read was by Larry Klein, which was heavily econometric, *The Keynesian Revolution* I guess it was called. I can remember viscerally reacting, partly to Hansen but reinforced by Larry Klein—who is a wonderful guy, I later discovered—but thinking it can't be all that simple. You know, the world doesn't operate this way. They seemed to encompass it all in this nice consumption function, but I just had this visceral suspicion that the world was a lot fuzzier than laying it out quite so neatly as they did.

I had gone through Princeton and I did a lot of economics there. I remember taking as an undergraduate the advanced theory course even when I was a freshman or sophomore. There was one course they had then, called Business Cycles, but I can't remember the word Keynes ever being pronounced. We certainly did not learn about the *General Theory*. My introduction was when I went to Harvard, because at Princeton they were a bunch of Austrians. They were teaching us Böhm-Bawerk and the Austrian school. What von Morgenstern mostly taught in the advanced theory course came straight out of that school. I skipped over the elementary economics course, but even that I think didn't have much Keynes.

Mehrling: Your mention of business cycles reminds me of your 1978 Moskowitz Lecture, "Rediscovery of the Business Cycle," where you say fine-tuning basically is a thing of the past, and not only that but also maybe the long cycle has turned down.

Volcker: Is that what I said? I said the business cycle is kind of a psychological affair, didn't I?

Mehrling: Yes, you did say that. Yes. "Greed, fear, and hubris."

Volcker: Did I say that? I've concluded in my old age that hubris is a besetting human sin, but I didn't know I was saying it then. I still say that in my recent speeches!

Mehrling: I wonder about the extent to which that view of business cycles in 1978 comes from your Princeton training, whether it came from Hansen, or what?

Volcker: Well, it certainly didn't come from Hansen. There wasn't much hubris and fear and greed in his theories. It was all more from observing markets at Chase, my intellectual background from sitting at the trading desk in the Federal Reserve, from sitting in banks in New York.

Mehrling: We'll get to that in a minute, but before that, you went to the London School of Economics, right?

Volcker: Well, I didn't spend a lot of intellectual time at LSE. I was supposed to be writing my thesis, but I found London a little distracting.

Mehrling: I can understand that!

Volcker: But it was useful intellectually in one respect. I'm sorry I never—well, I don't know that I'm really sorry I didn't write a thesis. The primary thing I did at the London School of Economics was take a graduate banking seminar, a monetary seminar from Richard Sayers. It consisted mainly of him bringing in people from the City of London or otherwise, from government, talking a bit about the real world of banking and monetary policy in Britain, which was of course an interest of mine at the time. The thesis was supposed to be on the avenues of transmission of monetary policy, a contrast between Britain and the United States: the United States with a unitary banking system, very diffuse and diverse; Britain with at that point I guess five big banks and two pretty big banks. This was back in the days of lending and credit controls—consumer credit controls, secondary reserve requirements, and primary reserve requirements, all that administrative intervention. That was very much bound up with monetary policy and attempts to deal with the business cycle.

I had a fellowship from Rotary. It amounted to quite a lot of money by student standards. Also, it gave you entree to the Rotary Clubs, wherever you traveled, which turned out to be a great thing. Here I was, this American student interested in banking, and I finally decided that I'd better do something. With my Rotary Club entree and with Sayers's help to some extent, I could go around England interviewing bankers, including the heads of some of the big banks. Hopping around outside of London, I got a pretty good view in a couple of months of how the British banking system worked. I went to the Bank of England and the Treasury, too. I could have written a good thesis! I did have an opportunity to get a pretty good view of how monetary policy functioned and the institutional side, but otherwise I was impatient about the life of a scholar.

Mehrling: So you didn't read at that time the classic banking texts, for example, Bagehot's *Lombard Street*?

Volcker: Well I read some of Bagehot, and I read a lot of Hawtrey. I remember I read a lot of Hawtrey.

Mehrling: *Currency and Credit? The Art of Central Banking?*

Volcker: I don't remember the names of the books, just being in London. In those days I used to read *The Economist* and the *Financial Times*, so I kept up with what was going on in the money markets.

Mehrling: So already you're getting your knowledge about how the monetary system works from looking at it, instead of from reading books about it.

Volcker: Yes, well you know I did some of both. I didn't regularly attend Lionel Robbins's lectures, which were considered the core of LSE economics. They were much more theoretical and abstract than Sayers's seminar. But to put that in perspective, I'd had a good deal of theory at Princeton and Harvard, at least as advanced as that in Robbins's seminar.

I remember there was this one banker who came down from the City of London to the Sayers seminar. He pointed out that there wasn't much international finance in those days. This was in the aftermath of World War II and there were controls, destruction, and lack of confidence. But, he said, someday it's going to change and international lending will start again. He said there was one thing that he'd learned from experience. If there's a lot of international lending, it had better be done in the banks. Then in the end, when the crisis comes, as it inevitably will, it will be more manageable than if the lending is done in the open market, because you can never get the creditors together when they are diffused in the open market. I've never forgotten that. It happens to be true! It was a lot easier to manage international financial crisis in the eighties than in the nineties precisely for that reason.

Mehrling: I want to get to that, but the next stage of the education of Paul Volcker was the New York Fed. You got a job there under Robert Roosa, then moved on to the open-markets desk. Am I right that that was an education?

Volcker: Well, if you're going to be chairman of the Federal Reserve Board, I had a pretty good education! The first part of the time I was at the Federal Reserve Bank of New York, I was involved in forecasting factors affecting banking reserves, highly technical stuff but a direct input into open-market operations. I used to know the Federal Reserve statement and all that went into changes in bank reserves backward and forward: Federal Reserve float, currency in circulation, Treasury cash—daily movements, seasonal movements, weekly movements. I was expert in that, and it gave me insight into the money market from a technical and intellectual standpoint. Then, I got the chance to go to the trading desk, and could observe the market in action. That was a rare privilege, unprecedented for an economist. In those days everything was much more hierarchical and constrained. The feeling was that unless you had been sitting on the trading desk for a long time you were not capable of talking to a government securities dealer and making a purchase or sale. You wouldn't use the right phraseology, you wouldn't have a market feel, and you would clumsily give the wrong signal. The fact that I was there at all meant that this had begun to change. Bob Roosa was there in a senior position, and he broke the dichotomy between the market operations and the economists at a management level. I was the first one to actually sit on the trading desk who was from an economics background.

My responsibilities were not all that enormous. I used to write endless reports, detailing exactly what the market did every day, and what the Federal Reserve did and why we did it. Some of it was dull, but I really did get a feeling for how financial markets worked, and what shaped attitudes, which most economists don't have. I began to realize the importance of expectations, watching the market move the most when there was very little trading. It jumped because of some psychological factor. You couldn't sit there watching the market every day without realizing that it was changing expectations that usually moved markets on a daily basis.

In those days if you got a move of 4/32nd's in the government securities market, it was considered a turbulent day. Of course, now that is all changed. Then you couldn't imagine the market moving a point in a day, which it does rather frequently nowadays.

Mehrling: So the next stage was Chase Manhattan?

Volcker: That was good training, too. All this money market stuff which I'd seen from the technical and Federal Reserve viewpoint, I could see it from the inside of a big bank. I used to make projections for the bank—how our deposits would change, how much we had to make loans, the implications for interest rates and lending policy. In those days, the deposit base was constricted, there were official interest-rate limitations, the negotiable CD hadn't been invented, and other restrictions were still in place. I provided a liaison between the economics department and the rest of the bank, at least for financial analysis.

Also, I did a lot of work for the Commission on Money and Credit, partly because David Rockefeller was both President of Chase and a member of the Commission. *De facto*, I was almost an official staff member. That was interesting because it brought me into contact with some of the leaders of the profession and the leaders of the business community that were on the Commission. Among other things, I came into contact with Marriner Eccles.

Mehrling: I think of your education as ending and your public service career beginning in earnest in 1962, when you go to the Treasury. Is that what it felt like at the time?

Volcker: In retrospect, I think you are right. I don't know how old you are, but probably. . . .

Mehrling: Forty.

Volcker: Well, that period may all seem ancient history to you. It is a little hard to reconstruct for somebody your age the feeling that existed when Kennedy was elected. Before that, the United States emerged from World War II feeling king of the world, confident and exuberant. We won the war, and defeated the great evil. Beyond that, as the clear leader of the world, and certainly the economic leader, there was a real excitement about working in government. That's where the action was, and that's where a lot of able people wanted to be. That was exciting. That initial enthusiasm maybe got dulled a bit during the Eisenhower years, but then this handsome young fellow came in, full of zest, and confidence, and leadership for America. "We'll bear every burden and we'll solve every problem." I was caught up in it, along with many in my generation.

In the second Kennedy year, I had the opportunity to go to Washington because of Bob Roosa, who had become Treasury Undersecretary for Monetary Affairs. I remember I was worried they were going to solve everything before I could get down there! It was a great feeling of challenge and excitement. You felt part of something important. I've always had a feeling about government that way, because of the way I grew up. But this was a great opportunity, all the more so because the Treasury was in a key position and Bob Roosa was the intellectual force.

Mehrling: Reading through your speeches, one of the things I noticed was your very consistent interest in the international monetary order, beginning already in 1962 with the first little cracks around the edges of the Bretton Woods system, and then escalating from there. This became a focus of your public service career?

Volcker: Well, I think that's probably right. You know it's hard to remember again how domestically focused economics teaching in the United States was in the forties, fifties, even in the sixties. In most economics courses, the international side was hardly mentioned. Any introductory textbook in those days would have a chapter or two at the end of the book, but the professor would often never get to it. And it was pretty superficial anyway. The international side was just not important to most people. Of course, the Keynesian analysis itself was very domestically oriented. I don't remember Hansen much getting into the international side of things. Unlike Williams, he was very, very domestically oriented.

I can remember with some embarrassment going to Chase from the very bureaucratic Federal Reserve Bank of New York, and assuming that all banks were equally bureaucratic. Of course, Chase was a bureaucracy too, but it was much less rigid than the Federal Reserve Bank of New York. I hadn't been there more than a month or two when I got invited up to the President's office to explain something I had written. I don't recall the subject, but when I finished, he sat me down and said he wanted to talk about his worries about the international situation, about the dollar, the balance of payments, the balance of trade. You know, the President of the Federal Reserve Bank of New York had never asked me to sit down in his office to talk about anything, much less a conversation as freewheeling as that!

I remember to my embarrassment that he was worried about our competitive position, which in those days was not considered a great concern by economists, but the President was very conservative, he was a banker, and he sensed things were becoming more difficult. This was in late 1957 or early 1958. I parroted the standard analysis at the time: "The more things we buy abroad, given the dollar shortage, other countries will spend the dollars as fast as they get them. Nothing to worry about there." Right about then it was that the gold stock began to go downhill. My reaction was pretty naïve. This practical banker knew more about what was going on than I did!

I really got pulled into the international side when I was in the Treasury. Roosa was very international-minded. The Federal Reserve Bank of New York was the focus of international attention within the Federal Reserve, though I was not particularly involved when I was there. To the extent that there was an international concern, it was concentrated very heavily in the Federal Reserve Bank of New York, which had relationships with all the foreign central banks. You would not have found much interest in international affairs at the Board of Governors, certainly not at the Board itself, apart from the staff. The attitude at the Treasury was quite different as the convertibility of the European currencies was restored and the gold stock dwindled. Roosa was intent upon maintaining the stability of the dollar through thick and thin. Nobody in the Administration was permitted ever to raise any question about changing the exchange rate or changing the price of gold.

Mehrling: This was in 1963, with the interest equalization tax and various other administrative controls to shore up system. Was there much of a sense, as you recall, that this was going to be an ongoing problem?

Volcker: Well, in the Treasury at least, we were not sitting down speculating much about changes in the system. There was an implicit assumption through this period that somehow the fundamentals were going to straighten themselves out, that what was needed was a kind of temporary defense operation, that it was going to work out. It was only after Roosa left in 1964 that there was a willingness to think in terms of a more fundamental reform. The SDR negotiations only blossomed after Roosa left. He was opposed to all initiatives in that area, basically, I think, because of a feeling that psychologically further questions would be raised about the value of the dollar.

Mehrling: You left the Treasury shortly after Roosa, returned to Chase for a while, and then returned to the Treasury in 1969, under Nixon, when you were Undersecretary for Monetary Affairs, basically watching the Bretton Woods system dissolve little by little.

Volcker: Yep, agonizing over every step of the way.

Mehrling: And you fought every step of the way, and the people around you, that was the general attitude?

Volcker: Well, I had even had my suspicions, unvoiced pretty much in the Treasury in the earlier 1960s, that the dollar was a bit overvalued, though we were still running a trade surplus in those days. We were never sure, but I didn't take a lot of convincing that sooner or later we were going to have to do something about the dollar. I didn't relish the thought of being the Undersecretary for Monetary Affairs with direct responsibility in this area, to preside over the dissolution of Bretton Woods or devaluation of the dollar. But I was there and I came to the conclusion that was the game that had to be played.

I was still a little naïve! You could see that something was going to have to be done. It was just a question of how much you could do at the time, how to go about it, how much exchange-rate change was necessary and could be negotiated, and whether you could pick the time rather than having it forced upon you. By the latter part of 1970, there was not much question in my mind that we were going to have to go off gold for a while, basically to make an exchange-rate change. We had already been through gold crises in the 1960's and the policy of sticking to the official price of gold had been stated and restated. The idea of reforming the system by doubling, or tripling, or quadrupling the price of gold would have been considered an enormous psychological defeat for the United States, as well as financially unsettling. I didn't think we were going to make a change in exchange rates without, in effect, suspending dollar convertibility into gold for a while.

I always had in mind that this would be a relatively short transitional phase to a reformed system. I had some preliminary plans developed, but when push came to shove you couldn't interest anybody in that kind of planning. When the crisis came, President Nixon and Secretary of the Treasury Connally were willing to bite the bullet and take step one, suspending convertibility. They weren't willing to think much beyond that, which was a great frustration to me. But I was very naïve to think you could reform the system very quickly.

Mehrling: What about Burns [Chairman of the Board of Governors of the Federal Reserve System]?

Volcker: Burns was different because Burns didn't want to do any of this. He was holding out to the end. I didn't think he had any realistic ideas as to how to reform the system, except he seemed to think we could negotiate a change in the price of gold without suspending convertibility. I could always talk to him, and we were allies on the domestic side of policy in a sense, though I didn't want to go as far as he did in advocating incomes policies and all that.

I had become convinced that when we floated the dollar or devalued —since we already had an inflationary problem—that the psychological repercussions of that would be severe and carry the threat of aggravating the inflation. We had this stagflation, and there was frustration in the country about what was then considered a high rate of inflation, with sluggish growth. I had become enamored with the idea that when the time came to float the dollar, we ought to also have a temporary price freeze, which was not so off the wall then as it sounds now. And that's what we ended up doing, but it lasted longer than the 90 days I had endorsed. All we needed to do, I thought, was to give expectations a chance to settle down. But 90 days became two years, or whatever it was, and monetary policy was much too loose.

Mehrling: So the thing blew up after.

Volcker: That's right. It's a sad story, engraved on my mind.

The attitude of foreign leaders of course was quite different. Much as they had criticized us and thought things were bad, when we finally acted to devalue the dollar, they were stunned and didn't know how to react. They were not at all prepared. At that point, we wanted some exchange-rate change, we wanted some more basic reform. But their idea of an appropriate exchange-rate change was very small—certainly well under 10%—and then simply put the old system back together again. That didn't make any sense, from our perspective. So there was a lot of confrontation.

Mehrling: So you are saying there was no real constituency for reform, and that America failed its responsibility to create such a constituency? I sense in your writings a touch of "city on a hill," America as a model, showing others the way.

Volcker: Well, it should be.

We went through this effort, first the devaluation and the Committee of Twenty. That took almost two years. It's now forgotten, but that was the effort to reform the system. I was in the Treasury and I was the American negotiator for reforming the system. I don't know how close we really came to an agreement. It was very difficult. But about the time when maybe an agreement was in sight, the oil price shock was used as an excuse to end the effort.

What remains from that reform effort is the Interim Committee and the Development Committee, the C25's. In fact, I take some credit for inventing the Interim Committee and the Development Committee as a means for improving the governance of the financial system and broadening the discussion to include developing countries. I can't say it all worked out as well as we hoped. The issues then were the same as those being pressed now. You know, nothing changes. You get older, the arguments are recycled! We wanted to broaden constituencies, so to speak. We wanted to bring the developing world into the discussions. And we wanted to get more intimate and more meaningful exchange of views. We wanted to get the Ministers and Secretaries, the politically responsible officials, more in contact with each other and more taken up with dealing with these problems on a face-to-face basis. The idea was that the Interim Committee should become the Governor's Committee and then eventually become the active governing body of the IMF. But we had so much bureaucratic resistance that that didn't happen *de jure*, but *de facto* it has happened to some degree.

Mehrling: And then you were on to the New York Fed in the aftermath of the oil shock, and then stagflation in earnest in the mid-seventies. What was it like to be President of the New York Fed at that time?

Volcker: Frustrating. It was a somewhat frustrating job, not so much on the policy side because I did have an opportunity to have as much influence on policy as anybody else in the Federal Reserve apart from the Chairman himself. But there had been a long, long history of personal and institutional rivalry between the New York Fed and Washington. Of course, over the years, New York lost relative influence, and the Bank's feeling of independence and autonomy within the system got whittled away. It just was frustrating administratively because the Board would intervene in what were essentially administrative decisions, big things to small things. For example, I was not particularly eager about building a new building, but I inherited extensive planning for a project at the New York Fed. The Board equivocated and then wanted to cancel it. That was a big issue. It didn't break my heart substantively because I felt they had good reasons, but it also entailed a lot of picky concerns. Things like reviewing the salaries of the senior officers were a constant source of friction. So there was a lot of frustration. On the other hand, there were benefits too. For all its frustrations, the presidency of the

New York Bank is the second best job in the Federal Reserve System, or should be anyway, and I think the relationships are a lot smoother now. After all, I had both jobs!

Mehrling: And then, in the year or so before you went to the Board, it seems you started making speeches?

Volcker: The only two speeches I really remember are the Hirsch lecture on the international monetary system ["The Political Economy of the Dollar"] plus another one which was just on monetary policy, in 1978 at the AEA convention ["The Role of Monetary Targets in an Age of Inflation"]. The idea in that speech came to be labeled "practical monetarism" because, for the first time, I began rumbling about how it might make sense for the Federal Reserve to pay more attention to money-supply targets to discipline policy. It reflects the fact that I had begun thinking about how one could practically adopt some of these monetarist ideas, not just to create a constituency but actually to make policy more coherent and predictable.

Mehrling: That's interesting. You mention the Hirsch lecture, which is mainly about the changing position of the dollar in the international monetary system. As I remember it, one of your themes was about how international monetary stability is a prerequisite for economic growth. You suggest that the Depression of the thirties was to some extent, if not

Figure 8.2   Paul Volcker addressing the MBIA conference.

caused, certainly lengthened and made worse, by the breakdown of the international monetary system.

I wonder, as you look back at the decision in 1979 to embrace "practical monetarism" operationally, how important were these international considerations as compared to more purely domestic concerns such as inflation?

Volcker: As I look back on that decision, I think my concern was primarily domestic . . . well, it's all mixed up together; you can't separate. I guess that's become my theme, you can't separate them. That speech wasn't explicitly directed to the external side, but the external stability of the dollar is mixed up with it. I'm sure what stood out as my concern was the accelerating rate of inflation.

Mehrling: In terms of implementing this policy, you knew there was going to be pain associated with this, and you must have realized that in a democratic country you've got to find some way of getting people to go along, some way of explaining it to the people. Otherwise, they'll boot you out and you won't be able to do anything. The language of monetarism proved quite effective in that regard, didn't it?

Volcker: I used to rankle when some of the members of the Board who were all enthusiastic about this turn of policy would say, "Isn't this just a kind of public relations ploy to avoid being blamed for the rise in interest rates?" I never thought it was that, but a lot of people did think it was largely that. It was a very common thing to say that we just did it to obfuscate.

There is no question that I thought we needed to get support for a highly restrictive policy. You can always debate about raising interest rates, even by a quarter percent, which is almost not noticeable in the larger scheme of things. Recently, the Federal Reserve has acted to raise interest rates five times. We've raised interest rates five times by a figurative inch, and three of those times were to offset what had been done in the midst of the Asian crisis. On balance, we've had very little tightening. But we've had a great deal of focus on even small deliberate actions to change interest rates, and it's hard to explain how those higher interest rates affect inflation.

It always seemed to me that there is a kind of commonsense view that inflation is too much money chasing too few goods. You could oversimplify it and say that inflation is just a monetary phenomenon. There are decades, hundreds of years, of economic thinking relating the money supply to inflation, and people to some extent have that in their bones. So I did think we could explain what we had to do to stop inflation better that way than simply by saying that we've got to raise interest rates. It was also true that we had no other good benchmark for how much to raise interest rates in the midst of a volatile inflationary situation.

At least as important was the idea to discipline ourselves. People in the Federal Reserve don't like to raise interest rates. So the danger is you're always too little too late. I think that would apply to the current situation. So, when inflation really had the upper hand, it was, I think, very important to put something out there so you could discipline yourself. For that kind of a commitment, you've got to know what's at stake, and it does make some broad sense if you have that much inflation.

Mehrling: You say you had already been thinking about this idea of practical monetarism before you came to the Board. There were others, staff in various places around the Federal Reserve System, who had also been thinking along these lines, weren't there?

Volcker: Some version of it. The Federal Reserve Bank of St. Louis was always promoting a strictly monetarist line. It wasn't exactly the fount of my wisdom, but there was a lot of frustration in the Federal Reserve and there had been some talk about operational changes along these lines. There had actually been a study of it before I became chairman. You're right, there was a lot of restiveness in the Federal Reserve and a lot of very general talk about doing something, but nothing had ever come close to being operational.

Mehrling: I'm interested in the role of the staff in the 1979 shift in operating policy. What role did they play?

Volcker: The Federal Reserve had a very good staff, a very professional staff. But they were professional enough so that by and large they were very reluctant to speak their mind about policy. Sometimes they would get very uncomfortable when, once in a while, I'd have one of them up and ask, "What do you think we ought to do?" The basic answer you'd get was, "That's your job." In my experience, they were always very reluctant to go beyond analysis of the alternatives.

Now in this case very few staff people knew about it. There were two or three that did. The principal staff member involved was Steve Axilrod, and I think he was sympathetic. He seemed to share the anxiety for a new approach. I don't think the staff in general were sympathetic. They were not monetarist, traditionally, and this to some degree sounded too monetarist for them, I'm sure. But there was all this background of frustration—staff, as well as others that may not have liked the idea of what was viewed as a monetarist approach—but there was so much frustration that people were ready for a change. There is no doubt about that.

What really propelled me to make the change was when we raised the discount rate for the second time, when I was first down there. The vote was 4–3. I thought it was a reasonably strong move and we'd get a favorable reaction in the market, but we didn't. The response was, "Well, gee, the Federal Reserve is behind the curve anyway, the vote was 4–3, and that's the last increase of the discount rate we'll see." So the market reacted badly, which surprised me. I guess I was a little naïve. I remember this very clearly. I didn't bend over backwards to try to twist the arms of the three people who voted the other way. I knew I had four votes. If we had to increase the discount rate again, we'd have another 4–3 vote. But that's not the way the market read it. Then I realized that we had this credibility problem worse than I thought. That got me off and really thinking operationally about the other approach. But when it was sprung on them, everybody was very much in favor, even those who were voting against the increases in interest rates.

Mehrling: You mean the Board.

Volcker: The Board and the Open Market Committee. The Board was more surprising. It got me a little worried. I don't know if they've ever published the minutes, but they should. I remember when we had that meeting and I said before the vote, "Are you sure you want to do this? I mean, this is going to be a big deal. We don't know where interest rates are going to go. Are you really on board here?" I couldn't get anybody to express any reservations.

Mehrling: Then there was this brief flirtation with credit controls.

Volcker: That was a sad story. By that time, early 1980, interest rates were about 17–18%, whatever they were. President Carter, of course, was coming up to an election year, and there wasn't much progress against inflation. The budget was issued and it was poorly received in the market, despite the fact that the Federal Reserve at that time was unambiguously tight. This is all clear in my mind, though it's not so clear when you go back and read the press. There was an enormous amount of skepticism, and the budget added to that skepticism. Carter felt all that pressure and felt he had to go back and redo the budget, which of course I thought was a good idea.

Mehrling: To make it tighter fiscally?

Volcker: To make it tighter, yes. That was an interesting experience for me, just to see how that process worked. He insisted that I accompany his people up to the Hill, that I attend meetings where he was making all these decisions about the budget. That was kind of an eye opener to me for other reasons—the effort to balance constituent pressures and party doctrine against the need to reduce the deficit.

Anyway, there was a law that had been passed in the early 1970s to embarrass President Nixon, authorizing the President to call for credit controls. It was a two-stage thing. He could call for controls but the

Federal Reserve would have to implement them. So Carter took the view that he wanted credit controls.

I didn't like the idea and the Board didn't like the idea. We discussed it. We had introduced some voluntary restraints on bank lending for speculative purposes in October. But the idea of really having more comprehensive and mandatory credit controls seemed undesirable. First of all, that was not the problem. We couldn't find any general excesses of credit. Housing credit was going down, so there was no problem with housing, which is a big credit user. The automobile industry was not using too much credit either, no problem. But President Carter wanted to do something, I think, to demonstrate to the American people that we had a serious problem that would require restraint all around.

The Board was very reluctant, and I was reluctant. But I finally took the view that, look, we were putting the country through hell, interest rates are rising way up, the budget is being redone, and the President wants us to do this, and the President has been broadly supportive of what we are trying to do. At least, he wasn't criticizing us even though he had a lot of provocation. If he wants to do this, and he is bound and determined to announce it, then we in the Fed can hardly say we are going to refuse to implement the controls. Whether that judgment was right or wrong, I don't know, but I said to the Board, "Let us do as little as we possibly can, consistent with the request or demand that we have some credit controls." So we developed a scheme: We would exempt housing credit, we would exempt automobile credit, we would exempt home repair credit, and the only things we would cover on the consumer side were credit cards and what in those days was nonsecured installment credit. Neither of those were very big in the general scheme of things. We said, we will put on a special reserve requirement for increases above the present level of outstandings, so it was a marginal reserve requirement on all lenders. We were trying to mimic the market as best we could, in effect raising the cost of some limited forms of consumer credit.

Mehrling: It shouldn't have done anything.

Volcker: It shouldn't have done anything, logically. We didn't want it to do very much. We wanted to make a gesture. So we put them on one day, with a big White House announcement by the President, and the economy collapses the next day. I never saw anything like it in my life! Of course, it took a while to sort this out, but to the very day, to the very week, there was a sharp reaction. Suddenly the stuff that was covered, like I guess automobile trailers or mobile homes, sales went to zero the next week. People were tearing up their credit cards, and sending them in to the White House. "Mr. President, we want to be patriotic." Consumption just collapsed for a couple of months.

And the money supply—because people were taking their cash balances and repaying their credit cards—the money supply went down like a rock. And so all the liberal economists, as well as the monetarists, began to say, "You say you're following the money supply, you've got to ease." We were kind of stuck. "We stayed with you when you were restraining the growth of the money supply, and now the money supply is down 6% in a month,"—or whatever it was, maybe it wasn't that much but it was very sharp—"you've got to ease."

The economy, after resisting months of rising interest rates, seemed to have fallen off a cliff and so we eased. And we eased more than I would have liked, but we were trying to follow the money supply. After three or four months of this, when the extent of the downturn became clear, we took the credit controls off. We took them off the first time we had an excuse. As soon as we got them on, we wanted to get them off. Businesses selling to consumers were up in arms, going up to the White House. Department stores particularly were worried about these credit controls. What they were worried about was the credit cards, and what would happen to outstanding credit with the usual seasonal increase in November and December. That's when they have their big sales, that's when credit card outstandings go up, and the fear was we were going to discourage Christmas shopping. It hadn't occurred to me. I had no idea when we put them on that they were still going to be in force six or eight months from then. Of course, you couldn't announce that they weren't going to be on in six or eight months, but that was my whole mental attitude. But what they were worried about was not what was happening currently, because credit card outstandings were going down anyway for seasonal reasons. They were worried about what was going to happen in six months.

Mehrling: It sounds like a lesson in expectations.

Volcker: Exactly! I mean it was a big lesson, again if you needed any reinforcement, about how that kind of direct intervention can really have unexpected expectational consequences. Anyway, we took the controls off as soon as we could, and of course interest rates had declined and money had got quite easy. The economy just took off as fast as it had gone down. Then we really got behind the eight ball. It was hard to catch up with the economic strength and continuing inflation. It was a sad experience, because we basically lost, I suppose we lost eight months or so.

Mehrling: So it took three years instead of two years before you could really change expectations.

Volcker: Exactly. I don't blame anybody. President Carter called for controls, in part, because he thought he was being supportive, right? I suppose in the end I could have said, "Mr. Carter, I don't care what you do, we're not going to implement controls." But I didn't think that extreme confrontation was appropriate.

Mehrling: So you say you took off the credit controls more or less as soon as you could. I wonder, would you say the same about practical monetarism in terms of October 1982? Once the back of inflation was broken, and Drysdale was falling, and Penn Square, Continental, and Mexico, you took off practical monetarism?

Volcker: I don't remember all the detailed circumstances at the time, but early and mid-1982 was a tense period.

The Fed staff—there's no sense blaming the Fed staff, it wasn't only them—but they had forecast some recovery in the spring, and the money supply was running very high against our targets. With that combination, I didn't feel comfortable about easing, even though the economy was not in very good shape. In particular, the inflation rate was still high, with a lot of skepticism remaining. I remember very well—all these figures have been revised, so it might not appear in just the same way in the data now available—it was some time in July that the money supply suddenly came within our target band. The Mexican crisis was brewing. The economic recovery had not appeared. I thought, ahah, here's our chance to ease credibly. So we took the first small easing step. I don't remember whether it was July or August. Of course that was all the market needed. It got a little sniff of easing and the stock market took off, the bond market took off.

Then in October, or whenever it was, the money supply (by some measures) was increasing again rather rapidly. We had a tough explanation to make, but I thought we had come to the point that we were getting boxed in by money supply data that was, in any event, strongly distorted by regulatory changes and bank behavior. We came to the conclusion that it was not very reliable to put so much weight on the money supply any more, so we backed off that approach.

Mehrling: One consequence of defeating inflationary expectations is that the dollar took off over the next couple years and the dollar became the strongest world currency. It seems to me from the record that your next move was to try to think about the international side. Is that how you remember it?

Volcker: Well, for a while it was nice having the dollar go up. I don't remember when, it was probably in 1984 or so, but at some point it clearly became a problem. We had a question what to do about it. We could have gone out and eased policy, more than policy already was eased. I didn't want to do that, because I didn't think we had won the game yet, expectations were so fragile and all the rest. All of the difficulty was made worse because we were running up against a great big budget

Figure 8.3 Paul Volcker fly fishing for trout, at Balsam Lake, Beaverkill Area, New York.

deficit. Obviously, if I had a choice of using restrictive fiscal policy action, that would have been helpful, but that was not in the cards. Also, we had a Treasury at that point that was ideologically supportive of a strong dollar as an indicator of policy success, and was adamantly opposed to intervention, so we really didn't have the option of trying intervention as a signal that we were concerned.

I concluded we were stuck; there was nothing much we could do. We could have eased money or intervened on our own, but I didn't want to ease money any further than it was already being eased, in the face of a remarkably fast economic rebound. And we certainly didn't want to intervene on our own if the Treasury was going to say, "We're in charge of intervention; you're doing terrible things." It wouldn't have achieved our purpose. Among other things, we would have endangered our institutional position. So there was nothing much to do, at least until the Treasury changed its mind.

Finally, I'm told, it was Mrs. Thatcher who told President Reagan he had to do something. The pound was approaching a historic low of one dollar to one pound and she couldn't stand that. Mrs. Thatcher was apparently much more persuasive than anybody else, but we were heading that way anyway. The Bundesbank, which was generally reluctant to do anything to stabilize currencies, did a big intervention in the summer of 1984 when the dollar really spiked up, but the effect was temporary. It seemed to me crazy that we couldn't do that in a coordinated way.

Mehrling: One way to read this record is that the collapse of the exchange rate system in the early seventies is followed by confusion and then reestablishment of the dollar, which turns out to be the beginning of a move toward a key currency system that revolves around a couple of dominant currencies. The negotiations in the eighties at Plaza and Louvre are the tentative first baby steps in that direction. Is that how you saw it at the time? Is that how those things came about? Is that the way those negotiations took place?

Volcker: Well, the Plaza was basically a Treasury-inspired operation, which I was not terribly keen about. By that point, I thought the dollar was going down anyway, and the new Baker Treasury had already taken a more flexible attitude toward intervention. Given my history with an excessively weak dollar and inflation and all the rest, I didn't think that we had to hit the dollar on the way down for fear that it would get out of control. We had long debates about that and, in the end, the planning for the Plaza Agreement reflected much of my concern. But that was a straight get-the-dollar-down operation.

The Louvre was, in a sense, more interesting. Both Secretary Baker and his deputy, Dick Darman, had become intrigued by the idea of target zones, target ranges, or something of that sort, and I was very encouraged by this. It seemed a reasonable approach if it started with the dollar at a reasonable level. There had been a long period when Baker would go up to the Hill to testify that the dollar should be lower, and the next day I would testify that I liked a reasonably strong dollar. On balance, the contrasting statements came out not too badly, but it seemed kind of stupid at the time.

Anyway, for whatever reason, the Secretary became intellectually intrigued by the target zones, and there was pressure from Japan and Europe that didn't want to see the dollar, from their perspective, too weak. He decided that, in practice, there were things to be gained by stabilizing currencies, and so, we had the Louvre Agreement, which I was much more in sympathy with than the Plaza, not so much in the technical details but the general philosophy. Technically, the agreed ranges seemed to me too narrow, and there was no clear agreement about how to support them. It's one thing setting ranges, but in the end you've got to worry about who is going to act if the ranges are threatened, and how. If you need to change monetary policy, which side and how much? There was not sufficient attention to the fact that monetary policy was even a relevant consideration.

Mehrling: Let's move now from the past to the future. If I understand right, you expect 25 years from now that there will be a single currency in the Western Hemisphere, and 50 years from now there will be a single currency in the world. Is that right?

Volcker: Yes, I say that now all the time. I don't mean to be taken absolutely literally, but in fact, the prospect of decidedly fewer currencies is a little more serious than I thought even a year ago. Things are happening. I think *de facto* all this e-commerce stuff, all the information revolution around it, is an important contributing factor. You're not going to communicate around the world so instantaneously, buy and sell on the Internet internationally and efficiently, and be faced with all these currencies at floating rates moving with a high degree of volatility. It's just illogical.

The European experiment with the euro I think will help demonstrate that. I think it will be successful. Back in 1989 or so, I gave the first Arthur Burns Memorial Lecture in Frankfurt and I said, "You're going to be on the way to a European currency. That's a good thing and it's going to happen before the end of the century." That was not very popular doctrine in Frankfurt at the time, but it did happen and before the end of the century. It's one forecast I got right, so I remember it! So now I think the integration of the world economy pushes us further in that direction.

And second, every generation of economists has a tendency to reject at least part of what the previous generation thought. In the 1960s and 1970s, economic doctrine turned toward floating and against the Bretton Woods system of parities. It was embedded in the textbooks. But the floating system has been much more volatile than the models suggested. Now, we just begin to get a little feeling that the new generation of economists feel that floating models don't fit and policy went off the deep end. The logic of world currency, which would have seemed a wild idea 50 years ago, can at least be discussed. So, I think intellectually the ground is beginning to shift a little bit.

I used to say we'd have a world currency before the end of the next century. Then, I guess I said in 50 years. Then I would say, not in my lifetime. I'd like to say I feel well enough so that I'm beginning to think I might live to see it!

Mehrling: Well, good luck to you!

Volcker: I think it's basically a battle, that the world currency implies certain political decisions. You're going to see that happen some day, I think, even if I am realist enough to know it's beyond my lifetime. First, you're going to have a contest between regional currencies and a single currency. We're not going to have a lot of little currencies.

The whole idea that a floating currency provides great advantages for economic management—the idea often advanced for pedagogical purposes: "Wouldn't it be great if New England had their own currency, or California"—this idea is very deeply ingrained in anybody who has taken economics in the past 30 or 40 years. The central point is that you can have independent monetary policy only if you've got a floating-currency arrangement.

Obviously, that is a logical proposition. But what we are finding out is that for many countries, particularly small and open countries, a floating currency is more trouble than the independent monetary policy is worth. Many small countries have found it difficult to sustain noninflationary policies, and extreme exchange-rate volatility has strong economic reper-cussions. Stabilizing against a major currency, which is itself relatively stable in purchasing power, can help stabilize the price level in a small country. One of the big concerns about maintaining an independent monetary policy ought in this case to be moderated. Still, the United States, most of all, seems to have very little to gain from currency stability. It is already a big relatively integrated and self-sufficient area. It is top dog. It doesn't want to be constrained in a lot of directions by what goes on in the rest of the world, at least not very much.

So I think one danger is that we'll get more stability all right, by small currencies attaching to big currencies. You'll have a big euro zone and you'll have a big dollar zone, and just maybe we'll have a China RMB zone in another 25 years. But is that the kind of world we really want to cultivate, with the danger that each of the areas will become inward, and all that comes with that? To assure stability and cooperation between the areas, we will need to think in terms of some truly international standard, the role that gold used to play at the beginning of the twentieth century. Without gold or a substitute gold, you'll have to have a world central bank of some sort, which I'm not quite ready to visualize.

Mehrling: So one of the obstacles to achieving this goal is the paro-chial interest of the regions. Another obstacle, which is a theme in your work, is the parochial interest of the private sector, of the financiers who are benefiting from volatility?

Volcker: And the ideological trap of the economists, the intellectuals. [*Laughs*]

Mehrling: Tell me what you mean by that.

Volcker: Well, you know, this whole generation of economists has been brought up on the idea that floating exchange rates are the answer to the need to reconcile national monetary autonomy with international economic integration. There is this wonderful vision of floating exchange rates. Read all of Milton Friedman's stuff of 30 or 40 years ago. He says floating rates will very nicely equilibrate for inflationary differentials, struc-tural differences, and the business cycle. If there is a little differential shock, you'll have nice orderly adjustment of the exchange rate.

In practice, I don't think we've seen any of those orderly adjustments.

Mehrling: You're saying it doesn't happen. Now, in terms of bringing the private sector along?

Volcker: I think that financial deregulation has been another big strand of what I've been concerned about. We are dealing with a situation in which markets have become much more fluid, and there is much less control by the authorities, whether it is the Federal Reserve or somebody else. There is a lot more volatility and there are more financial crises. After the extreme crisis of the thirties, we went without a financial crisis until the middle of the seventies. In the United States, we went for 40 years without a financial crisis worth recalling. When I was in the Treasury in the sixties, Wright Patman, an extreme populist from Texas and chairman of the House Banking Committee, made a speech complaining that we had too few bank failures and too little risk taking. Well, we have fixed that problem!

How we get the advantages of an open competitive flexible financial system and deal with its proclivity toward volatility and crisis has been an unsolved problem, one that has preoccupied me. I'll tell you the Federal Reserve paid a lot more attention to banking regulation when I was there than it had before. Maybe I didn't do a good enough job, but the problem is chronic.

Mehrling: You mean supervision of individual institutions?

Volcker: Both individual institutions and the system. Really, I'm going to get a little self-serving, but I worked hard to get the capital standards of U.S. banks right. Then, with the help of the Bank of England, we set the framework for the Basle Accord capital requirements. There was a lot of resistance to it, and a feeling that international agreement was impossible. They are not perfect, and they're arbitrary, and they need to be changed, and so forth. But I think they are better than nothing. Because you are going to have to be arbitrary in this area. There are no sophisticated capital requirements sustainable for international application.

I'm very skeptical of the effort of the banks to develop so-called "modern" risk management approaches based on some theoretical modeling by mathematicians who never saw a financial market. All of this is summed up in the "value at risk" concept, which I think is borrowed from statistical and mathematical theory. The whole concept rests on the idea of normal distribution curves, but there ain't no normal distribution when it comes to financial crises, I think. They tend to run to extremes. The banks want to run a risk management system based upon the idea that we have a normal distribution of outcomes but, as has been demonstrated by the Asian and the LTCM crises, there are lots of problems there.

One of my hobbyhorses, which you haven't yet mentioned, has been the value in separating, I used to say banking and commerce, now I have to say finance and commerce. From a conflict-of-interest standpoint, from a systemic standpoint of minimizing the risk of contagious crises, from the governance standpoint, the idea of a banking system that is not beholden to industrial firms is attractive. It's getting harder and harder to find the line between them, I have to confess.

Mehrling: . . . in this market where firms can issue their own scrip.

Volcker: Both banks and commercial companies can do things with modern technology that they couldn't do before.

Mehrling: So, if I can sum up, one of the themes that emerges from your work is that markets don't manage themselves. There is a need for some, not so much a watchdog as a coordinator, or something to give direction to the system. By itself, the system can wander off in some strange direction.

Volcker: I guess that's fair. Put some limits on it at some point.

Mehrling: And that shows up in this idea about the exchange rate, trying to give some direction for market expectations because otherwise they fly all over the place?

Volcker: No question. I think that the market has no sense of what a sustainable equilibrium is now, but I don't think it's beyond imagination that it could be given a sense of a reasonable equilibrium, because there is enough to economic theorizing that there is some equilibrium out there. And it's better to stay reasonably close to it than to wander way away from it.

Mehrling: So markets don't manage themselves, and also bankers don't manage themselves given the greed, fear, and hubris combination.

Volcker: This is true. Also bureaucrats left unchecked probably don't manage themselves either.

Mehrling: Okay, also bureaucrats. And yet, with this anti-laissez faire attitude, you are also very pro-market. I'm interested in this combination.

Volcker: I would argue, and we don't have time to develop all this philosophy, that there is a role for supervision and a role for some sense of giving the market a broad sense of direction. But you can't get into the details of the markets, you can't attempt to manage it in a bureaucratic way, because it just doesn't work. It's a natural central banking attitude. Typically, central bankers like to work through indirect instruments. That's the habit, that's the way they think.

Go back to the interest equalization tax. I don't recall exactly how that arose, but the reason it was so attractive to Bob Roosa, the Undersecretary of the Treasury at the time, was the concept that this was a market-oriented thing. We weren't going to dictate particular controls, we weren't going to have exchange controls. We were going to mimic the market as best we could do it by the application of a broad tax on the export of portfolio capital. Now it turned out there was a certain implication that developed from the interest equalization tax almost immediately.

Mehrling: Arbitrage?

Volcker: Well, people did say, and it was true, that you've got to do a lot of detailed controls to avoid the arbitrage. But they also said, "Look, if the United States government thinks they don't like this capital export, and they are going to tax it, then I am not going to borrow in the United States even if I can afford to pay the tax. It's unsocial, it's unpatriotic." So it was a little bit like those other credit controls in 1980. A tax doesn't really mimic the market. It had unanticipated expectations and market effects. In fact, you know, I had to learn that lesson twice. The interest equalization tax, while it tried to mimic the market, it really didn't. What we tried to do with the credit controls in the eighties was the same. We tried to mimic the market, and we got a different kind of reaction.

Mehrling: I want to finish here by talking about the issue of the independence of the Fed. I know that you had fights about this when you were at the Fed, and a lot of it was about maintaining independence from the government. I wonder if you would accept the idea that what this is really about is about having autonomy to take the long-term interest and the general interest, instead of the particular interest of the moment, or the particular interest of the group in power at the moment. Is this independence more than just keeping government from financing itself by printing money?

Volcker: Oh, I think it's more than that. The traditional root of this concern about independence is that the executive would use the money creation power to finance itself, but I think it is a general feeling that the money creation process, even if not directly financing government, peculiarly lends itself to abuse for short-term political purposes and the consequences are longer term. I don't want to say you can't trust the political process, because in some ways I trust the political process to delegate that authority to the Federal Reserve, to the central bank. It does have something to do with taking the longer-term view, sure, and not being corrupted, if that's the right word, by very particular political pressures.

It's a grand question of money creation but also, to the extent the central bank has regulatory responsibility, banking regulation in particular is susceptible to being politicized. I think it doesn't work very well when it's politicized as we see in some countries around the world today. The Federal Reserve does pretty well at avoiding that kind of political influence to the point that I almost never had any pressure from a congressman or senator to do something for a leading constituent, which is very unusual.

I do have some kind of a grandiose view, not quite exactly what you say, that we need some public institutions that have integrity and are recognized to have integrity. People can respect them for their professionalism and continuity and so forth. There is a certain scarcity of that in the United States, as well as other countries, today. I think it's a national asset and that puts a very heavy responsibility on those institutions to behave in a way that deserves independence. It means they have to be operated with a special degree of competence, professionalism, and particularly integrity.

It's an extremely damaging thing in itself for a central bank to get caught up in politics and corruption. The central bank of Russia is pretty well destroyed by accusations, rightly or wrongly, that they are corrupt in the most egregious sense. As a result, I think Russia has lost an asset, an important institutional asset. They will need to rebuild, and it takes time. At the same time, you have to build in some accountability. But how do you get that balance of independence and accountability? It's not so easy.

Mehrling: Good place to end. Thank you.

REFERENCE

Neikirk, W.R. (1987) *Volcker, Portrait of the Money Man*. New York: Congdon and Weed.

9

An Interview with Martin Feldstein

Interviewed by James M. Poterba
MASSACHUSETTS INSTITUTE OF TECHNOLOGY
January 30, 2002

Martin Feldstein is one of the most influential empirical economists of the late twentieth century. In the 1960s, as a research fellow at Oxford University, where he earned a D.Phil. in economics, he pioneered the empirical analysis of production functions for hospitals and for other health care providers. In the process, he helped to launch the modern field of health economics. In the 1970s, shortly after moving from Oxford to Harvard, his research expanded from health economics to a broader range of social insurance programs, particularly Social Security and unemployment insurance. He developed theoretical models for analyzing how these programs affected the incentives facing households and firms, and then marshaled empirical evidence to document the substantive importance of these program-induced distortions. Feldstein's work sparked an active public policy debate on the economic effects of these programs, and this debate continues to the present day.

Feldstein was one of the first to use household-level data from surveys and administrative records to analyze how taxes and government transfer programs affect household behavior. His research contributions, and his pedagogical role in training dozens of graduate students, accelerated the diffusion of new empirical strategies in the field of applied economics. Researchers in public finance still make widespread use of the TAXSIM computer model, a household-level program for computing tax liabilities, which Feldstein began to build during the 1970s.

Reprinted from *Macroeconomic Dynamics*, 7, 2003, 291–312. Copyright © 2003 Cambridge University Press.

Figure 9.1 Martin Feldstein.

In the early 1980s, Feldstein spent two years as the Chairman of the Council of Economic Advisers. During that time, he warned frequently of the long-term economic costs of large budget deficits, even though this was a very unpopular view on political grounds. Feldstein's time in Washington expanded his interests still further, to encompass international economic policy issues as well as domestic questions. When he returned to Harvard and the NBER in the mid-1980s, Feldstein directed several projects on the sources of, and policy responses to, international economic crises.

Throughout the late 1980s and early 1990s, Feldstein continued to make central contributions to his primary field of public finance. In a series of papers on how taxable income responds to changes in marginal tax rates, Feldstein developed a new framework for evaluating the efficiency cost of income taxation. These papers also contributed in a very significant way to the debate on how congressional tax analysts should compute the revenue effects of tax reforms. He also continued his long-standing interest in social insurance policy. His 1995 Ely Lecture to the American Economic Association was a clarion call drawing economic researchers to the analysis of Social Security reform proposals, and it anticipated the very active policy debate of the last half decade.

Feldstein has been actively involved in both undergraduate and graduate teaching during his 35 years on the Harvard faculty. He has served on the dissertation committees of more than 60 graduate students, and he has trained many of the current leaders in the field of public economics. He currently directs and lectures in Harvard's Principles of Economics course, which is the largest undergraduate course at Harvard.

Martin Feldstein has made landmark contributions in many subfields of applied economics. He has also played a critical role in shaping the direction of economic research more generally in his position as President of the National Bureau of Economic Research, a post he has held since 1977. Feldstein has made the NBER a clearinghouse for a wide range of current policy-relevant economic research, and he has directed numerous research projects that have generated important new economic insights. During Feldstein's tenure as NBER President, yellow-covered NBER working papers and, increasingly, the NBER Internet site, www.nber.org, have become standard starting points for researchers investigating many topics in applied economics.

In 1977, Martin Feldstein received the John Bates Clark Medal from the American Economic Association, recognizing him as the outstanding economist under the age of 40. Twenty-five years later, in 2002, he was elected President of that association.

This interview was conducted at Martin Feldstein's office at the NBER. One wall of the small conference room in which we worked is decorated with original drawings of some of the political cartoons that lampooned Feldstein's deficit worries during his time at the Council of Economic Advisers. Outside the conference room, a glass case contains literally hundreds of books that are the results of NBER research studies dating back to 1920. The interview follows a loose chronological pattern.

Poterba: Marty, let's start talking about how you became interested in economics. You began your economics career as a health economist, and

Figure 9.2   From left to right: Michelle White, Wen Hai, Gay Auerbach, Roger Gordon, and Martin Feldstein during the June 2001 NBER–Chinese Center for Economic Research Joint Conference.

your undergraduate economics thesis was about health issues. What drew you to these issues?

Feldstein: Well, actually, my undergraduate thesis grew out of the fact that I was a premed student and I had worked during the summer for a cancer research organization at Sloan-Kettering. I knew something about cancer research and I guess it has always been a habit of mine to build on real-world information.

Poterba: What issue in health economics did you study?

Feldstein: The thing that I looked at was how much the government should spend for cancer research. In retrospect, it was a very naïve thesis. I did a survey of people who had National Institutes of Health cancer research grants. I asked them if the government spent twice as much or five times as much, what would be the probability of various kinds of outcomes.

What I learned was that if the spending numbers were 50, 100, and 250, you got certain answers. If you multiplied those all by two and asked the same questions, you got the same answers at the same relative points. So that was good evidence that these people had no idea of the payoff from research spending, and that my question was very naïve. This was not a way in which you could find out what the payoff was for additional spending on research. Of course, that was not what I expected to find when I started the research.

Poterba: What was your economics training as an undergraduate at Harvard like? Was there any discussion of statistics, any discussion of mathematics in what you studied?

Feldstein: There was no undergraduate econometrics course. Those few people who were more mathematically inclined could presumably find their way into the graduate program, although I think, truth be told, it was not very mathematical at the time either.

Poterba: Now after this undergraduate experience, you headed off to England to do graduate work. Can you say a bit about how that came to pass?

Feldstein: Well, I thought I was going to be a doctor. I had been admitted to Harvard Medical School, but I thought taking a year off to see the world would be a good idea. And the people at the Fulbright Commission were nice enough to accommodate that. So I packed my bags and went off to Oxford, expecting that I'd come back at the end of one year and go to medical school.

Then I discovered I rather liked this economics work and decided to spend more time in Oxford. I wrote to Harvard Medical School and they agreed to postpone my admission for another year. And we repeated that process so that I'd been admitted three times before I worked up the courage to say, no, I was going to be an economist.

Poterba: When you were at Oxford, your graduate adviser was Terence Gorman, who is known primarily for his work on demand systems. How did he affect your development as an economic researcher?

Feldstein. The first person I had as an adviser was actually Ian Little. He was an expert on welfare economics, and I think he had an important impact. I didn't spend a lot of time with him, nothing like what I did with Terence, but Ian had written a book called *The Critique of Welfare Economics*, which essentially developed the theory of the second best, arguing that you can't make welfare judgments about specific public policies if there are any imperfections in the economy.

But Ian was too smart to settle for that conclusion. Having written a brilliant book, he then went on to do applied welfare economics. He wrote a book about the nationalized coal industry in England. He acknowledged in the introduction all of the things that he had written before—that in a "second-best" world it is not possible to make rigorous judgments—but then he proceeded to give sensible comments. And I suppose that has been my attitude: I understand that welfare economics is an approximation but I believe it can be useful.

Terence was a phenomenon. He showed me in a way that nobody at Harvard had what technical professional economics was all about. He also introduced me to econometrics. He was a one-man show: He taught us linear algebra, mathematical economics, and econometric theory.

Poterba: What was Terence teaching in econometrics?

Feldstein: His teaching in econometrics built on linear algebra rather than on mathematical statistics. In addition to the traditional OLS estimator, we studied instrumental variable estimation and saw LIML as a special case of the k-class linear estimators. Although big macro models were in vogue at the time, Terence was very much a single-equation man who thought that the chance that you could specify one of these large systems well enough to gain anything from cross-equation restrictions was very small. I'm sure that lesson stuck with me.

Poterba: Were there other key figures in your graduate school experience who affected the way you came to do research?

Feldstein: I went to John Hicks's seminar and to the Nuffield Colege economics seminar, but the major stimulus was talk with some of my fellow graduate students—particularly John Flemming and John Helliwell.

Poterba: What did you learn in your doctoral dissertation research on the British National Health System?

Feldstein: Well, I discovered that you could do useful econometric research about a health care system. That hardly comes as a surprise now since many people now do research on health care, but it was very novel at that time, in the United States as well as in England. The British system was good in that it had a lot of microeconomic hospital data that were publicly available.

One of the specific things that I looked at was the effect of resource availability on patterns of utilization. Different areas of England were differently endowed with hospitals and doctors. I studied how these differences in endowments in a nonmarket system affect the amount of care given to different kinds of illnesses. I showed clinical people the results and asked whether the things that were most sensitive to resource supply were the things that should be most sensitive. The answer was "Certainly not."

I also studied questions such as economies of scale and optimal hospital size. I estimated cost functions, and production functions with multiple inputs so that I could evaluate the marginal product of nurses and doctors in the production of case-mix-adjusted output.

Poterba: After six years in the United Kingdom, you returned to Harvard. Were there major challenges in shifting from a research program on health economics in the United Kingdom, where health care was largely provided in the public sector, to studying health economics in the United States?

Feldstein: No. It was much easier here because health care was provided in the market. There were prices, so there were more questions. It wasn't just about studying the technology. You could actually ask what does insurance do, and why do people buy insurance, and why are the prices rising faster in one area than in another? There were a whole set of questions that came very naturally to an economist. So I stopped doing the kind of microtechnology things that I had done in England.

Poterba: Had anyone done empirical work on these issues about insurance and related things before?

Feldstein: Not much. Ken Arrow had written a paper about the theory of health insurance. There were two or three economists who were working on the economics of health, but it was just not a field and there was no modern econometric research.

Poterba: Did any of the work that you did on insurance or health economics in the late 1960s and early 1970s give you any insights on what was going to happen in the health care economy for the next three decades, in particular, the rising share of GDP we devote to health care and the shift toward managed care?

Feldstein: Well, the rising share I think was foreseeable. In the hospital area, which was the big expenditure area, there was a dynamic in which the higher the price the more insurance you wanted, and the more insurance you had the higher the equilibrium market price. I wrote a few papers that worked that out and showed how tax rules were driving the demand for insurance. Moreover, my estimates implied that the existing system was on an explosive path in which some exogenous force would be needed to stop the rise in the relative cost of hospital care.

I did not see managed care as a solution. My view—and I think it was true of other economists who, by then, were joining the fraternity—was that more co-payment and deductibles would make the health care market work better. Although managed care and HMOs have been used to limit costs, public dissatisfaction and changing technology may lead to renewed interest in co-payments.

Poterba: Let me shift for a moment to the Harvard Economics Department that you returned to in the late 1960s. This was a time of great change at Harvard. You, Ken Arrow, Zvi Griliches, and Dale Jorgenson all arrived within a few years of each other. Was there a sense that you were part of a wave of change in the way economics was being taught and practiced?

Feldstein: Sure. It was an explicit decision by the department to go out and recruit. These people didn't just happen to come; they came as a package. I wasn't part of that package, but I came at the same time and I knew they were coming and that was part of the lure of Harvard. It was clearly a revolution in the way in which the first-year courses were going to be taught.

In the 1960s, the first-year course was being taught by people such as Wassily Leontief. Wassily was a Nobel Prize winner with a great track record behind him, but he was not the person to teach current microtheory. He may have been communicating more wisdom than the average microtheory course, but he was not teaching the material that graduate students needed to know.

Poterba: You mean students were not getting modern tools.

Feldstein: Right. Then a group of young Turks took over. Within the first year or so that I was at Harvard, Sam Bowles and Herb Gintis were teaching the introductory micro course and had written a little textbook for that purpose. And, no doubt, this brought the students closer to the frontier, but it wasn't the same as having Ken Arrow doing it.

John Meyer and Hank Houthakker were the teachers of econometrics, and that wasn't really their specialty in the sense that it was for Zvi and Dale. So, the arrival of the new faculty produced a real change in the way the first year was structured.

Poterba: Now, also about this time, around 1970, the set of issues you were working on seemed to broaden enormously. You moved beyond health economics and began thinking about topics in corporate finance, in macro, in labor economics, and even in theory and theoretical econometrics. What accounted for this shift?

Feldstein: Well, some of it had actually happened earlier. I started working on issues in public finance and wrote several papers about cost–benefit analysis while I was still in Oxford. They all grew out of an interest in the question of how costs and benefits should be discounted. Also, while I was still in England, I did some work on dividends and the British tax law. So I really had been working on a fairly wide range of things before I came back. And I think I more or less kept them going in parallel.

Poterba: Was the technology of using graduate students in the research process different at Harvard than at Oxford?

Feldstein: I was one of the unusual researchers in Oxford. For five shillings an hour—that was 70 cents at that time—I got some very bright undergraduates who worked for me. And of course everything then was very labor-intensive. There was no such thing as machine-readable data. When I came back here, it was more or less the same. The computers were somewhat better, and you had punch cards instead of punch tape, but you still needed people to transcribe things from books.

Poterba: When students and researchers read your papers from the 1960s and 1970s today, they read them primarily for their contribution to substantive issues such as taxes and health insurance or the effect of tax policy on corporate investment. When you were doing this work and presenting it within the economics profession at the time, was it viewed as econometrics research or was it typically in an allied microeconomics workshop?

Feldstein: In England, it was certainly econometrics. The thesis that I did there was published by North-Holland in their series of econometric monographs. I used to go to the European econometric society meetings and places like that. And I cared a lot about heteroskedasticity corrections and the autocorrelation corrections. When I came back here, I remember very distinctly that people seemed much less interested in the econometric techniques. It was taken for granted that applied work would use the state-of-the-art econometrics. Although I was an active participant in the Harvard–MIT econometrics seminar, I wasn't a technology maker. I wanted to study substantive issues. I wanted to use whatever was best-practice technology. So I was a consumer of econometrics.

Poterba: Can you say a little bit about the change in econometrics sophistication in applied economics that you have seen take place over the past three decades, and reflect on the benefits that we've taken from that or any costs that there may have been?

Feldstein: I think it's been enormous. Every graduate student now comes out with quite a lot of technical sophistication. But there have been waves of fashion, if you want to call it that. As I said before, big macroeconometric models were very much in vogue at a certain point. That then faded away. And there's still the ongoing debate between the people who want fully specified parametric structural models, and those who rely on the difference in difference estimates.

But the graduate students seemed very comfortable with all of that. Part of it is the software, too. Today, you decide what you want to do, you press a button on your PC, and it happens. That was certainly not true 30 years ago.

Poterba: Let me now shift to some of the substantive issues that you've worked on. In the early 1970s, after you did an influential study of the unemployment rate for the Joint Economic Committee, you began working on unemployment insurance (UI) issues and the role of UI in affecting temporary layoffs. That's a topic that has continued to attract your interest for nearly 30 years. You've worked recently on unemployment insurance savings accounts. What do your broad research findings suggest about the right way to design an unemployment insurance system?

Feldstein: I distinguish two ways to think about reform: parametric reforms within the given program structure and changes in the basic structure itself. Within the existing structure, there is a trade-off between protection and distortion. More complete insurance provides more protection but also distorts more, causing greater efficiency losses. The research suggests ways to change the parameters of the program to reduce distortion and indicates how protection would be affected. Such changes include the level of benefits and the time until benefits are paid (like the deductible in an insurance policy). I've also studied the incentive effects of the employer tax and the experience rating system.

Unemployment benefits are now part of taxable income. In the past, when they were not, some individuals could actually get more net income by remaining unemployed than by returning to work.

The magnitude of the distortions in unemployment is critical to the policy decisions and my research focused on measuring those distortions.

If we can think about restructuring UI and not just changing the parameters of the existing system, then some form of unemployment insurance savings accounts makes a lot of sense.

Poterba: We've had a lot of debate in the United States in the past few years about what the NAIRU is. What's your guess about the impact of policies such as unemployment insurance on the level of the NAIRU?

Feldstein: I think that the changes in the unemployment insurance system have probably reduced the NAIRU by about a half a percent, perhaps even more. It doesn't sound like a lot, but 1% is more than 1 million unemployed people.

Poterba: Let me ask a particular question about the unemployment insurance saving accounts that you recently suggested. Is unemployment distributed widely enough in the U.S. population to make such mandatory self insurance a feasible option?

Feldstein: Well, the data that we looked at, which was for male heads of households, certainly indicated that it was. More work needs to be done on other population groups.

Poterba: Let me move on now to Social Security, one of the other issues that has attracted your interest for many years. How did you first become interested in the issues surrounding that program?

Feldstein: Again, this goes back to England. I was lecturing about consumption behavior. I read the studies by Milton Friedman and others and was very impressed. They had a theory of consumption and analyzed data that supported their theory. But I then realized that Social Security wasn't in their analysis even though Social Security was the major form of "saving" for most people. So I first began research on Social Security in order to improve the specification and estimation of the consumption function. I'm sure I thought of Social Security because I was teaching public finance while others with a more purely macroeconometric perspective had not thought of it.

The same sort of thing happened when I did this work for the Joint Economic Committee. They didn't say, "Go study UI." Quite the contrary. They said, "Tell us how we can get the unemployment rate down to 3%," hoping that I would say stronger expansionary macro policies. But with my public finance hat on, things like UI jumped up at me.

Poterba: So when someone reads the 1974 *JPE* paper on Social Security today, one can think of it essentially as taking the Ando–Modigliani style of consumption function that was a building block in the macro models, recognizing that there was a missing variable, Social Security wealth, measuring that variable, and plugging it in.

Feldstein: Right. But once I got started on that, it became clear that Social Security was an interesting thing in itself. And like all interesting things in economics, its effect cannot be decided by theory alone. Social Security arguably could displace ordinary savings, but when one took into account the induced retirement effect, it could lead to more savings.

Poterba: Was the concept of Social Security wealth a concept that was discussed before your work?

Feldstein: No. I remember one day when I was thinking about how to introduce Social Security into a consumption function, I realized that the natural way to do so was a "wealth" variable, the present value of benefits that individuals can expect to receive.

Poterba: What's your current best estimate of the amount by which an additional dollar of unfunded Social Security wealth reduces national saving?

Feldstein: I think that a marginal dollar of Social Security wealth reduces private wealth accumulated by about 50 cents.

Poterba: The work that you did on Social Security and consumption behavior sparked a substantial empirical debate in the 1970s and early 1980s with people estimating those types of models and debating the coefficients. There's relatively little recent empirical work on that question. Why do you think that happened? Is it a shift away from single-equation consumption function models? Is it a change in interest in the underlying issue?

Feldstein: Well, a lot of work has been done. When people can read survey articles about it they might ask, "Do I really want to write another paper about this?" I can imagine another paper on this that would be different and that would build on some of the more recent work on savings behavior and would utilize some of the new data. So, researchers may come back again to this issue.

Poterba: Looking back on the work you did in the 1970s and also more recently on individual accounts in Social Security, how would you say the research that you and others have done has affected the public policy debate?

Feldstein: It's always hard to know. Even when you're a very active participant in it, it's hard to know what exactly affects it. But the policy debate today—for example, the Presidential Commission on Social Security—puts a lot of emphasis on the savings effect of all tentative reforms and on the need to increase savings in order to offset the dissaving effect of an unfunded program. Would that all have happened anyway? Maybe. It's very hard to know.

Poterba: In the mid-1990s, your Ely Lecture was an early wake-up call about the importance of Social Security reform. When you talked about those issues, there was relatively little attention to them in the economics profession. That has changed dramatically since then. If you were going to dictate policy today, how would you reform the current U.S. Social Security system?

Feldstein: I would move gradually to a mixed system that preserves some of the current pay-as-you-go structure but at a reduced level and combines it with personal retirement accounts so that, in the long run, it's possible to meet essentially the current kinds of benefit replacement rates without raising taxes. That option is now in the public policy debate because research has shown that it is feasible in a way that was not understood just a decade ago.

Poterba: Moving beyond Social Security, the rate of national saving has been another long-standing concern of yours. You generally argue the United States saves too little. Can you explain why you believe that's the case and whether you believe it's the case today?

Feldstein: Yes, I think it's the case today. I think one way of summarizing it is to say the marginal product of capital is quite high relative to what I would regard as relevant rates of substitution between current and long-term future consumption. This is a reflection of the tax wedges created by the corporate and personal income taxes.

The Social Security system puts a lot of people essentially at a corner solution where the only saving they do is for precautionary purposes. They don't have to do life-cycle saving. And yet they could provide the same retirement income at lower cost if they saved more. So I would say yes, there is too little saving today.

Poterba: What are the policies you would offer to raise national saving?

Feldstein: Tax reform comes high on the list, moving in the direction of a consumption tax or reducing the rates of tax on investment income. Social Security reform with individual accounts would be another thing. You would not get a lot of saving out of a system of unemployment insurance saving accounts, but that would also basically be moving in the right direction.

Poterba: On a somewhat different topic, one of your most successful papers was your 1980 study with Charles Horioka on the cross-national relationship between national saving and investment. I remember that when you were working on that paper, a number of the graduate students were surprised that you had shifted fields and were writing a paper on international economics.

This was your first foray into open-economy macro and it was a paper that subsequently stimulated a great deal of work. Did you have any idea when you were writing that paper that it was going to be such an important contribution?

Feldstein: No, not at all. It was published in the *Economic Journal* and it was delivered at a seminar at Queens University in Canada, so it was not exactly presented in a way that would maximize its impact. It grew out of going to an OECD meeting at which all the participants had the view that the global capital market was completely integrated so that capital earned the same real rate of return everywhere.

That struck me as really very, very important if true. If it were true, why bother to raise the saving rate in the United States? Most of the money would go elsewhere. And why worry about Social Security depressing saving? Foreign money would come in. Government policy should focus on investment: the money would come from elsewhere to finance desired investment and the corporate tax paid on the existing resulting profits would remain here as well. So that made me wonder whether in fact it was true. It struck me that it was probably just not true, given the little bit that I knew about the current account balances.

Charles Horioka was a Harvard graduate student at the time. It was very easy for us to put together the OECD data to study the relation between investment and saving. That, I think, also contributed to the popularity of the research because everybody could put those data together and reexamine our results. And it really was a very striking result and very robust.

Poterba: Now, along with Social Security, the effects of taxation on household behavior has been a repeated theme in your research, first on charitable gifts, then on portfolio investment and capital gains regulation, and then on total taxable income. Yet, despite the research by you and many others, there seems to remain a tremendous amount of empirical controversy over some of these basic relationships in empirical public finance. How do you explain this? Is it because the questions are complicated, the data are weak, or because tax policy changes too infrequently or too little?

Feldstein: Tax policy changes frequently enough, so that one, I wouldn't put on the list. Having good panel data would make a tremendous difference in this area, and we don't have very much of that. Also, some of the behavior is very complicated. Think of labor supply— we don't begin to know how to measure it.

So, the endless amount of study of "labor supply" that focuses on hours and participation strikes me as a very small part of the true dimensions of labor supply.

At a fundamental level, what matters is the effect of tax rates on taxable income. That is what we should care about, both because we care about revenue effects and because of the effect of taxes on deadweight losses. For both, what matters is how tax rates affect taxable income. And if the world were relatively static, if there weren't the opportunity to move money over time, then I think we know how to estimate that with existing data. But what we don't know is the extent to which high-income people also reduce their taxable income by perfectly legal tax avoidance strategies that defer income in a tax-favored way.

We also don't have good capital gains tax data. We have realizations, but we don't know what people are holding. We often do not know what the basis is for what they hold. So, it's really hard to do research on capital gains in a totally convincing way.

And then these are very "political" subjects in many cases. They involve income distribution and the rich and the poor. That creates an emotional response to a lot of these questions that make people very hard to convince of the facts.

Poterba: Now, a hard question, given your interest in taxes and health insurance, taxes and savings, and similar issues. If you were going to pick only one aspect of the current U.S. income tax to change, what would it be?

Feldstein: This assumes that it was going to be revenue-neutral, I assume.

Poterba: Absolutely.

Feldstein: I would move toward a consumption tax, toward a more unlimited deduction for saving.

Poterba: Essentially expanded IRA-type accounts.

Feldstein: Right.

Poterba: Let me now shift to the NBER. You've been President of the NBER since 1977 and during that time the organization has gone through a truly remarkable transition. I remember walking around in 1050 Massachusetts Avenue when it was still being renovated to become the new home for the Bureau. Which of the NBER's many achievements during your tenure as President would you say you're the proudest of?

Feldstein: I would not do it in terms of any specific project. I would say that it is creating this environment that reinforces empirical research in so many different ways. That was the goal and it has worked. Empirical research is hard because if you don't know the institutions and you don't really know the data, there's a good chance that you'll make mistakes. So, having a group of people who know a subject is much more important than it is in theoretical research, where if you specify an interesting model and you don't make a mistake, you get an acceptable answer. But the chance that there will be two people in an economics department who are experts on a particular applied subject is very small. So, by bringing together people from dozens of departments, we create a national community of researchers working on similar topics.

Poterba: So this is essentially the creation of the program meetings where people come together, and of the Summer Institute, which is a clearinghouse for empirical research.

Feldstein: Right. And then the "top-down" projects became a way of picking really important subjects that people may have found interesting but were reluctant to start working on. Someone might say: "Pensions are important but I don't know enough to venture into studying pensions. But if 12 of us are doing it, then I've got other people to talk to." In that way, NBER projects actually move the direction of research. The Bureau cannot tell people what to do because the researchers are certainly not employees in the normal sense, but being able to create teams and to create the sense that this is going to be an interesting group and an interesting subject has been very effective.

Poterba: Have there been major challenges that you have faced in leading the NBER?

Feldstein: Well, at first there was a credibility problem. Would this really work? Would top-quality researchers really want to sign up and be part of this? That was a challenge, but it didn't last long. I recruited program directors in the first instance who were very good and who brought credibility with them. They offered me good advice about who to bring into their programs, and we had enough resources that we could start interesting program meetings. We had enough credibility, plus the good name of the National Bureau, to go out and raise some money for projects, things like capital formation and international policy coordination, that people wanted to work on, so we could move forward.

Poterba: Let's shift and talk for a minute about Washington. Your most direct involvement in policy was during your stint as the Chairman of the Council of Economic Advisers in 1982–84. What were the central macro policy challenges during that time in Washington?

Feldstein: I arrived in the fall of 1982 and we were certainly still worried about inflation and inflation expectations and whether they had really been brought down. We also worried about the recession getting worse. And it soon became clear that the budget deficit was going to be an enormous problem. Even after the economy began to recover, and the cyclical deficits went away, there would be large structural deficits to be dealt with.

So those three things—inflation, the recovery, and budget deficits—were the challenge. A fourth one was the dollar and the trade deficit. And in Washington the trade deficit was often viewed as the result of actions by foreign governments. I had a hard time persuading people that the reason for the trade deficit was the strong dollar. They also didn't understand why the dollar was so strong if we were having large budget deficits, since in the Third World countries' large budget deficits usually had the opposite effect. I spent a lot of time trying to persuade people that it wasn't because of the evil actions of other governments that we had these large trade deficits.

Poterba: Did the research that you did before going to Washington help in any way to improve your effectiveness as the CEA Chair?

Feldstein: Sure. You don't accumulate a lot of technical economic information on that job. The fact that I knew a lot about things meant I could deal with them. And you don't get a lot of time to go and study the literature either. So you use your human capital. But previous research and teaching allows you to speak with authority and to structure decisions and analysis.

Poterba: How would you say your Washington experience affected either the type of research you did when you came back to academic life or the kinds of projects you encouraged others at the NBER to become involved in?

Feldstein: I don't think it changed the basic research that I did personally all that much, but it did get me more interested in international issues. And I wrote about that, about international policy coordination, about the dollar, and so on, but none of that was research in the normal sense of the word. Similarly, I felt much more comfortable with monetary economic issues after my weekly breakfasts with Paul Volcker and just more at ease in dealing with the macro numbers. But again, I don't think that specifically changed the kinds of things I was doing. I think the work I did on taxes and inflation and social insurance all began prior to my Washington experience.

What did it do to the research agenda of the Bureau? Well, I would say things like the work on international policy coordination grew out of my time in D.C. Having heard an endless amount about what I thought was an empty shell, it seemed worth our exploring that in various ways. I'm sure Washington broadened my interests and therefore the scope of things at the NBER.

Poterba: When you were in Washington, you were criticized, at least by political figures, for your concern about budget deficits. History certainly proved your concerns to be well grounded. If your concerns had been heeded in 1982 and 1983, how do you think fiscal policy would have evolved over the subsequent 20 years?

Feldstein: We would have had smaller budget deficits. Over the period from 1977 to 1997, we accumulated more than $3 trillion of national debt. We wouldn't have accumulated that much.

Poterba: That little statistic brings me to the issue of data availability. It is a constant concern for empirical researchers. Do you think the federal government currently spends enough, too much, or too little on data collection? If you were going to change our statistical infrastructure in any way, how would you do it?

Feldstein: I think I would make more of the existing data available. In mean, in our field, in public finance, it would be nice if we had better access to the kind of data that the Treasury research staff has internally. And it wouldn't surprise me if there were similar things in other areas that I know less well.

But, in general, of course, researchers have enormously more data now than we had 30 years ago, and that has made a tremendous difference. For today's researchers, its hard to imagine what empirical research was like then. My generation of researchers was the first to have machine-readable data. I recall the excitement of getting access to a CPS tape, to the TAXSIM data, and to the Federal Reserve Board's 1962 survey of consumer finances. So, the world of economic research has come a long way since then.

Poterba: One of the most notable features of your research is the constant focus on issues that are first-order topics in public policy. In many cases, this work was years ahead of the policy debate. Can you offer any advice to younger or older researchers who are trying to learn the art of choosing which topics to work on?

Feldstein: Pick real issues as opposed to issues that just are currently consuming the journals. Pick big issues. And if possible, pick new issues, issues that people aren't working on.

Poterba: Are there topics that you would have liked to work on but that given all the other things you were doing you simply never got around to tackling?

Feldstein: Well, there's always some new thing coming along. I've been doing work on the Social Security reform for the past few years. I've asked myself why didn't I do it earlier? One reason is that I didn't understand conceptually how to structure the transition that has been the focus of my recent research.

A broad topic, that I've thought about for the past several years but that I'm only now starting to do something about, is the economics of national security. This is a subject that is the ultimate public good and yet it's a virtually empty slate in terms of economics. It's real, it's big, it's new. I think economists should be able to contribute to this important subject.

Poterba: On that note, thank you very much.

10

An Interview with Christopher A. Sims

Interviewed by Lars Peter Hansen
UNIVERSITY OF CHICAGO
November 5, 2003

Christopher Sims is a well-known intellectual leader in time-series econometrics and applied macroeconomics. Among his many honors and distinctions, he has been the President of the Econometric Society and he is a member of the National Academy of Sciences. He has made fundamental contributions to both statistical theory of time series and empirical macroeconomics. Sims's work is influential precisely because it was motivated by important problems in macroeconomics. Not only did Sims study questions of statistical approximation in abstract environments, he showed how to apply the resulting apparatus to a variety of specific problems confronting applied researchers. The applications include seasonality in economic time series, aggregation over time, and approximation in formulating statistical models with economic underpinnings. Moreover, Sims's contributions to causality in time series and to the development of vector autoregressive methods were complemented by an important body of empirical research. Sims has served as an effective advocate and critic of the extensively used vector autoregressive statistical methods. Motivated by his own and related empirical research, Sims is one of the leaders in rethinking how monetary policy should be modeled and reconsidering the channels by which monetary policy influences economic aggregates. This interview with Chris Sims gives an opportunity to explore further the context of many of these contributions. Sims typically has a unique

Reprinted from *Macroeconomic Dynamics*, 8, 2004, 273–294. Copyright © 2004 Cambridge University Press.

Figure 10.1   Christopher A. Sims.

perspective on many economic problems, a perspective that is articulated in his answers to a variety of questions.

Hansen: In looking back at your time as a graduate student at Berkeley and Harvard in the mid-sixties, what were the important influences that shaped your thinking about economics and econometrics?

Sims: Actually, I started taking graduate courses in statistics and econometrics when I was an undergraduate at Harvard. I was a math major as an undergraduate, and in my senior year, I started taking some economics. I took a graduate course in econometrics from Henk Houthakker, who later became my adviser; and I took a graduate statistics course from Dempster.

Both classes were influential, but by that time I already knew that I was interested in both economics and statistics. I did contemplate going

Figure 10.2   The meeting of the National Academy of Sciences, 1999. From left to right: Buz Brock, Roy Radner, Chris Sims, John Chipman, and D. Gale Johnson.

to graduate school in mathematics, and I remember discussing that with my adviser early in my senior year, but in the end I decided to go to graduate school in economics. I went to Berkeley for one year in 1963, where I had first year econometrics from Dale Jorgenson and first-year economic theory from Dan McFadden. I then moved to Harvard, not because I was discontented with Berkeley academically, but for personal reasons. At Harvard, I took some more economic theory, but I'm not sure I took econometrics at that point. I worked with Houthakker on my dissertation. I wrote on embodied technological progress, in which all previous models were posed in discrete time. Houthakker had just written a book on formulating models of consumption in continuous time, so he told me I should formulate my models in continuous time. Following this advice forced me to learn a lot of mathematics. Most importantly, he put me in contact with Chipman who was at Harvard at the time, and knew the relevant mathematics. All of this probably had some influence on the fact that I later wrote papers about approximation in continuous and discrete time.

Hansen: Your early research considered a variety of problems connected to statistical approximation. This work includes the study of discrete-time approximation of continuous-time models [Sims (1971)], the approximation of finite-parameter distributed-lag models to more general dynamic economic models [Sims (1972)], and the general problem of statistical approximation in rich or high (infinite) dimensional parameter spaces [Sims (1971)]. Much of this research predated related work in statistics and elsewhere. What was the original impetus for this work?

Sims: Some of the impetus for thinking about continuous- and discrete-time modeling was due to Houthakker. The vintage models I was working with easily let one express output as a function of the history of investment, but I needed to express productivity as a function of the history of output. This involved finding the inverse of linear operators whose kernels were nice functions. In discrete time, this is fairly straightforward, but in continuous time it leads to generalized functions. This was mathematically much more complicated than what Houthakker had done in his own work on consumption. I learned the technical tools that allowed me to address this and related approximation problems. The impetus for my work on approximation was then partly that I was technically ready to address these issues in approximation and partly that I was not very satisfied with the big gap between economic theory and econometric theory. Dynamic economic theory was often posed in continuous time and econometric theory presumed an econometrician was supposed to have a true model, written down in discrete time, about which nothing was unknown except parameter values.

Hansen: How were these papers originally received? They must have looked technically intimidating to many economists at the time.

Sims: Well I think at the time a lot of people didn't read them. So they didn't get intimidated. The paper [Sims (1971c)] on continuous and discrete approximation was submitted to *Econometica* for consideration. The less sympathetic referee report claimed that everything done in the paper had already been done before. While Dale Jorgenson had previously discussed the rational approximation of lag distributions, the implied sense of approximation was too weak for statistical approximation. This issue had nothing to do with continuous- and discrete-time approximation, however. So, the referee hadn't even realized that there was a difference between approximation of a lag distribution and approximation of a continuous-time model by the estimated discrete-time model.

Since the work on infinite-dimensional spaces was technically beyond what was appearing in economics journals, I sent Sims (1971d) to the *Annals of Mathematical Statistics*. After what, for an economics journal, was a relatively short time, the editor wrote: "Sorry it's taken so long. I had a hard time finding any referees. Here's a referee report." The referee report said, "I really don't understand what this paper is about, but I've checked some of the theorems and they seem to be correct, so I guess we should publish it."

At the time I don't think that many econometricans or economists read it. Tom Sargent was an exception. He read my papers on approximating continuous-time models and my *Journal of the American Statistical Association* paper [Sims (1974e)] on approximation of discrete-time distributed-lag models that use frequency-domain methods, and he became a promoter of them. Tom was, of course, an important reader, and his influence got the work some attention, but it's true that most economists found these methods hard to follow.

Hansen: Your first job was as an assistant professor at Harvard. What was it like being a junior faculty member there?

Sims: It was probably not that much different from being a junior faculty member almost anywhere. Harvard was certainly different from Minnesota where I moved to later, though. I actually contemplated leaving Harvard immediately for Minnesota, when I finished my Ph.D. The reason I didn't was that they announced, during the time when I was finishing my degree, that they were hiring Griliches and Jorgenson. I thought it would be interesting to overlap with them for a little while, and it was. But after two years there, I decided to move to Minnesota, which was a much livelier place. There was a sense of intellectual excitement at Minnesota that I didn't have at Harvard at that time.

Hansen: I know that macroeconomists in the seventies, including Friedman, were intrigued by your paper: "Money, Income and Causality" [Sims (1972b)]. Was this the first of your applied papers to attract considerable interest? What type of reactions did it elicit from macroeconomists?

Sims: It is fair to say that this was the first of my macroeconomic papers that elicited considerable interest. There were two other things that I can think of that went before it that were applied. My paper [Sims (1969)] on double deflation of value added still does occasionally get cited by people. Index number theory is something that not many people today pay attention to. Every few years somebody thinks about it again, but there are not that many references in the down-to-earth application area. I also had a paper on evaluating Dutch macroeconomic forecasts [Sims (1967)], which I think attracted very little attention. "Money, Income and Casuality" attracted a lot of interest because it came out in the peak of the monetarists–Keynesian controversy. A lot of macroeconomics research was centered on this controversy. I was a Harvard Ph.D. who had nothing to do with Chicago, writing a paper that seem to say that Friedman was right and all Keynesians were wrong. So, there was a lot of artillery brought to bear against the conclusions in my paper.

I had a conversation with Tobin when I presented the paper at Yale. He was skeptical, but not nearly as critical as a lot of other people were. He recognized that even if you accept money in the income regression as exogenous and interpret the regression equation as characterizing the response of the economy to the money stock, the estimated equation still implies that only a fairly small fraction of all output variation was explained by the money stock. What was true then and is still true now is that it's very hard to get evidence that monetary policy is as important as most people seem to think it is, and certainly as Friedman seemed to think it was, at the time, in generating business cycles. Tobin saw that this result really didn't undermine the view that there was a lot else going on in the economy and possibly a lot of other policies would be important.

The first time I talked to Fisher Black about it, he said this result is entirely spurious, and he was essentially right. He said that, by a Granger causality test, stock prices would appear to cause everything because stock prices are unpredictable. While I knew that and I agreed with him on that point, I argued that money is very different. Money stock, as Friedman would explain to us over and over again, is actually quite tightly controlled by the Federal Reserve System. So we have to think of its moving in response to deliberate action by policymakers and being nothing like an asset price. That was my answer to him at the time, but in fact it is not a good answer. Fisher Black was the only person who really saw this objection. Most of the criticisms were either from Keynesians who just didn't believe it and didn't trust the methodology, or from statisticians, and econometricians, who bridled at calling this test a test for causality.

Hansen: Let me follow up on two of the aspects of your answers. While the formulation of causal restrictions on time-series representations has proved to be of very considerable value, the term "causality" itself seemed to generate much controversy. Were the resulting dialogs productive or merely distracting?

Sims: They were mostly distracting. I still think "causality test" is good terminology for these tests. I wrote a paper [Sims (1977a)] that virtually nobody has read and understood. Some people have told me they have read it and couldn't understand any of it. This paper treats formally the semantics of causality, discussing the different ways it's been used. Most people think they understand intuitively what causality means and what it means to say that object x causes object y. I think it's also fair to say that most people would have a hard time explaining exactly what the precise meaning is. We actually use the term "cause" in a variety of different ways.

The term "causality" has been used over and over again. Granger and I used it as a recursive ordering amongst the things determining something. In fact, in engineering, causality was used in this way before Granger and I used the term. Causality has also been used to refer to one-sided distributed-lag relationships in which the right-hand-side variables are exogenous. Econometricians have argued that good econometrics was not just looking for correlations, it is looking for regression relationships in which right-hand-side variables were being conditioned on. In applied work, when people put variables on the right and on the left, there was always an implicit notion of a causal ordering involved in making those decisions. Yet, nobody was discussing formally what the connection was between a causal ordering and a statistically legitimate right-hand-side variable in a regression equation. Granger causality perfectly links these notions.

It's true that the intuitive causal orderings are not necessarily Granger causal orderings and vice versa. Fisher Black's insight was perfectly correct on that. He had an example in mind where a Granger causal ordering would not correspond to any intuitive causal ordering. But there are many cases, probably most cases in applied work that involve estimating a regression equation, where intuitive notions of a causal ordering correspond precisely to a Granger causal ordering. It would be better if people understood that. Because the first application of this idea was to a very controversial subject, there are a lot of people who think that the one thing they know about Granger causal orderings is that they don't have anything to do with causality. I think this is a big mistake.

Hansen: Let me return to the substantive component to your "Money, Income and Causality" paper. In comparing this contribution to your later work, there is an interesting evolution in thought. The endogeneity of money is emphasized in your subsequent empirical work, and you were one of the originators of what is now called the fiscal theory of the price level. Could you comment on this evolution, and how it was driven by empirical findings and changes in macroeconomic policymaking?

Sims: I realized at the beginning that a policy authority that systematically controlled the money stock would try to offset business-cycle fluctuations. This could create a situation where money would appear to be exogenous, but the relationship would have nothing to do with the causal relationship between money and the business cycle. I thought at first that that was very unlikely, partly because monetarists had conditioned us so well to accept the idea that the money stock was the relevant instrument for monetary policy. Monetarists argued this despite the fact that week to week it was hard to control the money supply, and despite the fact that the money supply wasn't directly controlled by the monetary authorities. Then one of my first students at Minnesota, Yash Mehra, who had learned about causality from me, decided to do causality testing on money demand equations [Mehra (1978)]. These equations had money on the left-hand side of the equation, interest rates and output on the right. To my surprise, he found that those equations passed tests for exogeneity of interest rates and output. This finding was qualitatively the opposite of what I had found in Sims (1972b). In a later paper, Sims (1980a), I followed up on this idea. I looked at systems, not just single equations, but systems with interest rates among the variables. I realized that, with interest rates in the system, money was quite predictable and that it was this predictable part of money that was most strongly associated with output. None of these findings fit the simple monetarist framework or its rational-expectations natural rate variant.

It is because of these findings that I also started thinking about what happens in an equilibrium model when monetary authorities smooth interest rates. It doesn't take very long fiddling with such models to realize that if the monetary authority is smoothing interest rates, all of a sudden Fisher Black is right. The money stock starts moving in line with asset prices. While, strictly speaking, money will be statistically endogenous, it's likely to be very close to being causally prior in a Granger sense for the same generic reason that asset prices are. My view now is that it is likely in countries where interest rates are held fairly smooth and the monetary authority is not attempting to tightly control monetary aggregates that the Granger causality of monetary aggregates to other macroeconomic variables is not a true causal relationship.

I often say that the Phillips curve is not the best example of the Lucas critique. The best example of a spurious statistical relationship that we can discover from a rational expectations equilibrium model not to be usable as a mechanical policy trade-off is the regression of GDP on money.

Hansen: There have been a variety of papers devoted to theoretical underpinnings of the fiscal theory of the price level that you [Sims (1980a)], Mike Woodford, and others have been advocating. Have you found this work to be a useful elaboration and clarification?

Sims: Woodford and I were writing from different perspectives on this topic at about the same time. Woodford continued to write on the topic. Eric Leeper, who was a student of mine at Minnesota, worked out the local existence and uniqueness characterizations for a fiscal theory [Leeper (1991)]. John Cochrane helped explain the fallacy of thinking that the government budget constraint is no different from private budget constraints [Cochrane (2003)]. This work elaborating, explaining, and examining underpinnings of the theory has been useful.

Now there have also been other papers on this topic that may be what you had in mind. These papers question whether the theory makes any sense at all. I've tried to understand what underlies those objections. My current view is that the strongest objections come from people who really have in mind a model unlike any of the standard models in use in macroeconomics today. In such a model the central bank and the treasury have separate budget constraints and we can contemplate them going bankrupt independently. Actually, I have some work underway now that discusses models with this separation [Sims (2000a)]. In the United States, they seem quite irrelevant, but they may be relevant in the European Union where the institutional setup makes it very clear that it's contemplated that treasuries can go bankrupt without the European Central Bank going bankrupt. It also appears that the European Central Bank could quite easily fail without the treasuries failing. In an environment like this, game-theoretic notions come into play and you can get conclusions from the fiscal theory that do not follow from traditional monetarist theory by any means. I view this type of model really as an interesting elaboration of the fiscal theory.

But the critics who have taken this line—for example, McCallum (2001) and Buiter (2002)—have used intuitive notions that could only be backed up in a model with separate central bank and treasury budget constraints to criticize the theory as it works out in models with a unified government budget constraint. And the criticisms, when considered in a model with two government budget constraints, turn out in my view to be basically wrong-headed.

Another line of criticism was from people who argued that the notion of competitive equilibrium in FTPL (fiscal theory of the price level) models, unlike that in standard models, could not be embedded in a careful game-theoretic framework. Marco Bassetto's (2002) work was seen initially as supporting this view. In its final form, though, Bassetto's work pointed out that the incompleteness, from a game-theoretic viewpoint, of the specification of policy in FTPL models was no different from similar incompleteness in standard macroeconomic models. Furthermore, it is straightforward to resolve this incompleteness so that the FTPL equilibria emerge in exactly the form originally put forward under simple competitive notions of equilibrium.

Hansen: Let me change gears here a little bit. After you were an Assistant Professor at Harvard for a few years, you came to Minnesota in 1970. Tom Sargent and Neil Wallace were there at the time. This subsequently proved to be a rather influential group of young macroeconomists at the time. What was Minnesota like in those days?

Sims: It was an exciting place to be. Jack Kareken was important in recruiting Wallace and Sargent. Sargent helped to recruit me with a phone call. The process of Sargent developing his approach to teaching macro was great to watch and there were new ideas just bubbling up around the place. Sargent, Wallace, Kareken, and Meunch all had joint

Figure 10.3 Returning to Minneapolis from a year on leave at MIT and NBER, 1980, Chris Sims with children (left to right) Nancy, Ben, and Jody.

projects at various times related to monetary policy, partly stimulated by the Minneapolis Fed where these guys had part-time research appointments. I was teaching both econometrics and macroeconomics then, but the macroeconomics was on a one-quarter-a-year or sometimes one-quarter-every-other-year basis. Sargent's teaching put heavy emphasis on the value of empirical work with explicit stochastic models, so it created a demand for the teaching of econometrics. It was also clear that anybody who wanted to work with Sargent on a dissertation needed to know time-series econometrics. So it was a very good environment to be in, even though there were some differences among us, certainly political and some methodological. The atmosphere in the department then was as positive and mutually intellectually supporting as any place I've ever been.

Hansen: Your work on vector autoregressions (VARs) has had an enormous impact on applied research in macroeconomics. Presumably this was due to both the tractability and the appeal of the method. While the appeal of VAR models is based in part on skepticism of the empirical validity of tightly parameterized models, shocks must still be identified through the use of theory. Has your thinking about this identification changed over time? As I recall, the research reported in your paper "Macroeconomics and Reality" [Sims (1980b)], used primarily a recursive identification scheme?

Sims: I actually considered two identified models in that paper. Some of the people who cite it seem to never have read it in any detail. I've often seen it cited as a reference for the viewpoint that conclusions can be drawn from unidentified models or that identification is impossible. The fact that there are actually two identified models in that paper is sometimes missed, but it's true they were recursive.

I'm still skeptical of tightly parameterized models. I think the most reliable way to do empirical research in macroeconomics is to use assumptions drawn from "theory," which actually means intuition in most cases, as lightly as possible and still develop conclusions. Now of course there is not a one-dimensional ranking of theoretical restrictions for how light they are. So, this approach tends to lead to experimentation with different kinds of models and different restrictions, and essentially informally or formally averaging across the results. I thought that was the best way to do research when I wrote that paper and still do.

My thinking has changed in a few ways. First, I now better appreciate the importance, for getting people to use a model, that they be able to tell stories with the model. Even if you don't have a detailed identification scheme that provides a behavioral interpretation that you trust for every shock, it may be worthwhile to experiment with such schemes.

Figure 10.4 After a talk at the University of Saskatchewan, 1993. From left to right: Chris Sims, Tao Zha, Manjira Datta, Robert F. Lucas, and David Cushman.

People feel more comfortable if you can provide at least one story about what's going on inside the model so it doesn't look to them like a black box. And in part that's what led to my paper with Leeper [Leeper and Sims (1994)] called "Towards a Modern Macro Model Usable for Policy Analysis."

The other change in perspective began when I did forecasting seriously for awhile. There were several years during which I was providing a fresh forecast every quarter. I discovered that to get a model that really fits I had to have quite an elaborate reduced-form setup that allowed for time-varying variances, nonnormal disturbances, and time-varying parameters. By the time this was all set up, the dimensionality of the disturbance vector in the model was extremely high; every coefficient required a separate disturbance. I felt that the whole setup was becoming unwieldy, and it was clearly higher dimension than necessary. Another motivation for the work with Leeper was the idea that by using a theoretical model with a relatively small number of parameters as a base, one might have a starting point for modeling time variation and nonstationarity in a manner that is not inherently so high dimensional. So those are the directions of the evolution of my thinking about VARs.

Hansen: Often, structural VAR identification looks like Cowles Commission-style exclusion restrictions but applied to either the instantaneous response matrices or the long-run response matrices of multiple time series to economic shocks. Is this a fair characterization?

Sims: There are two versions of identification in VAR models that have been used with some frequency. One is a version in which you leave the lag coefficients unrestricted and restrict only the contemporaneous responses to the shock. Those restrictions by themselves would fit perfectly into a Cowles Commission setup. The important difference from Cowles-style restrictions is that, in the identified VAR setup, the structural disturbances are typically independent of, or at least orthogonal to, one another. This orthogonality is absent from the Cowles Commission framework.

My view is that this restriction is an advance over the Cowles Commission framework. People who use the Cowles Commission framework almost always back into making assumptions of orthogonality in structural disturbances anytime they really try to use the model to project effects of an intervention. If you have structural disturbances that are correlated, anytime you intervene and change the parameters of a structural equation in a model you have to ask yourself what was the source of the correlation and how should it be altered by the intervention. You always have the two extreme choices. One possibility is that the correlations reflect passive responses of the equation's disturbances to other disturbances. Changing the equation itself won't change the correlation structure of the rest of the disturbances. Or you can take the opposite view: To the extent that a money demand equation has residuals that are correlated with the money supply shock, this represents a causal impact of money supply decisions on money demand. Under this interpretation, you extract all the covariation from the other disturbances before you arrive at policy-invariant disturbances. There is no theory in the Cowles Commission approach for how you do this extraction. You have to take a stand on these issues if you are going to really use the model. This is the reason for the added structure in the VAR literature. In most applications, I think that it is the right way to go.

The second approach is to make restrictions on the long-run response matrices, but again to assume that the shocks are orthogonal. Restrictions on long-run response matrices are probably not as widespread because when they lead to overidentification, they can result in unwieldy computational problems. In contrast, you can handle overidentification in restrictions on the contemporaneous covariance matrices with much less computational difficulty.

There is another informal aspect to identification. Researchers will make some explicit restrictions and then look at the plausibility of the results. For instance, specifications in which responses to what are purported to be monetary policy shocks that are clearly ridiculous tend not to be reported. This informal aspect has bothered some people, including

Uhlig (2001), Faust (1998), and others. They have explored what happens if you make these prior plausibility restrictions formal. With modern computational methods, this approach can be feasible. The result of these exercises is that the empirical findings are very robust. Faust doesn't explain his results that way, but my reading of his paper is essentially a finding of robustness.

In this VAR literature, you see a phenomenon that is not treated in econometrics texts. We almost always really have fewer reliable identifying restrictions than we need to identify the full set of parameters. We are always experimenting with a variety of identification schemes, all of which are hard to reject. We evaluate this identification partly on the basis of how well the resulting econometric model fits the data and partly on the basis of how much sense the identification makes.

Hansen: What do you see as being the important empirical insights that emerged from the VAR literature.

Sims: I think the most important ones have been the ones about sorting out endogeneity of monetary policy that I've already talked about a little bit. I think that literature has had a really major impact on the way people think about monetary policies. The basic dynamics of the estimates from the VARs showing that the effect on output and prices of monetary policy shocks are quite smooth and slow are widely accepted now, even among policymakers. This pattern holds up under many different variations of a VAR specification.

Hansen: You have had a longstanding interest in Bayesian statistics and econometrics. Your research in Bayesian econometrics has targeted situations in which Bayesian and classical perspectives can lead to important differences in practice, as in Sims and Uhlig (1991). A leading example of this is research on unit roots. Is this a fair assessment, and are there other important examples?

Sims: Early on in my career, I didn't see that the difference between Bayesian and classical thinking was very important. So I didn't get involved in defending Bayesian viewpoints or get into arguments, because I thought that was irrelevant. Then, I noticed that it really made a difference in the unit-root literature. The construction of the likelihood function

Figure 10.5 Chris and Cathie Sims, August 2000.

for an autoregression conditioned on the initial values of the time series proceeds in the same way whether or not nonstationarity is present. So, the form of inference implied by the likelihood principle should be the same for stationary and nonstationary cases. Classical distribution theory seems to imply that we must use very different procedures when we have an autoregression that may include a unit root.

The Bayesian perspective implies that any special character of inference in the presence of possible nonstationarity should arise from differing implications (in stationary and nonstationary cases) of conditioning on initial conditions and from the related fact that "flat" priors can imply bizarre beliefs about the behavior of observables. So when such differences arise in the way you handle models that are dynamic and might have a unit root, they should come from the imposition of a reasonable prior for use in scientific reporting, and that's a very different problem formally and intuitively from the unit root classical distribution theory.

Another example of when it makes a lot of difference whether you take a Bayesian or classical perspective is in testing for break points. When you are testing for one break point, both Bayesian and some non-Bayesian approaches will trace out the likelihood as a function of the break point (though non-Bayesians are more likely to trace out the maximized, and Bayesians the integrated, likelihood). The Bayesian, or likelihood principle, approach would tell you that in a change-point problem, the precision of your knowledge about the change point, given the sample, is determined by the shape of the likelihood you confront in the sample. Classical approaches can lose track of this point, by thinking about the distribution of the likelihood function over all possible samples, rather than focusing on the likelihood function that's in front of you.

Though there is relatively little Bayesian work on instrumental variables I think there could be more, and it might make a distinct contribution. Instrumental variable estimation is not likelihood-principle based, but it applies to models for which there may be a likelihood. Also, one can ask the question of what is good inference conditional on the moments that go into the instrumental variable estimate instead of conditional on the whole data set. I think one may be able to get conclusions there that provide a more solid foundation for the discussion of weak instruments, which is an important applied topic.

Hansen: As a researcher, you have been a great example of someone for whom methodological and empirical interests are intertwined. As economics and econometrics become more developed, there is an inevitable pull toward specialization. Econometric theory is becoming a separate field in many places. Is there a good reason to be concerned about econometrics becoming too specialized too quickly?

Sims: In all kinds of fields, including economics, there's a split between more abstract and more applied theorists, and between theory and empirical work in general. Within econometrics, there's a division between econometric theory and applied econometric work. It is important that people work on connecting these areas. There's an internal social dynamic that makes people respond more to work within their own specialty, and that can leave people who actually bridge specialties without firm constituencies in the profession. Moreover, there is value to having economists involved in policy issues, because that creates a pressure to connect theory and practice and to contribute to economic research explicitly connected to real-world problems.

So I agree that excessive separation of econometrics from the rest of economics is not a good thing, and that there is, at least in some places, momentum in that direction. There is an opposite danger, though: By insisting that only people who have strong credentials in a substantive area of research are real, or useful, econometricians, some departments have, in my view, created environments hostile to theoretical econometrics, and thereby also to rigorous thinking about empirical methodology. Communication between econometricians and noneconometrician economists is important, but this happens best when there are econometricians who are truly dedicated to their subject rubbing shoulders with substantively oriented economists. When the strong abstract econometrician and the substantive researcher happen to be the same person, that's great, but it's rare.

Hansen: I know that you have continual contact with research in Federal Reserve banks. What role do you see time-series econometrics playing in research that supports the formulation and implementation of monetary policy?

Sims: I wrote a paper [Sims (2002)] recently that is concerned in part with this issue. I argue there that econometricians have failed to confront the problems of inference that are central to macroeconomic policy modeling. The first serious policy models inspired, and then used, the Cowles methodology, but, as the models expanded to try to incorporate all the important sources of information about the economy, they reached a point where non-Bayesian approaches to inference ceased providing answers. The models had many equations, many predetermined variables, and relatively few observations. Two-stage least squares using all the available instruments simply reproduced, or nearly reproduced, OLS. Maximum likelihood estimators tended to be hard to compute, and then once computed tended to be often unreasonable, because they corresponded to isolated peaks. Use of small-sample distributions of estimators to form confidence intervals and tests was impossible at models

Figure 10.6   Chris Sims commenting from the floor at the Swedish Riksbank, 2003.

of this scale, and the asymptotic theory clearly was unreliable because of the scant degrees of freedom.

Academic time-series modeling was focusing on unit roots and cointegration, suggesting hierarchical layers of statistical tests to pin down the cointegration structure before estimation. However, in very large models, carrying out such layers of tests is generally impractical.

Academic macroeconomic theorizing was focusing on rational expectations, which was not in itself a problem. But leading figures, such as Sargent and Lucas, associated rational expectations with the fallacious view that there is a fundamental distinction between analyzing a change in policy "rule" and analyzing a change in a policy variable. A change of policy rule can in fact be only consistently modeled as a particular, nonlinear sort of stochastic shock. The fallacious contrary view led to a generation of graduate students who believed that the bread and butter of quantitative policy analysis—making projections conditional on values of random variables that appear explicitly in a model—was somehow deeply mistaken or internally contradictory. The result was a long period with little or no academic interest in contributing to or criticizing the models actually used in making monetary policy.

The models are now in a sorry state, but we may be at the point where Bayesian methods and thinking can address these problems and begin to close the gap between academic macro and econometrics and the actual practice of quantitative policy modeling. Some recent papers by Smets and Wouters (e.g., 2002, 2003) are particularly promising along this line.

Hansen: You recently published a paper on "rational inattention" [Sims (2003a)] in which you apply results from information theory to build a model of sluggishness in decisionmaking. What led you to use this formalism, and where do you see this research headed?

Sims: I wrote a paper called "Stickiness" (Sims 1998b) a few years ago in which I set out to show that variations on standard theoretical assumptions about menu costs and inertia could match the qualitative behavior of the macro data. I noted, though, that the usual theoretical setups implied that either prices were sticky and real variables "jumpy," or real variables were sticky and prices jumpy. The data show that both classes of variables are about equally inertial. Furthermore, any sort of adjustment cost formulation tends to imply not only that the variables subject to adjustment costs should respond slowly and smoothly to other variables, but also that they should have smooth time paths. The data show the slow and smooth cross-variable responses, but not the correspondingly smooth time paths. The stickiness paper showed how you could get both, but via a kind of hierarchical adjustment cost setup that seems hard to connect to data or even to economic intuition.

At the end of that paper is an appendix pointing out that there might be reason to think that inertia due to information-processing constraints, modeled using the notion of Shannon channel capacity, could account for the way the data behave in a more intuitively appealing way. The more recent paper you mention works out the application of the method to general linear-quadratic dynamic optimization problems, and shows that it does in fact account for the qualitative nature of observed inertia.

Few economists know any information theory, though many have told me they find the intuition behind the formalism appealing. For the time being, these ideas are propagating slowly because there are few people able to actually advance the formal frontier. I'm working on the area myself, trying to construct easily used software that will let these methods be applied more widely. The rational inattention setup implies that people will behave as if they face signal extraction problems even when there are no external costs to obtaining precise information. This should encourage more attention to models with imperfectly informed agents, and in fact has already done so to some extent [e.g., Woodford (2001)], even before models that ground the form of the signal extraction problems in information theory are available.

REFERENCES

Bassetto, M. (2002) A game-theoretic view of the fiscal theory of the price level. *Econometrica* 70, 2167–2195.

Buiter, W.H. (2002) The fiscal theory of the price level: A critique. *Economic Journal* 112, 459–480.

Cochrane, J.H. (2003) Money as Stock. Discussion paper, University of Chicago, GSB, http://gsbwww.uchicago.edu/fac/john.cochrane/

Faust, J. (1998) The robustness of identified VAR conclusions about money. *Journal of Monetary Economics* 49, 207–244.

Leeper, E.M. (1991) Equilibria under active and passive monetary and fiscal policies. *Journal of Monetary Economics* 27, 129–147.

Leeper, E.M. & C.A. Sims (1994) Toward a modern macroeconomic model usable for policy analysis. *NBER Macroeconomics Annual* 81–117.

McCallum, B.T. (2001) Indeterminacy, bubbles, and the fiscal theory of price level determination. *Journal of Monetary Economics* 47, 19–30.

Mehra, Y.P. (1978) Is money exogenous in money-demand equations. *Journal of Political Economy* 86(2, p. 1), 211–228.

Sims, C.A. (1967) Evaluating short-term macroeconomic forecasts: The Dutch performance. *Review of Economics and Statistics* 49, 225–236.

Sims, C.A. (1969) A theoretical basis for double-deflation of value added. *Review of Economics and Statistics* 51, 470–471.

Sims, C.A. (1971a) Discrete approximation to continuous time distributed lags in econometrics. *Econometrica* 39, 545–563.

Sims, C.A. (1971b) Distributed lag estimation when the parameter-space is explicitly infinite-dimensional. *Annals of Mathematical Statistics* 42, 1622–1636.

Sims, C.A. (1972a) Money, income, and causality. *American Economic Review* 62, 540–552.

Sims, C.A. (1972b) The role of approximate prior restrictions in distributed lag estimation. *Journal of the American Statistical Association* 67(337), 169–175.

Sims, C.A. (1974) Seasonality in regression. *Journal of the American Statistical Association* 69(347), 618–626.

Sims, C.A. (1977) Exogeneity and causal orderings in macroeconomic models. In C.A. Sims (ed.), *New Methods in Business Cycle Research*, pp. 23–43. Federal Reserve Bank of Minneapolis.

Sims, C.A. (1980a) Comparison of interwar and postwar business cycles: Monetarism reconsidered. *American Economic Review* 70, 250–257.

Sims, C.A. (1980b) Macroeconomics and reality. *Econometrica* 48, 1–48.

Sims, C.A. (1998) Stickiness. *Carnegie–Rochester Conference Series on Public Policy* 49, 317–356.

Sims, C.A. (2000) Fiscal Aspects of Central Bank Independence. Technical report, Princeton University.

Sims, C.A. (2002) The role of models and probabilities in the monetary policy process. *Brookings Papers on Economic Activity* 2002(2), 1–62.

Sims, C.A. (2003) Implications of rational inattention. *Journal of Monetary Economics* 50, 665–690.

Sims, C.A. & H.D. Uhlig (1991) Understanding unit rooters: A helicopter tour. *Econometrica* 59, 1591–1599.

Smets, F. & R. Wouters (2002) An Estimated Stochastic Dynamic General Equilibrium Model of the Euro Area. Working paper, European Central Bank and National Bank of Belgium.

Smets, F. & R. Wouters (2003) Shocks and Frictions in U.S. Business Cycles: A Bayesian DSGE Approach. Discussion paper, European Central Bank and National Bank of Belgium.

Uhlig, H. (2001) What Are the Effects of Monetary Policy on Output? Results from an Agnostic Identification Procedure. Discussion paper, Humboldt University, Berlin.

Woodford, M. (2001) Imperfect Common Knowledge and the Effects of Monetary Policy. Discussion paper, Princeton University.

11

An Interview with Robert J. Shiller

Interviewed by John Y. Campbell
HARVARD UNIVERSITY
January 4, 2003

A recent article in *The Economist* magazine divided economists into "poets" and "plumbers," the former articulating radical new visions of the field and the latter patiently installing the infrastructure needed to implement those visions. Bob Shiller is the rare economist who is both poet and plumber. Not only that, he is also entrepreneur and pundit. His work has fundamentally changed the theory, econometrics, practice, and popular understanding of finance.

Starting in the late 1970s, Bob boldly challenged the prevailing orthodoxy of financial economics. He showed that financial asset prices often deviate substantially from the levels predicted by simple efficient-markets models, and he developed new empirical methods to measure these price deviations. In the early 1980s, Bob went on to argue that economists need a much more detailed understanding of investor psychology if they are to understand asset price movements. He pioneered the emerging field of behavioral economics and its most successful branch, behavioral finance. At the end of the century, Bob articulated his vision of finance in a wildly successful popular book, *Irrational Exuberance*. He became so well known that TIAA-CREF asked him to appear in a series of full-page advertisements in the popular press.

Although Bob does not believe that investors use financial markets in a perfectly rational manner, he does believe that these markets offer great

Reprinted from *Macroeconomic Dynamics*, 8, 2004, 649–683. Copyright © 2004 Cambridge University Press.

Figure 11.1 Robert J. Shiller.

possibilities to improve the human condition. His recent work asks how existing financial markets can be used, and new financial markets can be designed, to improve the sharing of risks across groups of people in different regions, countries, and occupations. He has explored risk-sharing possibilities not only in journal articles, but also in business ventures and a 2003 book, *The New Financial Order: Risk in the 21st Century*.

It was a great privilege for me to interview Bob Shiller. Bob's arrival at Yale when I was a Ph.D. student there set the course of my career as an economist. Bob reinvigorated the Yale tradition of macroeconomics, with its emphasis on the central role of financial markets in the macroeconomy and its idealism about the possibility of improving macroeconomic outcomes. First as a thesis adviser, then as a coauthor, mentor, and friend, Bob showed me how to contribute to this tradition.

The interview took place at the 2003 annual meetings of the Allied Social Science Associations in Washington, D.C. We met in a hotel suite, ate a room service meal, and had the enjoyable conversation that is reproduced below.

Campbell: Bob, I'd like to start right at the beginning by asking you when you first encountered economics. How did you get started with it?

Shiller: The earliest memory that I have is Samuelson's *Economics*, his introductory textbook. My brother is four years older than I. He took an introductory economics course in college and was assigned this book. He brought it home on a college recess when I was a freshman in high school; I happened to find it and read some of it. I discovered that elementary economic analysis has great power when applied to the major problems of the world and this discovery was an unexpected pleasure.

It may seem odd that I would read my older brother's textbook. I have always been a voracious reader, and whatever is around . . .

Campbell: You would just pick up whatever is there?

Shiller: My mother used to tell the story about when I was in the early years of elementary school. She had a minor foot problem, and went to the library to get a book on care of the feet. She left it on the table and I read it.

Campbell: I'm surprised you didn't become a podiatrist.

Shiller: I read just about everything, though not all things made such an impression on me as economics.

Campbell: Did you think then that you might become an economics major in college?

Shiller: No, not until much later. The formative experience for me was more with mathematics. When I was 14 years old I had a geometry teacher, Roger Souci, who inspired me in mathematics. And he gave me the idea of doing research. We had just learned formulas for the circumference of a circle and the volume of a sphere. From his inspiration, I wrote a paper for him in which I derived the formula for the length of a spiral. I hadn't really had calculus yet, but I thought of a limiting argument. From this teacher I became excited about doing quantitative research, but the idea that it would be in the realm of economics did not crystallize until I was in college.

Campbell: So when you applied to college, you put down mathematics?

Shiller: I put down physics, though I didn't feel committed to that. An interest in physics is apparently very common among economists. I didn't decide on economics until well into college. I tried to keep all my options open for as long as possible.

What really struck me at that age was the incredible range of career choice that our free modern society allows young people. No longer are we expected to follow in our father's career, or anything like it, or even anything like what we have seen as children. This freedom to choose seemed such a precious gift, an opportunity to involve one's inner purposes in a life's work, a gift that must not be squandered. I did not want to let chance or inertia dictate where I went.

I was very impressed by the gravity of the career decision, and the schedule that imposed on me that decision as part of choosing a major and a field for graduate school. In my junior year in college at the University of Michigan I went on long walks thinking about what I wanted to do with my life. I became a wanderer on campus. I remember getting a sore foot, and so I went to the doctor. He told me then that I had a stress fracture in a metatarsal, the kind of thing that happens to soldiers on long forced marches.

Campbell: So then how did you end up with economics?

Shiller: I could perfectly well have chosen another field, but economics came in because of a conviction that grew in me of an alignment of my personality with this field. Maybe it has to do with the emotional weights I place on quantitative reasoning, and an appreciation of the impact of economic outcomes on our lives, the importance of economic forces in our lives, and the possibility of taking control of them. I could feel a real sense of purpose in working in economics.

Campbell: Were there people in college, economics professors, who inspired you to go to graduate school or otherwise influenced you?

Shiller: At the University of Michigan, I remember getting the Stolper–Samuelson theorem from Wolfgang Stolper. I remember trying to understand the timing of devaluations with Robert Stern. Shorey Peterson was a guiding influence who helped me with my writing and with economic reasoning. George Katona gave me my first exposure to behavioral economics.

I should say I was also influenced by fellow undergraduates, who were heading to business careers. I probably learned just as much from talks with Bruce Wasserstein, then but a teenager, but later to found the investment bank Wasserstein Perella.

Campbell: But you decided to go to graduate school straightaway from college.

Shiller: Yes, well we didn't have a choice. We would either go there or go to Vietnam. I was adamantly opposed to our war in Vietnam, but also I wanted to get on with my immersion in economics. I had a National Science Foundation fellowship and so I didn't see any reason not to go to it directly.

Campbell: So, how did you decide on MIT for graduate school?

Shiller: I didn't put the same amount of thought into that as I did of going into economics. It seemed to be the place to go at the time. I was certainly impressed with the faculty there. I already mentioned Paul Samuelson. I had also acquired as an undergraduate an admiration for Franco Modigliani and Robert Solow.

Campbell: When you got to MIT what was it like? Was it what you expected? Also, what were the hot topics?

Shiller: The rational expectations revolution was emerging, long before the Lucas Critique [Lucas (1975)], and that was exciting. I well remember Richard Sutch, who overlapped one year with me at MIT, and who wrote a dissertation on the term structure of interest rates that involved testing whether the term structure is consistent with rational expectations and autoregressive forecasting equations for interest rates [Sutch (1978)]. My own dissertation [Shiller (1972)] grew out of his, through the intermediation of my adviser, Franco Modigliani. Later, Franco and I wrote a joint paper with some of these results [Modigliani and Shiller (1973)].

Figure 11.2 The Conference on Monetary Mechanisms in Open Economies, Helskinki, 1975. The speaker is Stanley Black. In the foreground, with a pipe, is Franco Modigliani. Row in foreground, from left to right: Robert Shiller, Benjamin Friedman, Jacob Frenkel, and Edmund Phelps. In the back row, Harry G. Johnson (with dark beard); diagonally opposite him, Karl Brunner (with white beard).

But, in truth, I didn't have a complete affection for this rational expectations theory. It was something to work on at that time. I didn't fully believe that people could be so calculating in their expectations. There were already elements of behavioral economics in my thinking, if not in my published research.

I met Jeremy Siegel practically on the day I arrived at MIT in 1967. I got to talking with him since MIT had all the incoming students scheduled alphabetically for our chest X-rays and Siegel comes right after Shiller. Jeremy impressed me immediately. And he always had a marvelous way of putting quantitative analysis into a real-world perspective, something I have enjoyed in his company ever since. I have long since used him to test the reality of theoretical notions.

Campbell: What was your first year like?

Shiller: I guess you could say that I spent that time orienting myself to the role of quantitative economics. It took me a while to consolidate

Figure 11.3 Poconos vacation, 1989. From left to right, front row: Jeffrey Siegel, Benjamin Shiller, and Andrew Siegel. Back row: Ellen Schwartz Siegel, Virginia Shiller (holding Derek Shiller), Jeremy Siegel, and Robert Shiller.

in my mind what role it, and the assumption of rational economic agents, should play.

Campbell: For the first year, you probably had star faculty.

Shiller: I actually relished Samuelson's lectures, which some other students found too much of a stream-of-consciousness. To me, they were a delight. There was no disagreement that Solow's growth theory lectures were gems. I also remember M.M. Postan, the historian of Europe, who was visiting from Cambridge University at the time. He was anything but a technical economist, but he inspired and supported me. Later, Robert Hall arrived from Berkeley, and rewarded us with his original, unconventional thinking.

Campbell: I am wondering whether people or topics or people that you came across in graduate school influenced your subsequent direction. You started to work with Franco Modigliani.

Shiller: I was attracted to Franco because he was building a really ambitious model of the economy. There was something real and tangible about his approach to economics that I found appealing. Today, I still believe that there is something solid and important about these ambitious large-scale econometric models, despite the profession's largely turning against them. Not so long ago I did some work with Ray Fair [Fair and Shiller (1990)] that showed that such large-scale model forecasts do indeed contain information not seen in vector autoregressive forecasts or judgmental forecasts either.

Anyway, Franco also impressed me because he made known his moral judgments. The war in Vietnam was going on then and we talked about that. There was also some turmoil about the relevance of abstract economic theory among other students I associated with. What I tried to do with rational expectations theory was to make it relevant and believable. I thought that it had some implausible assumptions about people calculating too much. So, one of my solutions was that if people have a greater information set than economists, then the projection of their expectations onto the common information set must be the same as the projection of the actual onto the information set. Obviously, people do not do elaborate calculations, but it seemed plausible that they would do even better than that.

Campbell: It would look as if they had estimated autoregressions.

Shiller: Right.

Campbell: But that is not a response to this criticism that they do too many calculations.

Shiller: Well, it is in the sense that it relieves us of assuming that they actually do the calculations. The smart money do not run autoregressions, but they do think a lot about the data, and so it seemed plausible that they could do even better than the autoregressions with their own different methods. That was the thought, anyway. I was just trying to make rational expectations theory somehow believable to myself and to understand how it could be even approximately valid. I attempted in my dissertation to make the case that patterns of change in the term structure of interest rates matched up somewhat well with what we would expect if investors had such abilities.

The other thing I did for my dissertation was to develop a distributed-lag estimator based on smoothness priors [Shiller (1973)]. I thought that distributed lags were an important topic, since practically nothing in economic relationships happens instantaneously, and lags are likely to be distributed over time. The effect of lagged variables may even grow with lag, and then decline asymptotically to nil, but the available econometric theory for lag estimation was just very arbitrary, and people were estimating relationships that I just could not believe. At their worst, they would impose a single one-quarter lag when using quarterly data, and a single one-year lag when using yearly data, letting the period of data collection dictate the length of the lag. Robert Solow had improved this practice with his rational lags, and Shirley Almon with her polynomial lags, but even these were really arbitrary parameterizations. They often produced funny lag patterns that were artifacts of the procedure.

I was wondering what we really wanted to assume about distributed lags. I was thinking that the existing approaches didn't capture our information. Their restrictions didn't correspond to our true priors. We should base our analysis on a good representation of our prior information about the lag structure, mostly just that the lag structure should be fairly smooth through time. So, I started reading Bayesian econometrics, and launched off on nonparametric estimation, using what I called smoothness priors. I later found out that Grace Wahba, in the Statistics Department at Wisconsin, was onto a similar smoothness idea, and her approach was more thoroughgoing than mine, though not applied to the estimation of distributed lags. Also, later, the same idea of smoothness was embodied in what is now called the Hodrick–Prescott filter. Anyway, the distributed-lag estimator I developed at the time had a good application in my dissertation to my study of the term structure of interest rates.

Since then, a lot of others have developed nonparametric estimation into a significant field, and there has been a lot of activity in Bayesian econometrics as well. Unfortunately, even today, the economics profession at large has not adopted any such methods on a substantial scale for applied work.

As far as I recall, no one had ever mentioned Bayesian methods at MIT, though I found Ed Leamer, an assistant professor at Harvard, who was deeply involved in using Bayesian foundations to adapt the scientific method to economics [Leamer (1978)].

Campbell: Who taught econometrics?

Shiller: Franklin Fisher had written a book on the identification problem in econometrics [Fisher (1966)]. We went through that whole book, an elegant treatise, but perhaps too much on that topic. The econometrics course I had with Edwin Kuh doesn't stand out in my memory, but I can say that he impressed me about the importance of regression diagnostics and of isolating influential observations, practices that not enough people implement even today [Belsley, Kuh, and Welsch (1980)]. I learned the essential lesson to be skeptical of econometric results. I remember when Leonall Anderson and Jerry Jordan came to MIT in 1968 to present the "St. Louis Model" of the U.S. economy [Anderson and Jordan (1968)]. The results were impressive, but not really received well at MIT. Later, our skepticism was borne out. Ben Friedman reestimated the same model in 1985 and found that the new data provided by the mere passage of time had destroyed their results [Friedman (1977)]. There are lots of ways econometric analyses can go wrong.

I then started reading time-series analysis on my own. I never took a course in that.

Campbell: Did you read Box and Jenkins?

Shiller: I certainly did, but I wanted to combine it with Bayesian methods. Arnold Zellner at the University of Chicago somehow discovered me; he invited me starting as a graduate student to a series of Bayesian econometrics conferences. It was at one of these conferences in 1972 that I first met Sandy Grossman, then only 19 years old, and already a dazzling intellect. I was fortunate to have the opportunity to work with him later on several papers.

I tend to attribute my interest in Bayesian statistics and time-series analysis to my physical-science orientation, which had been with me since childhood. I have long admired scientists. I thought that the Bayesian methods would help adapt the scientific method to economics, help us to base our analysis on what we do know, and let the data speak for what we do not know. The kind of science that appealed to me was the kind that was based on careful observation followed by induction that allowed you to discover a general principle. It was that discovery process that excited me. Bayesian econometrics appealed to me then as a good approach since it didn't impose some arbitrary model. In fact, the prior was supposed to come from some previous analysis; your prior was your earlier posterior.

I also thought that science is, at its core, really intuitive. Charles Darwin didn't follow a research program that was outlined for him. He was trying to think how this whole thing works and observed everything he could. Leamer referred to "Sherlock Holmes inference," in response to that fictional detective's attention to all the details, but I would prefer to call the ideal "Charles Darwin inference."

Campbell: You started to mention the Lucas Critique.

Shiller: When I first read Lucas's paper in 1975, I thought that there was nothing new in it. The idea of rational expectations was already prominent at MIT, through Modigliani and Sutch.

Campbell: But they didn't actually cause you to change your mind about econometric modeling. Their papers assume a fixed structure.

Shiller: If you were to take Franco aside then, and ask him, "isn't there a risk that if policy changes, the expectations structure might change," he would say, "obviously." But, Lucas presented this in a very forceful way. . . . Lucas is a great writer.

Campbell: Another idea that was floating around at the time was the efficient-markets hypothesis. Did you come across that in graduate school?

Shiller: Well, that was already well established.

Campbell: I am just wondering if that was a big part of the discussion in graduate school at the time?

Shiller: My dissertation was about the expectations theory of the term structure, which was an efficient-markets model. We talked a lot about efficient markets.

Campbell: Did you at the time already have seeds of the critiques that you later mounted so effectively?

Shiller: Well, as I just said, it didn't seem to me that ordinary people were estimating autoregressions as was represented in those models. There were already seeds of my later views of excess volatility in my mind. I noticed that when I estimated autoregressions, if I constrained the sum of coefficients to be one in the short-rate autoregression—that is, to have a unit root—I could come close to explaining the volatility of long rates. It bothered me that the difference between this sum and one wasn't well estimated, in other words, there seemed to be great uncertainty about whether there was a unit root. As you know, this has turned out to be a very contentious issue.

Campbell: This was before Dickey–Fuller and any of the other unit root literature in econometrics [Dickey (1975), Fuller (1976)].

Shiller: The issues of unit roots were very much bothering me then. I thought that maybe there was excess volatility. In the case of the term structure, if there is not a unit root in the short rate process, then there would appear to be excess volatility in long rates. That unit-root/excess-volatility issue is not in my dissertation, but I was wrestling with that as I wrote it.

Campbell: Let's move forward then for now. You left graduate school. Your first job was at Minnesota. What happened there?

Shiller: I had some wonderful colleagues there, such as Tom Sargent and Chris Sims. But, for me that was the slowest period of my life in terms of academics. I didn't publish for several years. I felt that I had to get on with my personal life. The biggest thing then was that I met my future wife Ginny. Now we have been happily married for almost 27 years.

Campbell: Then you picked up the theme of excess volatility after a few years.

Shiller: I had written about a rational expectations model of the term structure, but, after thinking about it intuitively, wondering what is causing the big movements in long rates, I cast about for other interpretations.

Campbell: The first paper was on long-term interest rates [Shiller (1979)].

Shiller: It seemed tangible and real to me that the long rates were not moving only for rational reasons.

Campbell: How then did you carry the analysis to the stock market?

Shiller: That was a very simple transition. As you know, the expectations theory of the term structure is a present-value model, and the efficient-markets theory of the stock market is also a present-value model. I thought that the stock market might be an even better example of excess volatility. Another advantage to the stock market was that one could get a lot of data. I found the Cowles data, and created from it time series of price, dividends, and earnings back to 1871. That was what I needed, since the present-value relation extends over so many years, as you know.

Campbell: As I learned from you! That is an interesting point, that you were doing work on historical financial data, very early on. Also, Jeremy Siegel has become known for that. I wonder if the two of you discussed that.

Shiller: Well, we did. Using only a short recent sample period *seems* scientific to many people, because they think that *the best* data, which are collected with greatest accuracy, should always be used. So, people thought that you should rely not on long historical time spans, but rather on high frequency of sampling. You can get daily data more recently, while if you sought long historical time series the best you could get further back was monthly, or annual. So, people wanted to stay with these recent data, and perhaps they thought that doing so was being very "scientific." But, I had a different concept of what "scientific" means, and I thought, from my own reading in science, that scientists have to look at discrepant data, at things that are not so well measured.

Campbell: You also were aware that with the long span of the present-value relation, the testing required a long sample.

Shiller: Well, that seemed very intuitive to me. My student Pierre Perron and I wrote a paper [Shiller and Peron (1985)] presenting a Monte Carlo study on power of tests as frequency of observation goes to infinity, holding the sample length, measured in years, fixed. In the cases we studied, power does not appear to go to infinity as the number of observations does. Later, Pierre teamed up with Peter Phillips and developed a real theory confirming this [Perron and Phillips (1988)]. Also, I should mention the work that my student Andrea Beltratti and I did to extend the excess volatility framework to consider excess covariance between assets' prices.

Campbell: So as you look at it now, some 20 years since the excess volatility work came out, how do you think it has affected the field of finance?

Shiller: I thought that excess volatility was an especially important anomaly regarding the efficient-markets theory. It certainly pointed to a possible failure of efficient markets.

Behavioral finance has emerged since then, but what exactly caused that I do not know. Excess volatility is an anomaly that is very different from other anomalies. The other anomalies, such as the Monday effect, or the January effect, do not seem fundamental. If you read Fama's "Efficient Capital Markets" [Fama (1970)], he talks about anomalies, but the ones he talks about sound like the result of a little bit of friction disrupting the otherwise precise predictions of the model. But, you wouldn't think that friction would cause excess volatility. Friction ought to slow things down or smooth them out, and the volatility seemed excess by a wide margin. It also accorded with intuitive feelings that people who look at the market have, and I wanted to try to show that there might be a scientific basis for those feelings.

Campbell: You mentioned behavioral finance, which is probably the big theme of your career. So, let us move beyond the excess-volatility work. But, then what you really did do was develop an alternative perspective. If the excess volatility grew out of your thesis with Franco, how did this alternative view develop?

Shiller: Well, I met Ginny in 1974. Soon after we married, she enrolled in a Ph.D. program in psychology at the University of Delaware, not far from the University of Pennsylvania, where I taught at the time. We lived in Newark, Delaware, and I commuted to Philadelphia. So, by day I was an economics professor, but by night I was living amongst a whole community of young psychologists. Some of their thinking made an impression on me.

Since our days together in Delaware, Ginny has accompanied me, first to Cambridge, Massachusetts, where I visited the National Bureau of Economic Research, and then to MIT, and then finally, in 1982, to Yale, where she got an appointment at the Yale Child Study Center. Over all these years, I have talked a lot with Ginny about my work, and her work. She was a big influence on me. She still is.

The next event was that I met Dick Thaler in 1982. I was invited to give a talk then at Cornell, where he was associate professor, and we immediately hit it off. He has a remarkable ability to put economics in a broader perspective than we are accustomed to seeing, a perspective informed by psychology. And over the years, his stature has grown and grown. I believe he was already connected then with Daniel Kahneman and Amos Tversky.

Campbell: So you learned about them through him?

Shiller: No, actually, Kahneman and Tversky's prospect theory appeared in 1979, and I had heard a lot about that paper before I met Dick. But, I think that Dick jumped onto their inspiration much faster than I, and had a lot of insights to convey to me.

Thaler's dissertation at Rochester in 1974 had been about measuring the value of a life for economic purposes, assuming that everyone was rational [see Thaler and Rosen (1976)]. It was somewhat later that he met Kahneman and Tversky, and that set the course of his career. He turned fundamentally against his earlier work. I did not have any such epiphany. I never came as close to psychology proper in my research as he did. My research remained more quantitative and centered more on conventional economics.

Dick Thaler and I have been working together since 1991 to organize a series of NBER conferences on behavioral finance, sponsored by the Russell Sage Foundation. Also, out of this grew a series of NBER conferences on behavioral macroeconomics that George Akerlof and I have been organizing since 1994.

Campbell: Well, there was this other strand in your work, the consumption-based asset pricing, the material with Sandy Grossman. Looking back on it, it was innovative.

Shiller: That research was very exciting to me, though I had doubts about that too. I thought there was some truth to the consumption-based asset pricing model, but again I didn't fully believe it. I had long talks with Sandy, and discussed models, and I remember saying that I just don't believe this model.

Campbell: And he said that he did believe it?

Shiller: Well, I can't summarize his thinking. He is a pretty practical guy, too. It becomes a subtle question of the philosophy of science, how far to pursue a model. This is an interesting model, and it seems to explain some things, as some of my work with Sandy revealed [Grossman and Shiller (1981)]. But there were also substantial problems with the consumption-based asset pricing model.

For example, I had derived an inequality that showed a lower bound on the variance of the intertemporal marginal rate of substitution, and found that this appeared to be widely violated by the data [Shiller (1982)]. Lars Hansen and Ravi Jagannathan later [1991] did a splendid job of establishing the scope and significance of such a violation.

Beyond this, I just wanted to move on to something else. And Sandy has moved on to something else, too.

Campbell: He certainly has. In the early years when you were doing behavioral finance it was extraordinarily controversial, and there were big fights. So, do you have any stories from that early time?

Shiller: This excess volatility got quite a hostile response. Well, I should say that a lot of people were quite friendly about it, but I think it was costly to me to do this. People didn't really receive it well. It was politically incorrect somehow.

Campbell: I remember you had a Brookings paper in 1984 where you laid out what has become the standard paradigm of behavioral finance, where you laid out the importance of social contagion and looked at the interaction of noise traders and rational arbitrageurs [Shiller (1984)]. Did that get a hostile reception at Brookings?

Shiller: No, not at Brookings, I don't think. The hostile reception that there was, was subtle. It was not that people started shouting at me, or, as you can testify, later, at you and me. Instead, some tried to marginalize or ignore what we were saying. They tended to try to dismiss the theory without even looking at it. They often described it as if we had made some egregious error, a stupid error. On the other hand, I didn't think it was a totally bad reception, even from the beginning. Our profession indeed includes a lot of open-minded people, who really look at the evidence, even though their own published work may not make obvious to readers the breadth of their understanding and personal desire to pursue the truth.

I remember from that 1984 Brookings paper that I had a paragraph that highlighted an important error in economists' thinking. If markets are perfectly efficient and expected returns exactly constant, it implies that price is exactly the expected value of the present value of expected future dividends. That is true. The widespread error is to assume that, from the assumption that expected returns are *approximately* constant, it follows that price is *approximately* equal to the present value of expected future dividends, approximated equally well. That error has inclined people to think that, given that short-term stock market returns are hard to forecast, the level of the stock market itself must be equally hard to distinguish from its fundamental value, the present value of expected future dividends. They conclude that every movement in the stock market must have a rational foundation. In that Brookings paper, I said that this error is "one of the greatest errors in the history of economic thought." Someone at the Brookings conference where I presented the paper said afterward that I should take that provocative line out of the paper. I asked Bill Nordhaus, who was also at the conference, for advice: Should I really delete that line? Bill said "No no, don't take it out!"

Thinking about approximation error led me further to examine how inadequate appreciation of the low power of some tests of market efficiency had misled researchers. It led them into widely accepting a theory, the expected present-value model for aggregate stock prices, that is egregiously wrong.

Campbell: That is an interesting story, because I remember seeing that line about the greatest error in the history of thought in the paper and thinking that most people are more aggressive in person than they are on paper, and thinking that perhaps you are the exception that proves the rule.

Shiller: Well, maybe I am a more aggressive person on paper. I think I become a different person when I am writing. That is, in part, why I have kept a diary all my life, continually since I turned 12 years old. Writing just stimulates my mind. I believe that people are stimulated by conversation: that is the way the brain works. Keeping a diary and talking in it to oneself creates a more idiosyncratic view.

Campbell: So, having a social influence on yourself.

Shiller: It seems to work that way. Do you keep a diary?

Campbell: I don't, but maybe I should.

Shiller: It seems to elevate my thinking, in the sense that writing down my thinking makes it come to fruition. If I am not writing it down, my mind would just drop it. It helps me to think things through systematically and adopt resolve to take action, and it reminds me of my own past thinking.

Campbell: Another thing that you started in the late 1980s was using survey methods. I remember you did surveys around the time of the 1987 stock market crash. And, many economists had been skeptical about surveys. Was that an influence from Ginny? How did you get started in this direction?

Shiller: It probably was in part an influence from Ginny. She gave me support in pursuing a line of research that made little sense from a career standpoint, but that I (or, should I say, we) really believed in.

I remember reading Milton Friedman's *Essays in Positive Economics* [1953], where he argues against relying on what people say when they explain their motives for their economic actions. There is even a tradition among psychologists against doing that. There is obviously a tradition there against asking people "Why did you do that?" and taking what they say at face value. That is not economics and it is not psychology.

But, on the other hand, economists, such as Milton Friedman, seemed to assume that is the only thing one could do with surveys, and to advise instead that economists should rely exclusively on formal optimizing models, and test them statistically using price and quantity data. But it seemed to me that economists often seemed to live in a rarified world. Often, there are very simple explanations of why people do what they do, and economists ignore them. We should ask people about what they do, at least find out the focus of their attention and the assumptions they were making, though still not take their answers at face value.

Economists often impute thoughts to people, implicitly in their optimizing models, that are not really in people's minds at all, it seemed to me. So, I thought we should find out what people say they were thinking, that this is interesting research. I viewed this as not career-optimizing research for me. But, I already had tenure when I began this research, and so I thought, this is what tenure is for. I do not have to do the same things others are doing.

There was a big stock market drop on September 11th and 12th of 1986, and I immediately thereafter did a little postcard questionnaire asking investors what they were thinking on those days. I learned from the reaction that I got from this and subsequent research that probably nobody else in the world was doing such research on what people think during crashes. Merton Miller later pointed me to a Securities and Exchange Commission interview study of participants in a stock market crash in 1946, but apparently no one else had ever done such a thing since.

I was thinking that science involves a lot of herd behavior: Too many scientists do the same thing. There are career reasons why they do, but scientists are often most effective for the long term when they move independently. From this perspective, I was noticing the volatility, and thinking about it.

Campbell: So you were ready when the crash happened.

Shiller: Yes, and when this big crash came in 1987, I thought that this might be the chance of a lifetime for research on speculative bubbles. I first worried that maybe somebody else would do such a survey about what people were thinking on the day of the biggest one-day stock market crash (and still today, biggest to date), making mine unnecessary. But, on further thought, I thought maybe not. I had learned that there was no organization that was set up to do this very fast. I concluded that there was a chance that no one else would do it. Months later, President Reagan's Brady Commission did do a survey of investment professionals as part of its report on the crash, but not only was it late, after people were possibly in a different frame of mind, but also it did not really ask what they had been thinking on the day of the crash.

To arrange this survey, I stayed up practically all night on both October 19th and 20th, 1987. I was exhausted, but happy to see the survey in motion within days of the crash: 2,000 questionnaires were mailed out to individual investors and 1,000 to institutions. Between the two, I got almost 1,000 responses.

I didn't even try sending this to a scholarly journal. I thought it would be rejected. I put it in my book, *Market Volatility* [1989].

Campbell: Now, I don't know a whole lot about psychology, but I am impressed that there is a trend away from strict behaviorism, toward studying what goes through people's minds. You seem to be saying that you are pursuing that same line of thought within economics, that if we have models that ascribe certain purposes to economic agents, we should look to what they say they are trying to do. So, maybe there is a parallel with psychology.

Shiller: I suppose. . . . Yes, there was a trend within the social sciences of studying intentions. It has been called interpretive or hermeneutic social science. Of course, intentions are part of classical economics. An optimizing model is a representation of intentions, but there is traditionally no attempt to collect data on what intentions, or associated worldviews

Figure 11.4   Red Square, Moscow, 1989. From left to right: Alan Auerbach, Robert Shiller, Lawrence Katz, David Wise, and Lawrence Summers.

and popular models, are. Economists try to observe actions rather than intentions to test these models.

In 1987, I thought I should do my survey since otherwise the chance would forever be lost. Even though it wasn't being used by practically anyone else in economics proper, I thought it would someday be useful.

Campbell: And then you found other applications of it.

Shiller: And then I found Chip Case. He has been a great colleague. A year after the stock market crash, in 1988, we did a questionnaire survey of recent homebuyers to study a housing bubble in California, and the end of a bubble in Boston [Case and Shiller (1988)]. We compared across cities, boom, postboom, and nonboom, in Milwaukee. We learned some very basic things. For example, we learned that Milwaukeeans are very uninterested in real estate. Fascination with and attention to speculative markets is something that varies geographically, presumably because of different market experiences.

Campbell: So, that is something that leads to my next question. How did you get interested in real estate? Was it just a natural idea, "Oh, there is volatility in real estate too so let us look at that too?"

Figure 11.5   The founders of Case Shiller Weiss, Inc., 1991. Front row, Robert Shiller and Charles Longfield; back row, Karl Case and Allan Weiss.

Shiller: Well, partly my sense of herd behavior influences a lot of my thinking. Economists themselves are herd-like in their research directions, and so there is a lot to be gained by staying away from these common topics. Well, maybe not career opportunities, but intellectual opportunities, to go off onto topics that no one is studying. So, I did a survey of the literature to see what was known about the efficiency of real estate prices. Are they a random walk? In my survey of the literature, there was almost nothing about the efficiency of home prices. And, when you think of it, real estate is just about as important as the stock market, in terms of total market value. Why was there all this study about the stock market and not of real estate?

Campbell: So, did you look for a housing economist? Was that how you found Chip?

Shiller: He was connected with Ray Fair, who was writing a textbook with him. Also, Chip is a kindred spirit: he had written an article in 1986 about the Boston housing market, looking at all the fundamentals, and concluding that there was nothing there that would justify the nearly 40% increase in housing prices in one year in the mid-1980s [Case (1986)]. He was a great collaborator, and I think we learned a lot about what was going on in people's minds during this bubble.

Campbell: So, then, in the real estate context, you went beyond academic work and started a company.

Shiller: Well, my student at Yale, Allan Weiss, after he graduated in 1989, wanted to work with me on the producing the indexes Chip and I had developed, to produce these on an ongoing basis as a commercial enterprise. Also, Allan had been thinking about how to manage real estate risk, and he thought that getting into the index business might somehow be a way to make take these thoughts into action. We set up Case Shiller Weiss, Inc., in 1991, and Allan was president; Chip and I were board members. We initially hoped to make the indexes the basis for futures contracts, but that still hasn't happened. We became forecasters of housing prices. We expanded the company to be a provider of an automated valuation model, an econometric model that provides instant online valuations of homes. We were lucky in our timing, for our first efforts here coincided with a rapid transition to online lending in the mortgage and home equity loan industry, and so these lenders became our customers. Allan made this company a big success. In 2002, we sold the company to Fiserv, Inc., but it continues to function independently as Fiserv CSW, Inc.

All of this happened because, in the late 1980s, Chip and I had to create real estate price indexes for our purpose of testing real estate market efficiency. At that time, there were really no available real estate price indexes that could be used to test market efficiency. The available median price was extremely choppy through time, and we thought that was due to the changing mix of houses sold. Chip, in his article in 1986, had created a repeat-sales price index for Boston. I discovered that while Chip had independently discovered that method, there had been a treatise on the repeat-sales price index in the early 1960s by Martin Baily, Richard Muth, and Hugh Nourse [1963]. But, they never seriously implemented it. Twenty-five years had gone by and there were still no repeat-sales home price indexes produced on a continuing basis or for any substantial geographic areas. So, we had to develop them. We improved the repeat-sales method, found the data, and started producing indexes. My student Will Goetzmann wrote his dissertation here at Yale on repeat-sales indexes, which he applied to the market for paintings, and he is now back at Yale as my colleague, and head of the International Center for Finance here.

Chip and I hadn't expected to get into the index number business, but we published an article on real estate price indexes, for four cities. Then, we tested (and soundly rejected) the efficient-markets hypothesis for single-family home prices using these indexes [Case and Shiller (1989)]. We found some very substantial momentum in home prices. It seems as

Figure 11.6 Robert Shiller in his office at Yale University, 2003, with colleagues (from left to right) William Goetzmann, William Brainard, Stefano Athanasoulis, and Carol Copeland.

if my excitement then was not entirely unlike that which Leeuwenhoek must have experienced when he looked through the microscope for the first time. We *saw* from our plots what real estate prices were doing, that they behaved very smoothly through time, unlike stock prices. People must have intuitively been assuming that there was price inertia, but they had never actually seen it. One cannot clearly see home price movements without some careful econometrics, because of the noisiness of individual home prices and the incommensurability of dates of sale of houses.

My student Allan Weiss thought there was a business in providing real estate price indexes. He started the business, and pursued all the difficulties of creating a kind of business where there was no prior model to copy. I was an adviser. Well, I was more than an adviser. I did all the econometrics initially and wrote the computer program to construct the indexes, the same program that our company still uses today. I worked with Allan and Chip on developing applications for our indexes. The three of us made a tour of futures exchanges and other risk management companies to try to get markets for real estate risk started.

That was an interesting experience. For an academic economist, it is a good experience to run a business. Allan would discuss with me everything about the business. In the early days, Allan and I even had to loan money to the company so that we could meet the payroll, so we really experienced the anxieties of the business world, and I believe this has affected my thinking about economics.

Campbell: I would like to talk now about the stock market overvaluation of the late 1990s, and the fact that you were watching the market in light of your earlier work and a concern that the market was becoming overvalued.

Shiller: Well, my book, *Irrational Exuberance* [2000], is a case in point. Well, before that, of course, in 1996, you and I were invited to testify before the Federal Reserve Board.

Campbell: My impression, for what it is worth, is that Greenspan had already been formulating his opinion about irrational exuberance before that meeting.

Shiller: You are no doubt right. How could he really have been suddenly swayed at that meeting, there were so many different opinions expressed there. So, . . .

Yes, this reminds me, we have skipped over *our* collaborations. I have written over a dozen papers with you, more than with anyone else. You were a very big influence in my life. You made my analysis rigorous. We developed vector autoregressive, and cointegrated, models, and you helped deal very much with various criticisms, notably the unit root criticisms. It was your idea, I believe, to have a cointegrated vector autoregression, involving the dividend-price or earnings-price variables as an information variable.

Campbell: Yes, I remember when I was on the job market going to San Diego and learning about cointegration. Robert Engle and Clive Granger were just doing this stuff on cointegration. They were thinking about it in terms of disequilibrium adjustments, or partial adjustments, to an equilibrium that relates to the long run and not the short run, and I remember thinking it needn't be that way. The same economic model that generates the long-run equilibrium might also determine the short-run adjustment to that equilibrium. It fit very nicely with the issues that were being raised by critics of your excess volatility.

Shiller: That was in a sense the final step. My work on testing for excess volatility never progressed further after that. That led to your decomposition of returns into a component relating to new information about future dividends and a component relating to information about future returns.

Campbell: Well, that was another thing in our joint work. The loglinearization we developed together allowed us to think of a present-value

Figure 11.7 Robert J. Shiller and John Y. Campbell, 2003, at the Littauer Center, overlooking Harvard Square.

model with time-varying interest rates [Campbell and Shiller (1988)]. And let us now give credit to you, you came up with that extension that allows a log-linearization in terms of interest rates, and I ran with it in different directions, in terms of consumption and all that. But, the idea that you could log-linearize the equation was fundamental. That was an eye-opening moment for me, an epiphany for me.

Shiller: That was a beginning of a number of papers.

Campbell: Well, let's go back though to the late 1990s. After going public that we thought the stock market might be too high, there were several years when the market kept going higher. By 1998, we published a paper saying that the market was perilously high; we published that in the *Journal of Portfolio Management* [Campbell and Shiller (1998)].

Shiller: That was our joint testimony that we prepared for publication. That was when we first really went public with it. That was when there weren't so many caveats as in our earlier statements.

Campbell: I guess I'm just asking whether it was personally hard for you to stick to your guns during this period. I certainly found it hard. You stuck to your guns with a vengeance, and you wrote *Irrational Exuberance*.

Shiller: I felt propelled by the market, and the collective delusions about the economy we were experiencing then, to write something against it. The book came out in March 2000, the very top of the market. That timing was luck. Well, it wasn't entirely luck; I had a sense this market had to come to an end soon, and so I rushed to write that book.

Campbell: With a feeling that it was now or never?

Shiller: I wrote that book at breakneck speed.

Campbell: And I believe that Jeremy Siegel encouraged you to do that.

Shiller: That's right. I had been thinking of coming out with another edition of my collection of papers *Market Volatility*, and Jeremy said I should just write a whole new book, and this was the time.

Campbell: Did he say this was the time because he too thought that the market was overvalued?

Shiller: I think, . . . interesting question . . . he did say it was the time for me to write this book. I think that he did share some of my concerns. Nine months later, in March 2000, he wrote a *Wall Street Journal* piece [Siegel (2000)] about the overpricing of technology stocks. He sounded very much like me then, except that he was confining his attention to a certain class of stocks—technology stocks—rather than to the whole market.

Often, a lot has been made of our differences—that he is the bull and I the bear—but as a matter of fact we were very much on the same wavelength in many ways. I think that what he was saying was "I don't know if you're right Bob, but this is an interesting argument and this is the time to get a book out." Maybe he thought with my book I would produce something that focused only on technology stocks. Note, too, that the latest edition of his book *Stocks for the Long Run* [Siegel (2002)], contains a chapter on behavioral finance.

I have a philosophy that one must start big projects immediately on inspiration; otherwise, one will never start them. So, after the phone call with Jeremy, I started writing the book immediately.

Campbell: Like the survey after the stock market crash.

Shiller: Yes, in a way, it was impulsive. Fortunately I didn't have any appointments that afternoon. I immediately went on a long walk, thinking about this idea, and I started writing before I lost the inspiration, so that it would be framed in my mind as a going project. Then I started calling publishers, including Peter Dougherty at Princeton, who became an important formative influence on this book.

I was writing a different book at the time, and I abruptly dropped it. That is an emotional thing to do: when one is writing a book, one doesn't want to stop it, and one fears that it will never be done.

Campbell: What other book was that?

Shiller: That is the book that was finally entitled *The New Financial Order: Risk in the 21st Century*, and appeared in 2003. I started that book in 1997, so I had been working a year and a half on that book when I had to set it aside. Fortunately, I was later able to rekindle my enthusiasm for that book, with Peter Dougherty's encouragement and help. Dougherty was a terrific editor for *Irrational Exuberance*, and I am very lucky to have him again with *New Financial Order*. A really good editor can offer subtle guidance that makes all the difference in the final product. I should add that my wife, Ginny, also read and marked up the entire manuscript, and helped me organize my thinking for that book.

Campbell: Do you think that *Irrational Exuberance* has affected people's understanding of the stock market?

Shiller: Well, at least it affected mine, in the sense it was writing up, consolidating, my thinking. I thought about all the different things that I had studied over the years, and tried to state their relevance to the current situation. I don't view it as a popular book. Some people would say that it was a popularization. But it was a popularization only in the sense that I left the math out. It was a bit like the discussion or conclusion to one of our joint papers, John. There are actually two equations in *Irrational Exuberance*, though they are buried in the endnotes.

In a sense I was writing this book for myself. It was just exactly my thinking. It reflected the inner thoughts I have when I try to put financial research in a broader perspective. So, I was surprised that the book ended up on *The New York Times* nonfiction bestseller list. This is a very unusual event for a university press book. The only significant thing that I did to appeal to a broader audience was just to try to make it interesting, interesting to me.

There is something to be said for a very broad focus in economics. Economics is different from a lot of other fields. One thing is that it is harder to compartmentalize and be useful. In chemistry, one can take some particular compound and do an analysis of it, but, to be useful in economics, one has to have a broader perspective. There seems to be a greater risk in economics than in chemistry of doing something useless.

Campbell: Yes, I think that is right. There are some disciplines where there are many little bricks that have to be assembled to make the wall, but perhaps less so in economics.

Shiller: Yes, of course we have data collection, like that done by the Census Bureau, lots of very little bricks put together for a foundation. Then we economists build on these foundations some very flimsy superstructures, some tenuous economic models.

Campbell: You talk about economists being useful. Some of the things you have done advocating financial innovation are certainly potentially very useful. And maybe your work on inflation indexation. . . .

Shiller: Some of that is joint with you.

Campbell: Some of it is. You also did some work on inflation with Jeremy Siegel very early in your career. And you have solo work on inflation. So, how did you first get the idea this was an important topic?

Shiller: That is another question that I can't answer exactly. Well, I keep getting back to things that I was taught about science. Getting back to physics, one of the most important things that I learned there was the importance of getting your units right. And, in economics, some of the most important fallacies in the history of thought have had to do with problems of units. The nineteenth-century wage fund theory is an example, where economists confused a fund with a flow. My instructor, Shorey Peterson, at Michigan, stressed this, but it was also my physics professors that stressed to me the importance of units of measurement. We write most of our long-term contracts in terms of dollars, a unit of measurement that changes through time, and that is just a changing yardstick. It is odd that we in the twenty-first century would be using such archaic measures.

Now, the history of thought on this is interesting: The first person to propose the compensated dollar was Simon Newcomb, an astronomer, in the 1870s [Newcomb (1879)]. He was an expert on systems of measurement.

And then Irving Fisher, another formative influence on me (though I never met him), also emphasized human foibles in designing monetary policy [Fisher (1928)]. And this is the real beginning of behavioral economics.

It strikes me that, so often, economists build models that portray people as effectively paying attention to certain quantities that I suspect they are not even looking at. People are not even thinking in those terms, but are using an entirely different system of coordinates.

So much of the theory of the term structure of interest rates is a theory of *real* interest rates. When you point out to theorists that we have not had, until very recently, a term structure of real interest rates to observe, they sometimes say that a theory of the nominal term structure would be messy, inelegant. Nominal interest rates involve an inflation component that is not elegant to model.

Given the difficulties people have in behaving as economists assert they ought to behave, it has just seemed to me that the world should be more indexed, indexed in a way that is very easy for them. We should define an inflation-indexed unit of measurement, like the *unidad de fomento* in

Chile. That way, we change people's psychological frame of reference. And, in fact, we should at the same time establish units of measurement for many such things. This is in my new book, *The New Financial Order*. As well as an inflation unit, there should be a wage unit that reflects the average wage. For this, we need better wage indexes. Wage indexes today are not repeated-measure indexes, and so they do not accurately reflect changes in individuals' compensation. Then, we would have also a productivity measure, different market baskets for the elderly, et cetera. And you should be able to write a check measured in any of these measures, not just in terms of currency, use your credit card with these units, and so on.

I wanted to call the unit that is indexed to inflation "baskets," referring to the market basket that underlies the consumer price index, and so ideally one could write a check in terms of baskets instead of dollars. Writing such a check for 10 baskets, say, would be like handing over 10 baskets of an array of real goods, and so, the name would help people to understand that in writing such a check they were in fact doing just this.

Campbell: Well, that is sort of like going back to the Middle Ages where feudal dues were specified in hogsheads of agricultural products.

Shiller: And yet, it draws on economic theory. Index number theory is an important area of progress in economic theory that I think ought to be applied so that it can yield more tangible benefits to society. The indexed units of account may in some sense seem like going back to the Middle Ages, but in fact it would be going forward with some very sophisticated theory.

Campbell: Back to the future.

Shiller: Yes indeed. It also relates to new electronic technology. Irving Fisher, when he proposed his compensated dollar, assumed that we needed to base our transactions on a hand-to-hand currency [Fisher (1913)]. It was difficult to conceive of a way to make the real value of currency absolutely stable. Irving Fisher was worried about the calculations required by indexation: One cannot expect people to do complex calculations every time they buy a newspaper. His way to solve this problem was the compensated dollar. Today, it is much easier to achieve that with electronic money, where the real value of the unit can be defined in terms of an index that is computed automatically and continually by computers. Now, with credit cards, smart cards, and the like, we really ought to have sophisticated units of measurements that are taught to children and established in our economy, so that it is easy to make sensible contracts. These are themes in *New Financial Order*.

Campbell: So, you mentioned the book, but that is just part of the whole research agenda, and the mission to promote new financial instruments to enhance risk sharing. And you had your earlier book, your Clarendon Lectures book on macro markets [Shiller (1993)]. Some people would say, "Isn't it surprising that the same Bob Shiller who argues that markets are excessively volatile is also promoting the further extension of financial markets." How would you respond to that?

Shiller: Yes, well it would be oversimplifying in the real world to say that just because there is excess volatility, we should not have markets. You know, no one has proposed, and I never proposed, that in response to excess volatility we should shut down the stock market.

Campbell: Well, Alan Blinder once told me that he thought that the stock market should be open one day a year.

Shiller: Well, that is a bit of a "sand in the wheels" theory. Jim Tobin might have gone along with that, but even Blinder is not advocating shutting the markets down. Excess volatility is just one example of how the inconsistency of human behavior is a potent force. The human mind is incredibly powerful; it is capable of computations that can dazzle you, but can also be very blundering and foolish at times. So, we have to design things so that they work well for real people.

For example, airplanes are designed so that they are very stable—do not go wildly off course when there is a minor pilot error. We have to design our financial institutions in the same way. It is a difficult problem, how to achieve this. One has to engineer around human limitations, and make it possible for people to do what they can do very well. Most people are quite capable of managing their lives and their own risks, and so we want to create the vehicles that enable them to do this, but also to have default options set up so that if they do nothing they will still fare fairly well.

So, excess volatility is a manifestation of a certain inconsistency in human behavior, and that same inconsistency has other manifestations, even things like wars, rebellions, things that have nothing to do with markets. So, I think that, overall, expanding markets is the right thing to do.

Campbell: You have also sought to expand markets, create new markets, partly through your company, and through efforts at persuasion.

Shiller: A lot of things are happening now. I get phone calls from many people who are thinking of creating some new derivative market or some new way of achieving social goals through incentives. That would go on whether I had been here or not, but one will never know what influence I had on that, if any.

Campbell: So, do you feel you understand the obstacles, from talking to people at futures exchanges, for example, or talking with people through the company you and Allan Weiss recently created, Macro Securities

Research? You've become perhaps more savvy about the obstacles, the inertia that prevents these markets from becoming successful.

Shiller: Yes, Allan and I, and now Sam Masucci, who is Chief Operating Officer of Macro Securities Research, have been working for years to try to make better risk management happen. And we have learned very much about institutional inertia.

One reason why I wanted to create a more sensible system of indexation is precisely because of such institutional inertia. We were thinking of creating vehicles for people to hedge the value of their houses. When we went to futures exchanges to propose that, it occurred to us that a simple risk management product for homeowners should be one that protects the real value of their home, not its nominal value. For if people hedged the nominal value in a time of uncertain inflation, they could be creating bigger fluctuations in the real value than they would have had if they had not hedged. I asked people at these exchanges if we could create a hedging vehicle that was defined in terms of real values, and they just looked blankly at me. "What are you talking about?" So, it seemed that one could not do anything sensible if we have to make all of our economic contracts in terms of some crazy unit (money), so that people cannot manage such a simple construct as indexation. That is an example of what I observed from trying to get these things started. So, we need to set up an economic infrastructure that will make these things more possible.

Campbell: You have this new book coming out, *The New Financial Order.* So, how did you come to write that book? You started it back in 1997, and then dropped it.

Shiller: Well, I wrote *Macro Markets* in 1993. That book had a very technical side, where I talked about repeated-measures indexes, for example, and sources of volatility. But it also got into a side that is broader, about how institutional change will transform our markets and our lives. It was reviewed in *The New York Times*, and the reviewer, Peter Passell, called me up and said that I should really write a version of this book that is accessible to a broader audience. He said, all that math is intimidating and not necessary for the basic ideas. But, I told him that I didn't know how to write a book for a broader audience on this topic, which seemed to be an inherently technical topic. So, I put that idea on the back burner. I didn't think I could do it.

Some years went by. My student Stefano Athanasoulis and I advanced the mathematical theory of fundamental risk management in the context of institutional design in several papers [Athanasoulis and Shiller (2001)]. Working with Stefano really was very productive; we have a much clearer idea of the theory of these new risk markets now. We have written four major papers on this topic, and continue to work together. He has been a very important force in my work in this area, and has given me many ideas.

At the same time I began to think that there is in fact a lot to say without reference to these technical issues. Again, I started to write the book for myself, to try to understand the issues better myself.

Part of my motivation is that, after I wrote the book *Macro Markets*, people for the most part just did not react to it. They didn't see that it contained a good idea, an idea that was workable. So, I needed myself to come up with better arguments, and that meant integrating the risk management notions into a bigger picture.

Handling the real obstacles to risk management was the basic motivation. I wanted readers to see how analogous innovation has fitted into history, to see that radically new financial innovation is not unprecedented, and that it is not implausible that we would find ways to deal with barriers in human psychology, especially if new institutions are designed right to work around human foibles. I wanted it to be a serious book, and I thought I could put the vector autoregressions somewhere else. Anyone who wants to read about that can read some of our papers, for example.

I really got very excited about this book, but it has been very hard to write. In contrast, I wrote *Irrational Exuberance* basically in nine, months. Though there were some notes I incorporated that I wrote in 1987, the basic project really took only nine months. Writing *The New Financial Order* was very hard, and took a long time.

Campbell: One of the things that you say in the preface to your new book is that your 20 years at Yale have had a certain influence on your thinking.

Shiller: Well, I came to Yale because I admired a number of people there: Jim Tobin, Bill Brainard, Bill Nordhaus, and others. There was the Brainard–Dolbear article [1971] that talked about hedging risks to livelihoods. And that is the earliest reference I could find to that idea. Tobin is implicit in his work about hedging idiosyncratic risks. He was concerned a lot about institutional change. He was the inventor of the Yale Tuition Payment Option, the institution that allowed student loan contracts to work toward managing lifetime income risks. And he made it happen, albeit only on a small scale. He got Yale University to implement it.

Campbell: But this has backfired for the university, because people who owed big payments under the program are people who would otherwise give big donations and they are claiming to be so annoyed at the bills they get that they refuse to give money.

Shiller: Well, so they ended the program, and finally forgave the rest of the loans. The original plan had some shortcomings. Another problem is that the payments were defined by a line on the Federal Income Tax form. Unfortunately, when people married later, they wound up taxing the spouse. People hadn't anticipated this, and it seemed unjust. Now, there is a big question about how to handle that.

Campbell: You could be married and file separately.

Shiller: Well, but that is costly under current tax law. It will be easier once the income tax is more computerized, and you can push a button and the forms can come out in different ways. The reason that the Yale TPO had to be defined in terms of a line on the tax form is that they didn't have this technology. Now, one of the points of my new book is that technology is advancing so fast that the complexity of our institutions can go very far forward now.

Campbell: Well, if you look at the tax code, it has been doing that. The tax code has become more complicated because it is possible to do the calculations now.

Shiller: Well, obviously, for good risk management purposes, complexity may be necessary. But, anyway, as far as the Yale tradition . . . going back to Irving Fisher, a lot of people admire him. He was an innovator. He tried to get indexed bonds started. He had a kind of practical approach to economics. And he even did survey work.

Campbell: Really? I didn't know that.

Shiller: In his book *Money Illusion*, he reported an informal survey of shopkeepers in Germany during the hyperinflation, and asked them why they raised their prices, and concluded that they didn't really understand the role of inflation in their decision. So, there is a sort of tradition at Yale for down-to-earth policy-focused research.

Incidentally, there is another article in *Macroeconomic Dynamics* about the Yale Tradition. David Colander interviewed Jim Tobin and me about the Yale Tradition in economics [Colander (1999)].

Campbell: I have a last question. Looking forward, are there any research topics that are going to be especially productive for you or for the profession in the next 10 years? If a graduate student comes to you and says I am looking for a field to work in or an idea to work on, what would you say?

Shiller: Well, it is hard to predict very far out what we will be doing. I have never known very far out what my own research will be. I think that there are a number of things to say.

One of the things I would say that perhaps most economists would not say in answer to such a question is that the information revolution is lowering the costs of doing things, and we have to think about what we as economists can do with that new opportunity. And so, economic researchers should be thinking more about what they can do constructively to develop more complex economic institutions.

It is starting to happen. We have a lot more research on financial engineering and mechanism design. It is an emerging thing.

I think that there is a lot of fundamental work to do on the integration of the theory of risk management into broader economic theory. It is very important to try to advance this fundamental theory. Unfortunately, the day-to-day life in the profession has a tendency to distract one from such basic research with a million little diversions. I have to thank my administrative assistant for many years, Carol Copeland, for helping me to manage my time and to steer clear of distractions. People need to listen both to others' advice as well as to their own conscience to keep their research from becoming diluted.

A lot of what economists do is, though, very abstract. I would also encourage more economists to do practical things, like write patents, rather than just NSF proposals. There is a lot to be gained from the application of our theory.

I imagine myself in the coming decade celebrating and supporting others' efforts to do such things. It is hard to be an innovator because it is not a traditional course in the profession. It tends to look nutty. Well, the Wright brothers were thought of as nutty by many when they tried to develop the airplane. Today, new designers of airplanes are fully respected. But, today, in mechanism design or other constructive aspects of economics, we are in the Wright Flyer stage.

So, one of my missions in the years ahead is to help support innovation in finance. I get a lot of proposals now that cross my desk or my e-mail. The typical story is that "I have this idea that nobody will listen to." Sometimes the idea *is* nutty, but often not. Sometimes it just seems to be an idea that there is no current momentum for. I believe that eventually many of these ideas will be heard. There will be a lot of fundamental financial and social insurance innovations in coming years, coming from people all over the world who are inspired by financial theory and the rapid advance of information technology.

REFERENCES

Anderson, L.C. & J.L. Jordan (1968) Monetary and fiscal actions: A test of their relative importance. *Federal Reserve Bank of St. Louis Review* 50, 11–23.

Athanasoulis, S. & R.J. Shiller (2001) World income components: Measuring and exploiting risk sharing opportunities. *American Economic Review* 91, 1031–1054.

Baily, M.J., R.F. Muth, & H.O. Nourse (1963) A regression method for real estate price index construction. *Journal of the American Statistical Association* 933–942.

Belsley, D.A., E. Kuh & R. Welsch (1980) *Regression Diagnostics: Identifying Influential Data and Sources of Collinearity*. New York: Wiley.

Brainard, W. & F.T. Dolbear (1971) Social risk and financial markets. *American Economic Review* 61, 360–370.

Campbell, J.Y. & R.J. Shiller (1988) The dividend-price ratio and expectations of future dividends and discount factors. *Review of Financial Studies* 1, 195–228.

Campbell, J.Y. & R.J. Shiller (1998) Valuation ratios and the long-run stock market outlook. *Journal of Portfolio Management* 24(2), 11–26.

Case, K.E. (1986) The market for single-family homes in Boston. *New England Economic Review* (May/June) 38–48.

Case, K.E. & R.J. Shiller (1988) The behavior of home buyers in boom and post-boom markets. *New England Economic Review* (Nov./Dec.) 29–46.

Case, K.E. & R.J. Shiller (1989) The efficiency of the market for single family homes. *American Economic Review* 71, 325–331.

Colander, D. (1999) Conversations with James Tobin and Robert Shiller on the "Yale Tradition" in macroeconomics. *Macroeconomic Dynamics* 3, 116–143.

Dickey, D.A. (1975) Hypothesis Testing for Nonstationary Time Series. Manuscript, Iowa State University.

Fair, R.C. & R.J. Shiller (1990) Comparing information in forecasts from econometric models. *American Economic Review* 80, 375–389.

Fama, E. (1970) Efficient capital markets: A review of empirical work. *Journal of Finance* 25, 383–417.

Fisher, F. (1966) *The Identification Problem in Econometrics*. New York: McGraw-Hill.

Fisher, I. (1913) A compensated dollar. *Quarterly Journal of Economics* 27, 213–235.

Fisher, I. (1928) *The Money Illusion*. New York: Adelphi.

Friedman, B.M. (1977) Even the St. Louis model now believes fiscal policy. *Journal of Money, Credit, and Banking* 9, 365–367.

Friedman, M. (1953) *Essays in Positive Economics*. Chicago: University of Chicago Press.

Fuller, W.A. (1976) *Introduction to Statistical Time Series*. New York: Wiley.

Grossman S. & R.J. Shiller (1981) The determinants of the variability of stock market prices. *American Economic Review* 71, 222–227.

Hansen, L.P. & R. Jagannathan (1991) Restrictions on intertemporal marginal rates of substitution implied by asset returns. *Journal of Political Economy* 99, 225–262.

Kahneman, D. & A. Tversky (1979) Prospect theory: An analysis of decision under risk. *Econometrica* 17, 263–291.

Learner, E. (1978) *Specification Searches: Ad Hoc Inferences with Nonexperimental Data*. Wiley.

Lucas, R.E. (1975) Econometric policy evaluation: A critique. In K. Brunner & A. Meltzer (eds.), *The Phillips Curve and Labor Markets. The Journal of Monetary Economics Supplement*, pp. 19–46. New York: Elsevier.

Modigliani, F. & R.J. Shiller (1973) Inflation, rational expectations and the term structure of interest rates. *Economica* 40(157), 12–43.

Newcomb, S. (1879) The standard of value. *North American Review* 58, 223–237.

Perron P. & P. Phillips (1988) Testing for a unit root in time series autoregression. *Biometrika* 75, 335–346

Shiller, R.J. (1972) Rational Expectations and the Term Structure of Interest Rates. Ph.D. Dissertation, MIT.

Shiller, R.J. (1973) A distributed lag estimator derived from smoothness priors. *Econometrica* 41, 775–788.

Shiller, R.J. (1979) The volatility of long term interest rates and expectations models of the term structure. *Journal of Political Economy* 87, 1190–1219.

Shiller, R.J. (1982) Consumption, asset markets and macroeconomic fluctuations. *Carnegie–Rochester Conference Series on Public Policy* 17, 203–238.

Shiller, R.J. (1984) Stock prices and social dynamics. *Brookings Paperson Economic Activity* 2, 457–498.

Shiller, R.J. (1989) *Market Volatility.* Cambridge, MA: MIT Press.

Shiller, R.J. (1993) *Macro Markets: Creating Institutions for Managing Society's Largest Economic Risks.* Oxford: Oxford University Press.

Shiller, R.J. (2000) *Irrational Exuberance.* Princeton, NJ: Princeton University Press.

Shiller, R.J. (2003) *The New Financial Order: Risk in the 21st Century.* Princeton, NJ: Princeton University Press.

Shiller, R.J. & P. Perron (1985) Testing the random walk hypothesis: Power versus frequency of observation. *Economic Letters* 18, 381–386.

Siegel, J.J. (2000) Big-cap tech stocks are a sucker bet. *Wall Street Journal,* Mar. 14, op-ed page.

Siegel, J.J. (2002) *Stocks for the Long Run.* 3rd ed. New York: McGraw-Hill.

Sutch, R.C. (1968) *Expectations, Risk, and the Term Structure of Interest Rates.* Ph.D. Dissertation, MIT.

Thaler, R. & S. Rosen (1976) The value of saving a life: Evidence from the labor market. In N.E. Terleckyj (ed.), *Household Production and Consumption. Studies in Income and Wealth,* vol. 40. New York: NBER and Columbia University Press.

12

An Interview with Stanley Fischer

Interviewed by Olivier Blanchard

MASSACHUSETTS INSTITUTE OF TECHNOLOGY

May 2004

This interview was completed in May 2004, well before Stan Fischer had any idea he would become Governor of the Bank of Israel, a position he took up in May 2005. The interview took place in April 2004 in my office at the Russell Sage Foundation in New York City, where I was spending a sabbatical year. We completed it while running together in Central Park during the following weeks.

Our meeting at Russell Sage was just like the many meetings we have had over the years. I was not sitting with a Master of the Universe, a world VIP, but with the same Stan Fischer I had first met in 1973 when he was a young associate professor, freshly imported from Chicago. There was the same ability to listen carefully, the same ability to talk and to explain simply and straightforwardly. In addition, there was the accumulated wisdom of a professional life spent developing and applying macroeconomics to the very real world.

When I arrived as a Ph.D. student at MIT in 1973, it was clear that Stan would quickly play a central role in the department. Within a few years, he was one of the most popular teachers, and one of the most popular thesis advisers. We flocked to his office, and I suspect that the only time for research he had was during the night. What we admired most were his technical skills—he knew how to use stochastic calculus —and his ability to take on big questions and to simplify them to the

Reprinted from *Macroeconomic Dynamics*, 9, 2005, 244–262. Copyright © 2005 Cambridge University Press.

point where the answer, *ex post*, looked obvious. When Rudi Dornbusch joined him in 1975, macro and international quickly became the most exciting fields at MIT. Imitation is the sincerest form of admiration, and this is very much what we all did.

When I came back to MIT in 1982, this time as a faculty member, Stan had acquired near-guru status. Teaching the advanced macro courses with him, and writing *Lectures on Macroeconomics*, which we finished in 1988, was one of the most exciting intellectual adventures of my life. We both felt that there was a new macroeconomics, more micro-founded and full of promises, and that we understood its architecture and its usefulness. Although we had not thought of it as a textbook, it quickly became one, and it is nice to know that it still sells surprisingly well today.

As the years had passed, Stan had taken more and more interest in applying theory to the real world, working with Rudi on hyperinflation, being involved in the economics of peace with George Shultz in the Middle East. In 1988, he decided to jump from academia to the real world, and became Chief Economist of the World Bank. After a brief return to MIT, he then returned to Washington in 1994 to become First Deputy Managing Director of the IMF, where he remained until 2001. That part of his life has been well documented in newspapers and magazines: While at the IMF, he was on the front lines during the Mexican crisis, the Russian crisis, the Asian crises, and many others. From the peeks I got of him during those times, what strikes me most is how he remained the same as he had been at MIT: calm, careful about the facts, analytical, using macroeconomic theory even in the middle of the most intense fires. Many thought and hoped that he would become the managing director of the IMF. Antiquated rules and country politics prevented it from happening. The IMF's loss turned out to be the private sector's gain. In 2002, Stan joined Citigroup, where he is the President of Citigroup International. He is still active in macro policy debates and remains one of the wise men of our profession.

Blanchard: When and why did you decide to go into economics?

Fischer: I was a schoolboy in what was then Southern Rhodesia, later Rhodesia, later yet, Zimbabwe. The educational system was British, which meant you had to specialize during the last two years of high school. I originally specialized in physics, math, and chemistry, thinking I would become an engineer or maybe a scientist or a mathematician. At some point I had a conversation with the son of friends of my parents. He had studied at the LSE, and told me I should become an economist. He gave me a few lessons, which were interesting—I think we used Samuelson's introductory book. Also, amazingly enough, I took an economics course during my last year at high school.

Figure 12.1   Stanley Fischer.

Blanchard: An economics course at school. This sounds very unusual.

Fischer: Well, this was the British sixth form, where students have to specialize. The teacher was extremely good. We studied Hicks's *Social Framework*, and I was introduced to Keynes. In the vacation between school and college, I read the *General Theory* and was hooked by Keynes's use of language, although I'm not sure I understood the book. I had decided to study in England and ended up at the LSE.

Blanchard: Why LSE? Why not the United States?

Fischer: We didn't think of the United States then. For us, England was the center of the universe. My teachers told me the choice was Cambridge or the LSE. I ended up at the LSE, partly because the person who had introduced me to the subject had gone there and partly because they were willing to give me a very early decision (the academic year in the Southern Hemisphere ends in December instead of June). Although the LSE had the reputation for being left wing, that was not true of economics. We took very conventional courses. Richard Lipsey taught the first principles course, and he was very good. Frank Paish taught an applied economics course. I recall his showing his slides early in 1963 and saying: "You see, it goes up and it goes down and then it goes up again. And that's why we're going to have a balance of payments crisis in 1964." The crisis took place on the appointed date, and I was very impressed.

Blanchard: This was an exciting time at LSE. Did you pick up a sense of that excitement?

Fischer: I had a great time at the LSE. This was my first experience of the big world and I took advantage of London and of the continent, but I was quite unsophisticated about academic life and intellectual life. That was not something you picked up in my high school—good as it was as a teaching institution. I thought the main aim of studying was to get through the exams.

In retrospect, I realize there was intellectual excitement there at the time. The LSE was then in the midst of the controversy about the Radcliffe committee report. Richard Sayers, who was at the LSE, was the main intellectual force behind the report. It suggested that monetary policy worked, and was later seen as the beginning of the revival of monetary policy in the United Kingdom, but it was full of qualifications. It featured a three-gear view of monetary policy: If you changed gear drastically enough, you could have an impact. Still, it marked the end of the period in which it was believed in the United Kingdom that monetary policy didn't work, and the beginning of a new era in which monetary policy has increasingly been seen as a powerful driver of the economy.

Karl Popper was the dominant force in the philosophy department, and everyone became a Popperian in methodology. Phillips of the Phillips curve was there, though I didn't take a course from him, but I did see his machine of the economy. And, there was a lot of work being done on the Phillips curve.

Other memories include a lecture by Bob Solow. He must have been about 40 at the time, but he looked much younger, and was very funny, even in talking about production functions. I remember him saying: "When I say K, I mean Kuznets. Capital is that thing that Kuznets measures." I also remember on one occasion being incredibly excited when someone explained to me what an econometric model was—that you could use data to estimate parameters, and then if you put the whole thing together, you had a set of equations that described the economy. That was really exciting; it meant you could control the economy, and it was obvious that was immensely important.

At the LSE then, you wrote exams only at the end of the first and third years (it was a three-year degree), and you didn't get course grades. So, I didn't really know whether I was a good student or an average student. I had won an economic history prize and some other prize at the end of the first year, but I had no real idea of where I stood in the class. So, I planned to work in a bank when I graduated.

Blanchard: [*Laughing*] It eventually happened, but it took a long time.

Fischer: Touché. I wrote the first degree, and it turned out that I did very well. I had gone to Israel to work for the summer, where I got a telegram indicating that I had gotten a scholarship and should come back to do graduate work. So, I didn't know I was going to be an academic until after the first degree.

Blanchard: So, passion was not there yet.

Fischer: No, it was not there. I really liked the subject, but research was not central to what we did. That came later, with the graduate studies at MIT. Even though I did a master's degree at LSE, up to that point my view of economics was always that it was what these great professors did and do. Your job as a student was to study what they said.

Blanchard: Was MIT the logical choice for you when you wanted to go on, or was Chicago in the picture?

Fischer: To me, MIT was the logical choice. Everybody said "Why do you want to go to MIT?" And I'd say "Samuelson and Solow." Even though Harry Johnson, who was at LSE while I was there, recommended Chicago, and even though we read Friedman's restatement of the quantity theory, I thought MIT was the best. And I got in there and went there.

Blanchard: How was MIT?

Fischer: Because I hadn't thought of going to graduate school until after completing my first degree, I had done a one-year master's degree at the LSE. So I was better prepared when I went to MIT than most of the students, but that wore off pretty quickly. The faculty member I was closest to, almost by geographic accident, was Miguel Sidrauski, who was a Chicago graduate—an Argentine—who started as an assistant professor at MIT the same year I arrived. We happened to live in the same apartment building in Cambridge, and became very friendly.

Miguel was a terrific mentor. The relationship of the young assistant professor with the student is a very nice one, because you are so close in age. I worked a lot with Miguel in my first summer as a research assistant for him and Duncan Foley. Tragically, Miguel died of cancer at the end of his second year at MIT. I also worked for Don Patinkin, who was visiting MIT and was one of my heroes. So I really got into things.

My MIT experience was truly formative. The professors were great and the courses were great. The department emphasized good teaching, and most of the professors were available if you wanted to talk to them. And, we had enough term papers to do to be drawn into research. Samuelson used to say interesting things in class and throw out interesting problems. Sidrauski was an excellent teacher who made you understand the economics that was represented in his phase diagrams, and Bob Solow did that too. Frank Fisher taught econometrics, and had a big influence on the students, and there were many others who influenced us.

No less important, I was with a really remarkable group of fellow students. The class above me, in particular, included a whole host of people whose names you know. Bob Hall was there, as was Bill Nordhaus, Avinash Dixit, Bob Gordon, Ray Fair, Mike Rothschild, Joe Stiglitz, and others who later made their mark. Avinash Dixit could do *The Times* crossword puzzle in about 10 seconds. Bob Merton arrived a year after me, and we shared an office for a year.

Blanchard: Your thesis was on macro. Why?

Fischer: I focused on macro as a graduate student, as I had at the LSE. I think I liked macro because I was interested in big questions, but that may be an *ex post* rationalization. Maybe it was because I had read Keynes's *General Theory* and was intrigued. I had this image of the world as we knew it having nearly collapsed in the 1930s, and that these guys had saved it.

My thesis was actually on lifetime portfolio choice. We were very much into the microfoundations of macro at the time, and that topic was about the microfoundations of portfolio choice and saving, in the presence of life insurance. In part, I chose that topic because Paul Samuelson was working on lifetime portfolio choice at the time, as was Bob Merton.

Blanchard: Then, you moved to Chicago.

Fischer: I went to Chicago as a postdoc, financed partly through Al Harberger's Latin America workshop. It was the best university that made me an offer. My first year as postdoc, I went to the Money Workshop, Harberger's Latin American workshop, the trade workshop, Milton Friedman's money course, and, no doubt, much else. That was also the year I met Rudi Dornbusch and Jacob Frenkel, and other outstanding students, including Mike Mussa. Chicago enabled me to combine MIT's analytics with the policy relevance that Milton Friedman typified.

Blanchard: MIT was more in theory mode?

Fischer: That was the impression I had at the time. I remember a discussion at MIT with the faculty during the student disturbances at Harvard in 1968 when I said that "we know a lot of economics, but we don't know much about the economy." And Chicago *then* was the perfect antidote for this. Plus, Chicago too had an extraordinary group of students. I taught micro with Harberger and later taught macro.

But as I reflect on the question, I realize I must have been thinking of what I did at MIT, rather than what was happening there in the late 1960s. After all, that was when Franco Modigliani and his students were working on the FRB–MIT–Penn macromodel, and Bob Solow was the devotee *par excellence* of using small tractable analytic models to get to the essence of a problem.

Blanchard: How central was Milton Friedman in all of this?

Fischer: To the macro? Absolutely central. Macro was the money workshop. It was his workshop. In those days, I regretted that they did not have people from another tradition except for a few of us, Bob Gordon in particular. Later, I decided that if Chicago wasn't Chicago, who would be? It was all right for them to pursue a particular line, but, as an assistant professor, although I benefited in the long run, it was at times difficult.

Blanchard: But did it change the way you did macro? The way you thought about macro? Your choice of topics?

Fischer: It did have a long-run impact. I started working then on monetary rules with Phil Cooper, an MIT fellow-student, who became an assistant professor at the Chicago Business School. I also talked a lot to Rudi Dornbusch and served on his thesis committee, and wrote a few papers with Jacob Frenkel.

Blanchard. You went back to MIT in 1973?

Fischer: During the time I was at Chicago I had taken a six-month sabbatical at the Hebrew University, and we had very seriously thought about living in Israel. When I went back to MIT in the fall of 1973, I thought that it might be an interesting two-year interlude on the way to living in Israel and teaching at the Hebrew University.

The first course I co-taught when I got back to MIT was monetary economics with Paul Samuelson. That was intimidating. He would insist on taking the chalk and explaining things better than me. Then, I sort of eased into the role with which you are familiar. You came in 1973, right?

Blanchard: Right. 1973.

Fischer: And gradually I became a decent teacher. I taught the introductory macro, got a lot of students over the course of time. Coming from Chicago where the money workshop was so central, I built up the money workshop at MIT. Franco Modigliani was the star attraction. I loved advising on theses. Then in 1975, I persuaded my colleagues to bring Rudi Dornbusch to MIT. He had taught at Rochester and then went back to Chicago. He was very analytic. Not very interested in the real world. Very pure. He wrote his "overshooting" article within a few months of coming to MIT. Our collaboration grew, and that also made a huge difference. So I had terrific elder colleagues, terrific students, and a great contemporary colleague in Rudi. Probably an ideal setup.

Blanchard: Did Israel recede as an option?

Fischer: We always maintained a close contact, and we took several sabbaticals there, but after we made up our minds to live in the States, around 1975, we didn't look back. At least not more than once every two weeks or so. . . . But we never really came close to changing our minds because MIT was such a wonderful place to be. And because we liked Boston. And our kids were growing up.

Blanchard: When did you shift toward more applied topics?

Fischer: I should have mentioned that one of the things that got me interested in economics, peculiarly, was that Dag Hammarskjold was an economist. When I was in high school, Dag Hammarskjold was this great man. Then he was killed in the then-Belgian Congo, right next door. I knew he had done good in the world and my parents had brought me up to believe I should do good in the world. I realized that economics would help you do good. So I always wanted to use what I had learned. That factor was probably there and moved me over the course of time.

My first really intense applied work was when I visited the Bank of Israel and spent a month there in 1979. They gave me a lot of applied questions, since they were suffering from high inflation. My real opportunity came in 1983 when George Shultz asked me join an advisory group he was creating on the Israeli economy. I had in the meantime become somewhat of an American expert on the Israeli economy.

That was when I got into the policy game. It was a very fortunate introduction. It's extremely unusual to have the Secretary of State take some young guy he doesn't know and appoint him as an adviser, and then let him have an active role. Herb Stein and I were appointed as George Shultz's advisers on the Israeli economy. On the occasions Herb and I traveled to Israel, we essentially had George Shultz's authority behind us, and we could say, "The Secretary of State believes this." As a professor, that didn't especially impress me, but when you say "the Secretary of State believes" to a government that depends on the United States, they are not listening only to the economics.

Blanchard: Was the shift to more applied topics in the air in the 1980s? Rudi Dornbusch moved in a similar way at the same time.

Fischer: Well, there were all those high inflations around, and we'd studied and taught about them. There were countless conferences on what to do about inflation and that seemed to be the general policy problem of most of the countries we were working with. Also, foreign travel was exciting. I went to Japan in 1981, together with Ben Friedman and Jeff Sachs, on a trip organized by Ezra Vogel of Harvard. I had never been to the East. There was this incredibly exciting economy, Japan, which was doing the most amazing things, growing by leaps and bounds. It was exciting. So, I can't quite explain my transition, except that these opportunities came along and they were interesting. I guess it was a combination of being interested in the real world, wanting to be useful, being able to travel, and being given interesting problems.

Blanchard: That's the right transition to the next stage: the World Bank.

Fischer: The World Bank was another opportunity to be in the policy world, and so I was very happy to take the offer.

Blanchard: What did you know about development at the time?

Fischer: I had studied development and taken development economics as one of my fields in the MIT generals. And on the macro side, I did know the economies of developing countries. Also, at that time, the main issues were stabilization and the debt crisis, and I knew a lot about them.

At the World Bank, I got into structural adjustment and associated issues. I visited China, visited India for the first time. I spent 10 days in China and met Zhou Ziang, then the premier, about six months before Tiananmen Square. I was impressed by how much he knew about Western economics. He told me that my views differed from those of Milton Friedman and from those of Lawrence Klein. I couldn't imagine that the Prime Minister was studying all these matters, but he was. Visiting India was also a wonderful experience.

I was gripped by the problem of development. And that problem hasn't left me. I grew up in a very small town in Northern Rhodesia for the first 13 years of my life, living among Africans. So, the development issue was with me all the time. I also began to understand a lot both about the way organizations work, because the World Bank is an unusually complex organization, and also about the problems confronting the world. And so, I left with a much better idea of what mattered and what needed to be done.

Blanchard: You stayed at the World Bank for two years?

Fischer: It was originally a two-year term and it ended up being two and a half years. I did think about staying, and giving up my MIT tenure, but because I was not ready to give up MIT tenure, and for family reasons, we decided to go back to MIT. It was hard readjusting. I remember going to theory seminars and saying to myself, what difference does it make whether this guy is right or wrong, why should anyone care about that theorem, and so forth. But I did somewhat readjust. I was obviously more interested in the policy side of things. I continued my involvement with Israel. I began writing a column for an Italian newspaper. I tried my hand at writing occasional columns for American newspapers. I was interested in both international problems and American problems, but I became tagged as an international expert more than a macro expert.

When I got back, everyone thought I would revolutionize development at MIT, but I didn't. The younger generation, which came not so long after, including Abhijit Banerjee, probably did.

Blanchard: Do you think we have today the macro tools we need to understand the world?

Fischer: The quantity theory goes a very long way in dealing with inflation. And the intertemporal budget constraint, and the equation for debt dynamics, take you further along. . . . I'd say the political economy is much harder. There's a bunch of guys who try to get policies done and the question is how they get them done. This became clear to me even before the World Bank, when, in 1985, I was involved in the implementation of the Israeli stabilization. That stabilization was the work of Michael Bruno and colleagues. Discussions about how to do it were exciting, and I learned a tremendous amount; but, I learned even more watching the administrative and political battles that had to be fought in making the program work.

Blanchard: How much does it matter at those critical moments to have people with clear minds?

Fischer: Oh! It matters entirely. The Bruno team understood what it was doing in a way politicians wouldn't. These guys knew what to fight about and what not to fight about. Some of the fights were very vigorous; politicians always think "Well okay, we've done it now so let's open up for business again in the same old way." If you hadn't had Bruno appointed central bank governor soon after the stabilization, it probably would not have worked. It certainly would not have worked as well.

So, yes, it matters to have people who understand the environment in which they are working.

Blanchard: I think we are coming to the IMF. Being chairman of the MIT department was not enough?

Fischer: Being chairman of MIT was only partly inspiring. You know Alfred Kahn's description of the role of the Dean at an academic institution: the dean is to the faculty as the fire hydrant is to the dog. It wasn't quite like that, but it had certain elements in common. I was quite involved in various academic and quasi-academic initiatives on Middle East peace during 1990–93. I did a lot of work on the economics of Middle East peace, which looked very prescient until recently. Unfortunately, I fear it has not had much influence in practice.

And then I joined the IMF. I took to that job like a duck to water. I was ready for it. Having been in the World Bank, I had a good idea of what these institutions were about. Having studied and taught macro and about macro stabilization, I was probably better suited for the IMF than for the World Bank. Having lots of my students all over the Fund, and in many of the member country governments, helped. Having Larry Summers as Undersecretary of Treasury certainly helped, since we were friends. It was just a terrific place to work.

I had an enormously gifted boss in Michel Camdessus, who, however, did not take to me initially. It took a while till we hit it off. I think he thought of me as a critic of the IMF when I arrived. I may well have criticized the IMF before I arrived, but, within about a year or two, our relationship was a very good one. Within a few months of my arriving, we had the Mexico crisis, which was a good learning experience for everyone, including the U.S. Treasury.

Blanchard: Was this because the mechanisms of the crisis were different?

Fischer: Well, it was a different sort of crisis, and the first economic crisis for the Clinton administration. The United States tried to handle the crisis on its own, and then realized that it couldn't. It is much harder for one country to impose conditions on another than for an international organization to have one of its members sign up to those conditions. The United States also realized that the IMF had a team and a way of dealing with countries in crisis.

As you know, the Mexican crisis was subsequently called the first financial crisis of the twenty-first century. It was set off by massive capital flows. I learned a lot in that crisis, including from Michel Camdessus. He was so much calmer throughout the entire crisis than I was. I thought Western civilization as we knew it was coming to an end. But he had seen this particular play before.

Blanchard: Was there a sense that you were all flying without a parachute, that this crisis was more complicated than you understood?

Fischer: Yes. Events would happen. You would suddenly discover about tessobonos. You knew they existed, but the difference between knowing something and realizing what it implies can be quite intense. There are 47 factors in the background. Always. The key to managing a crisis is to figure out which of them really matters.

In every crisis, something takes prominence that you hadn't thought was necessarily going to be critical. You could understand events in game theory terms. I understand fully why they issued tessobonos: That was a signal that a devaluation would be very costly for Mexico, therefore implying that a devaluation was less likely. That was quite right. The problem was that making the devaluation less likely didn't prevent it— and it *was* very costly.

Fortunately, the Mexican crisis was over relatively quickly. Mexico was back in the market within six months. There was another jittery period in November 1995, but that was soon overcome. Nonetheless, for a few months the Mexican crisis seemed chaotic. And, there were days I felt the crisis would just get worse and worse. For instance, there was a day in January 1995 when Asian markets tanked as a result of contagion from the Mexican crisis. I thought this was one of the most insane things that had ever happened, because I thought Asia was in great shape.

Blanchard: Did you have the sense that you understood at least the basics? For example, in the Mexican or the Russian or the Asian crisis?

Fischer: I thought I did; possibly I didn't initially understand just how severely the financial sector had been hit. Initially, in Thailand, the Asian crisis looked like an old-fashioned balance-of-payments crisis. We knew the banks were in deep trouble. We knew the government was going to have to bail them out in some way. But, in the Asian crisis, I don't think I initially appreciated just how costly it would be to bail out the banks. Financial system weaknesses were central in almost all the crises of the 1990s, except Brazil.

In dealing with the crises, I couldn't get quite as excited about moral hazard as most of the critics. The issue was prominent in the case of Mexico, but it was important to help Mexico come back to economic health quickly. And, everyone who had invested in Mexico, except for the tessobono holders, had taken a terrific hit. Given that, and given the contagion in so many countries, I couldn't see why people thought investors believed they would always be bailed out in future crises. So I couldn't figure out why so many people argued that investors hadn't learned their lesson about the dangers of investing in emerging markets from this crisis. I still believe that today.

Blanchard: What else did you take away from the Mexican crisis?

Fischer: The importance of having a coherent government and having very good technocrats—Mexico had them, but many countries don't. President Zedillo's steadiness, and the steadiness of the team, with lots of American support of course helping them stay steady, was very, very important. I took that for granted at the time, because the team I'd worked with in Israel, which was my previous crisis experience, was also very steady, but that is not a common feature.

Following the Mexico crisis, we got into the whole architecture discussion and what to do to prevent future crises. We focused on statistics and transparency and more macro and on the financial sector. But, I suspect the main lesson I took away was: Don't run balance-of-payment deficits of 8% of GDP financed by short-term borrowing. Seemed to me a good lesson to have learned. [*Laughing*]

I don't think I internalized fully how dangerous the fixed exchange rate system was. I knew that was the proximate cause of the problem. But that such a system was a standing invitation to a crisis, I don't think I internalized fully at that stage.

Blanchard: Why?

Fischer: All the Asians were doing well with more or less pegged rates, and I thought they could adjust in time. What I hadn't figured out was the political economy of a firm peg. If you really peg the exchange rate, then the longer the peg has been in place, the more the entire economic policy and the entire structure of the financial system depend on the continuance of the peg. The longer you stay with it, the more costly it is to depart from this system. Argentina suffered from this problem, in spades. I knew how dangerous the political economy of strong pegs was by the time of the Argentine crisis, but there wasn't much you could do about it at that stage. One reason it took me a while to figure that out is because I was still struck by the Israeli experience, where they pegged the rate, but adjusted it a few times, then began a crawl, and eventually floated; Poland did something similar. But Israel had enough control over capital flows to manage that, whereas the Mexicans didn't.

Blanchard: What about the later crises?

Fischer: The Asian crisis, followed by the Russian crisis, the LTCM crisis in the United States, and then the Brazilian crisis, certainly kept us busy, and at times frightened. From about October 1997 till March

1999, when it became clear that Brazil was stabilizing, there was an almost physical pressure hanging over us. I once read an account of some aspect of the Korean crisis, and wondered why I couldn't fully remember that event—and then realized that was because we were dealing simultaneously with the Indonesian crisis, which was at its height at the same time.

The Russian crisis was particularly dramatic. We saw the storm clouds gathering, especially from May 1998, but there was nothing that in the end could be done to stop the crisis from happening. The last hope was the IMF loan plus the attempted debt restructuring in July 1998. When that failed, the collapse was guaranteed. It was just a matter of how it would happen, and what the consequences would be for Russia and the rest of the world.

Global capital markets were hit very hard after the Russian devaluation and debt default in August 1998, and in September it seemed that the emerging market debt crisis was spreading to industrialized country financial markets. Fortunately, the Fed acted resolutely by cutting interest rates in October 1998. It was followed a bit later by the ECB, and a few months later the global crisis seemed to be over.

Of course, we did much more than deal with crises at the IMF. I was there during the transition process of the former Soviet-bloc economies, and I think we helped those countries a lot. And then there were other economies that were not in the headlines, where I thought we made a positive difference, for instance, Jordan.

So my time at the IMF was really an absolutely fabulous experience. I was fortunate enough to be at the center of a financial storm in a period of immense historical interest, with highly talented colleagues. It was a great privilege to be in that position at that time.

Blanchard: On to your most recent move, you joining Citigroup.

Fischer: I decided to leave the Fund at an age when I could still have another career. I debated long and hard, very hard, about going to an academic or research institution, or becoming an independent—to work at home, act as an economic adviser, take part in conferences, and sit on boards—or joining a financial institution. I decided I would like to join a financial institution, to try my hand at something at which I might be good, and for which my previous experience would be a benefit. I'd never been in a private sector and it interested me. That's how I decided. And among the alternatives, Citigroup looked the most attractive. Bob Rubin and Jeff Shafer, and other colleagues I knew, were there.

Working in the private sector is very interesting. Our team is as good as you are going to find anywhere. The challenges are intellectually as tough as you are going to find anywhere. The organizational problems in an organization of 280,000 people are more severe than you are going to find almost anywhere. And I am able to continue to do economics because among other assignments, I am the head of the country risk committee. I think about finance because a lot of the guys are doing finance; I think about the macro because we are talking about what is going to happen in the United States and other economies all the time. There are fascinating human interactions all around the place. So, it is a very exciting, intellectually very exciting, life.

Blanchard: Is having been an academic an enormous plus or minus?

Fischer: I used to say in the IMF, when someone would try to dismiss an argument by saying that it was academic, "You mean the conclusions follow from the assumptions, and the arguments are logical?"

At the IMF, my background was probably an ideal fit. Here, the finance side is more important, and fortunately I do have a lot of finance from various stages of my MIT career. It is immensely useful to have the intellectual framework of a macroeconomist. It probably doesn't matter that much for the guys who are trading. Some of them are very good at trading, even though they probably don't have a macroeconomic framework in mind. What they have is experience and smarts. They probably do have some framework, but it is not the one I have. We can have good conversations, and we probably educate each other, but I don't think like they do and they don't think like I do, and they are better at what they do, and I am probably better at what I do.

Blanchard: Are there weaknesses of being an academic in a place like that? Do we think too much? Do we see both sides too much? Are we a bit slow?

Fischer: The caricature would be that we dither. A possible weakness of being an academic is that you don't understand you have to make decisions even when you don't know everything. But I don't think most academics would be subject to this problem when put in a situation where decisions have to be made. If they didn't like making decisions, that isn't where they would end up. It was the same at the IMF. At the end of meeting, you had to make a decision, so you did.

Blanchard: How often did you find you had to make a decision based on much less information than you'd have wanted?

Fischer: In a crisis, much of the time. That's almost the definition of a crisis. In a crisis you find yourself saying, we have to choose A or B or C. You would always look for the D or the E. But things are collapsing now, and if they collapse, many people's lives and well-being will be even more badly damaged. The situation has to be saved in some way. You object to moral hazard and you object to bailouts, but in the end you ask what's the best among several difficult choices. You would like a few more days or weeks to think about it but you don't have that time.

It's the same here in the private sector. You cannot sit something out when you are not sure of what is happening, for you are never sure; you have to take bets. One of the many strengths of Bob Rubin is that he is totally calm about that. Very rational, committed to probabilistic thinking. That means he does not commit the fallacy of, "If I lost money yesterday, I made a mistake yesterday." A fallacy many of us are inclined to commit. Of course, if you lose money every day for a year you probably made a mistake.

Blanchard: Back to academic economics. How do you see the state of macro today?

Fischer: I am very happy the field seems to come back to dealing with a world I can recognize, or at least is trying to deal with a world that I can recognize. There was a long period during which arguments were more about methodology than about the way the world worked—the rational expectations revolution or the equilibrium revolution—seemed set to conquer the world and you didn't know what to do about it. That tension is reflected in our book *Lectures in Macroeconomics*, because we allowed those somewhat [*laughing*] inconsistent chapters in the end of the book. I was very happy to have them in the book. There just *is* a useful macroeconomics.

I see two evolutions today. One is that there is a bunch of researchers who do a lot of really relevant and very good work, which I think is much better today than it has ever been. There is also much progress in our use of data. For many years, we said "With the data we now have available, we should be able to understand much more." Well, finally this is happening and we are learning a lot from these large databases. The second, which makes me very happy, is the beginning of the end of the great split between freshwater and saltwater economics. Although the split is still evident, convergence is also clearly under way. And I think that is very healthy for the profession. I pick up the *QJE* frequently, the *AER* likewise, even the *JPE*, and find myself even if not reading the articles then at least interested in the conclusions and saying "Gee, this is really interesting. Gee, this really makes a difference." So, I think we are way better off. And I am glad that all this happened. Many people get the credit, Larry Summers prominently among them, and many others at the National Bureau.

Blanchard: The next question is related. Tell us about macro seen from the various seats that you've had. Are there big holes, big issues that we are not working on?

Fischer: When I had to deal with a problem, I was more impressed by the fact that there was typically a model that was useful than by the fact that nobody had ever worked on something. I don't know what the big holes are. Are we working on the right issues? The right issues in macro are the ones about what determines long-term growth, what determines productivity growth, what determines why some economies have these structural problems. We are certainly working on it very intensely, and I think with considerable insight. The hard part, as I said before, is the political economy, and how to make things happen.

Let me take the risk of saying something that I cringe at when I hear it: "I think we more or less know the policies that would work." Saying that always makes me nervous, but now I've said it.

Blanchard: Including Africa? Forgetting political economy issues, we know what should be done?

Fischer: You're right. I am less convinced of that for Africa than I am for Asia. Then I have to ask myself why. It comes down to human capital. We have underestimated how much work needs to be done on two things: human capital creation and the closely correlated issue of the creation of institutions supportive of economic activity and growth. So, those issues are there, but to say nobody is working on them is certainly not right. Everybody is working on them. So, I don't expect some blinding revelation to emerge that will say that, if only people would work on X, Y, and Z, we could all do things much, much better.

Blanchard: You just focused on the long run, not on the short run at all. Are you buying the Lucas argument that it is less important? Or do you think we actually understand it well enough?

Fischer: I think we are in somewhat better shape on the short run. There are two aspects of the Lucas argument. One is: In the long run, growth is all that matters. That's something that has been understood since the days of Adam Smith. That is why people worked on growth theory for so long. The other proposition is that recessions don't really matter because the loss of consumer surplus is five decimal places down. That strikes me as a problem with the calculation or in the welfare function. So, that is not what leads me to focus on growth. It's that, growth problems aside, we know a lot of what to do on the macro end. You may say "Well, you need to tell me how to get fiscal budgets balanced at times of prosperity so I can use fiscal policy actively in recessions." Well, that's political economy again. And there it's harder.

Blanchard: One last question here. You can answer it if you want. Advice to young researchers.

Fischer: It is critical to get yourself the right set of tools when you are young.

Blanchard: You used to say this when I was a student. You haven't changed your mind.

Fischer: I haven't changed my mind on this topic in the least. If you look at our profession, there are people I know who are extremely gifted, but who spend all their lives apologizing for not being able to do econometrics or algebra. Some, like the late Charlie Kindleberger, manage to surmount that. Some don't. And you need to get yourself the self-confidence of knowing you can handle these techniques, and can operate at a fully professional level.

Once you've got that, then you need to find a problem that is both interesting and important—potentially important. I've been surprised over the years by how often friends who worked on things I didn't think mattered but later turned out to have hit a jackpot. One of my MIT graduate student friends wrote a thesis on gas pipelines in Canada. It seemed to me as totally lacking in interest, even though he was interested. But his ship came home in 1973. And so, you need to believe your topic has the potential to be important at some time. And you should certainly find it interesting.

Once you've done that once, it becomes easier and easier to find interesting problems as you do more research.

13

An Interview with Jacques Drèze

Interviewed by Pierre Dehez
UNIVERSITÉ CATHOLIQUE DE LOUVAIN

and

Omar Licandro
EUROPEAN UNIVERSITY INSTITUTE

May 2004

Jacques Drèze was born in Verviers, Belgium, in 1929 and completed his Ph.D. in economics in 1958 at Columbia. His contribution to economics is exceptional, opening up new paths of research in various areas including general equilibrium, decision theory, game theory, econometrics (in particular, Bayesian econometrics), followed by contributions to macroeconomics and economic policy. Drèze has been President of the Econometric Society as well as associate editor and co-editor of *Econometrica*, founding member and first President of the European Economic Association, President of the International Economic Association, and honorary member of the American Economic Association and the National Academy of Sciences. He has received 15 honorary doctorates, including one from the University of Chicago. He has engaged in the promotion and development of research and higher education in Europe, being a founding member of the Center for Operations Research and Econometrics (CORE) and of the European Doctoral Program in Quantitative Economics (EDP). He has also actively participated in the most pressing economic problems in Europe.

Reprinted from *Macroeconomic Dynamics*, 9, 2005, 429–461. Copyright © 2005 Cambridge University Press.

The interview mainly aims at inviting Jacques Drèze to explain what have been his major contributions and what avenues he suggests for future research in macroeconomics. The interview has been conducted sequentially. It started in October 2002 at the European University Institute. The long material collected along these highly illuminating talks was polished and condensed in the following pages. They are organized in the following way. The first section refers to Jacques's initial experiences in Belgium, followed by his study of economics in the United States. The second section is devoted to the unity underlying an apparent diversity in his research interests. The third section is devoted to his more recent contributions to macroeconomics, which may be stated as "incomplete markets drive multiplicity of equilibria, calling for active economic policies." The interview concludes with his contribution to the promotion of research and, in particular, research institutions across Europe.

Both Pierre Dehez and Omar Licandro were students of Jacques Drèze. Dehez and Drèze co-authored several papers, some of which are mentioned in the interview.

Licandro: Different stories were told at the time I was a student at the University of Louvain concerning the reasons that motivated you to study economics: your banking experience, your contacts with unions, your studies at the University of Liege. Were these initial times important for your intellectual development? What have you learned from them and

Figure 13.1 Jacques Drèze in the CORE office, in the late eighties, illustrating second-best wage rigidities.

Figure 13.2   London embankment, 1949, selling sterling forward on behalf of Belgian wool washers.

how they have influenced your research?

Drèze: When I graduated from high school in 1946, I enrolled for a degree in philosophy at Louvain. The plan did not materialize due to the accidental death of my older brother a few weeks before commencement. This was a very hard blow for my parents, and I decided to stay with them, go to work for my father, serving as a secretary, chauffeur, and assistant, but mostly keeping him company and providing the stimulation of introducing me to his trade. At the same time, I enrolled for a degree in business and economics at the nearby University of Liege. My father was a small-town banker, in a one-industry town: textiles and textile machinery. His business was very modest, but these were the years of postwar reconstruction, and my father's customers faced all sorts of new financial problems. As I had no fixed duties at the bank, and had progressively acquired a basic understanding of finance, I went on a number of special assignments that were very instructive—like finding counterparts in London, for forward transactions on foreign currencies, negotiating barter agreements in Finland to enable a local firm to pay for textile machinery with pig iron, raising equity capital for a small family-owned firm, or even serving as mediator for a labor conflict.

So, by the age of 20 or 21, I had come to grips with a set of real economic problems of some sophistication. This was more challenging than the curriculum in business and economics at Liege, where I was not attending classes anyhow. In these early postwar years, modern economics had not yet come to Liege. I managed to graduate without suspecting the existence of a scientific discipline of economics.

Dehez: Then, the American experience came. How did you decide to go to the States, and to work for a Ph.D.? Why did you go to Columbia?

Drèze: When I graduated from Liege, the University urged me to apply for a fellowship to study in the United States. University authorities were disappointed to find few Liege students among the bursaries of the Belgian American Educational Foundation, and chased up graduates with honors as potential applicants. One of my Liege professors explained that the best economics program in the United States was at Columbia, where John Maurice Clark taught. Little did he realize that Clark had retired nine years earlier. . . . Actually, I was lucky, because Columbia in the early 1950s had some excellent faculty members, including three that I worked with more closely: my adviser George Stigler; my thesis supervisor William Vickrey, and Abram Bergson (of welfare-function fame).

I did a standard first year, culminating in the Ph.D. qualifying examinations. At the beginning of my second year, Stigler took issue with my plan to spend the year at Columbia preparing for the field exams, prior to my impending military service in Belgium. Stigler told me: "Do not go back to Belgium having attended only Columbia; to become an independent thinker, you must listen to people who disagree with us. Take the field exams as soon as possible and then visit some other university or universities before returning to Belgium."

That is the best advice I ever got. I followed it with enthusiasm. I took the field exams in January, with four fields (theory, mathematical economics, welfare, and cycles) that Stigler described as four names for theory, and proceeded to Cambridge, Massachusetts, for the spring term. There, I could attend the seminars of Samuelson, Leontief, and Haberler, as well as interact with younger people like Daniel Ellsberg (I was probing for a thesis topic related to uncertainty). May and June I spent at the Cowles Commission, where I met Marschack, Koopmans, and Debreu, as well as Houthakker, Beckman, or Telser. Next I attended summer school in Ann Arbor, where the Survey Research Center had set up the large database of the Survey of Consumer Finance and was pioneering microeconometrics. Klein was there, also Jim Morgan, and of course, George Katona, the psychologist who had founded the Center.

In the meantime, I had in December 1953 heard Franco Modigliani present the life-cycle model, which I found very convincing. But lifetime income is far from certain. I wrote to Modigliani, stating a potential interest in extending the model to uncertainty. At his invitation, I visited him in Pittsburgh in May 1954. Our conversation lasted six hours, during which we understood the difference between immediate and delayed resolution of uncertainty, with application to savings decisions—the root of a paper published in 1972.

This was my first personal experience with progress in research. It was also the start of a life-long association with Franco Modigliani, which was to prove influential for my own career.

So, thanks to a three-month deferment granted by the Belgian army, I spent the fall of 1954 at Carnegie, associating with Modigliani and Miller,

Figure 13.3 With lifelong friend Franco Modigliani (right) in Rome, 1992, after the Baffi Lecture.

but also Herbert Simon, Charnes and Cooper, Cyert and March or Jack Muth, and the team developing linear decision rules. I took a course there in multivariate statistics, to make up for the absence of any econometric teaching at Columbia, and discovered operations research, which proved valuable when I did my military service as an OR specialist [*sic*] working for the Quarter Master General.

Licandro: This brings us to the diversity of your contributions to our science: from economic theory to economic policy, from econometrics to operations research, from general equilibrium to game theory, from micro- to macroeconomics. Why have you decided to extend your research in so many different areas? What are the connecting themes behind this variety of research subjects?

Drèze: There are actually two quite distinct answers to that question: the first brings out the substantial unity underlying an apparent diversity, whereas the second accounts for the residual diversity. As an economist primarily interested in real-world problems, my theoretical interests have been driven in part by the substantive theme of allocation under uncertainty, in part by the persistent desire to integrate theoretical advances into a unified approach, namely, general equilibrium theory—a field that I taught at Louvain for 25 years.

Regarding uncertainty, my interest originates in early work related to decision theory. Thus, my Ph.D. thesis was entitled "Individual decision-making under partially controllable uncertainty." It dealt with two extensions of the model of individual decision in games against nature as developed by L.J. Savage (1972) in *The Foundations of Statistics*. The extensions concern state-dependent preferences and moral hazard. The relevance of these extensions is clearly brought out in the application to safety that I pursued in the early sixties [Drèze (1962)].

Dehez: That is indeed an interesting application, which I enjoyed developing further with you 20 years later [Dehez and Drèze (1982)]! Can you explain a bit?

Drèze: In 1960, two French engineers were wondering how much should be spent on investments enhancing road safety. So they tried to define the economic value of a life saved. They suggested measuring that economic value by the future income of a potential victim—a consideration also retained in the compensation to the heirs of the 9/11 victims—and stumbled on the question: Should the value of future consumption be subtracted, in order to appraise society's *net* loss? I realized at once that this very question pointed to the basic flaw of the approach: people want to survive and consume, not starve! Going back to the root of the problem, I introduced what is known today as the "willingness to pay" approach to valuing lives in safety analysis. How much would an individual be willing to pay to reduce his probability of accidental death? That is for the individual to decide, given his resources on the one hand, given the subjective importance he attaches to survival on the other hand. That subjective value is not reducible to objective calculations; also, it is diminishing in the size of the probability gain. Road safety being a public good, individual willingness to pay should then be aggregated as in the Lindahl–Samuelson theory of public goods.

Dehez: Indeed, my dear Watson! But how does that relate to your thesis?

Drèze: When the "state of the world" is either life or death, it is clear that preferences among "consequences" are state dependent! Also, when the decisions aim at enhancing safety, it is clear that the probabilities of the states are not given, but depend upon the chosen "course of action." So, Savage's model is not suitable; it must be extended to state-dependent preferences and action-dependent probabilities. These were the very extensions pursued in the thesis. Note that the literature is loaded with models where agents maximize expected utility over actions that entail not only consequences but also variable probabilities. I was after the axiomatic foundations of such behavior.

Dehez: Did your thesis already provide these foundations?

Drèze: The thesis dealt with a model with three states of the world only. The generalization to $n > 3$ states, calling for more advanced tools, came in installments, first in 1961, then in the definitive formulation of 1987 [Drèze (1987a)], somewhat simplified more recently [Drèze and Rustichini (2004)]. Also, I conjectured in the thesis that the logic of subjective expected-utility maximization also applied to games of strategy. That conjecture is proved, at long last, in current work with Robert Aumann (2004)—a clear illustration of continuity of research interests, if I may say so.

Dehez: You are jumping over 45 years! What came after the thesis?

Drèze: While working on the thesis, I started working with Franco Modigliani on savings decisions under uncertainty [Drèze and Modigliani (1972)]. I soon realized that many other chapters of microeconomic theory similarly called for extension to uncertainty. My volume of collected papers, *Essays on Economic Decisions Under Uncertainty*, consists of several parts: individual as well as public decisions, market equilibrium, consumer as well as producer decisions, human capital, and labor contracts —a breadth singled out for praise by John Hey (1988) in his kind review of the book. My alertness to the need of spelling out the extensions to uncertainty of many economic models is no doubt rooted in my early exposure to practical business situations: Coping with uncertainty was part of the daily life of my father and of his customers.

Dehez: The collected papers appeared in 1987. You are again jumping ahead! Can you single out a few intermediate landmarks?

Drèze: In 1953, Arrow wrote a path-breaking paper, introducing states of the world and an event tree as the primitive description of exogenous uncertainties for general equilibrium analysis—a topic soon picked up by Gérard Debreu (1959) in *Theory of Value*. That was exciting, but it called for interpretation. How do subjective probabilities (and state-dependent utilities, for that matter) affect prices for contingent claims? My paper on "Market Allocation Under Uncertainty" (1971), largely conceived during my visit to the University of Chicago during 1963–64, establishes the martingale property for contingent prices, an important result further generalized by Harrison and Kreps (1979).

Yet, complete insurance or asset markets are an abstraction, no doubt essential for theoretical understanding, but devoid of empirical realism. Thus, securities traded on all U.S. primary and secondary markets account for a mere 7% of GDP! So, incomplete markets are the rule. That observation was in the foreground of my thinking on uncertainty through the sixties. When I discovered Peter Diamond's (1967) path-breaking paper on "The Role of a Stock Market in a General Equilibrium Model," I immediately sought to extend his analysis—limited to ray technologies, so that firms only choose investment levels—to more general technologies. I could not replicate his efficiency result, and eventually proved the opposite: stock-market equilibria need not be efficient, not even constrained-efficient, under incomplete markets [Drèze (1974b)]! And this, even though each firm is adopting a production plan that is Pareto efficient from the viewpoint of its shareholders, and the stock market is competitive!

Dehez: You are referring now to the so-called "Drèze criterion" for firm decisions under incomplete markets, when profit maximization is not well defined. Did you pursue that theme further?

Drèze: In several directions. Some work extended the criterion to more complex decision structures within the firm [Drèze (1987b, 1989)]. Other work applied the same analysis to nonprofit organizations [Drèze and Marchand (1976)] or to labor-managed firms [Drèze (1976b, 1989)]. A joint paper [Geanakoplos et al. (1990)] establishes the generic inefficiency of stock-market equilibria in a general model. Right now, I am extending the so-called "Drèze criterion" to many periods, thereby integrating the concern voiced by Grossman and Hart (1979), but using more general assumptions.

Dehez: Another instance of continuity in your research interests! From what you have said so far, it seems that your persistent interest in uncertainty has taken you in a variety of directions, confirming an inclination toward diversity.

Drèze: I must indeed plead guilty on that score. It is not without ground that my friend Agnar Sandmo likes to introduce me as a "Jacques of all trades." But remember: there is also a persistent quest toward integration. If I look back at the major developments of our thinking about uncertainty over the 50 years of my professional career, I trace their origins to three interacting disciplines, namely, statistical decision theory, individual decision theory, and general equilibrium. Familiarity with statistical decision theory, especially the work of Abraham Wald (1950), was a clear source of inspiration to both Jimmy Savage (1972), in his work on decision theory, and to Ken Arrow (1953), in his work on general equilibrium. I was active on both fronts. And, there is yet another offspring of that interaction, in which I too became involved, namely Bayesian statistics.

Dehez: How did that come about?

Drèze: The significant development of Bayesian statistics over the past half-century owes a lot to the pioneering research of the fifties at Harvard Business School by Pratt, Raiffa, and Schlaifer. In 1958, I was hired by Université Catholique de Louvain to teach statistics, econometrics, and OR. In statistics, I was following their lead and expounding Bayesian techniques. This was a natural approach for someone immersed in decision theory. Going from decision theory to Bayesian statistics to the economics of uncertainty was a natural route [Drèze (1972a)]. But the econometrics of the time, centered on simultaneous equations, was classical. Hence my students, who went from Bayesian statistics to classical econometrics, faced a breach of continuity. So, I went to work and wrote in 1962 a paper on the Bayesian analysis of simultaneous equations, a paper that was never published as such but was rather influential and paved the way for my own later work [Drèze (1974a, 1976a), Drèze and Morales (1976)] and that of my students Morales, Mouchart, Palm, and Richard. That explains my involvement in Bayesian econometrics, and the birth of what has sometimes been referred to as "the Louvain Bayesian school."

Dehez: So, you have been active on all three fronts just mentioned. You mentioned current work with Aumann. There were earlier forays into game theory with him.

Drèze: I do not regard myself as a professional game theorist. Bob and I did two earlier papers [Aumann and Drèze (1975, 1987)] combining his technical expertise with my economic interests. Also close to my heart is a paper with Yossi Greenberg on "hedonic coalitions" [Drèze and Greenberg (1980)], which brings in preferences of the players over the identity of the other members of the coalition in which they belong—a natural concern, as every member of an economics department knows! I wish that I could someday get back to that interesting topic . . .

Figure 13.4 With Robert Aumann (left) in Louvain-la-Neuve, 1986, celebrating the twentieth anniversary of CORE, which Aumann described as "a unique breeding ground: a place where cross-fertilization leads to the conception of new ideas, as well as a womb—a warm, supportive environment in which these ideas can grow and mature."

Dehez: Please do not bring in the future . . . We are not done with the past yet! Are we done with the recurrent theme of uncertainty?

Drèze: If I may add a final note: There is a direct link from uncertainty to macroeconomics; every macrotheorist realizes that today.

In my own thinking, the link materialized via price rigidities. Let me read to you footnote 1 of my 1975 paper on "Existence of an Exchange Equilibrium Under Price Rigidities". "The present note was motivated by research in progress on the rational aspects of wage rigidities and unemployment compensation, viewed as a form of income insurance for which market opportunities offer no substitute." Said research in progress matured progressively [Drèze (1990, 1993)], leading to my joint paper with Christian Gollier on "Risk Sharing on the Labour Market and Second-Best Wage Rigidities" [Drèze and Gollier (1993)], and to other papers on reconciling risk-sharing efficiency with productive efficiency on the labor market [Drèze (2000, 2002)]. But in the meantime, equilibrium under price rigidities had attracted the attention of macroeconomists, and the recession initiated by the oil price hikes of the seventies had gained momentum. Prompted by these real concerns, my research interests veered toward macroeconomics, but, here again, uncertainty matters, under incomplete markets. Incomplete markets not only provide the rationale for wage rigidities just mentioned, they also account for the volatility of investment and aggregate demand, which is central to macroeconomic fluctuations. My current research on "The Macroeconomics of Uncertainty and Incomplete Markets" [Drèze (2001a)] brings together my concerns for uncertainty and macroeconomics, restoring again the unity of apparently diverse themes. And it adds the dimension of endogenous, macroeconomic uncertainties. So, macroeconomics brings me back to uncertainty, which closes the loop.

Licandro: So, you are claiming again underlying homogeneity. We will come back to wage rigidities and macroeconomics, but, first, let me ask "Jacques of all trades" how he became interested in labor management?

Drèze: It all came from being a Professor-at-large at Cornell University, and being assigned the office of Jaroslav Vanek during his sabbatical. One day at lunch, the department head, T.C. Liu, said: "When Jaroslav can explain to me when a labor-managed firm will adopt labor-saving innovations, I will become interested—but not until then." In the afternoon, I was sitting in Vanek's armchair, facing a bookcase containing all the published work on labor management, and reflecting upon Liu's stricture. As my reflections took shape, they eventually led to the general equilibrium model of labor-managed economies [Drèze (1976b)]. Liu's question is answered unequivocally by my equivalence result for competitive equilibria and labor management equilibria—a result comparable to that of Oskar Lange and Fred Taylor (1938) for planned economies. Of course, I immediately went on to consider uncertainty, and the funding of labor-managed firms. That line of research merged naturally with

Figure 13.5 With Gérard Debreu (right) in 1989, during the Sixth International Symposium in Economic Theory and Econometrics, held at CORE on the occasion of Jacques Drèze's early retirement from teaching. Debreu had tallied Drèze's "48 coauthors, whose list goes from Aumann to Zellner."

my interests in incomplete markets and second-best wage rigidities, as evidenced by my Jahnsson Lectures entitled *Labour Management, Contracts, and Capital Markets* [Drèze (1989)].

Other apparent outliers came from pursuing themes linked to my mainstream research. This remark applies, for instance, to papers on stability of dynamic processes. At an early stage of research on the normative theory of the firm under uncertainty, I followed a wise suggestion of Gérard Debreu (then a visitor to CORE) and looked first at the simpler problem of efficient provision for public goods. That led to "A Tâtonnement Process for Public Goods" [Drèze and de la Vallée Poussin (1971)], the mathematics of which are generalized in Champsaur et al. (1977) and applied to macroeconomic issues in the nineties [Drèze (1991, 1999)].

Dehez: You have made several other contributions to public economics, ranging from discount rates for public investment [Sandmo and Drèze (1971)] and public sector pricing [Drèze (1985a)] to public goods with exclusion [Drèze (1980)]. Is that diversity within an outlier?

Drèze: Public economics is another field in which I had no formal training and "learned by doing." The initial investment came from writing a survey of postwar contributions of French economists [Drèze (1964)]. That was highly educational, and introduced me to second-best pricing at the hand of Marcel Boiteux. My paper on "Public Sector Pricing in a Keynesian Regime" [Drèze (1985a)] extends the Ramsey–Boiteux analysis to an economy with price rigidities—another attempt at integrating different approaches. It was influential in convincing me that looking for the macroeconomic implications of microeconomics could be more fruitful than looking for the microeconomic foundations of macroeconomics.

Dehez: How is that?

Drèze: I was curious to see what happens to inverse-elasticity pricing rules when private goods are allocated not only by prices, but also in part by quantity constraints. While extending the pricing rules, I saw a multiplier emerge! There is a specific formula in that paper, which I interpret as a multiplier. I was not looking for anything like that. It just came out of the analysis. A multiplier was at work, in an economy where some prices are rigid, and the public authorities affect the allocation of resources through their pricing policies. This came as a surprise to me: Why should a multiplier emerge in this second-best analysis? Lightning struck, and I foresaw the possibility of doing general equilibrium macroeconomics!

Dehez: Well, you were starting there from price rigidities—a natural starting point for you! I remember vividly the interest at the mid-seventies and early eighties in equilibrium under price rigidities and quantity rationing. Indeed, that work has reconciled the Keynesian and general equilibrium approaches, but that interest was mostly on the European side—not surprisingly, since the seminal contributions came from you, Bénassy, Younès, and Malinvaud. Why, in your opinion, did that interest eventually fade away?

Drèze: I have all along regretted the extent to which macrotheorists have privileged the special case of fixed prices over the more general case of imperfectly flexible prices with quantity rationing of supply allowed only when downward rigidities are binding. Though, of course, I realize that the fixed-prices case has been useful to understand the variety of market configurations (classical, Keynesian, repressed inflation) and the need to allow for a mixture of these configurations at the micro level—as is done, for instance, in the econometric work of the *Europe's Unemployment Problem* [Drèze et al. (1990)]. In a sense, I too reject the fixed-prices paradigm—while remaining convinced of the relevance and significance of price rigidities and quantity rationing. My own explanation of the disregard in which so-called "disequilibrium theory" has fallen, especially in the Anglo-Saxon world, is simple. I agree with Blanchard and Fischer (1989) that *price or wage rigidities need to be explained, not just assumed*! Providing such an explanation, and testing it empirically, is prominent on the agenda of new Keynesian economics.

In my 1986 EEA Presidential Address [Drèze (1987c)], I claim that "increasing returns, price dynamics and uncertainty" bring along market allocations that "involve rationing in a natural way." I still regard today these features, especially the last one, as leading explanations of price–wage rigidities and the associated rationing. Once the existence of uninsurable risks is recognized, an inescapable conclusion emerges: Sequential competitive clearing of spot markets can be dominated, according to second-best Pareto efficiency, by market clearing with price rigidities and quantity rationing.

Licandro: That is a bold statement! Can you outline your justification?

Drèze: Efficient risk sharing requires that the resources of every agent be independent of idiosyncratic risks and related only to society's risks. We have known this at least since the work of Karl Borch in the sixties. Under complete markets, trading in contingent claims brings that property about, but not so under incomplete markets. Thus, for a worker with no property income, risk-sharing efficiency would call for wages indexed on national income. But allocative efficiency calls for wages reflecting marginal productivities. Yet, at times of depressed labor demand, market-clearing wages would fall to reservation levels. There is thus a conflict between two dimensions of efficiency. Note that we are discussing efficiency, not redistribution.

A first-best outcome could be implemented through wage taxes and subsidies. Wage costs could be kept at marginal productivities while labor incomes would follow national income. I have pursued that theme in several papers. Edmund Phelps (1997), proceeding from a complementary motivation, has devoted a full book to the working of the scheme. In the absence of the wage subsidies, downwards wage rigidities cum unemployment benefits provide a second-best alternative.

Licandro: Jacques, this is not obvious. Do you have an intuitive explanation of how wage rigidities may imply a second-best allocation under incomplete markets?

Drèze: Downward rigidity insures labor incomes against depressed market-clearing wages, but there is a loss of productive efficiency when wages exceed the real opportunity cost of labor. Sufficient conditions for the insurance benefits to outweigh the productive inefficiencies appear in my paper with Gollier (1993). To me, that argument provides the most fundamental explanation—and perhaps justification—of observed wage rigidities. It is an extension to prospective job seekers of the reasoning first developed in the seventies by Azariadis (1975), Baily (1974), and

Figure 13.6 With Jean-Jacques Herings (right) in the CORE lounge, 2003: a coffee break away from the continuum of supply-constrained equilibria!

Gordon (1974) for workers under contract. Our extension covers general equilibrium with risk-averse firms (Dréze and Gollier, 1993).

Dehez: Incomplete markets may have motivated your work on equilibria with price rigidities, known as "Drèze equilibria" in the literature, but, motivation aside, where did the new equilibrium concept take you?

Drèze: There was some further work on efficient rationing [Drèze and Müller (1980)], or with you on supply-constrained equilibria [Dehez and Drèze (1988)]. And there was some empirical work in disequilibrium econometrics [Sneessens and Drèze (1986)], leading to *Europe's Unemployment Problem* [Drèze et al. (1990)]. While supervising that 10-country study, I became increasingly aware of an underlying multiplicity of equilibria, but the econometric model did not make room for that. Later, in the early nineties, general equilibrium theory confirmed my intuition: Price rigidities may lead to a continuum of equilibria!

When a market is not cleared by price but by quantity constraints, as under unemployment, the extent of rationing introduces an extra degree of freedom: An equality has been replaced by an inequality. For a specific market, like unskilled labor in a given area, that is obvious enough: As demand evolves, alternative rates of unemployment are compatible with the same minimum wage and unemployment benefits. General equilibrium endogenizes the demand side. The new feature is the multiplicity of macroeconomic equilibria.

My first foray in this intriguing domain, inspired mostly by early work of John Roberts (1989) and Jean-Jacques Herings (1996), dates back to 1997 [Drèze (1997)]. It is surveyed in my Presidential Address to the International Economic Association [Drèze (2001a)]. A general model, studied in a recent joint paper [Citanna et al. (2001)] is now being extended with Jean-Jacques Herings to the incomplete markets framework. This work illustrates the merits of the general equilibrium methodology for tackling macroeconomic issues. Although coordination failures have come to the attention of macrotheorists along other routes—partial equilibrium or macromodels, surveyed by Cooper and John (1988)—the link to price rigidities emerged from the general equilibrium analysis.

Licandro: Once again, we face a technical issue that deserves some explanation . . .

Drèze: Let me try. Consider first an economy consisting of one firm turning labor, supplied by households, into output. Returns are diminishing. Nominal wages are given. Households jointly supply N units of labor, collect wages and profits, and buy output. The firm maximizes profits. Any level of output using no more than N units of labor defines an underemployment equilibrium, with output price equal to marginal cost. Indeed, the firm maximizes profits, households optimize under a constraint on labor supply, and markets clear.

Dehez: That is at variance with the three-good model of Barro–Grossman (Barro and Grossman, 1976) and Malinvaud (1977), where classical equilibria are unique?

Drèze: With reference to that model, the equilibria just proposed define the frontier between classical and Keynesian unemployment, a locus indexed by output prices at given nominal wages. In the three-good model, all nominal prices are fixed. I explain in my 1997 EER paper how this implies a particular selection from the continuum associated with flexible output prices. Actually, the continuum is a general property. Thus, consider an Arrow–Debreu economy with two sets of commodities, say F commodities with flexible prices and R commodities with downward rigid nominal prices. Quantity constraints are allowed on supply alone; we are looking for a "supply-constrained equilibrium." When the rigidities bite, the R fixed nominal prices imply that $R - 1$ relative prices are given. But R markets are allowed to clear through supply constraints. There is thus one degree of freedom left. It corresponds to either the overall ratio of the flexible prices to the rigid prices, or to the overall extent of rationing for the commodities with rigid prices. Walras's Law links these two macroeconomic variables as per a Phillips curve of sorts. There remains a single degree of freedom, corresponding to the selection of a point on that Phillips curve. The question then arises. How is an element from the continuum selected? Note that competitive equilibria also exist in my economy, at nominal prices high enough.

My provisional conclusion is that the intertemporal equilibrium model must be complemented with a specification of the short-run adjustment process that links successive equilibria. That specification should embody the sources of price stickiness; it should cover the transition from one multivariate equilibrium to the next—possibly as per a tâtonnement or nontâtonnement in prices and quantity constraints, of which I have studied some examples [Drèze (1991, 1999)]; and it should perform the selection of a specific equilibrium from the equivalent of a Phillips curve, especially when the latter is multidimensional.

Licandro: Why multidimensional?

Drèze: When we move from Arrow–Debreu to the more realistic specification of incomplete markets, the degree of indeterminacy may rise, but that is really technical! Well, you asked for it. In the two-period stock-market economy with S states and J assets, J less than S, we may expect $S - J + 1$ degrees of freedom, that is, a set of equilibria of dimension $S - J + 1$! I have not encountered such a Phillips curve in the macroeconomic literature yet. Not surprising, given the limited popularity of multiple equilibria. But general equilibrium theory aims for generality. If your premises entail multiple equilibria, you had better find out, and face the consequences!

Dehez: Your answers to the last two questions refer to nominal rigidities. Your own interest in money is rather recent, I think. How does it fit into the broader picture?

Drèze: In joint work with Herakles Polemarchakis (2001) and then also Gaetano Bloise [Bloise et al. (2005)], we use a consistent and natural definition of a monetary economy: Money balances are used for transactions; they are supplied by banks, which lend them at nominal interest rates set by themselves. Thus, we are considering "inside money," the only kind issued by central banks with balanced accounts. At competitive equilibria under given nominal interest rates, there remains in such a model indeterminacy of the overall price level. In a one-period model, one would say that all relative prices are determined, but the overall price level is arbitrary—a standard feature of the Arrow–Debreu model. In a multiperiod model with certainty, the same property holds, and the inflation rates relating the price levels at successive dates are determined through a Fisher equation. That is the starting point from which different authors proceed toward determinacy along different routes, like feedback rules or the fiscal theory.

However, in the intertemporal model with uncertainty—that is, with alternative states of the world at any date—there is further indeterminacy to the following extent: At any date event, the expected rate of inflation between today and tomorrow is pinned down by interest rates, but the variability of inflation rates across alternative realizations tomorrow is unrestricted. Understandably, a single instrument, namely, the nominal interest rate, implies a single constraint, at each date event.

Licandro: Of course, price-level determinacy in monetary economies is a debated issue. Exactly what is your stance?

Drèze: The extent of indeterminacy just stated is both a headache and a blessing: a headache because we all know that price levels do not jump around like puppets, but also a blessing because indeterminacy in the abstract model leaves room for endogenous nominal rigidities to pin down price levels.

Licandro: Another enigmatic assertion! Can you explain?

Drèze: I started my Baffi Lecture at Banca d'Italia (1992) with the question: "When warfare in the Gulf bids up oil prices, do you expect the prices of books or magazines to go down?" Because many prices are set at intervals, and because many are downward rigid, the answer is clear. As relative prices vary, price stickiness generates some core inflation. This is part of the short-run adjustment process selecting an equilibrium from my continuum, from my Phillips curve if you wish.

Many macromodels of the New Keynesian vein go that route—through staggered prices, menu costs, and the like. I differ on two scores: the explanations of price stickiness—we talked about that, and the formal analysis of its implications—which brings us back to the real and nominal indeterminacy associated with price rigidities.

Licandro: And the upshot for macroeconomics is . . .

Drèze: The upshot is both substantive and methodological. On the substantive side, I feel that coordination failures associated with price–wage rigidities—whatever the origins of these rigidities may be—have their place in macroeconomic theory and policy. I only wish that I could measure the extent of coordination failures empirically, but that lies probably beyond my own horizon. On the methodological side, I am now investigating some macroeconomic implications of microeconomics in a general equilibrium model extended simultaneously to incomplete markets, money, price and wage stickiness, but also increasing returns [Dehez and Drèze (1988)] and imperfect competition [Dehez et al. (2003)]. The works! And a long way from the competitive Arrow–Debreu model. . . . As we discussed, these extensions lead to multiple equilibria, and the static intertemporal model remains to be complemented by a specification of short-run adjustments, for which generality is an open challenge.

Dehez: What equilibrium concept, or concepts, are you using?

Drèze: There is always a trade-off between generality, hence scope for realism, and tractability! In models with arbitrary finite horizons, which are also the basic tool for infinite-horizon analysis, the perfect foresight equilibrium of Radner (1972) is the easier starting point. It lends itself well to my extensions, and to the analysis of coordination failures, but perfect foresight is a strong assumption, especially under multiple equilibria, and I want to pursue more general formulations in the spirit of "temporary equilibrium" à la Grandmont (1977). Arbitrary horizons then create logical as well as technical difficulties, with which I am currently struggling.

Licandro: All that seems quite remote from contemporary macroeconomics!

Drèze: Indeed. My vision is that the extended model is susceptible of encompassing macroeconomics! What I mean is: Most of the models used in macroeconomics concern economies that fit within the general model just outlined. Mostly, of course, macrotheory uses specific models —and reaches specific conclusions, but a general approach adds perspective to the more specialized contributions. The clear identification of additional assumptions that lead from the general model to a tractable special case permits relating alternative specific models to each other, and facilitates transfers of results or techniques across specific models. These benefits largely account for the success of microeconomics as an integrated discipline within the broad framework of general equilibrium theory. I foresee today the possibility of integrating formally micro- and macroeconomic analyses in a common theoretical framework. And I stress again the intellectual comfort of a unified approach to both fields, a comfort no doubt aspired to by students and teachers alike. Of course, I realize that this is not the alpha and omega of macroeconomics. I am all the more interested in special models yielding specific results, especially dynamic models, that I envision how they can be fitted into a unified structure.

Licandro: We have taken up a number of questions relating to macroeconomic theory, but not to policies. Does your eclectic approach to macroeconomics suggest specific policy recommendations?

Drèze: Definitely so! Not that they are particularly original, but at least they are clear-cut. They aim at coping with situations of underemployment of resources, including an element of coordination failure— that is, of underemployment not due entirely to wrong prices and wages —but reflecting in addition a demand gap under incomplete markets. Investment is postponed at a second-order cost to firms but with a first-order effect on aggregate demand. Savings correspond to postponed spending not confirmed to producers. Reflating aggregate demand could sustain an equilibrium with more activity and employment, possibly at unchanged prices and wages. Here lies my different rationale for demand management policies.

Licandro: Why do you say "different"? Aren't we simply back to good old Keynesian deficit spending?

Drèze: Wait, I am not done yet. One should be aware of the fact that coordination failures are potentially recurrent: Whatever we do today, we will again be faced by a continuum of equilibria tomorrow. If a bad equilibrium comes about, we may be able to remedy it through a suitable policy, but we must realize that we may have to repeat the policy over and over again. So, a policy aimed at overcoming a coordination failure through deficit spending, a fiscal expansion, could, if repeated over time, lead to a continuous increase in the level of the public debt. That would result in another type of disequilibrium, which would call for corrective action; it would not be a sustainable policy in the long run.

That is also the reason why I have increasingly advocated coping with coordination failures, not through deficit spending or digging holes, but through socially profitable investments [Drèze et al. (1998)]. Under price–wage rigidities, there exist investment projects that are socially profitable, though not privately profitable—if only because private wage costs do not reflect the social opportunity cost of labor. These investments will have the same merits for reflating aggregate demand as other forms of fiscal expansion, but they will not lead to instability in the long run, because the service of the debt will be covered by the returns to the investments. And they will have no reason to be offset by private savings, thus avoiding the Ricardian equivalence trap. Of course, the policy is less easy to implement: It is straightforward to decree a tax cut; it is much more difficult to engineer a profitable investment program of similar impact on aggregate demand.

Licandro: Let me press this point. You say that if there is a coordination failure, there is a role for economic policies. In a dynamic framework, as displayed by the real world, the multiplicity of equilibria will occur not only today but also tomorrow, and the day after tomorrow, et cetera. So agents need to coordinate their expectations not only today but also over the whole future. What is wrong with following simple policy rules?

Drèze: I do not put much emphasis on the notion of coordination of expectations. For me, it is natural that different agents hold different expectations, and surveys confirm that view, but what matters to avoidance of severe coordination failures, of severe underutilization of resources, is a certain degree of optimism in anticipations. In that sense, one could talk about coordinating expectations on reasonably favorable outcomes.

Contemporary theorists, such as Michael Woodford, stress that monetary policy rules aim primarily at anchoring inflation expectations. Let us transpose this reasoning to forestalling high unemployment. Suppose the government had a large portfolio of investment projects that are ready to be implemented, projects concerning public housing, urban renewal, urban transportation, high-speed communication, what not. Let the government announce: Should we see signs of a deep recession setting in, we would immediately release investment programs to reflate aggregate demand. If the agents believe that, they will expect economic activity to remain at levels reasonably close to full employment, in exactly the same way that they would anticipate monetary policy to keep inflation rates within a narrow band. There lies the scope for intervention offered by the continuum of short-run equilibria.

Licandro: So, your policy recommendations are definitely demand-oriented?

Drèze: When participating in policy exercises in Europe [Drèze et al. (1988, 1994), Drèze and Bean (1991)], I have been a consistent advocate of two-handed policies addressing simultaneously the demand side and the supply side. And more recently, I have advocated wage subsidies for the low skilled, as an alternative to wage floors, a point that we have discussed earlier. This is related to coordination failures, which I trace back to price or wage rigidities. Unfortunately, the second-best analysis for wages that we discussed earlier does not take that dimension into account. There is thus an extra reason to be wary of excessive wage rigidities—while still realizing that *ex ante* stabilization of labor incomes is part of economic efficiency. Wage subsidies are an answer, to which I draw the attention of the profession as well as of policymakers.

Licandro: This brings us to the many debates on crucial issues for the future of Europe you were involved in. How do you explain that economists still have a limited influence on the political debate in Europe? Is there something important to be learnt from the American experience?

Drèze: There is one item on which the position paper "Growth and Employment, the Scope for a European Initiative" [Drèze et al. (1994)] produced in the early nineties by 13 Belgian and French economists, convened by Edmond Malinvaud and myself, has been influential. In very brief summary, that position paper advocated the two sets of measures that I have just reviewed with you: demand-side measures in the form of public investment and supply-side measures in the form of reduced labor costs for low-skilled workers. The position paper was one of the first public documents to stress the deterioration in the market position of unskilled workers. So, for the unskilled workers, we advocated eliminating employers' contributions to social security. That was a fairly drastic suggestion, which would have reduced the cost of low-skilled labor by something like 30% to 40%.

Of these two measures, the first has been completely ignored; it remains so that in official European circles, aggregate demand is not a preoccupation. This reflects in part neglect by economists, in part ineffectiveness at the national, as opposed to the EU level. Anyhow, our recommendation of wage subsidies at the low end of the wage scale did retain attention. Immediately, the staff of the European Commission initiated a set of simulations, which suggested that indeed the proposed measure would have a positive effect on aggregate employment, and especially on employment of the low skilled. Several countries have introduced such measures. Today, I know better about France and Belgium. The rate of social security abatements at the minimum wage is roughly 18% in France and 15% in Belgium. That is less than what we were recommending, but it is still substantial. So, I feel that here is one instance where suggestions by economists have been taken seriously by decisionmakers.

Licandro: Are you pointing to this episode as exceptional?

Drèze: It is indeed the standard view that economists are less influential in Europe than in the United States. Two comments on that issue. First, in Europe there is no economic authority comparable to the U.S. government. Why? Because Europe is a Union, a confederation of states, so the prerogatives at the level of the Union are limited; the decision process at that level is complicated and carries limitations. Economic advisers to the Commission are remote from the decision-making body, namely the Council of Ministers. In contrast, in the United States, the chief economic adviser attends the meetings of the cabinet where the decisions are made. So, there is no chain of communication; the economic adviser is right there. In addition, the cabinet in the United States has much more direct authority than the Council of Ministers in Europe. In that sense, there is much less influence of economic advisers on policy decisions in Europe than in the United States.

Dehez: You announced two comments. . . .

Drèze: Indeed, there is another aspect to the question: the debate among professional economists, and the communication from the professional economists to the general public. Here again, there is a big difference between the United States and Europe. It has been customary for a number of leading U.S. economists to write columns in periodicals. Also, panels regularly organized at the AEA meetings, by Brookings or the NBER, and so on, nourish the debate among economists. We do not have the same habit in Europe, even though I wish to commend CEPR and the journal *Economic Policy* for their valuable forum.

Licandro: Your contribution to the development of economics in Europe exceeds your own research: the creation of CORE, the European Doctoral Program in which some of the more famous European departments participate, and the European Economic Association, of which you were the first President, are noticeable examples. Why did you attach so much importance to institutions? What were the roles of these three institutions in the progress of economic research in Europe and why is economic research still led by American universities?

Drèze: You are indeed right that my contribution to economics in Europe has consisted mostly in encouraging, promoting, and facilitating the work of others rather than in my own research. In fact, if I look at it from a strictly personal viewpoint, perhaps my main contribution to economics has been to sire Jean Drèze, who has contributed very positively and significantly to development economics, and nowadays plays an active role in promoting a form of social security in India.

To get to your question, and to start with CORE, let me recount the following. I came to Louvain—Leuven in those days—in 1958, after holding my first academic appointment at Carnegie during 1957–58. I was extremely happy professionally in the Carnegie environment, which was more supportive and stimulating than anything I have seen elsewhere, and that is saying a lot for someone who has spent so many years at CORE. The situation in Belgium was extremely different. I was lucky to have an offer from Louvain and to start working there, but the stimulation and the excitement of Carnegie were of course no longer present, and my immediate conclusion was: I cannot stay here unless I have colleagues. That explains why I was eager to organize a small research unit that could bring several people together.

Dehez: By "a small research unit," you mean CORE—an understatement, no doubt.

Drèze: Not initially! The opportunity to start CORE arose in 1964 when Hans Theil, who had developed the Econometric Institute in Rotterdam, left for the United States. The endorsement he was receiving from the Institute of Management Science (in which my Carnegie friends were influential) could be transferred to Louvain. That was helpful in convincing the university to support a small research unit in operations research, econometrics, and mathematical economics. The university would provide some premises and a small budget, with professors from the business school, engineering, and economics getting together. I was coming back from a visit to the University of Chicago in 1964 with the feeling that there was a place for some outfit in Europe where Americans could spend their sabbaticals. I immediately advertised to my friends in the United States that CORE would be glad to accommodate visitors.

Indeed, during the first two years, we had visitors such as Merton Miller and Jack Hirshleifer. In 1966, CORE was a small operation, but it was distinctly international.

Dehez: And then?

Drèze: Then we had a piece of good luck: My good friend George Shultz tipped us that the Ford Foundation was eager to intervene on the European scene of business and economics. The Foundation had done that in the United States, felt that it had been successful, wanted to do something similar in Europe, but was eager to do it at an international level, not at the level of a single country. I could go at some length into anecdotes about how we eventually received the support from the Ford Foundation. Be it enough to say that by 1968, two years after the creation of CORE, we were partly—and temporarily—financed by the Ford Foundation. We had received adequate facilities from the University, at the request of the Ford Foundation in fact, and we had seven or eight visitors for the whole academic year. In 1968, the names that come to mind, besides Ton Barten and Werner Hildenbrand who had joined CORE on a standing basis, include Gérard Debreu, the late Karl Vind and Birgit Grodal, David Schmeidler from Israël, Truman Bewley, et cetera. CORE had become a lively place.

Dehez: CORE at the time was rather unique on the European continent—a monopoly that has eroded over time.

Drèze: I am truly gratified and proud that several other European universities have over the years emulated CORE. The contribution of CORE to economics in Europe is again less the research output produced in-house than the stimulus to others by the simple example that it could be done. The developments at Bonn, at Tilburg where CentER started as a mirror image of CORE with Ton Barten as director, at Delta in Paris, at GREQAM in Marseille, were all inspired by the CORE experience and organized along similar lines by former CORE members or visitors. So, in that sense, CORE has been very influential on the European scene.

Dehez: CORE is a research center. How did it impact on teaching?

Drèze: Inside CORE, there soon developed a debate about the advisability of having our own doctoral program. Some members of CORE were strongly in favor of doing that, both in order to firm-up university support, and because doctoral students are stimulating and helpful in research. The counter-argument said: If we cannot offer a program of the highest quality, better send students abroad and let them study, say in the United States or in London. For a number of years, the two camps were holding their position and nothing happened. In 1975, there had been another debate at the CORE board, and I was mulling over the issue. Among the visitors that year was David Hendry, then a professor at LSE. In thinking about the issue, I told myself: Why don't we cooperate with the LSE? Then: Why stop there? Werner Hildenbrand had moved from CORE to Bonn; he was still in close contact with us and eager to cooperate. So the idea came up: Why not have a joint doctoral program with LSE, and Bonn? Of course, my own experience (being kicked out of Columbia by George Stigler to listen to people who disagreed with him) was not forgotten. If students engaged in a joint degree between Bonn, LSE, and Louvain, with obligation to attend at least two of these institutions, they would necessarily listen to people from two different schools of thought! When I talked with Hendry and Hildenbrand, both were immediately enthusiastic. That is how the European Doctoral Program in Quantitative Economics, better known as EDP, was started in 1978. It has some 120 graduates to date. The first of these, a certain Pierre Dehez, set the standards! One of the indicators of success is that EDP has been copied and emulated by several others. These joint degrees, with obligation for the students to spend time at two institutions, are now part of the educational landscape of economics in Europe, and I regard this as a very positive development. The road toward emulating American excellence in higher education and research is the road of cooperation, pending concentration.

Dehez: Did the European Economic Association also matter?

Drèze: The idea of the European Economic Association came up at CORE in discussions between Jean Gabszewicz and Jacques Thisse. Then, Louis Phlips convened the first meeting of about 30 economists from different European countries where the project was discussed. Most of the participants soon agreed on what should be the basic features of the EEA; they decided to go ahead and launch it. It took a good start. For the first year of official activity, including the first congress in Vienna in 1986, we reached 1,800 dues-paying members. To date the number hovers around 2,000. That, I must say, is my disappointment about the EEA. It is today part of the economic scene in Europe. It is playing a useful role in issuing a journal of internationally recognized quality, in holding annual meetings, in organizing summer schools for young Ph.D.'s and progressively in serving as a platform for the European labor market for economists, but somehow these services are not valued sufficiently by large numbers to have an increased membership. It is significant that people become members when they attend a congress, but in later years, if they do not attend the congress, they do not renew their membership, indicating that they do not value the services to individuals.

Licandro: In your CV, you used to include the long list of your Ph.D. students, most of them well-known economists. Were they the output of your tireless work or a major input in your research technology?

Drèze: The list is not that long: 20 Louvain Ph.D.'s (there were a couple elsewhere) over 20 years (1968–89), that is, one per year,

Figure 13.7 With another kind of big fish, April 1995: underway from Panama to Galapagos during circumnavigation under sail with wife Monique.

meaning that I would supervise three or four students at a time. It is unquestionably true that I had the privilege of supervising a majority of first-rate dissertations, by students who remained active in research and have acquired notoriety. When I retired from teaching in 1989, 19 out of these 20 Louvain Ph.D.'s were active in research. Many, but by no means all of them worked in areas where I had made a research investment myself. Some of them introduced me to areas new to me: general equilibrium theory with Jean Gabszewicz in the mid-sixties, or disequilibrium econometrics with Henri Sneessens in the late seventies. In all cases, I learned a lot from them, and I remain most grateful. In 1989, I made the mistake of giving up Ph.D. supervision, a mistake that I regret to this date. I mention this for the benefit of other early retirees. There is no doubt that my work in Bayesian econometrics or in empirical estimation of macroeconomic models with rationing, for instance, was substantially extended by my students, and enriched through interaction with them. A majority of these Ph.D. students had taken courses from me here, so the transition to a thesis topic was natural. I would not describe it as "technological," but it illustrates the virtue of including in taught courses some visions of the research frontier. Remembering your student days and looking at both your careers, I feel gratified!

REFERENCES

Arrow, K. (1953) The role of securities in the optimal allocation of risk bearing. *Econometrie* 11, 41–47.

Aumann, R.J. & J.H. Drèze (1975) Cooperative games with coalition structures. *International Journal of Game Theory* 3, 217–237.

Aumann, R.J. & J.H. Drèze (1987) Values of markets with satiation or fixed prices. *Econometrica* 54, 1271–1318.

Aumann, R.J. & J.H. Drèze (2004) Assessing Strategic Risk, DP 361, Center for the Study of Rationality, Hebrew University of Jerusalem.

Azariadis, C. (1975) Implicit contracts and underemployment equilibria. *Journal of Political Economy* LXIII, 1183–1202.

Baily, M.N. (1974) Wages and unemployment under uncertain demand. *Review of Economic Studies* XLI, 37–50.

Barro, R.J. & S.J. Grossman (1976) *Money, Employment and Inflation*. New York: Cambridge University Press.

Blanchard, O.J. & S. Fisher (1989) *Lectures on Macroeconomics*. Cambridge, MA: MIT Press.

Bloise, G., J.H. Drèze & H. Polemarchakis (2005) Monetary equilibria over an infinite horizon. *Economic Theory* 25, 51–74.

Champsaur, P., J.H. Drèze & C. Henry (1977) Stability theorems with economic applications. *Econometrica* 45, 273–294.

Citanna, A., H. Crès, J.H. Drèze, P.J.-J. Herings & A. Villanacci (2001) Continua of underemployment equilibria reflecting coordination failures, also at Walrasian prices. *Journal of Mathematical Economics* 36, 169–200.

Cooper, R. & A. John (1988) Coordinating coordination failures in Keynesian models. *Quarterly Journal of Economics* 103, 441–463.

Debreu, G. (1959) *The Theory of Value: An Axiomatic Analysis of Economic Equilibrium*. New York: Wiley.

Dehez, P. & J.H. Drèze (1982) State-dependent utility, the demand for insurance and the value of safety. In M.W. Jones-Lee (ed.), *The Value of Life and Safety*, Proceedings of a Conference held by The Geneva Association, pp. 41–65. Amsterdam: North-Holland.

Dehez, P. & J.H. Drèze (1984) On supply-constrained equilibria. *Journal of Economic Theory* 33, 172–182.

Dehez, P. & J.H. Drèze (1988) Competitive equilibria with quantity-taking producers and increasing returns to scale. *Journal of Mathematical Economics* 17, 209–230.

Dehez, P., J.H. Drèze & T. Suzuki (2003) Imperfect competition à la Negishi, also with fixed costs. *Journal of Mathematical Economics* 39, 219–238.

Diamond, P. (1967) The role of a stock market in a general equilibrium model with technological uncertainty. *American Economic Review* 57, 759–776.

Drèze, J.H. (1961) Les fondements logiques de l'utilité cardinale et de la probabilité subjective. In *La Décision*, Colloques Internationaux du CNRS, pp. 73–97. Paris: CNRS.

Drèze, J.H. (1962) L'utilité sociale d'une vie humaine. *Revue Française de Recherche Opérationnelle* 23, 93–118.

Drèze, J.H. (1964) Some postwar contributions of French economists to theory and public policy. *American Economic Review* 54 (2), 1–64.

Drèze, J.H. (1971) Market allocation under uncertainty. *European Economic Review* 2, 133–165.

Drèze, J.H. (1972a) A tâtonnement process for investment under uncertainty in private ownership economies. In G.P. Szegö & K. Shell (eds.), *Mathematical Methods in Investment and Finance*, pp. 3–23. Amsterdam: North-Holland.

Drèze, J.H. (1972b) Econometrics and decision theory. *Econometrica* 40, 1–17.

Drèze, J.H. (1974a) Bayesian theory of identification in simultaneous equations models. In S.E. Fienberg & A. Zellner (eds.), *Studies in Bayesian Econometrics and Statistics*, pp. 159–174. Amsterdam: North-Holland.

Drèze, J.H. (1974b) Investment under private ownership: optimality, equilibrium and stability, Ch. 9. In *Allocation Under Uncertainty: Equilibrium and Optimality*. London: Macmillan.

Drèze, J.H. (1975) Existence of an exchange equilibrium under price rigidities. *International Economic Review* 16, 301–320.

Drèze, J.H. (1976a) Bayesian limited information analysis of the simultaneous equations model. *Econometrica* 44, 1045–1075.

Drèze, J.H. (1976b) Some theory of labour management and participation. *Econometrica* 44, 1125–1139.

Drèze, J.H. (1980) Public goods with exclusion. *Journal of Public Economics* 13, 5–24.

Drèze, J.H. (1985a) Second-best analysis with markets in disequilibrium: public sector pricing in a Keynesian regime. In M. Marchand, P. Pestieau & H. Tulkens (eds.), *The Performance of Public Enterprises: Concepts and Measurement*, pp. 45–79. Amsterdam and New York: North-Holland; also reprinted in *European Economic Review* 29, 263–301.

Drèze, J.H. (1985b) (Uncertainty and) the firm in general equilibrium theory. *Economic Journal* 95 (Suppl.: Conference Papers), 1–20.

Drèze, J.H. (1987a) Decision theory with moral hazard and state-dependent preferences. In J.H. Drèze, *Essays in Economic Decisions Under Uncertainty*, Ch. 2. Cambridge, U.K.: Cambridge University Press.

Drèze, J.H. (1987b) Underemployment: from theory to econometrics and policy. *European Economic Review* 31, 9–34.

Drèze, J.H. (1989) *Labour Management, Contracts, and Capital Markets: A General Equilibrium Approach*. Oxford and New York: Basil Blackwell.

Drèze, J.H. (1990) The role of securities and labor contracts in the optimal allocation of risk-bearing. In H. Loubergé (ed.), *Risk, Information and Insurance. Essays in the Memory of Kark H. Borch*, pp. 245–270. Boston: Kluwer Academic.

Drèze, J.H. (1991) Stability of a Keynesian adjustment process. In Barnett, W.A., B. Cornet, C. d'Aspremont, J.J. Gabszewicz & A. Mas-Colell (eds.), *Equilibrium Theory and Applications*, pp. 197–231. Cambridge, U.K.: Cambridge University Press.

Drèze, J.H. (1992) *Money and Uncertainty: Inflation, Interest, Indexation*. Rome: Edizioni Dell' Elefante.

Drèze, J.H. (1993) Can varying social insurance contributions improve labour market efficiency? In A.B. Atkinson (ed.), *Alternative to Capitalism: The Economics of Partnership*, pp. 161–200. London: Macmillan.

Drèze, J.H. (1997) Walras–Keynes equilibria: coordination and macroeconomics. *European Economic Review* 41, 1737–1762.

Drèze, J.H. (1999) On the dynamics of supply-constrained equilibria. In Heerings, P.J.-J., G. van der Laan & A.J.J. Talman (eds.), *Theory of Markets*, pp. 7–25. Amsterdam: North-Holland.

Drèze, J.H. (2000) Economic and social security in the twenty-first century, with attention to Europe. *Scandinavian Journal of Economics* 102, 327–348.

Drèze, J.H. (2001a) On the macroeconomics of uncertainty and incomplete markets. *Recherches Economiques de Louvain* 67, 5–30; reprinted in J.H. Drèze (ed.), *Advances in Macroeconomics*, Ch. 3. London: Macmillan.

Drèze, J.H. (2001b) Introduction: advances and challenges in Macroeconomics. In J.H. Drèze (ed.), *The Theory of Unemployment Reconsidered*, pp. 1–16. New York: Palgrave.

Drèze, J.H. (2002) Economic and social security: the role of the EU: 15th Tinbergen Lecture. *The Economist* 150, 1–18.

Drèze, J.H. & C. Bean (1990) Europe's unemployment problem: introduction and synthesis. In J.H. Drèze, C. Bean, J.-P. Lambert, F. Mehta & H. Sneessens (eds.), *Europe's Unemployment Problem*, Ch. 1. Cambridge, MA: MIT Press.

Drèze, J.H. & C. Gollier (1993) Risk sharing on the labour market and second-best wage rigidities. *European Economic Review* 37, 1457–1482.

Drèze, J.H. & J. Greenberg (1980) Hedonic coalitions: optimality and stability. *Econometrica* 48, 987–1003.

Drèze, J.H. & M. Marchand (1976) Pricing, spending and gambling rules for non-profit organisations. In R.E. Grieson (ed.), *Public and Urban Economics: Essays in Honor of William S. Vickrey*, pp. 59–89. Lexington, KY: Lexington Books.

Drèze, J.H. & F. Modigliani (1972) Consumption decisions under uncertainty. *Journal of Economic Theory* 5, 308–335.

Drèze, J.H. & J.-A. Morales (1976) Bayesian full information analysis of simultaneous equations. *Journal of the American Statistical Association* 71, 919–923.

Drèze, J.H. & H. Müller (1980) Optimality properties of rationing schemes. *Journal of Economic Theory* 23, 131–149.

Drèze, J.H. & H.M. Polemarchakis (2001) Monetary equilibria. In G. Debreu, W. Neuefeind & W. Trockel (eds.), *Economics Essays, A Festschrift for Werner Hildenbrand*, Ch. 5. Berlin, Heidelberg, and New York: Springer.

Drèze, J.H. & A. Rustichini (2004) State-dependent utility and decision theory. In S. Barbera, P. Hammond & C. Seidl, (eds.), *Handbook of Utility Theory*, Vol. 2, pp. 839–892. Dordrecht, The Netherlands: Kluwer.

Drèze, J.H. & D. de la Vallée Poussin (1971) A tâtonnement process for public goods. *Review of Economic Studies* 38, 133–150.

Drèze, J.H., A. Durré & H. Sneessens (1998) Investment stimulation, with the example of housing. *Recherches Economiques de Louvain* 66, 33–53.

Drèze, J.H., C. Bean, J.-P. Lambert, F. Mehta & H. Sneessens (eds.) (1990) *Europe's Unemployment Problem*. Cambridge, MA: MIT Press.

Drèze, J.H., C. Wyplosz, C. Bean, F. Giavazzi & H. Giersch (1988) The two-handed growth strategy for Europe: autonomy through flexible cooperation. *Recherches Economiques de Louvain* 54, 5–52.

Drèze, J.H., E. Malinvaud, P. De Grauwe, L. Gevers, A. Italianer, O. Lefebvre, M. Marchand, H. Sneesens, A. Steinherr, Paul Champsaur, J.-M. Charpin, J.-P. Fitoussi & G. Laroque (1994) Growth and employment: the scope for a European initiative. *European Economy, Reports and Studies* 1, 75–106.

Gabszewicz, J.J. & J.H. Drèze (1971) Syndicates of traders in an exchange economy. In Kuhn, H.W. & G.P. Szegö (eds.), *Differential Games and Related Topics*, pp. 399–414. Cambridge, MA: MIT Press.

Geanakoplos, J., M. Magill, M. Quinzii & J.H. Drèze (1990) Generic inefficiency of stock-market equilibrium when markets are incomplete. *Journal of Mathematical Economics* 19, 113–151.

Gordon, D.F. (1974) A neoclassical theory of contracts. *Economic Inquiry* 12, 431–459.

Grandmont, J.-M. (1977) Temporary general equilibrium theory. *Econometrica* 45, 535–572.

Grossman, S.J. & O.D. Hart (1979) A theory of competitive equilibrium in stock market economies. *Econometrica* 47, 293–329.

Harrison J.M. & D.M. Kreps (1979) Martingales and arbitrage in multiperiod securities markets. *Journal of Economic Theory* 20, 381–408.

Herings, P.J.-J. (1996) *Static and Dynamic Aspects of General Equilibrium Theory.* Dordrecht: Kluwer.

Hey, J. (1988) Review of "Essays on economic decisions under uncertainty." *Economic Journal,* 196–197.

Lange, O. & F. Taylor (1938) *On the Economic Theory of Socialism.* Minneapolis: The University of Minnesota Press.

Malinvaud, E. (1977) *The Theory of Unemployment Reconsidered.* Oxford: Basil Blackwell.

Phelps, Edmund (1997) *Rewarding Work: How to Restore Participation and Self-Support to Free Enterprise.* Cambridge, MA: Harvard University Press.

Radner, R. (1972) Existence of equilibrium of plans, prices, price expectations in a sequence of markets. *Econometrica* 40, 289–303.

Robert, J. (1989) Equilibrium without market clearing. In Cornet, B. & H. Tulkens (eds.), *Contributions to Operations Research and Economics.* Cambridge, MA: MIT Press.

Sandmo, A. & J.H. Drèze (1971) Discount rates for public investments in closed and open economies. *Economica* 38, 152, 395–412.

Savage, L.J. (1972) *The Foundations of Statistics.* New York: Dover.

Sneessens, H. & J.H. Drèze (1986) A discussion of Belgian unemployment, combining traditional concepts and disequilibrium econometrics. *Economica* 53, 89–119.

Wald, A. (1950) *Statistical Decision Functions.* New York: Wiley.

14

An Interview with Thomas J. Sargent

Interviewed by George W. Evans
DEPARTMENT OF ECONOMICS,
UNIVERSITY OF OREGON

and

Seppo Honkapohja
FACULTY OF ECONOMICS, UNIVERSITY OF
CAMBRIDGE

January 11, 2005

The rational expectations hypothesis swept through macroeconomics during the 1970s and permanently altered the landscape. It remains the prevailing paradigm in macroeconomics, and rational expectations is routinely used as the standard solution concept in both theoretical and applied macroeconomic modelling. The rational expectations hypothesis was initially formulated by John F. Muth, Jr. in the early 1960s. Together with Robert Lucas, Jr., Thomas (Tom) Sargent pioneered the rational expectations revolution in macroeconomics in the 1970s.

Possibly Sargent's most important work in the early 1970s focused on the implications of rational expectations for empirical and econometric research. His short 1971 paper "A Note on the Accelerationist Controversy" provided a dramatic illustration of the implications of rational expectations by demonstrating that the standard econometric test of the natural rate hypothesis was invalid. This work was followed in short order

Reprinted from *Macroeconomic Dynamics*, 9, 2005, 561–583. Copyright © 2005 Cambridge University Press.

Figure 14.1   Thomas J. Sargent.

Figure 14.2   Minnesota boundary waters, August 1974.

by key papers that showed how to conduct valid tests of central macroeconomic relationships under the rational expectations hypothesis. Imposing rational expectations led to new forms of restrictions, called "cross-equation restrictions," which in turn required the development of new econometric techniques for the study of macroeconomic relations and models.

Tom's contributions were wide-ranging. His early econometric work in the 1970s includes studies of the natural rate of unemployment, the neutrality of real interest rates with respect to money, dynamic labor demand, empirics of hyperinflation, and tests for the neutrality of money in "classical rational" expectations models. In the 1980s, Sargent (with Lars Hansen) developed new econometric methods for estimating rational expectations models.

In addition to these seminal contributions to rational expectations econometrics, Sargent made several key contributions during this period to theoretical macroeconomics, including the saddle path stability characterization of the rational expectations equilibrium and the policy ineffectiveness proposition (both developed with Neil Wallace), and the observational equivalence of rational and nonrational theories of monetary neutrality. In later work Tom continued to extend the rational expectations equilibrium paradigm into new areas. Two prominent examples are the implications of the government budget constraint for inflation and "unpleasant monetarist arithmetic" (with Neil Wallace) and the sources of the European unemployment problem (with Lars Ljungqvist).

Tom's impact on macroeconomics in the early days of rational expectations extends well beyond this research. His 1979 textbook *Macroeconomic Theory* introduced a generation of graduate students around the world to a new vision of macroeconomics in which time-series analysis is fully integrated into macro theory, and in which macroeconomic equilibrium is viewed as a stochastic process.

Sargent's contributions have not been confined to the development and application of the rational expectations paradigm. As a true scholar, he became interested in the theoretical foundations of rationality. As he describes here, the initial criticisms of the concept of rational expectations led him in the 1980s to join a line of research called "learning theory," in which the theoretical underpinnings of rational expectations were examined.

Tom became one of the pioneers in this area as well. His 1989 papers with Albert Marcet showed how to use the tools of stochastic approximation to analyze convergence of least squares learning to rational expectations equilibrium in a general framework. His 1993 book *Bounded Rationality in Macroeconomics* helped to disseminate the learning approach

Figure 14.3 Hawaii, September 1980.

to a broader audience, and was part of the rapid growth of research on learning in the 1990s. Tom's 1999 book *The Conquest of American Inflation* called attention to the possibility of "escape routes," that is, occasional large deviations from an equilibrium, and led to a surge of interest in persistent learning dynamics. Closely related to the research on learning are issues of robustness and model misspecification to which Tom (with Lars Hansen) has recently made key contributions.

The depth and range of the contributions we have listed is huge, yet this is not the full extent. Sargent also has done important research in economic history. His work in the 1980s on episodes of moderate and rapid inflations and the recent research on monetary standards (with François Velde) is much less technical, but the rational expectations viewpoint remains clearly visible in these works.

Many collaborators, researchers, and students have experienced Tom's remarkable intellectual depth and energy personally. His thinking is well reflected in this interview, which has a somewhat unusual format. It gets to the key issues very quickly. Only at the end is there commentary on some of his personal experiences as a scholar.

Rational Expectations Econometrics

Evans and Honkapohja: How did you first get interested in rational expectations?

Sargent: When I was a graduate student, estimating and interpreting distributed lags topped the agenda of macroeconomists and other applied economists. Because distributed lags are high-dimensional objects, people like Solow, Jorgenson, Griliches, Nerlove, and Almon sought economical ways to parameterize those distributions in clever ways; for example, by using ratios of low-order polynomials in a lag operator. As beautiful as they are, where on earth do those things come from? Cagan and Friedman interpreted their adaptive expectations geometric distributed lag as measuring people's expectations. At Carnegie, Mike Lovell told me to read John Muth's 1960 *JASA* paper. It rationalized Friedman's adaptive expectations model for permanent income by reverse engineering a stochastic process for income for which Cagan's expectation formula equals a mathematical expectation of future values conditioned on the infinite history of past incomes. Muth's message was that the stochastic process being forecast should dictate both the distributed lag and the conditioning variables that people use to forecast the future. The

Figure 14.4 With grandson Addison, January 2005.

point about conditioning variables primed us to see the importance of Granger–Wiener causality for macroeconomics.

Evans and Honkapohja: When did you first use rational expectations to restrict a distributed lag or a vector autoregression in empirical work?

Sargent: In a 1971 paper on testing the natural unemployment rate hypothesis. I figured out the pertinent cross-equation restrictions and showed that in general they didn't imply the "sum-of-the-weights" test on distributed lags that was being used to test the natural-rate hypothesis. That was easy because for that problem I could assume that inflation was exogenous and use a univariate process for inflation. My 1973 and 1977 papers on rational expectations and hyperinflation tackled a more difficult problem. Those papers found the cross-equation restrictions on a VAR for money and prices by reverse engineering a joint process for which Cagan's adaptive expectations formula delivers optimal forecasts. This was worth doing because Cagan's model fit the data so well. Imposing rational expectations exposed a lot about the Granger causality structure between money and prices that prevailed during most of the hyperinflations that Cagan had studied.

Evans and Honkapohja: Econometrically, what was the big deal about rational expectations?

Sargent: Cross-equation restrictions and the disappearance of *any* free parameters associated with expectations.

Figure 14.5 With Carolyn at Santorini, 2001.

Evans and Honkapohja: What do you mean "disappearance"?

Sargent: In rational expectations models, people's beliefs are among the outcomes of our theorizing. They are not inputs.

Evans and Honkapohja: Do you think that differences among people's models are important aspects of macroeconomic policy debates?

Sargent: The fact is that you simply cannot talk about those differences within the typical rational expectations model. There is a communism of models. All agents inside the model, the econometrician, and God share the same model. The powerful and useful empirical implications of rational expectations—the cross-equation restrictions and the legitimacy of the appeal to a law of large number in GMM estimation—derive from that communism of models.

Evans and Honkapohja: What role do cross-equation restrictions play in Lucas's Critique?

Sargent: They are everything. The positive part of Lucas's Critique was to urge applied macroeconomists and econometricians to develop ways to implement those cross-equation restrictions. His paper had three examples. What transcends them is their cross-equation restrictions, and the absence of free parameters describing expectations. In a nutshell, Lucas's Critique of prerational expectations work was, "you have ignored cross equation restrictions, and they are all important for policy evaluation."

Evans and Honkapohja: What do those cross-equation restrictions have to say about the evidence in favor of coefficient volatility that Bob Lucas talked about in the first part of his "Critique"?

Sargent: Little or nothing. Lucas used evidence of coefficient drift and add factors to bash the Keynesians, but as I read his paper, at least, he didn't claim to offer an explanation for the observed drift. His three examples are each time-invariant structures. Data from them would not have coefficient drift even if you fit one of those misspecified Keynesian models. So the connection of the first part of his paper to the second was weak.

Evans and Honkapohja: Do you feel that your work contributed to the Lucas Critique?

Sargent: It depends what you mean by "contribute." Lucas attended a conference on rational expectations at the University of Minnesota in the spring of 1973. The day after the conference, I received a call from Pittsburgh. Bob had lost a manuscript and thought he might have left it at the conference. I went to the room in Ford Hall at which we had held the conference and found a folder with yellow sheets in it. I looked at the first few pages. It was Bob's Critique. I mailed the manuscript back to Bob. So, yes, I contributed to the Critique.

Evans and Honkapohja: What were the profession's most important responses to the Lucas Critique?

Sargent: There were two. The first and most optimistic response was complete rational expectations econometrics. A rational expectations equilibrium *is* a likelihood function. Maximize it.

Evans and Honkapohja: Why optimistic?

Sargent: You have to believe in your model to use the likelihood function. It provides a coherent way to estimate objects of interest (preferences, technologies, information sets, measurement processes) within the context of a trusted model.

Evans and Honkapohja: What was the second response?

Sargent: Various types of calibration. Calibration is less optimistic about what your theory can accomplish because you'd only use it if you didn't fully trust your entire model, meaning that you think your model is partly misspecified or incompletely specified, or if you trusted someone else's model and data set more than your own. My recollection is that Bob Lucas and Ed Prescott were initially very enthusiastic about rational expectations econometrics. After all, it simply involved imposing on ourselves the same high standards we had criticized the Keynesians for failing to live up to. But after about five years of doing likelihood ratio tests on rational expectations models, I recall Bob Lucas and Ed Prescott both telling me that those tests were rejecting too many good models. The idea of calibration is to ignore some of the probabilistic implications of your model but to retain others. Somehow, calibration was intended as a balanced response to professing that your model, though not correct, is still worthy as a vehicle for quantitative policy analysis.

Evans and Honkapohja: Why do you say "various types of calibration"?

Sargent: Different people mean and do different things by calibration. Some people mean "use an extraneous estimator." Take estimates from some previous study and pretend that they are known numbers. An obvious difficulty of this procedure is that often those extraneous estimates were prepared with an econometric specification that contradicts your model. Treating those extraneous parameters as known ignores the clouds of uncertainty around them, clouds associated with the estimation uncertainty conveyed by the original researcher, and clouds from the "specification risk" associated with putting your faith in the econometric specification that another researcher used to prepare his estimates.

Other people, for example, Larry Christiano and Marty Eichenbaum, by calibration mean GMM estimates using a subset of the moment conditions for the model and data set at hand. Presumably, they impose only a subset of the moment conditions because they trust some aspects of their model more than others. This is a type of robustness argument that has been pushed furthest by those now doing semiparametric GMM. There are ways to calculate the standard errors to account for vaguely specified or distrusted aspects of the model. By the way, these ways of computing standard errors have a min–max flavor that reminds one of the robust control theory that Lars Hansen and I are using.

Evans and Honkapohja: We know what question maximum likelihood estimates answers, and the circumstances under which maximum likelihood estimates, or Bayesian counterparts to them, have good properties. What question is calibration the answer to?

Sargent: The best answer I know is contained in work by Hansen and others on GMM. They show the sense in which GMM is the best way to estimate trusted features of a less than fully trusted model.

Evans and Honkapohja: Do you think calibration in macroeconomics was an advance?

Sargent: In many ways, yes. I view it as a constructive response to Bob's remark that "your likelihood ratio tests are rejecting too many good models." In those days, the rational expectations approach to macroeconomics was still being challenged by influential people. There was a danger that skeptics and opponents would misread those likelihood ratio tests as rejections of an entire *class* of models, which of course they were not. (The internal logic of the likelihood function as a complete model should have made that clear, but apparently it wasn't at the time!) The unstated case for calibration was that it was a way to continue the process of acquiring experience in matching rational expectations models to data by lowering our standards relative to maximum likelihood, and emphasizing those features of the data that our models could capture. Instead of trumpeting their failures in terms of dismal likelihood ratio statistics, celebrate the features that they could capture and focus attention on the next unexplained feature that ought to be explained. One can argue that this was a sensible response to those likelihood ratio tests. It was also a response to the scarcity of resources at our disposal. Creating dynamic equilibrium macro theories and building a time-series econometrics suitable for estimating them were both big tasks. It was a sensible opinion that the time had come to specialize and to use a sequential plan of attack: let's first devote resources to learning how to create a range of compelling equilibrium models to incorporate interesting mechanisms. We'll be careful about the estimation in later years when we have mastered the modeling technology.

Evans and Honkapohja: Aren't applications of likelihood-based methods in macroeconomics now making something of a comeback?

Sargent: Yes, because, of course, a rational expectations equilibrium *is* a likelihood function, so you couldn't ignore it forever. In the 1980s, there were occasions when it made sense to say, "It is too difficult to maximize the likelihood function, and besides if we do, it will blow our model out of the water." In the 2000s, there are fewer occasions when you can get by saying this. First, computers have gotten much faster, and the Markov Chain Monte Carlo algorithm, which can be viewed as a clever random search algorithm for climbing a likelihood function, or building up a posterior, is now often practical. Furthermore, a number of researchers have constructed rational expectations models with enough shocks and wedges that they believe it is appropriate to fit the data well with complete likelihood-based procedures. Examples are the recent models of Otrok and Smets and Wouters. By using log-linear approximations, they can use the same recursive representation of a Gaussian likelihood function that we were using in the late 1970s and early eighties.

Of course, for some nonlinear equilibrium models, it can be difficult to write down the likelihood. But there has been a lot of progress here thanks to Tony Smith, Ron Gallant, and George Tauchen and others, who have figured out ways to get estimates as good, or almost as good, as maximum likelihood. I like the Gallant–Tauchen idea of using moment conditions from the first-order conditions for maximizing the likelihood function of a well fitting auxiliary model whose likelihood function is easy to write down.

Evans and Honkapohja: Do you see any drawbacks to likelihood-based approaches for macro models?

Sargent: Yes. For one thing, without leaving the framework, it seems difficult to complete a self-contained analysis of sensitivity to key features of a specification.

Evans and Honkapohja: Do you think that these likelihood-based methods are going to sweep away GMM-based methods that don't use complete likelihoods?

Sargent: No. GMM and other calibration strategies will have a big role to play whenever a researcher distrusts part of his specification and so long as concerns about robustness endure.

Learning

Evans and Honkapohja: Why did you get interested in nonrational learning theories in macroeconomics?

Sargent: Initially, to strengthen the case for and extend our understanding of rational expectations. In the 1970s, rational expectations was severely criticized because, it was claimed, it endowed people with too much knowledge about the economy. It was fun to be doing rational expectations macro in the mid-seventies because there was lots of skepticism, even hostility, toward rational expectations. Critics claimed that an equilibrium concept in which everyone shared "God's model" was incredible. To help meet that criticism, I enlisted in Margaret Bray's and David Kreps's research program. Their idea was to push agents' beliefs away from a rational expectations equilibrium, then endow them with learning algorithms and histories of data. Let them adapt their behavior in a way that David Kreps later called "anticipated utility" behavior: here you optimize, taking your latest estimate of the transition equation as though it were permanent; update your transition equation; optimize again; update again; and so on. (This is something like "fictitious play" in game theory. Kreps argues that while it is "irrational," it can be a smart way to proceed in contexts in which it is difficult to figure out what it means to be rational. Kreps's Schwartz lecture has some fascinating games that convince you that his anticipated utility view is attractive.) Margaret Bray, Albert Marcet, Mike Woodford, you two, Xiaohong Chen and Hal White, and the rest of us wanted to know whether such a system of adaptive agents would converge to a rational expectations equilibrium. Together, we discovered a broad set of conditions on the environment under which beliefs converge. Something like a rational expectations equilibrium is the only possible limit point for a system with adaptive agents. Analogous results prevail in evolutionary and adaptive theories of games.

Evans and Honkapohja: What do you mean "something like"?

Sargent: The limit point depends on how much prompting you give agents in terms of functional forms and conditioning variables. The early work in the least squares learning literature initially endowed agents with wrong coefficients, but with correct functional forms and correct conditioning variables. With those endowments, the systems typically converged to a rational expectations equilibrium. Subsequent work by you two, and by Albert Marcet and me, withheld some pertinent conditioning variables from agents, e.g., by prematurely truncating pertinent histories. We found convergence to objects that could be thought of as "rational expectations equilibria with people conditioning on restricted information sets." Chen and White studied situations in which agents permanently have wrong functional forms. Their adaptive systems converge to a kind of equilibrium in which agents' forecasts are optimal within the class of information filtrations that can be supported by the functional forms to which they have restricted agents.

Evans and Honkapohja: How different are these equilibria with subtly misspecified expectations from rational expectations equilibria?

Sargent: They are like rational expectations equilibria in many ways. They are like complete rational expectations equilibria in terms of many of their operating characteristics. For example, they have their own set of cross-equation restrictions that should guide policy analysis.

They are "self-confirming" within the class of forecasting functions agents are allowed. They can also be characterized as having forecasting functions that are as close as possible to mathematical expectations conditioned on pertinent histories that are implied by the model, where proximity is measured by a Kullback–Leibler measure of model discrepancy (that is, an expected log-likelihood ratio). If they are close enough in this sense, it means that it could take a very long time for an agent living within one of these equilibria to detect that his forecasting function could be improved.

However, suboptimal forecasting functions could not be sustained in the limit if you were to endow agents with sufficiently flexible functional forms, e.g., the sieve estimation strategies like those studied by Xiaohong Chen. Chen and White have an example in which a system with agents who have the ability to fit flexible functional forms will converge to a nonlinear rational expectations equilibrium.

Evans and Honkapohja: Were those who challenged the plausibility of rational expectations equilibria right or wrong?

Sargent: It depends on how generous you want to be to them. We know that if you endow agents with correct functional forms and conditioning variables, even then only *some* rational expectations equilibria are limit points of adaptive economies. As you two have developed fully in your book, other rational expectations equilibria are unstable under the learning dynamics and are eradicated under least squares learning. Maybe those unstable rational expectations equilibria were the only ones the critics meant to question, although this is being generous to them. In my opinion, some of the equilibria that least squares learning eradicates deserved extermination: for example, the "bad" Laffer curve equilibria in models of hyperinflations that Albert Marcet and I, and Stan Fischer and Michael Bruno also, found would not be stable under various adaptive schemes. That finding is important for designing fiscal policies to stabilize big inflations.

Evans and Honkapohja: Are stability results that dispose of some rational expectations equilibria, and that retain others, the main useful outcome of adaptive learning theory?

Sargent: They are among the useful results that learning theory has contributed. But I think that the stability theorems have contributed something even more important than equilibrium selection. If you stare at the stability theorems, you see that learning theory has caused us to

318 George W. Evans and Seppo Honkapohja

refine what we mean by rational expectations equilibria. In addition to the equilibria with "optimal misspecified beliefs" that I mentioned a little while ago, it has introduced a type of rational expectations equilibrium that enables us to think about disputes involving different models of the economy in ways that we couldn't before.

Evans and Honkapohja: What do you mean?

Sargent: Originally, we defined a rational expectations equilibrium in terms of the "communism of models" that I alluded to earlier. By "model," I mean a probability distribution over all of the inputs and outcomes of the economic model at hand. Within such a rational expectations equilibrium, agents can have different information, but they share the same model. Learning theories in both macroeconomics and game theory have discovered that the natural limit points of a variety of least squares learning schemes are what Kreps, Fudenberg, and Levine call "self-confirming equilibria." In a self-confirming equilibrium, agents can have different models of the economy, but they must agree about events that occur sufficiently often within the equilibrium. That restriction leaves agents free to disagree about off-equilibrium outcomes. The reason is that a law of large numbers doesn't have enough chances to act on such infrequent events. In the types of competitive settings that we often use in macroeconomics, disagreement about off-equilibrium-path outcomes among small private agents don't matter. Those private agents need only to predict distributions of outcomes along an equilibrium path. But the government is a large player. If it has the wrong model about off-equilibrium-path outcomes, it can make wrong policy choices, simply because it is wrong about the counterfactual thought experiments that go into solving a Ramsey problem, for example. No amount of empirical evidence drawn from within a self-confirming equilibrium can convince a government that it is wrong about its model, because its model is correct for all frequently observed events. To be motivated to change its model, the government must either experiment or listen to a new theorist. The theorist has to come up with a model that is observationally equivalent with the government's model for the old self-confirming equilibrium outcomes, but that improves the analysis of counterfactuals relative to those outcomes.

Evans and Honkapohja: Are there interesting examples of this kind of thing occurring in the macroeconomy?

Sargent: You can tell a story that this is what Lucas was up to with his 1972 *JET* paper on the natural rate. If you alter Kydland and Prescott's 1977 version of Lucas's story a little, you can alter their timing protocol and reinterpret Kydland and Prescott's suboptimal time-consistent equilibrium as a self-confirming equilibrium that could be improved with a better government model of off-equilibrium-path outcomes.

Evans and Honkapohja: Wasn't this part of your story in *The Conquest of American Inflation*?

Sargent: Yes.

Evans and Honkapohja: So it seems that you can talk about disagreements among models within a rational expectations framework if you extend the concept of rational expectations to mean "self-confirming."

Sargent: Yes. This is a nice feature of self-confirming equilibrium models. My reading of disputes about economic policy is that they are not merely struggles based on different information or different interests—which is all they could possibly reflect within a "communist" rational expectations model. Some disputes over government policy originate in the fact that advocates have different models of the way the economy functions, and it can be difficult to criticize their models on empirical grounds because they fit the data from the prevailing equilibrium.

Evans and Honkapohja: What else has learning theory contributed?

Sargent: A couple of important things. First, it contains some results about rates of convergence to a rational expectations equilibrium that can be informative about how difficult it is to learn an equilibrium. Second, we have discovered that even when convergence occurs with probability one, sample paths can exhibit exotic trajectories called "escape routes." These escape routes exhibit long-lived departures from a self-confirming equilibrium and can visit objects that qualify as "near equilibria." The escape paths can be characterized by an elegant control problem and contribute a form of "near rational" dynamics that can have amazing properties. I first encountered these ideas while working on my *Conquest* book. In-Koo Cho and Noah Williams have pushed these ideas further. I suspect that these escape routes will prove to be a useful addition to our toolkit. For example, they can sustain the kind of drifting parameters that Lucas brought out in the first part of his Critique, but that, until recently, most of us have usually refrained from interpreting as equilibrium outcomes. A good example of the type of phenomena that drifting coefficients with escapes from a self-confirming equilibrium can explain is contained in the recent *AER* paper on recurrent hyperinflations by Albert Marcet and Juan Pablo Nicolini.

Evans and Honkapohja: With your coauthor Tim Cogley, you have been studying drifting coefficients and volatilities. Did Lucas's Critique fuel your work with Cogley?

Sargent: Yes. Sims claims that while there is ample evidence for drifting volatilities, the evidence for drifting coefficients is weak. And he uses that fact to argue that U.S. data are consistent with time-invariant government monetary and fiscal policy rules throughout the post-World War II period. So when bad macroeconomic outcomes occurred, it was due to bad luck in the form of big shocks, not bad policy in the form of decision rules that had drifted into becoming too accommodating or too tight. It is true that detecting drifts in the AR coefficients in a VAR is much more difficult than detecting drifts in innovation volatilities—this is clearest in continuous time settings that finance people work in. (Lars Hansen has taught this to me in the context of our work on robustness.) Thus, Sims and other "bad luck, not bad policy" advocates say that the drift spotted by Lucas is misinterpreted if it is regarded as indicating drifting decision rules, e.g., drifting monetary policy rules. The reason is that, by in effect projecting in wrong directions, it misreads stochastic volatility as reflecting drift in agents' decision rules. These are obviously very important issues that can be sorted out only with an econometric framework that countenances both drifting coefficients and drifting volatilities. Tim and I are striving to sort these things out, and so are Chris and Tao Zha and Fabio Canova.

Economic History

Evans and Honkapohja: Your papers on monetary history look very different than your other work. Why are there so few equations and so little formal econometrics in your writings on economic history? Like your "Ends of Four Big Inflations" and your paper with Velde on features of the French Revolution? We don't mean to insult you, but you look more like an "old economic historian" than a "new economic historian."

Sargent: This is a tough question. I view my efforts in economic history as pattern recognition, or pattern imposition, exercises. You learn a suite of macroeconomic models that sharpen your mind by narrowing it. The models alert you to look for certain items, e.g., ways that monetary and fiscal policy are being coordinated. Then you read some history and economic history and look at a bunch of error-ridden numbers. Data are often error-ridden and incomplete. You read contemporaries who say diverse things about what is going on, and historians who put their own spins on things. From this disorder, you censor some observations, over-weight others. Somehow, you impose order and tell a story, cast in terms of the objects from your suite of macroeconomic theories. Hopefully, the story rings true.

Evans and Honkapohja: Do you find rational expectations models useful for understanding history?

Sargent: Yes. A difficult thing about history is that you are tempted to evaluate historical actors' decisions with too much hindsight. To understand things, you somehow have to put yourself in the shoes of the historical actor and reconstruct the information he had, the theory he was operating under, and the interests he served. Accomplishing this is an immense task. But our rational expectations theories and decision theories are good devices for organizing our analysis. By the way, to my mind, reading history immediately drives you away from perfect foresight models toward models in which people face nontrivial forecasting problems under uncertainty.

Evans and Honkapohja: Interesting. But you didn't answer our question about why your historical work is more informal than your other work.

Sargent: I don't know. Most of the historical problems that I have worked on have involved episodes that can be regarded as transitions from one rational expectations equilibrium to another. For example, the ends of hyperinflations; the struggles for new monetary and fiscal policies presided over by Poincaré and Thatcher; the directed search for a new monetary and fiscal constitution by a sequence of decisionmakers during the French Revolution; the 800-year coevolution of theories and policies and technologies for producing coins in our work with François on small change. I saw contesting theories at play in all of these episodes. We didn't see our way clear to being as complete and coherent as you have to be in formal work without tossing out much of the action. Analyzing the kinds of the transitions that we studied in formal terms would have required a workable model of the social process of using experience to induce new models, paradigm shifts and revolutions of ideas, the really hard unsolved problem that underlies Kreps's anticipated utility program. (You wouldn't be inspired to take Muth's brilliant leap to rational expectations models by running regressions.) We didn't know how to make such a model, but we nevertheless cast our narratives in terms of a process that, with hindsight, induced new models from failed experiences with old ones.

Robustness and Model Misspecification

Evans and Honkapohja: You work with Hansen and others on robust control theory. How is that work related to your work on rational expectations and on learning?

Sargent: It is connected to both, and to calibration as well. The idea is to give a decisionmaker doubts about his model and ask him to make good decisions when he fears that some other model might actually generate the data.

Evans and Honkapohja: Why is that a good idea?

Sargent: One loose motivation for both rational expectations theory and learning theories is that the economist's model should have the property that the econometrician cannot do better than the agents inside the model. This criterion was used in the old days to criticize the practice of attributing to agents adaptive and other naive expectations schemes. So rational expectations theorists endowed agents with the ability to form conditional expectations, i.e., take averages with respect to infinite data samples drawn from *within* the equilibrium. The idea of learning theory was to take this "take averages" idea seriously by giving agents data from *outside* the equilibrium, then to roll up your sleeves and study whether and at what rate agents who take averages from finite outside-equilibrium data sets can eventually learn what they needed to know in a population rational expectations equilibrium. It turned out that they could. The spirit was to "make the agents like econometricians."

Of course, the typical rational expectations model reverses the situation: the agent knows more than the econometrician. The agent inside the model knows the parameters of the true model while the econometrician does not and must estimate them. Further, thorough rational expectations econometricians often come away from their analyses with a battery of specification tests that have brutalized their models. (Recall my earlier reference to Bob's and Ed's early 1980s comments to me that "your likelihood ratio tests are rejecting too many good models.")

Using robust control theory is a way to let our agents share the experiences of econometricians. The idea is to make the agent acknowledge and cope with model misspecification.

Evans and Honkapohja: Is this just to make sure that agents are put on the same footing as us in our role as econometricians?

Sargent: Yes. And an agent's response to fear of model misspecification contributes behavioral responses that have interesting quantitative implications. For example, fear of model misspecification contributes components of indirect utility functions that in some types of data can look like heightened risk aversion, but that are actually responses to very different types of hypothetical mental experiments than are Pratt measures of risk aversion. For this reason, fear of model misspecification is a tool for understanding a variety of asset price spreads. Looked at from another viewpoint, models of robust decisionmaking contribute a disciplined theory of what appears to be an endogenous preference shock.

Another reason is that decisionmaking in the face of fear of model misspecification can be a useful normative tool for solving Ramsey problems. That is why people at central banks are interested in the topic. They distrust their models.

Evans and Honkapohja: What are some of the connections to learning theory?

Sargent: There are extensive mathematical connections through the theory of large deviations. Hansen and I exploit these. Some misspecifications are easy to learn about, others are difficult to learn about. By "difficult" I mean "learn at a slow rate." Large deviation theory tells us which misspecifications can be learned about quickly and which can't. Hansen and I restricted the amount of misspecification that our agent wants to guard against by requiring that it be a misspecification that is hard to distinguish from his approximating model. This is how we use learning theory to make precise what we mean by the phrase "the decisionmaker thinks his model is a good approximation." There is a race between a discount factor and a learning rate. With discounting, it makes sense to try to be robust against plausible alternatives that are difficult to learn about.

Evans and Honkapohja: Can this model of decisionmaking be recast in Bayesian terms?

Sargent: It depends on your perspective. We have shown that *ex post*, it can, in the sense that you can come up with a prior, a distorted model, that rationalizes the decisionmaker's choices. But *ex ante* you can't— the set of misspecifications that the agent fears is too big and he will not or cannot tell you a prior over that set.

By the way, Lars and I have constructed equilibria with heterogeneous agents in which the *ex post* Bayesian analysis implies that agents with different interests will have different "twisted models." From the point of view of a rational expectations econometrician, these agents look as if they have different beliefs. This is a disciplined way of modeling belief heterogeneity.

Evans and Honkapohja: Is this a type of behavioral economics or bounded rationality?

Sargent: Any decision theory is a type of behavioral economics. It is not a type of bounded rationality. The decisionmaker is actually smarter than a rational expectations agent because his fear of model misspecification is out in the open.

Evans and Honkapohja: Parts of your description of robustness remind us of calibration. Are there connections?

Sargent: I believe there are, but they are yet to be fully exploited. Robust versions of dynamic estimation problems have been formulated. In these problems, the decisionmaker does not use standard maximum likelihood estimators for his approximating model—he distrusts his likelihood function. Therefore, he distorts his likelihood function in preparing his estimates. This twisting is reminiscent of what some calibrators do, though the robustness procedure is more precisely defined, in the sense that you can answer your earlier question about "What question is calibration the answer to?"

Evans and Honkapohja: Why has Sims criticized your work on robustness?

Sargent: He thinks it is not wise to leave the Bayesian one-model framework of Savage. He thinks that there are big dividends in terms of ease of analysis by working hard to represent fear of model misspecifications in ways that stay within the Bayesian framework.

However, I should say that Lars's and my readings of Chris's early work on approximation of distributed lags were important inspirations for our work on robustness. Chris authored a beautiful approximation error formula and showed how to use it to guide the choice of appropriate data filters that would minimize approximation errors. That beautiful practical analysis of Chris's had a min–max flavor and was not self-consciously Bayesian. One version of Chris's min–max analysis originated in a message that Chris wrote to me about a comment in which I had argued that a rational expectations econometrician should never use seasonally adjusted data. My argument was very Bayesian in spirit, because I assumed that the econometrician had the correct model. Chris both read my comment and wrote his memo on a Minneapolis bus going home from the U in 1976—that's how fast Chris is. Chris's bus memo on seasonality and approximation error was pretty well known in the macro time-series community at Minnesota in the late 1970s. (At the time, I don't know why, I felt that the fact that Chris could write such an insightful memo while riding on his 20-minute bus ride home put me in my proper place.) By the way, in Eric Ghysels's 1993 *Journal of Econometrics* special volume on seasonality, Lars and I wrote a paper that went a long way towards accepting Sims's bus memo argument. That Ghysels-volume paper was one motivation for our robustness research agenda.

Minnesota Economics

Evans and Honkapohja: Along with Carnegie Mellon and Chicago, Minnesota during the 1970s was at the forefront in developing and propagating a new dynamic macroeconomics. What ingredients formed the Minnesota environment?

Sargent: Tension and tolerance. We took strong positions and had immense disagreements. But the rules of engagement were civil and we always built each other up to our students. Minnesota in those days had a remarkable faculty. (It still does!) The mature department leaders, Leo Hurwicz and John Chipman, set the tone; they advocated taking your time to learn carefully and they encouraged students to learn math. Chris Sims and Neil Wallace were my two best colleagues. Both were forever generous with ideas, always extremely critical, but never destructive. The three of us had strong disagreements but there was also immense respect. Our seminars were exciting. I interacted intensively with both Neil and Chris through dissertations committees.

The best thing about Minnesota from the mid-seventies to mid-eighties was our extraordinary students. These were mostly people who weren't admitted into top-five schools. Students taking my macro and time-series classes included John Geweke, Gary Skoog, Salih Neftci, George Tauchen, Michael Salemi, Lars Hansen, Rao Aiyagari, Danny Peled, Ben Bental, Bruce Smith, Michael Stutzer, Charles Whiteman, Robert Litterman, Zvi Eckstein, Marty Eichenbaum, Yochanan Shachmurove, Rusdu Saracoglu, Larry Christiano, Randall Wright, Richard Rogerson, Gary Hansen, Selahattin Imrohoroglu, Ayse Imrohoroglu, Fabio Canova, Beth Ingram, Bong Soo Lee, Albert Marcet, Rodolfo Manuelli, Hugo Hopenhayn, Lars Ljungqvist, Rosa Matzkin, Victor Rios Rull, Gerhard Glomm, Ann Vilamil, Stacey Schreft, Andreas Hornstein, and a number of others. What a group! A who's-who of modern macro and macroeconometrics. Even a governor of a central bank [Rusdu Saracoglu]! If these weren't enough, after I visited Cambridge, Massachusetts in 1981–82, Patrick Kehoe, Danny Quah, Paul Richardson, and Richard Clarida each came to Minneapolis for much of the summer of 1982, and Danny and Pat stayed longer as RAs. It was a thrill teaching classes to such students. Often I knew less than the students I was "teaching." Our philosophy at Minnesota was that we teachers were just more experienced students.

One of the best things I did at Minnesota was to campaign for us to make an offer to Ed Prescott. He came in the early 1980s and made Minnesota even better.

Evans and Honkapohja: You make 1970s–1980s Minnesota sound like a love-in among Sims and Wallace and you. How do you square that attitude with the dismal view of your work expressed in Neil Wallace's *JME* review of your Princeton book on the history of small change with François Velde? Do friends write about each other that way?

Sargent: Friends do talk to each other that way. Neil thinks that cash-in-advance models are useless and gets ill every time he sees a cash-in-advance constraint. For Neil, what could be worse than a model with a cash-in-advance constraint? A model with *two* cash-in-advance constraints.

But that is what Velde and I have! The occasionally positive multiplier on that second cash-in-advance constraint is Velde and my tool for understanding recurrent shortages of small change and upward-drifting prices of large-denomination coins in terms of small-denomination ones.

When I think of Neil, one word comes to mind: integrity. Neil's evaluation of my book with Velde was no worse than his evaluation of the papers that he and I wrote together. Except for our paper on commodity money, not our best in my opinion, Neil asked me to remove his name from every paper that he and I wrote together.

Evans and Honkapohja: Was he being generous?

Sargent: I don't think so. He thought the papers should not be published. After he read the introduction to one of our *JPE* papers, Bob Lucas told me that no referee could possibly say anything more derogatory about our paper than what we had written about it ourselves. Neil wrote those critical words.

15

An Interview with Robert Aumann

Interviewed by Sergiu Hart
THE HEBREW UNIVERSITY OF JERUSALEM
September 2004

Who is Robert Aumann? Is he an economist or a mathematician? A rational scientist or a deeply religious man? A deep thinker or an easygoing person?

These seemingly disparate qualities can all be found in Aumann; all are essential facets of his personality. A pure mathematician who is a renowned economist, he has been a central figure in developing game theory and establishing its key role in modern economics. He has shaped the field through his fundamental and pioneering work, work that is conceptually profound, and much of it also mathematically deep. He has greatly influenced and inspired many people: his students, collaborators, colleagues, and anyone who has been excited by reading his papers or listening to his talks.

Aumann promotes a unified view of rational behavior, in many different disciplines: chiefly economics, but also political science, biology, computer science, and more. He has broken new ground in many areas, the most notable being perfect competition, repeated games, correlated equilibrium, interactive knowledge and rationality, and coalitions and cooperation.

But Aumann is not just a theoretical scholar, closed in his ivory tower. He is interested in real-life phenomena and issues, to which he applies insights from his research. He is a devoutly religious man; and he is one of the founding fathers—and a central and most active member—of the

Reprinted from *Macroeconomic Dynamics*, 9, 2005, 683–740. Copyright © 2005 Cambridge University Press.

Figure 15.1   Bob Aumann, circa 2000.

multidisciplinary Center for the Study of Rationality at the Hebrew University in Jerusalem.

Aumann enjoys skiing, mountain climbing, and cooking—no less than working out a complex economic question or proving a deep theorem. He is a family man, a very warm and gracious person —of an extremely subtle and sharp mind.

This interview catches a few glimpses of Robert Aumann's fascinating world. It was held in Jerusalem on three consecutive days in September 2004. I hope the reader will learn from it and enjoy it as much as we two did.

Hart: Good morning, Professor Aumann. Well, I am not going to call you Professor Aumann. But what should I call you—Yisrael, Bob, Johnny?

Aumann: You usually call me Yisrael, so why don't you continue to call me Yisrael. But there really is a problem with my given names. I have at least three given names—Robert, John, and Yisrael. Robert and John are my given names from birth and Yisrael is the name that I got at the circumcision. Many people call me Bob, which is of course short for Robert. There was once a trivia quiz at a students' party at the Hebrew University, and one of the questions was, "Which faculty member has four given names and uses them all?" Another story connected to my names is that my wife went to get approval of having our children included in her passport. She gave me the forms to sign on two different occasions. On one I signed Yisrael and on one I signed Robert. The clerk, when she gave him the forms, refused to accept them, saying, "Who is this man? Are there different fathers over here? We can't accept this."

Hart: I remember a time, when you taught at Tel Aviv University, you were filling out a form when suddenly you stopped and phoned your wife. "Esther," you asked, "what's my name in Tel Aviv?"

Let's start with your scientific biography, namely, what were the milestones on your scientific route?

Aumann: I did an undergraduate degree at City College in New York in mathematics, then on to MIT, where I did a doctorate with George Whitehead in algebraic topology, then on to a postdoc at Princeton with an operations research group affiliated with the math department. There I got interested in game theory. From there I went to the Hebrew University in Jerusalem, where I've been ever since. That's the broad outline.

Now to fill that in a little bit. My interest in mathematics actually started in high school—the Rabbi Jacob Joseph Yeshiva (Hebrew Day School) on the lower east side of New York City. There was a marvelous teacher of mathematics there, by the name of Joseph Gansler. The classes were very small; the high school had just started operating. He used to gather the students around his desk. What really turned me on was geometry, theorems, and proofs. So all the credit belongs to Joey Gansler.

Then I went on to City College. Actually I did a bit of soul-searching when finishing high school, on whether to become a Talmudic scholar, or study secular subjects at a university. For a while I did both. I used to get up in the morning at 6:15, go to the university in uptown New York from Brooklyn—an hour and a quarter on the subway—then study calculus for an hour, then go back to the yeshiva on the lower east side for most of the morning, then go back up to City College at 139th Street and study there until 10 p.m., then go home and do some homework or whatever, and then I would get up again at 6:15. I did this for one semester, and then it became too much for me and I made the hard decision to quit the yeshiva and study mathematics.

Hart: How did you make the decision?

Aumann: I really can't remember. I know the decision was mine. My parents put a lot of responsibility on us children. I was all of 17 at the time, but there was no overt pressure from my parents. Probably math just attracted me more, although I was very attracted by Talmudic studies.

At City College, there was a very active group of mathematics students. The most prominent of the mathematicians on the staff was Emil Post, a famous logician. He was in the scientific school of Turing and Church—mathematical logic, computability—which was very much the "in" thing at the time. This was the late forties. Post was a very interesting character. I took just one course from him and that was functions of real variables—measure, integration, et cetera. The entire course consisted of his assigning exercises and then calling on the students to present the solutions on the blackboard. It's called the Moore method—no lectures, only exercises. It was a very good course. There were also other excellent teachers there, and there was a very active group of mathematics students. A lot of socializing went on. There was a table in the cafeteria called the mathematics table. Between classes we would sit there and have ice cream and—

Hart: Discuss the topology of bagels?

Aumann: Right, that kind of thing. A lot of chess playing, a lot of math talk. We ran our own seminars, had a math club. Some very prominent mathematicians came out of there—Jack Schwartz of Dunford–Schwartz fame, Leon Ehrenpreis, Alan Shields, Leo Flatto, Martin Davis, D.J. Newman. That was a very intense experience. From there I went on to graduate work at MIT, where I did a doctorate in algebraic topology with George Whitehead.

Let me tell you something very moving relating to my thesis. As an undergraduate, I read a lot of analytic and algebraic number theory. What is fascinating about number theory is that it uses very deep methods to attack problems that are in some sense very "natural" and also simple to formulate. A schoolchild can understand Fermat's last theorem, but it took extremely deep methods to prove it. A schoolchild can understand what a prime number is, but understanding the distribution of prime numbers requires the theory of functions of a complex variable; it is closely related to the Riemann hypothesis, whose very formulation requires at least two or three years of university mathematics, and which remains unproved to this day. Another interesting aspect of number theory was that it was absolutely useless—pure mathematics at its purest.

In graduate school, I heard George Whitehead's excellent lectures on algebraic topology. Whitehead did not talk much about knots, but I had heard about them, and they fascinated me. Knots are like number theory: the problems are very simple to formulate, a schoolchild can understand them; and they are very natural, they have a simplicity and immediacy that is even greater than that of prime numbers or Fermat's last theorem. But it is very difficult to prove anything at all about them; it requires really deep methods of algebraic topology. And, like number theory, knot theory was totally, totally useless.

So, I was attracted to knots. I went to Whitehead and said, "I want to do a Ph.D. with you, please give me a problem. But not just any problem; please, give me an open problem in knot theory." And he did; he gave me a famous, very difficult problem—the "asphericity" of knots—that had been open for 25 years and had defied the most concerted attempts to solve.

Though I did not solve that problem, I did solve a special case. The complete statement of my result is not easy to formulate for a layman, but it does have an interesting implication that even a schoolchild can understand and that had not been known before my work: alternating knots do not "come apart," cannot be separated.

So, I had accomplished my objective—done something that (i) is the answer to a "natural" question, (ii) is easy to formulate, (iii) has a deep, difficult proof, and (iv) is absolutely useless, the purest of pure mathematics.

It was in the fall of 1954 that I got the crucial idea that was the key to proving my result. The thesis was published in the *Annals of Mathematics* in 1956 [Aumann (1956)]; but the proof was essentially in place in the fall of 1954. Shortly thereafter, my research interests turned from knot theory to the areas that have occupied me to this day.

That's Act I of the story. And now, the curtain rises on Act II—50 years later, almost to the day. It's 10 p.m., and the phone rings in my home. My grandson Yakov Rosen is on the line. Yakov is in his second year of medical school. "Grandpa," he says, "can I pick your brain? We are studying knots. I don't understand the material, and think that our lecturer doesn't understand it either. For example, could you explain to me what, exactly, are 'linking numbers'?" "Why are you studying knots?" I ask: "What do knots have to do with medicine?" "Well," says Yakov, "sometimes the DNA in a cell gets knotted up. Depending on the characteristics of the knot, this may lead to cancer. So, we have to understand knots."

I was completely bowled over. Fifty years later, the "absolutely useless"—the "purest of the pure"—is taught in the second year of medical school, and my grandson is studying it. I invited Yakov to come over, and told him about knots, and linking numbers, and my thesis.

Hart: This is indeed fascinating. Incidentally, has the "big, famous" problem ever been solved?

Aumann: Yes. About a year after my thesis was published, a mathematician by the name of Papakyriakopoulos solved the general problem of asphericity. He had been working on it for 18 years. He was at Princeton, but didn't have a job there; they gave him some kind of stipend. He sat in the library and worked away on this for 18 years! During that whole time he published almost nothing—a few related papers, a year or two before solving the big problem. Then he solved this big problem, with an amazingly deep and beautiful proof. And then, he disappeared from sight, and was never heard from again. He did nothing else. It's like these cactuses that flower once in 18 years. Naturally that swamped my result; fortunately mine came before his. It swamped it, except for one thing. Papakyriakopoulos's result does not imply that alternating knots will not come apart. What he proved is that a knot that does not come apart is aspheric. What I proved is that *all* alternating knots are aspheric. It's easy to see that a knot that comes apart is not aspheric, so it follows that an alternating knot will not come apart. So that aspect of my thesis—which is the easily formulated part—did survive.

A little later, but independently, Dick Crowell also proved that alternating knots do not come apart, using a totally different method, not related to asphericity.

Hart: Okay, now that we are all tied up in knots, let's untangle them and go on. You did your Ph.D. at MIT in algebraic topology, and then what?

Aumann: Then for my postdoc, I joined an operations research group at Princeton. This was a rather sharp turn because algebraic topology is just about the purest of pure mathematics and operations research is very applied. It was a small group of about 10 people at the Forrestal Research Center, which is attached to Princeton University.

Hart: In those days operations research and game theory were quite connected. I guess that's how you—

Aumann: —became interested in game theory, exactly. There was a problem about defending a city from a squadron of aircraft most of which are decoys—do not carry any weapons—but a small percentage do carry nuclear weapons. The project was sponsored by Bell Labs, who were developing a defense missile.

At MIT I had met John Nash, who came there in '53 after doing his doctorate at Princeton. I was a senior graduate student and he was a Moore instructor, which was a prestigious instructorship for young mathematicians. So he was a little older than me, scientifically and also chronologically. We got to know each other fairly well and I heard from him about game theory. One of the problems that we kicked around was that of dueling—silent duels, noisy duels, and so on. So when I came to Princeton, although I didn't know much about game theory at all, I had heard about it; and when we were given this problem by Bell Labs, I was able to say, "This sounds a little bit like what Nash was telling us; let's examine it from that point of view." So I started studying game theory; the rest is history, as they say.

Hart: You started reading game theory at that point?

Aumann: I just did the minimum necessary of reading in order to be able to attack the problem.

Hart: Who were the game theorists at Princeton at the time? Did you have any contact with them?

Aumann: I had quite a bit of contact with the Princeton mathematics department. Mainly at that time I was interested in contact with the knot theorists, who included John Milnor and of course R.H. Fox, who was the high priest of knot theory. But there was also contact with the game theorists, who included Milnor—who was both a knot theorist and a game theorist—Phil Wolfe, and Harold Kuhn. Shapley was already at RAND; I did not connect with him until later.

In '56 I came to the Hebrew University. Then, in '60–'61, I was on sabbatical at Princeton, with Oskar Morgenstern's outfit, the Econometric Research Program. This was associated with the economics department, but I also spent quite a bit of time in Fine Hall, in the mathematics department.

Let me tell you an interesting anecdote. When I felt it was time to go on sabbatical, I started looking for a job, and made various applications. One was to Princeton—to Morgenstern. One was to IBM Yorktown Heights, which was also quite a prestigious group. I think Ralph Gomory was already the director of the math department there. Anyway, I got offers from both. The offer from IBM was for $14,000 per year. $14,000 doesn't sound like much, but in 1960 it was a nice bit of money; the equivalent today is about $100,000, which is a nice salary for a young guy just starting out. Morgenstern offered $7,000, exactly half. The offer from Morgenstern came to my office and the offer from IBM came home; my wife Esther didn't open it. I naturally told her about it and she said, "I know why they sent it home. They wanted *me* to open it."

I decided to go to Morgenstern. Esther asked me, "Are you sure you are not doing this just for *ipcha mistabra?*," which is this Talmudic expression for doing just the opposite of what is expected. I said, "Well, maybe, but I do think it's better to go to Princeton." Of course I don't regret it for a moment. It is at Princeton that I first saw the Milnor–Shapley paper, which led to the "Markets with a Continuum of Traders" [Aumann (1964)], and really played a major role in my career; and I have no regrets over the career.

Hart: Or you could have been a main contributor to computer science.

Aumann: Maybe, one can't tell. No regrets. It was great, and meeting Morgenstern and working with him was a tremendous experience, a tremendous privilege.

Hart: Did you meet von Neumann?

Aumann: I met him, but in a sense, he didn't meet me. We were introduced at a game theory conference in 1955, two years before he died. I said, "Hello, Professor von Neumann," and he was very cordial, but I don't think he remembered me afterwards unless he was even more extraordinary than everybody says. I was a young person and he was a great star.

But Morgenstern I got to know very, very well. He was extraordinary. You know, sometimes people make disparaging remarks about Morgenstern, in particular about his contributions to game theory. One of these disparaging jokes is that Morgenstern's greatest contribution to game theory is von Neumann. So let me say, maybe that's true—but that

Figure 15.2   Sergiu Hart, Mike Maschler, Bob Aumann, Bob Wilson, and Oskar Morgenstern, at the 1994 Morgenstern Lecture, Jerusalem.

is a tremendous contribution. Morgenstern's ability to identify people, the potential in people, was enormous and magnificent, was wonderful. He identified the economic significance in the work of people like von Neumann and Abraham Wald, and succeeded in getting them actively involved. He identified the potential in many others; just in the year I was in his outfit, Clive Granger, Sidney Afriat, and Reinhard Selten were also there.

Morgenstern had his own ideas and his own opinions and his own important research in game theory, part of which was the von Neumann–Morgenstern solution to cooperative games. And, he understood the importance of the minimax theorem to economics. One of his greatnesses was that even though he could disagree with people on a scientific issue, he didn't let that interfere with promoting them and bringing them into the circle.

For example, he did not like the idea of perfect competition and he did not like the idea of the core; he thought that perfect competition is a mirage, that when there are many players, perfect competition need *not* result. And indeed, if you apply the von Neumann–Morgenstern solution, it does not lead to perfect competition in markets with many people—that was part of your doctoral thesis, Sergiu. So even though he thought that things like core equivalence were wrongheaded, he still was happy and eager to support people who worked in this direction.

At Princeton I also got to know Frank Anscombe—

Hart: —with whom you wrote a well-known and influential paper [Aumann and Anscombe (1963)]—

Aumann: —that was born then. At that time the accepted definition of subjective probability was Savage's. Anscombe was giving a course on the foundations of probability; he gave a lot of prominence to Savage's theory, which was quite new at the time. Savage's book had been published in '54; it was only six years old. As a result of this course, Anscombe and I worked out this alternative definition, which was published in 1963.

Hart: You also met Shapley at that time?

Aumann: Well, being in game theory, one got to know the name; but personally I got to know Shapley only later. At the end of my year at Princeton, in the fall of '61, there was a conference on "Recent Developments in Game Theory," chaired by Morgenstern and Harold Kuhn. The outcome was the famous orange book, which is very difficult to obtain nowadays. I was the office boy, who did a lot of the practical work in preparing the conference. Shapley was an invited lecturer, so that is the first time I met him.

Another person about whom the readers of this interview may have heard, and who gave an invited lecture at that conference, was Henry Kissinger, who later became the Secretary of State of the United States and was quite prominent in the history of Israel. After the Yom Kippur War in 1973, he came to Israel and to Egypt to try to broker an arrangement between the two countries. He shuttled back and forth between Cairo and Jerusalem. When in Jerusalem, he stayed at the King David Hotel, which is acknowledged to be the best hotel here. Many people were appalled at what he was doing, and thought that he was exercising a lot of favoritism towards Egypt. One of these people was my cousin Steve Strauss, who was the masseur at the King David. Kissinger often went to get a massage from Steve. Steve told us that whenever Kissinger would, in the course of his shuttle diplomacy, do something particularly outrageous, he would slap him really hard on the massage table. I thought that Steve was kidding, but this episode appears also in Kissinger's memoirs; so there is another connection between game theory and the Aumann family.

At the conference, Kissinger spoke about game-theoretic thinking in Cold War diplomacy, Cold War international relations. It is difficult to imagine now how serious the Cold War was. People were really afraid that the world was coming to an end, and indeed there were moments when it did seem that things were hanging in the balance. One of the most vivid was the Cuban Missile Crisis in 1963. In his handling of that crisis, Kennedy was influenced by the game-theoretic school in international relations, which was quite prominent at the time. Kissinger and Herman Kahn were the main figures in that. Kennedy is now praised for his handling of that crisis; indeed, the proof of the pudding is in the eating of it—it came out well. But at that time it seemed extremely hairy, and it really looked as if the world might come to an end at any moment —not only during the Cuban Missile Crisis, but also before and after.

The late fifties and early sixties were the acme of the Cold War. There was a time around '60 or '61 when there was this craze of building nuclear fallout shelters. The game theorists pointed out that this could be seen by the Russians as an extremely aggressive move. Now it takes a little bit of game-theoretic thinking to understand why building a shelter can be seen as aggressive. But the reasoning is quite simple. Why would you build shelters? Because you are afraid of a nuclear attack. Why are you afraid of a nuclear attack? Well, one good reason to be afraid is that if you are going to attack the other side, then you will be concerned about retaliation. If you do not build shelters, you leave yourself open. This is seen as conciliatory because then you say, "I am not concerned about being attacked because I am not going to attack you." So building shelters was seen as very aggressive and it was something very real at the time.

Hart: In short, when you build shelters, your cost from a nuclear war goes down, so your incentive to start a war goes up.

Since you started talking about these topics, let's perhaps move to Mathematica, the United States Arms Control and Disarmament Agency (ACDA), and repeated games. Tell us about your famous work on repeated games. But first, what are repeated games?

Aumann: It's when a single game is repeated many times. How exactly you model "many" may be important, but qualitatively speaking, it usually doesn't matter too much.

Hart: Why are these models important?

Aumann: They model ongoing interactions. In the real world we often respond to a given game situation not so much because of the outcome of that particular game as because our behavior in a particular situation may affect the outcome of future situations in which a similar game is played. For example, let's say somebody promises something and we respond to that promise and then he doesn't keep it—he double-crosses us. He may turn out a winner in the short term, but a loser in the long term: if I meet up with him again and we are again called upon to play a game—to be involved in an interactive situation—then the second time around I won't trust him. Whether he is rational, whether we are both rational, is reflected not only in the outcome of the particular situation in which we are involved today, but also in how it affects future situations.

Another example is revenge, which in the short term may seem irrational; but in the long term, it may be rational, because if you take revenge, then the next time you meet that person, he will not kick you in the stomach. Altruistic behavior, revengeful behavior, any of those things, make sense when viewed from the perspective of a repeated game, but not from the perspective of a one-shot game. So, a repeated game is often more realistic than a one-shot game: it models ongoing relationships.

In 1959 I published a paper on repeated games [Aumann (1959)]. The brunt of that paper is that cooperative behavior in the one-shot game corresponds to equilibrium or egotistic behavior in the repeated game. This is to put it very simplistically.

Hart: There is the famous "Folk Theorem." In the seventies you named it, in your survey of repeated games [Aumann (1981)]. The name has stuck. Incidentally, the term "folk theorem" is nowadays also used in other areas for classic results: the folk theorem of evolution, of computing, and so on.

Aumann: The original Folk Theorem is quite similar to my '59 paper, but a good deal simpler, less deep. As you said, that became quite prominent in the later literature. I called it the Folk Theorem because its authorship is not clear, like folk music, folk songs. It was in the air in the late fifties and early sixties.

Hart: Yours was the first full formal statement and proof of something like this. Even Luce and Raiffa, in their very influential '57 book, *Games and Decisions*, don't have the Folk Theorem.

Aumann: The first people explicitly to consider repeated non-zero-sum games of the kind treated in my '59 paper were Luce and Raiffa. But as you say, they didn't have the Folk Theorem. Shubik's book *Strategy and Market Structure*, published in '59, has a special case of the Folk Theorem, with a proof that has the germ of the general proof.

At that time people did not necessarily publish everything they knew—in fact, they published only a small proportion of what they knew, only really deep results or something really interesting and nontrivial in the mathematical sense of the word—which is not a good sense. Some of the things that are most important are things that a mathematician would consider trivial.

Hart: I remember once in class that you got stuck in the middle of a proof. You went out, and then came back, thinking deeply. Then you went out again. Finally you came back some 20 minutes later and said, "Oh, it's trivial."

Aumann: Yes, I got stuck and started thinking; the students were quiet at first, but got noisier and noisier, and I couldn't think. I went out and paced the corridors and then hit on the answer. I came back and said, "This is trivial"; the students burst into laughter. So "trivial" is a bad term.

Take something like the Cantor diagonal method. Nowadays it would be considered trivial, and sometimes it really is trivial. But it is extremely important; for example, Gödel's famous incompleteness theorem is based on it.

Hart: "Trivial to explain" and "trivial to obtain" are different. Some of the confusion lies there. Something may be very simple to explain once you get it. On the other hand, thinking about it and getting to it may be very deep.

Aumann: Yes, and hitting on the right formulation may be very important. The diagonal method illustrates that even within pure mathematics the trivial may be important. But certainly outside of it, there are interesting observations that are mathematically trivial—like the Folk Theorem. I knew about the Folk Theorem in the late fifties, but was too young to recognize its importance. I wanted something deeper, and that is what I did in fact publish. That's my '59 paper [Aumann (1959)]. It's a nice paper—my first published paper in game theory proper. But the Folk Theorem, although much easier, is more important. So it's important for a person to realize what's important. At that time I didn't have the maturity for this.

Quite possibly, other people knew about it. People were thinking about repeated games, dynamic games, long-term interaction. There are Shapley's stochastic games, Everett's recursive games, the work of Gillette, and so on. I wasn't the only person thinking about repeated games. Anybody who thinks a little about repeated games, especially if he is a mathematician, will very soon hit on the Folk Theorem. It is not deep.

Hart: That's '59; let's move forward.

Aumann: In the early sixties Morgenstern and Kuhn founded a consulting firm called Mathematica, based in Princeton, not to be confused with the software that goes by that name today. In '64 they started working with the United States Arms Control and Disarmament Agency. Mike Maschler worked with them on the first project, which had to do with inspection; obviously there is a game between an inspector and an inspectee, who may want to hide what he is doing. Mike made an important contribution to that. There were other people working on that also, including Frank Anscombe. This started in '64, and the second project, which was larger, started in '65. It had to do with the Geneva disarmament negotiations, a series of negotiations with the Soviet Union, on arms control and disarmament. The people on this project included

Kuhn, Gérard Debreu, Herb Scarf, Reinhard Selten, John Harsanyi, Jim Mayberry, Maschler, Dick Stearns (who came in a little later), and me. What struck Maschler and me was that these negotiations were taking place again and again; a good way of modeling this is a repeated game. The only thing that distinguished it from the theory of the late fifties that we discussed before is that these were repeated games of incomplete information. We did not know how many weapons the Russians held, and the Russians did not know how many weapons we held. What we— the United States—proposed to put into the agreements might influence what the Russians thought or knew that we had, and this would affect what they would do in later rounds.

Hart: What you do reveals something about your private information. For example, taking an action that is optimal in the short run may reveal to the other side exactly what your situation is, and then in the long run you may be worse off.

Aumann: Right. This informational aspect is absent from the previous work, where everything was open and above board, and the issues are how one's behavior affects future interaction. Here the question is how one's *behavior* affects the other player's *knowledge*. So Maschler and I, and later Stearns, developed a theory of repeated games of incomplete information. This theory was set forth in a series of research reports between '66 and '68, which for many years were unavailable.

Hart: Except to the aficionados, who were passing bootlegged copies from mimeograph machines. They were extremely hard to find.

Aumann: Eventually they were published by MIT Press in '95 [Aumann and Maschler (1995)], together with extensive postscripts describing what has happened since the late sixties—a tremendous amount of work. The mathematically deepest started in the early seventies in Belgium, at CORE, and in Israel, mostly by my students and then by their students. Later it spread to France, Russia, and elsewhere. The area is still active.

Hart: What is the big insight?

Aumann: It is always misleading to sum it up in a few words, but here goes: in the long run, you cannot use information without revealing it; you can use information only to the extent that you are willing to reveal it. A player with private information must choose between not making use of that information—and then he doesn't have to reveal it—or making use of it, and then taking the consequences of the other side finding it out. That's the big picture.

Hart: In addition, in a non-zero-sum situation, you may *want* to pass information to the other side; it may be mutually advantageous to reveal your information. The question is how to do it so that you can be trusted, or in technical terms, in a way that is incentive-compatible.

Aumann: The bottom line remains similar. In that case you can use the information, not only if you are willing to reveal it, but also if you actually *want* to reveal it. It may actually have positive value to reveal the information. Then you use it *and* reveal it.

Hart: You mentioned something else and I want to pick up on that: the Milnor–Shapley paper on oceanic games. That led you to another major work, "Markets with a Continuum of Traders" [Aumann (1964)]: modeling perfect competition by a continuum.

Aumann: As I already told you, in '60–'61, the Milnor–Shapley paper "Oceanic Games" caught my fancy. It treats games with an ocean— nowadays we call it a continuum—of small players, and a small number of large players, whom they called atoms. Then in the fall of '61, at the conference at which Kissinger and Lloyd Shapley were present, Herb Scarf gave a talk about large markets. He had a countable infinity of players. Before that, in '59, Martin Shubik had published a paper called "Edgeworth Market Games," in which he made a connection between the core of a large market game and the competitive equilibrium. Scarf's model somehow wasn't very satisfactory, and Herb realized that himself; afterwards, he and Debreu proved a much more satisfactory version, in their *International Economic Review* 1963 paper. The bottom line was that, under certain assumptions, the core of a large economy is close to the competitive solution, the solution to which one is led from the law of supply and demand. I heard Scarf's talk, and, as I said, the formulation was not very satisfactory. I put it together with the result of Milnor and Shapley about oceanic games, and realized that *that* has to be the right way of treating this situation: a continuum, not the countable infinity that Scarf was using. It took a while longer to put all this together, but eventually I did get a very general theorem with a continuum of traders. It has very few assumptions, and it is not a limit result. It simply says that the core of a large market is the *same* as the set of competitive outcomes. This was published in *Econometrica* in 1964 [Aumann (1964)].

Hart: Indeed, the introduction of the continuum idea to economic theory has proved indispensable to the advancement of the discipline. In the same way as in most of the natural sciences, it enables a precise and rigorous analysis, which otherwise would have been very hard or even impossible.

Aumann: The continuum is an approximation to the "true" situation, in which the number of traders is large but finite. The purpose of the continuous approximation is to make available the powerful and elegant methods of the branch of mathematics called "analysis," in a situation where treatment by finite methods would be much more difficult or even hopeless—think of trying to do fluid mechanics by solving n-body problems for large n.

Hart: The continuum is the best way to start understanding what's going on. Once you have that, you can do approximations and get limit results.

Aumann: Yes, these approximations by finite markets became a hot topic in the late sixties and early seventies. The '64 paper was followed by the *Econometrica* '66 paper [Aumann (1966)] on existence of competitive equilibria in continuum markets; in '75 came the paper on values of such markets, also in *Econometrica* [Aumann (1975)]. Then there came later papers using a continuum, by me with or without coauthors [Aumann (1973, 1980), Aumann and Kurz (1977a,b), Aumann, Gardner, and Rosenthal (1977), Aumann, Kurz, and Neyman (1983, 1987)], by Werner Hildenbrand and his school, and by many, many others.

Hart: Before the '75 paper, you developed, together with Shapley, the theory of values of nonatomic games [Aumann and Shapley (1974)]; this generated a huge literature. Many of your students worked on that. What's a nonatomic game, by the way? There is a story about a talk on "Values of nonatomic games," where a secretary thought a word was missing in the title, so it became "Values of nonatomic war games." So, what are nonatomic games?

Aumann: It has nothing to do with war and disarmament. On the contrary, in war you usually have two sides. Nonatomic means the exact opposite, where you have a continuum of sides, a very large number of players.

Hart: None of which are atoms.

Aumann: Exactly, in the sense that I was explaining before. It is like Milnor and Shapley's oceanic games, except that in the oceanic games there were atoms—"large" players—and in nonatomic games there are no large players at all.

Figure 15.3 Werner Hildenbrand with Bob Aumann, Oberwolfach, 1982.

There are *only* small players. But unlike in Milnor–Shapley, the small players may be of different kinds; the ocean is not homogeneous. The basic property is that no player by himself makes any significant contribution. An example of a nonatomic game is a large economy, consisting of small consumers and small businesses only, without large corporations or government interference. Another example is an election, modeled as a situation where no individual can affect the outcome. Even the 2000 U.S. presidential election is a nonatomic game—no single voter, even in Florida, could have affected the outcome. (The people who did affect the outcome were the Supreme Court judges.) In a nonatomic game, large coalitions can affect the outcome, but individual players cannot.

Hart: And values?

Aumann: The game theory concept of value is an a priori evaluation of what a player, or group of players, can expect to get out of the game. Lloyd Shapley's 1953 formalization is the most prominent. Sometimes, as in voting situations, value is presented as an index of power (Shapley and Shubik 1954). I have already mentioned the 1975 result about values of large economies being the same as the competitive outcomes of a market [Aumann (1975)]. This result had several precursors, the first of which was a '64 RAND Memorandum of Shapley.

Hart: Values of nonatomic games and their application in economic models led to a huge literature.

Another one of your well-known contributions is the concept of correlated equilibrium (*Journal of Mathematical Economics*, '74 [Aumann, 1974]). How did it come about?

Aumann: Correlated equilibria are like mixed Nash equilibria, except that the players' randomizations need not be independent. Frankly, I'm not really sure how this business began. It's probably related to repeated games, and, indirectly, to Harsanyi and Selten's equilibrium selection. These ideas were floating around in the late sixties, especially at the very intense meetings of the Mathematica ACDA team. In the Battle of the Sexes, for example, if you're going to select *one* equilibrium, it has to be the mixed one, which is worse for *both* players than *either* of the two pure ones. So you say, "Hey, let's toss a coin to decide on one of the two pure equilibria." Once the coin is tossed, it's to the advantage of both players to adhere to the chosen equilibrium; the whole process, including the coin toss, is in equilibrium. This equilibrium is a lot better than the unique mixed strategy equilibrium, because it guarantees that the boy and the girl will definitely meet—either at the boxing match or at the ballet —whereas with the mixed strategy equilibrium, they may well go to different places.

With repeated games, one gets a similar result by alternating: one evening boxing, the next ballet. Of course, that way one only gets to the convex hull of the Nash equilibria.

This is pretty straightforward. The next step is less so. It is to go to three-person games, where two of the three players gang up on the third —correlate "against" him, so to speak [Aumann (1974), Examples 2.5 and 2.6]. This leads *outside* the convex hull of Nash equilibria. In writing this formally, I realized that the same definitions apply also to two-person games; also there, they may lead outside the convex hull of the Nash equilibria.

Hart: So, correlated equilibria arise when the players get signals that need not be independent. Talking about signals and information— how about common knowledge and the "Agreeing to Disagree" paper?

Aumann: The original paper on correlated equilibrium also discussed "subjective equilibrium," where different players have different probabilities for the same event. Differences in probabilities can arise from differences in information; but then, if a player knows that another player's probability is different from his, he might wish to revise his own probability. It's not clear whether this process of revision necessarily leads to the same probabilities. This question was raised—and left open—in Aumann (1974) [Section 9j]. Indeed, even the formulation of the question was murky.

I discussed this with Arrow and Frank Hahn during an IMSSS summer in the early seventies. I remember the moment vividly. We were sitting in Frank Hahn's small office on the fourth floor of Stanford's Encina Hall, where the economics department was located. I was trying to get my head around the problem—not its solution, but simply its formulation. Discussing it with them—describing the issue to them—somehow sharpened and clarified it. I went back to my office, sat down, and continued thinking. Suddenly the whole thing came to me in a flash— the definition of common knowledge, the characterization in terms of information partitions, and the agreement theorem: roughly, that if the probabilities of two people for an event are commonly known by both, then they *must* be equal. It took a couple of days more to get a coherent proof and to write it down. The proof seemed quite straightforward. The whole thing—definition, formulation, proof—came to less than a page.

Indeed, it looked so straightforward that it seemed hardly worth publishing. I went back and told Arrow and Hahn about it. At first Arrow wouldn't believe it, but became convinced when he saw the proof. I expressed to him my doubts about publication. He strongly urged me to publish it—so I did [Aumann (1976)]. It became one of my two most widely cited papers.

Six or seven years later I learned that the philosopher David Lewis had defined the concept of common knowledge already in 1969, and, surprisingly, had used the same name for it. Of course, there is no question that Lewis has priority. He did not, however, have the agreement theorem.

Hart: The agreement theorem is surprising—and important. But your simple and elegant formalization of common knowledge is even more important. It pioneered the area known as "interactive epistemology": knowledge about others' knowledge. It generated a huge literature—in game theory, economics, and beyond: computer science, philosophy, logic. It enabled the rigorous analysis of very deep and complex issues, such as what is rationality, and what is needed for equilibrium. Interestingly, it led you in particular back to correlated equilibrium.

Aumann: Yes. That's Aumann (1987). The idea of common knowledge really enables the "right" formulation of correlated equilibrium. It's not some kind of esoteric extension of Nash equilibrium. Rather, it says that if people simply respond optimally to their information—and this is commonly known—then you get correlated equilibrium. The "equilibrium" part of this is not the point. Correlated equilibrium is nothing more than just common knowledge of rationality, together with common priors.

Hart: Let's talk now about the Hebrew University. You came to the Hebrew University in '56 and have been there ever since.

Aumann: I'll tell you something. Mathematical game theory is a branch of applied mathematics. When I was a student, applied mathematics was looked down upon by many pure mathematicians. They stuck up their noses and looked down upon it.

Hart: At that time most applications were to physics.

Aumann: Even that—hydrodynamics and that kind of thing—was looked down upon. That is not the case anymore, and hasn't been for quite a while; but in the late fifties when I came to the Hebrew University that was still the vogue in the world of mathematics. At the Hebrew University I did not experience any kind of inferiority in that respect, nor in other respects either. Game theory was accepted as something worthwhile and important. In fact, Aryeh Dvoretzky, who was instrumental in bringing me here, and Abraham Fränkel (of Zermelo–Fränkel set theory), who was chair of the mathematics department, certainly appreciated this subject. It was one of the reasons I was brought here. Dvoretzky himself had done some work in game theory.

Hart: Let's make a big jump. In 1991, the Center for Rationality was established at the Hebrew University.

Aumann: I don't know whether it was the brainchild of Yoram Ben-Porath or Menahem Yaari or both together. Anyway, Ben-Porath, who was the rector of the university, asked Yaari, Itamar Pitowsky, Motty Perry, and me to make a proposal for establishing a center for rationality. It wasn't even clear what the center was to be called. Something having to do with game theory, with economics, with philosophy. We met many times. Eventually what came out was the Center for Rationality, which you, Sergiu, directed for its first eight critical years; it was you who really got it going and gave it its oomph. The Center is really unique in the whole world in that it brings together very many disciplines. Throughout the world there are several research centers in areas connected with game theory. Usually they are associated with departments of economics: the Cowles Foundation at Yale, the Center for Operations Research and Econometrics in Louvain, Belgium, the late Institute for Mathematical Studies in the Social Sciences at Stanford. The Center for Rationality at the Hebrew University is quite different, in that it is much broader. The basic idea is "rationality": behavior that advances one's own interests. This appears in many different contexts, represented by many academic disciplines. The Center has members from mathematics, economics, computer science, evolutionary biology, general philosophy, philosophy of science, psychology, law, statistics, the business school, and education. We should have a member from political science, but we don't; that's a hole in the program. We should have one from medicine too, because medicine is a field in which rational utility-maximizing behavior is very important, and not at all easy. But at this time we don't have one. There is nothing in the world even approaching the breadth of coverage of the Center for Rationality.

It is broad but nevertheless focused. There would seem to be a contradiction between breadth and focus, but our Center has both—breadth and focus. The breadth is in the number and range of different disciplines that are represented at the Center. The focus is, in all these disciplines, on rational, self-interested behavior—or the lack of it. We take all these different disciplines, and we look at a certain segment of each one, and at how these various segments from this great number of disciplines fit together.

Hart: Can you give a few examples for the readers of this journal? They may be surprised to hear about some of these connections.

Aumann: I'll try; let's go through some applications. In computer science we have distributed computing, in which there are many different processors. The problem is to coordinate the work of these processors, which may number in the hundreds of thousands, each doing its own work.

Hart: That is, how processors that work in a decentralized way reach a coordinated goal.

Aumann: Exactly. Another application is protecting computers against hackers who are trying to break down the computer. This is a very grim game, just like war is a grim game, and the stakes are high; but it is a game. That's another kind of interaction between computers and game theory.

Still another kind comes from computers that solve games, play games, and design games—like auctions—particularly on the Web. These are applications of computers to games, whereas before, we were discussing applications of games to computers.

Biology is another example where one might think that games don't seem particularly relevant. But they are! There is a book by Richard Dawkins called *The Selfish Gene.* This book discusses how evolution makes organisms operate as if they were promoting their self-interest, acting rationally. What drives this is the survival of the fittest. If the genes that organisms have developed in the course of evolution are not optimal, are not doing as well as other genes, then they will not survive. There is a tremendous range of applications of game-theoretic and rationalistic reasoning in evolutionary biology.

Economics is of course the main area of application of game theory. The book by von Neumann and Morgenstern that started game theory rolling is called *The Theory of Games and Economic Behavior.* In economics people are assumed to act in order to maximize their utility; at least, until Tversky and Kahneman came along and said that people do not necessarily act in their self-interest. That is one way in which psychology is represented in the Center for Rationality: the study of irrationality. But the subject is still rationality. We'll discuss Kahneman and Tversky and the new school of "behavioral economics" later. Actually, using the term "behavioral economics" is already biasing the issue. The question is whether behavior really is that way or not.

We have mentioned computer science, psychology, economics, politics. There is much political application of game theory in international relations, which we already discussed in connection with Kissinger. There also are national politics, like various electoral systems. For example, the State of Israel is struggling with that. Also, I just came back from Paris, where Michel Balinsky told me about the problems of elections in American politics. There is apparently a tremendous amount of gerrymandering in American politics, and it's becoming a really big problem. So it is not only in Israel that we are struggling with the problem of how to conduct elections.

Another aspect is forming a government coalition: if it is too small—a minimal winning coalition—it will be unstable; if too large, the prime minister will have too little influence. What is the right balance?

Law: more and more, we have law and economics, law and game theory. There are studies of how laws affect the behavior of people, the behavior of criminals, the behavior of the police. All these things are about self-interested, rational behavior.

Hart: So that's the Center for Rationality. I know this doesn't belong, but I'll ask it here. You are a deeply religious man. How does it fit in with a rational view of the world? How do you fit together science and religion?

Aumann: As you say, it really doesn't belong here, but I'll respond anyway. Before responding directly, let me say that the scientific view of the world is really just in our minds. When you look at it carefully, it is not something that is out there in the real world. For example, take the statement "the earth is round." It sounds like a very simple statement that is either true or false. Either the earth is round or it isn't; maybe it is square, or elliptical, or whatever. But when you come to think of it, it is a very complex statement. What does roundness mean? Roundness means that there is a point—the "center" of the earth—such that any point on the surface of the earth is at the same distance from that center as any other point on the surface of the earth. Now that already sounds a little complex. But the complexity only begins there. What exactly do we mean by equal distance? For that you need the concept of a distance between two points. The concept of distance between two points is something that is fairly complex even if we are talking about a ball that we can hold in our hands; it involves taking a ruler and measuring the distance between two points. But when we are talking about the earth, it is even more complex, because there is no way that we are going to measure the distance between the center of the earth and the surface of the earth with a ruler. One problem is that we can't get to the center. Even if we could find it we wouldn't be able to get there. We certainly wouldn't be able to find a ruler that is big enough. So we have to use some kind of complex theory in order to give that a practical meaning. Even when we have four points and we say the distance from A to B is the same as the distance from C to D, that is fairly complex already. Maybe the ruler changes. We are using a whole big theory, a whole big collection of ideas, in order to give meaning to this very, very simple statement that the earth is round.

Don't get me wrong. We all agree that the earth is round. What I am saying is that the roundness of the earth is a concept that is in our minds.

It's a product of a very complex set of ideas, and ideas are in people's minds. So the way I think of science, and even of fairly simple things, is as being in our minds; all the more so for things like gravitation, the energy that is emitted by a star, or even the concept of a "species." Yes, we are both members of the species *Homo sapiens*. What does that mean? Obviously we are different. My beard is much longer than yours. What exactly does species mean? What exactly does it even mean to say "Bob Aumann" is sitting here? Is it the same Bob Aumann as five minutes ago? These are very complex ideas. Identity, all those things that we think of trivially on a day-to-day basis, are really complex ideas that are in our minds; they are not really out there. Science is built to satisfy certain needs in our minds. It describes *us*. It does have a relationship with the real world, but this relationship is very, very complex.

Having said that, I'll get to your question. Religion is very different from science. The main part of religion is not about the way that we model the real world. I am purposely using the word "model." Religion is an experience—mainly an emotional and aesthetic one. It is not about whether the earth is 5,765 years old. When you play the piano, when you climb a mountain, does this contradict your scientific endeavors? Obviously not. The two things are almost—though not quite—orthogonal. Hiking, skiing, dancing, bringing up your children—you do all kinds of things that are almost orthogonal to your scientific endeavor. That's the case with religion also. It doesn't contradict; it is orthogonal. Belief is an important part of religion, certainly; but in science we have certain ways of thinking about the world, and in religion we have different ways of thinking about the world. Those two things coexist side by side without conflict.

Hart: A world populated by rational players—is it consistent with the religious view?

Aumann: Yes. Religion places a lot of emphasis on coliving with your fellow man. A large part of religion is, be nice to other people. We can understand this in the religious context for what it is and we can understand it scientifically in the sense of repeated games that we discussed before, and we can understand it from the evolutionary viewpoint. These are different ways of understanding the phenomenon; there is no contradiction there. Fully rational players could be deeply religious; religion reflects other drives.

Hart: This applies to person-to-person interaction. But isn't there, in a sense, an extra player, which would be G-d or something that you cannot understand by rational means, an extra nonrationally driven player?

Aumann: My response is that each player has to see to his own actions. In discussing the laws, the rules by which we live, the Talmud sometimes says that a certain action is not punishable by mortal courts but is punished by Heaven, and then discusses such punishments in detail. Occasionally in such a discussion somebody will say, "Well, we can only determine what the reaction of human courts will be to this or that action. We cannot dictate to Heaven how to react, and therefore it's useless for us to discuss it." That cuts off the discussion. As a religious person I must ask myself how *I* will act. I cannot discuss the rationality or irrationality of G-d.

Hart: The point is not the rationality or irrationality of that player, of G-d, but how that player affects what other players do and in what ways rational players can take this into account. Let me make it very simplistic. As you said, you don't know what Heaven will do, so how can I make rational decisions if I don't know that?

Aumann: We don't know what Heaven will do, but we do have rules of conduct. We have the Pentateuch, the Torah, the Talmud.

Hart: I am talking more on the philosophical level, rather than on a practical level. The point is that that player is not reducible to standard mortal arguments or understanding. Because if he were, he would not be a special entity, which G-d is. However, he is part of the world. Not only is he part of the world, he is an important part of the religious world. He is not just a side player. He is the main player. Not only is he the main player, he is a player who by definition cannot be reduced to rational analysis.

Aumann: I wouldn't say that He is irrational. By the way, it is interesting that this should come up just today, because there is a passage in the Torah reading of yesterday that relates to this. "This commandment that I command you today is not far away from you. It is not in Heaven so that one would have to say, 'Who will go up to Heaven and will take it from there and tell us about it?'" (*Deuteronomy* 30, 11–12). These verses were interpreted in the Talmud as saying that in the last analysis, commands in the Torah, the religious commandments, the whole of Scripture must be interpreted by human beings, by the sages and wise men in each generation. So the Torah must be given practical meaning by human beings.

The Talmud relates a story of a disagreement between one of the sages, Rabbi Eliezer ben Horkanos, and all the other sages. Rabbi Eliezer had one opinion and all the others had a different opinion. Rabbi Eliezer said, "If I am right then let the water in the aqueduct flow upwards." Sure enough, there was a miracle, and the water started flowing uphill. So the other sages said, "We are sorry; the law is not determined by the way the water flows in an aqueduct. It is determined by majority opinion." He asked for several other miracles and they all happened—Heaven was on his side. Nevertheless, his opinion was rejected. Each time the majority rejected it and said "This is irrelevant." In the end he said, "If I am right let a voice come from Heaven and say so." And sure enough, a voice came from Heaven and said, "Why do you argue with Rabbi Eliezer? Whatever he says is always right." This was again rejected by the majority, who quoted the verse I just cited, "It is not in Heaven." The Torah was given to *us* by Heaven, and now it is *our* prerogative to interpret it. The story goes on to say that Elijah (the prophet who never died and keeps going back and forth between Heaven and earth) was asked by one of the sages who met him, "Were you in Heaven when that happened?" He said, "Yes, I was there." The sage said, "How did G-d react to His opinion being rejected by the earthly sages?" So Elijah said, "G-d smiled and said, 'My children have vanquished me.'"

This is an example of what is behind the figure of G-d—call it a model, a way of thinking, a way of living. It is similar, broadly speaking, to the earth being round. G-d is a way of thinking of our lives; translated into practical terms, it tells us how to live as human beings.

Hart: This is very interesting. Let me try to summarize. On the one hand there is an emotional and aesthetic experience, to which I can very clearly relate, like going to a concert or seeing something beautiful. On the other hand, religion dictates certain rules of behavior. These rules, first of all, are not well defined. They are interpreted by human beings. Second, these rules may be justified in a rational way. Like in your work with Michael Maschler [Aumann and Maschler (1985)], where you gave a game-theoretic interpretation of a passage from the Talmud that nobody could understand, and suddenly everything became crystal clear. So you are saying that there are rules, which are good rules. And they are good not just because G-d gave them to us. We may not understand the reasons, but if we go deep enough and start analyzing, we may find good reasons for them. Moreover, if people are following these rules it leads perhaps to a better society—a Pareto improvement. Is that correct?

Aumann: Well, it is your way of putting it. Let me enlarge on it. The observance of the Sabbath is extremely beautiful, and is impossible without being religious. It is not even a question of improving society—it is about improving one's own quality of life. For example, let's say I'm taking a trip a couple of hours after the Sabbath. Any other person would spend the day packing, going to the office, making final arrangements, final phone calls, this and that. For me it's out of the question. I do it on Friday. The Sabbath is *there*. The world stops.

Hart: That's a good example. In fact my wife has said many times, after yet another guest suddenly dropped in on us on Saturday, or we had to go and do something or other: "I wish we would become religious and have a really quiet Saturday once in a while." So I can definitely understand the advantages of having a nice, quiet day of rest.

Aumann: The day before the Sabbath, Friday, is a very hectic day for the person in charge of the house, who has to prepare for the Sabbath. On Friday in Israel, like on Saturday in most of the Western world, many offices are closed. It is a semi-day-of-rest. But for religious people, especially for the houseperson, it is very hectic. We have a seminar series at the Center for Rationality called "Rationality on Friday"; my wife used to say that she could understand rationality on any other day, but *not* on Friday.

So, we have this one day in the week when nothing can come in the way and we are shut off from the world. We don't answer the phone, we don't operate electricity, we don't drive cars.

Hart: It is a self-committing device, if you translate it into rational terms.

Aumann: Exactly, it's a self-committing device.

Here is another example. There was a period 15, 20 years ago when stealing software was considered okay by many people, including many academics. There was an item of software that I needed, and I was wondering whether to "steal" it—make a copy of which the developers of the software disapprove. Then I said to myself, "Why do you have to wonder about this? You are a religious person. Go to your rabbi and ask him." I don't have to worry about these questions because I have a religion that tells me what to do. So I went to my rabbi—a Holocaust survivor, a very renowned, pious person. I figured he won't even know what software is—I'll have to explain it to him. Maybe there is a Talmudic rule about this kind of intellectual property not really being property. Whatever he'll say, I'll do. I went to him. He said, "Ask my son-in-law." So I said, "No, I am asking *you*." He said, "Okay, come back in a few days." I'll make a long story short. I went back again and again. He didn't want to give me an answer. Finally I insisted and he said, "Okay, if you really want to know, it's absolutely forbidden to do this, absolutely forbidden." So I ordered the software.

In short, you can be a moral person, but morals are often equivocal. In the eighties, copying software was considered moral by many people. The point I am making is that religion—at least my religion—is a sort of force, a way of making a commitment to conduct yourself in a certain way, which is good for the individual and good for society.

Hart: But then, in a world where everybody follows these rules, there is perhaps no reason for game theory. Of course, there is a problem in the details; the rules of conduct may not be enough to tell you exactly what to do in every situation. But in principle, in a world populated by religious people, do we need game theory?

Aumann: Certainly. The rules cover only the moral or ethical issues. There is a lot of room within these rules for strategic behavior. For example, the rules tell you that if you made an offer and it was accepted, then you can't renege. But they don't tell you how much to offer. The rules tell you that you must bargain in good faith, but they don't tell you whether to be tough, or compromising, or whatever. The rules tell you, "You may not steal software"; but they don't tell you how much to pay for the software, when to buy it and when not. The rules tell you to give a lot to charity, but not how much. There was a study made in the United States of income tax deductions to charity. It turned out that orthodox Jews were among the largest contributors to charities. It's a religious command.

Unfortunately it has been my lot to spend more time in hospitals than I would have wanted. I have witnessed some very beautiful things. People coming to hospital wards and saying, "Look, we have private ambulances. We can take people from this hospital to wherever you want to go, from Metulla to Eilat [the northern and southern extremities of Israel], for nothing. We'll take anybody, religious, irreligious, Jews, Arabs, anybody." These were people who obviously were religious. They were going around with a beard and sidelocks. You have people who come around on Friday afternoon to make *kiddush* for the sick, and people who come around at any time of the week playing the violin and things like that.

The religious community, by the way, is very close. This matter of *khessed*, of helping your fellow man, is very strong in religious communities; it is a commandment, like eating kosher and keeping the Sabbath.

Hart: Returning to the rules and their interpretation: do you mean that you would not go to the rabbi to ask him, say, whether to enter into a certain partnership, or how to vote in an election?

Aumann: Well, *I* would not, and many others like me would not. But others—for example, "Khassidim"—might well consult their rabbi on such matters. In Khassidic circles, the rabbi is often much more than a scholar and legal and spiritual authority. He is a fountain of advice on all kinds of important decisions—medical, business, family, whatever. And often he gives very good advice! How come? Is he smarter than others? Yes, he often is. But that's not the important reason. The important reason is that everybody comes to him, so he gets a whole lot of inside information. We have a very interesting strategic equilibrium there—it's optimal for everyone to go to him, given that everybody goes to him! Of course, for that it is important that he be honest and straightforward, and that's already dictated by the moral rules. But it's also part of the equilibrium, because the whole thing would fall apart if he weren't.

There is, incidentally, a phenomenon like this also among the "Mitnagdim," like me. There is a person in Israel called Rabbi Firer, who is absolutely the top source of medical information in the whole country, possibly in the whole world. And he is *not* a physician. Anybody who has an unusual or serious medical problem can go to him, or phone him. You make a phone appointment for, say, 1:17 a.m., you describe your problem, and he tells you where to go for treatment. Often the whole thing takes no more than a minute. Sometimes, in complicated cases, it takes more; he will not only direct you to a treatment center in Arizona, he'll arrange transportation when necessary, make the introductions, et cetera, et cetera. The whole point is that he is *not* a physician, so he has no special interests, no axe to grind. How it works is that he, like the Khassidic rabbi, gets information from everybody, patients and doctors alike, and he is also unusually brilliant. And he is deeply religious, which, again, is what keeps him honest. I have made use of him more often than I would have liked.

Up to now we have been discussing the normative side of game theory— advising individuals how to act—but there are also other sides. One is "public normative." The religion will not tell you how to conduct elections, or when to cut the discount rate, or how to form a government. It will not tell you how to build a distributed computer, or how to run a spectrum auction, or how to assign interns to hospitals.

Still another side is the "descriptive." Religion will not explain how evolution formed various species, or why competition works.

But I must immediately correct myself: the Talmud *does* in fact discuss both evolution and competition. Evolution is discussed in the tractate *Shabbat* on page 31a. The sage Hillel was asked why the eyes of certain African tribesmen are smaller than usual, and why the feet of other African tribesmen are broader than usual. Hillel's answers were adaptive: the eyes are smaller because these tribesmen live in a windy, sandy region, and the smallness of the eyes enables them better to keep the sand out; and the feet are broader because that tribe lives in a swampy region, and the broad feet enable easier navigation of the swamps.

Competition is also discussed in the Talmud. In the tractate *Baba Bathra* 89a, the Talmud says that the authorities must appoint inspectors to check the accuracy of the weights and measures used by marketplace vendors, but *not* to oversee prices. The twelfth-century commentator Samuel ben Meier (Rashbam) explains the reason: if a vendor overcharges, another vendor who needs the money will undercut him, all the customers will go to him, and the original vendor will have to match the lower price. The invisible hand—600 years before Adam Smith!

Other game-theoretic and economic principles are also discussed in the Talmud. The nucleolus makes an implicit appearance in the tractate *Kethuboth* 93a [Aumann and Maschler (1985)]; risk aversion shows up in *Makkoth* 3a [Aumann (2003b)]; moral hazard, in *Kethuboth* 15a, and the list can be made much longer.

But of course, all these discussions are only the barest of hints. We still need the game theory to understand these matters. The Talmud speaks about adaptation, but one can hardly say that it anticipated the theory of evolution. The Talmud discusses competition, but we can hardly say that it anticipated the formulation of the equivalence theorem, to say nothing of its proof.

Besides, one needs game theory to explain the ethical and moral rules themselves. *Why* not steal software? *Why* have accurate weights and measures? Why love one's neighbor as oneself? How did it come about, what function does it serve, what keeps it together? All these are game-theoretic questions.

Finally, let's not forget that the world is very far from being—to use your phrase—populated by religious people only.

In short, the Bible and the Talmud are fascinating documents, and they cover a lot of ground, but there still is a lot of room for game theory—and for all of science.

Hart: So, to summarize this point: game theory definitely has a place in a religious world. In the "micro," the rules of conduct are principles that cover only certain issues, and there is "freedom of decision." In the "macro," the structures that arise, and the rules of conduct themselves, are subject to game-theoretic analysis: how and why did they come about?

Is your view a common view of religious people?

Aumann: Maybe not. One doesn't discuss this very much in religious circles. When I was young, there were many attempts by religious people to "reconcile" science and religion. For example, each of the six days of creation can be viewed as representing a different geological era. There was—and perhaps still is—a view that science contradicts religion, that one has to reconcile them. It is apologetic, and I don't buy it.

Hart: Take, for example, the six days of creation; whether or not this is how it happened is practically irrelevant to one's decisions and way of conduct. It's on a different level.

Aumann: It is a different view of the world, a different way of looking at the world. That's why I prefaced my answer to your question with the story about the roundness of the world being one way of viewing the world. An evolutionary geological perspective is one way of viewing the world. A different way is with the six days of creation. Truth is in our minds. If we are sufficiently broad-minded, then we can simultaneously entertain different ideas of truth, different models, different views of the world.

Hart: I think a scientist will have no problem with that. Would a religious person have problems with what you just said?

Aumann: Different religious people have different viewpoints. Some of them might have problems with it. By the way, I'm not so sure that no scientist would have a problem with it. Some scientists are very doctrinaire.

Hart: I was just reminded of Newcomb's paradox, with its "omniscient being." We both share the view that it doesn't make much sense. On the other hand, perhaps it does make sense in a religious world.

Aumann: No, no. It's a little similar to this question of the omnipotence of G-d. If G-d is omnipotent, can He create an immovable object? Atheists will come up with a question like that, saying, "Here, I've disproved the whole idea of religion."

By the way, it's not a Jewish view that G-d is omnipotent. But that's not the point; the point is that the question is simply nonsense.

Altogether, the Jewish tradition is not very strong on theology, on what it is that G-d can or cannot do. But there is a very strong tradition of human free will in Judaism. There is definitely one thing that G-d *cannot* do, namely, influence a person's free will, his decisionmaking capacity. So there is a lack of omnipotence at least in that aspect of the Jewish tradition.

Hart: Rational people can very well exist in this religious world. You have reconciled that very nicely. That was very interesting.

Aumann: I haven't reconciled. I tried not to reconcile, but to say, "These are different things."

Hart: Reconciled in the sense that those things can coexist.

Let's move now to your personal biography.

Aumann: I was born in 1930 in Frankfurt, Germany, to an orthodox Jewish family. My father was a wholesale textile merchant, rather well to do. We got away in 1938. Actually we had planned to leave already when Hitler came to power in 1933, but for one reason or another the emigration was cancelled and people convinced my parents that it wasn't so bad. It will be okay, this thing will blow over. The German people will not allow such a madman to take over, et cetera, et cetera. A well-known story. But it illustrates that when one is in the middle of things it is very, very difficult to see the future. Things seem clear in hindsight, but in the middle of the crisis they are very murky.

Hart: Especially when it is a slow-moving process, rather than a dramatic change: every time it is just a little more and you say, "That's not much," but when you look at the integral of all this, suddenly it is a big change.

Aumann: That is one thing. But even more basically, it is just difficult to see. Let me jump forward from 1933 to 1967. I was in Israel and there was the crisis preceding the Six-Day War. In hindsight it was "clear" that Israel would come out on top of that conflict. But at the time it wasn't at all clear, not at all. I vividly remember the weeks leading up to the Six-Day War, the crisis in which Nasser closed the Tiran Straits and massed troops on Israel's border; it wasn't at all clear that Israel would survive. Not only to me, but to anybody in the general population. Maybe our generals were confident, but I don't think so, because our government certainly was not confident. Prime Minister Eshkol was very worried. He made a broadcast in which he stuttered and his concern was very evident, very real. Nobody knew what was going to happen and people were very worried, and I, too, was very worried. I had a wife and three children and we all had American papers. So I said to myself, "Johnny, don't make the mistake your father made by staying in Germany. Pick yourself up, get on a plane and leave, and save your skin and that of your family; because there is a very good chance that Israel will be destroyed and the inhabitants of Israel will be wiped out totally, killed, in the next two or three weeks. Pick yourself up and GO."

I made a conscious decision not to do that. I said, "I am staying." Herb Scarf was here during the crisis. When he left, about two weeks before the war, we said goodbye, and it was clear to both of us that we might never see each other again.

I am saying all this to illustrate that it is very difficult to judge a situation from the middle of it. When you're swimming in a big lake, it's difficult to see the shore, because you are low, you are inside it. One should not blame the German Jews or the European Jews for not leaving Europe in the thirties, because it was difficult to assess the situation.

Anyway, that was our story. We did get away in time, in 1938. We left Germany, and made our way to the United States; we got an immigration visa with some difficulty. In this passage, my parents lost all their money. They had to work extremely hard in the United States to make ends meet, but nevertheless they gave their two children, my brother and myself, a good Jewish and a good secular education. I went to Jewish parochial schools for my elementary education and also for high school. It is called a yeshiva high school, and combines Talmudic and other Jewish studies with secular studies. I have already mentioned my math teacher in high school, Joe Gansler. I also had excellent Talmud and Jewish studies teachers.

Figure 15.4   Bob Aumann with fiancée Esther Schlesinger, Israel, January 1955.

When the State of Israel was created in 1948, I made a determination eventually to come to Israel, but that didn't actually happen until 1956. In 1954 I met an Israeli girl, Esther Schlesinger, who was visiting the United States. We fell in love, got engaged, and got married. We had five children; the oldest, Shlomo, was killed in Lebanon in the 1982 Peace for Galilee operation. My other children are all happily married. Shlomo's widow also remarried and she is like a daughter to us. Shlomo had two children before he was killed (actually the second one was born after he was killed). Altogether I now have 17 grandchildren and one great-grandchild. We have a very good family relationship, do a lot of things together. One of the things we like best is skiing. Every year I go with a different part of the family. Once in four or five years, all 30 of us go together.

Hart: I can attest from my personal knowledge that the Aumann family is really an outstanding, warm, unusually close-knit family. It is really great to be with them.

Aumann: My wife Esther died six years ago, of cancer, after being ill for about a year and a half. She was an extraordinary person. After elementary school she entered the Bezalel School of Art—she had a great talent for art. At Bezalel she learned silversmithing, and she also drew well. She was wonderful with her hands and also with people. When about 50, she went to work for the Frankforter Center, an old-age day activities center; she ran the crafts workshop, where the elderly worked with their hands: appliqué, knitting, embroidery, carpets, and so on. This enabled Esther to combine her two favorite activities: her artistic ability, and dealing with people and helping them, each one with his individual troubles.

When she went to school, Bezalel was a rather Bohemian place. It probably still is, but at that time it was less fashionable to be Bohemian, more special. Her parents were very much opposed to this. In an orthodox Jewish family, a young girl going to this place was really unheard of. But Esther had her own will. She was a mild-mannered person, but when she wanted something, you bet your life she got it, both with her

Figure 15.5   Bob Aumann with his immediate family, Jerusalem, October 10, 2005.

parents and with me. She definitely did want to go to that school, and she went.

Hart: There is a nice story about your decision to come to Israel in '56.

Aumann: In '56 I had just finished two years of a postdoc at Princeton, and was wondering how to continue my life. As mentioned, I had made up my mind to come to Israel eventually. One of the places where I applied was the Hebrew University in Jerusalem. I also applied to other places, because one doesn't put all one's eggs in one basket, and got several offers. One was from Bell Telephone Laboratories in Murray Hill; one from Jerusalem; and there were others. Thinking things over very hard and agonizing over this decision, I finally decided to accept the position at Bell Labs, and told them that. We started looking around for a place to live on that very same day.

When we came home in the evening, I knew I had made the wrong decision. I had agonized over it for three weeks or more, but once it had been made, it was clear to me that it was wrong. Before it had been made, nothing was clear. Now, I realized that I wanted to go to Israel immediately, that there is no point in putting it off, no point in trying to earn some money to finance the trip to Israel; we'll just get stuck in the

United States. If we are going to go at all we should go right away. I called up the Bell Labs people and said, "I changed my mind. I said I'll come, so I'll come, but you should know that I'm leaving in one year." They said, "Aumann, you're off the hook. You don't have to come if you don't want to." I said, "Okay, but now it's June. I am not leaving until October, when the academic year in Israel starts. Could I work until October at Bell Labs?" They said, "Sure, we'll be glad to have you." That was very nice of them.

That was a really good four months there. John McCarthy, a computer scientist, was one of the people I got to know during that period. John Addison, a mathematician, logician, Turing machine person, was also there. One anecdote about Addison that summer is that he had written a paper about Turing machines, and wanted to issue it as a Bell Labs discussion paper. The patent office at Bell Labs gave him trouble. They wanted to know whether this so-called improvement on Turing machines could be patented. It took him a while to convince them that a Turing machine is not really a machine.

I am telling this long story to illustrate the difficulties with practical decisionmaking. The process of practical decisionmaking is much more complex than our models. In practical decisionmaking, you don't know the right decision until after you've made it.

Hart: This, at least to my mind, is a good example of some of your views on experiments and empirics. Do you want to expand on that?

Aumann: Yes. I have grave doubts about what's *called* "behavioral economics," but isn't really behavioral. The term implies that that is how people actually behave, in contradistinction to what the theory says. But that's not what behavioral economics is concerned with. On the contrary, most of behavioral economics deals with artificial laboratory setups, at best. At worst, it deals with polls, questionnaires. One type of so-called behavioral economics is when people are asked, what would you do if you were faced with such and such a situation. Then they have to imagine that they are in this situation and they have to give an answer.

Hart: Your example of Bell Labs versus the Hebrew University shows that you really can give the wrong answer when you are asked such a question.

Aumann: Polls and questionnaires are worse than that; they are at a double remove from reality. In the Bell Labs case, I actually was faced with the problem of which job to take. Even then I took a decision that was not the final one, in spite of the setup being real. In "behavioral economics," people ask, "What would you do if . . ."; it is not even a real setup.

Behavioral economists also do experiments with "real" decisions rewarded by monetary payoffs. But even then the monetary payoff is usually very small. More importantly, the decisions that people face are not ones that they usually take, with which they are familiar. The whole setup is artificial. It is not a decision that really affects them and to which they are used.

Let me give one example of this—the famous "probability matching" experiment. A light periodically flashes, three quarters of the time green, one quarter red, at random. The subject has to guess the color beforehand, and gets rewarded if he guesses correctly. This experiment has been repeated hundreds of times; by far the largest number of subjects guess green three quarters of the time and red one quarter of the time.

That is not optimal; you should always guess green. If you get a dollar each time you guess correctly, and you probability-match—three quarters, one quarter—then your expected payoff is five eighths of a dollar. If you guess green all the time you get an average of three quarters of a dollar. Nevertheless, people probability-match. The point is that the setting is artificial: people don't usually sit in front of flashing lights. They don't know how to react, so they do what they think is expected of them, which becomes probability-matching.

In real situations, people don't act that way. An example is driving to work in the morning. Many people have a choice of routes, and each route has a certain probability of taking less time. It is random, because one can't know where there will be an accident, a traffic jam. Let's say that there are two routes; one is quicker three quarters of the time and the other, one quarter of the time. Most people will settle down and take the same route every day, although some days it will be the longer one; and that is the correct solution.

In short, I have serious doubts about behavioral economics as it is practiced. Now, *true* behavioral economics does in fact exist; it is called empirical economics. This really *is* behavioral economics. In empirical economics, you go and see how people behave in real life, in situations to which they are used. Things they do every day.

There is a wonderful publication called the *NBER Reporter*. NBER is the National Bureau of Economic Research, an American organization. They put out a monthly newsletter of four to six pages, in which they give brief summaries of research memoranda published during that month. It is all empirical. There is nothing theoretical there. Sometimes they give theoretical background, but all these works are empirical works that say how people actually behave. It is amazing to see, in these reports, how well the actual behavior of people fits economic theory.

Hart: Can you give an example of that?

Aumann: One example I remember is where there was a very strong effect of raising the tax on alcohol by a very small amount, let's say 10%. Now we are talking about raising the price of a glass of beer by 2 2½%. It had a very significant effect on the number of automobile accidents in the States. There is a tremendous amount of price elasticity in people's behavior. Another example is how increasing the police force affects crime.

Hart: Let's be more specific. Take the alcohol example. Why does it contradict the behavioral approach?

Aumann: The conclusion of so-called behavioral economics is that people don't behave in a rational way, that they don't respond as expected to economic incentives. Empirical economics shows that people do respond very precisely to economic incentives.

Hart: If I may summarize your views on this, empirical economics is a good way of finding out what people actually decide. On the other hand, much of what is done in experimental work is artificial and people may not behave there as they do in real life.

Aumann: Yes. Let me expand on that a little bit. The thesis that behavioral economics attacks is that people behave rationally in a conscious way—that they consciously calculate and make an optimal decision based, in each case, on rational calculations. Perhaps behavioral economists are right that that is not so. Because their experiments or polls show that people, when faced with certain kinds of decisions, do not make the rational decision. However, nobody ever claimed that; they are attacking a straw man, a dead horse. What *is* claimed is that economic agents behave in a way that could be described as derived from rationality considerations; not that they actually are derived that way, that they actually go through a process of optimization each time they make a decision.

Hart: This brings us to the matter of "rule rationality," which you have been promoting consistently at least since the nineties.

Aumann: Yes, it does bring us to rule rationality. The basic premise there is that people grope around. They learn what is a good way of behaving. When they make mistakes they adjust their behavior to avoid those mistakes. It is a learning process, not an explicit optimization procedure. This is actually an old idea. For example, Milton Friedman had this idea that people behave *as if* they were rational.

Rule rationality means that people evolve rules of behavior by which they usually act, and they optimize these *rules*. They don't optimize each single decision. One very good example is the ultimatum game, an experiment performed by Werner Güth and associates in the early eighties.

Hart: And then replicated in many forms by other people. It is a famous experiment.

Aumann: This experiment was done in various forms and with various parameters. Here is one form. Two subjects are offered 100 deutsch marks, which in the early eighties was equivalent to 150–200 euros of today—a highly nonnegligible amount. They are offered this amount to split in whatever way they choose, as long as they agree how. If they cannot agree, then both get nothing. The subjects do not speak with each other face to face; rather, each one sits at a computer console. One is the offerer and the other, the responder. The offerer offers a split and the responder must say yes or no, once the proposed split appears on his computer screen. If he says yes, that's the outcome. If he says no, no one gets anything.

This experiment was done separately for many pairs of people. Each pair played only once; they entered and left the building by different entrances and exits, and never got to know each other—remained entirely anonymous. The perfect equilibrium of this game is that the offerer offers a minimum amount that still gives the responder something. Let's say a split of 99 for the offerer and one for the responder.

Hart: The idea being that the responder would not leave even one deutsch mark on the table by saying no.

Aumann: That is what one might expect from rationality considerations. I say "might," because it is not what game theory necessarily predicts; the game has many other equilibria. But rationality considerations might lead to the 99–1 split.

In fact, what happened was that most of the offers were in the area of 65–35. Those that were considerably less—let's say 80–20—were actually rejected. Not always, but that was the big picture. In many cases a subject was willing to walk away from as much as 20 deutsch marks; and the offerer usually anticipated this and therefore offered him more.

Walking away from 20 deutsch marks appears to be a clear violation of rationality. It *is* a violation—of *act* rationality. How does theory account for this?

The answer is that people do not maximize on an act-by-act basis. Rather, they develop *rules* of behavior. One good rule is, do not let other people insult you. Do not let other people kick you in the stomach. Do not be a sucker. If somebody does something like that to you, respond by kicking back. This is a good rule in situations that are not anonymous. If you get a reputation for accepting 20 or 10 or one deutsch mark when 100 deutsch marks are on the table, you will come out on the short end of many bargaining situations. Therefore, the rule of behavior is to fight back and punish the person who does this to you, and then he won't do it again.

Of course, this does not apply in the current situation, because it is entirely anonymous. Nobody will be told that you did this. Therefore, there are no reputational effects, and this rule that you've developed does not apply. But you have not developed the rule consciously. You have not worked it out. You have learned it because it works in general. Therefore you apply it even in situations where, rationally speaking, it does not apply. It is very important to test economic theories in contexts that are familiar to people, in contexts in which people really engage on a regular basis. Not in artificial contexts. In artificial contexts, other things apply.

Another example of rule rationality is trying to please. It is a good idea to please the people with whom you deal. Even this can be entirely subconscious or unconscious. Most people know that voting in elections is considered a positive thing to do. So if you are asked, "Did you vote?," there is a very strong tendency to say yes, even if you didn't vote. Camil Fuchs, one of the important polltakers in Israel, gave a lecture at the Center for Rationality, in which he reported this: in the last election in Israel, people were asked several hours after the polls closed, did you vote? Ninety percent of the people in the sample said yes; in fact, only 68% of the electorate voted.

Hart: It calls into question what we learn from polls.

Aumann: It sheds a tremendous amount of doubt; and it shows something even more basic. Namely, that when people answer questions in a poll, they try to guess what it is that the questioner wants to hear. They give that answer rather than the true answer; and again, this is not something that they do consciously.

That is another example of rule rationality. I am not saying that people do this because there is something in it for them. They do it because they have a general rule: try to please the people to whom you are talking; usually they can help you. If you are unpleasant to them it is usually not to your good. So people subconsciously develop tools to be pleasant and being pleasant means giving the answer that's expected.

Hart: What you are saying is that one should evaluate actions not on a decision-by-decision basis, but over the long run. Also, one has to take into account that we cannot make precise computations and evaluate every decision. We need to develop rules that are relatively simple and applicable in many situations. Once we take into account this cost of computation, it is clear that a rule that is relatively simple, but gives a good answer in many situations, is better than a rule that requires you to go to extreme lengths to find the right answer for every decision.

Aumann: That's the reason for it. You are giving the fundamental reason why people develop rules rather than optimize each act. It is simply too expensive.

Hart: Kahneman and Tversky say that there are a lot of heuristics that people use, and biases, and that these biases are not random, but systematic. What you are saying is, yes, systematic biases occur because if you look at the level of the rule, rules indeed are systematic; they lead to biases since they are not optimal for each individual act. Systematic biases fit rule rationality very well.

Aumann: That's a good way of putting it. If you look at those systematic biases carefully you may well find that they are rule optimal. In most situations that people encounter, those systematic biases are a short way of doing the right thing.

Hart: This connects to another area in which you are involved quite a lot lately, namely, biology and evolutionary ecology. Do you want to say something about that?

Aumann: The connection of evolution to game theory has been one of the most profound developments of the last 30 or 40 years. It is one of the major developments since the big economic contributions of the sixties, which were mainly in cooperative game theory. It actually predates the explosion of noncooperative game theory of the eighties and nineties.

It turns out that there is a very, very strong connection between population equilibrium and Nash equilibrium—strategic equilibrium—in games. The same mathematical formulae appear in both contexts, but they have totally different interpretations. In the strategic, game-theoretic interpretation there are players and strategies, pure and mixed. In the two-player case, for every pair of strategies, each player has a payoff, and there is a strategic equilibrium. In the evolutionary context, the players are replaced by populations, the strategies by genes, the probabilities in the mixed strategies by population proportions, and the payoffs by what is called fitness, which is a propensity to have offspring. You could have a population of flowers and a population of bees. There could be a gene for having a long nectar tube in the flowers and a gene for a long proboscis in the bees. Then, when those two meet, it is good for the flower and good for the bee. The bee is able to drink the nectar and so flits from flower to flower and pollinates them.

What does that mean, "good"? It means that both the flowers and the bees will have more offspring. The situation is in equilibrium if the proportions of genes of each kind in both populations are maintained. This turns out to be formally the same as strategic equilibrium in the corresponding game.

This development has had a tremendous influence on game theory, on biology, and on economic theory. It's a way of thinking of games that transcends biology; it's a way of thinking of what people do as traits of behavior, which survive, or get wiped out, just like in biology. It's not a question of conscious choice. Whereas the usual, older interpretation of Nash equilibrium is one of conscious choice, conscious maximization. This ties in with what we were saying before, about rule rationality being a better interpretation of game-theoretic concepts than act rationality.

Hart: Perhaps it is time now to ask, what is game theory?

Aumann: Game theory is the study of interactions from a rational viewpoint. Even though the rationality does not have to be conscious, it is still there in the background. So we are interpreting what we see in the world from a rational viewpoint.

In other words, we ask, what is best for people to do when there are other people, other decisionmakers, other entities who also optimize their decisions? Game theory is optimal decisionmaking in the presence of others with different objectives.

Hart: And where everyone's decision influences everyone's outcomes. One takes into account that everyone is doing his own optimization and everyone is trying to advance his own objectives.

Game theory started formally with the von Neumann and Morgenstern book in the 1940s. Probably the war had a lot to do with the fact that many people got interested. Just to see how it developed, in the first international game theory workshop in 1965 in Jerusalem there were 17 people.

Aumann: There were three conferences on game theory in Princeton in the fifties: '53, '55, and '57. Those were attended by more than 17 people. The 17 people in 1965 were 17 selected people.

Hart: The discipline has really grown—from a few dozen people in the fifties and sixties, to more than 600 at the last game theory congress in Marseille.

This is a good point to discuss the universality of game theory. In the Preface to the first volume of the *Handbook of Game Theory* [Aumann and Hart (1992–2002)], we wrote that game theory may be viewed as a sort of umbrella or unified field theory.

Aumann: It's a way of talking about many sciences, many disparate disciplines. Unlike other approaches to disciplines like economics or political science, game theory does not use different, ad-hoc constructs to deal with various specific issues, such as perfect competition, monopoly, oligopoly, international trade, taxation, voting, deterrence, animal behavior, and so on. Rather, it develops methodologies that apply in principle to all interactive situations, then sees where these methodologies lead in each specific application.

But rather than being an umbrella for all those disciplines, it's perhaps better to think of it as a way of thinking about a *certain aspect* of each

—the interactively rational aspect. There are many things in these disciplines that have nothing to do with this aspect. In law, in computer science, in mathematics, in economics, in politics, there are many things that have nothing to do with game theory. It is not like a unified field theory, which would cover *all* of gravitation, magnetism, and electricity.

Hart: Perhaps it is like mathematics applied to other sciences, which is a tool, a language for formalizing and analyzing.

Aumann: That's an interesting analogy. Mathematics helps in certain aspects of many sciences—those given to formalization. Game theory is similar in that respect: it helps in many disciplines, specifically in their interactively rational parts. Figure 15.6 is a stylized representation.

Hart: The Game Theory Society was established in '99. You were the first, founding president, up to 2003. By now you should have a good overview of what game theory is, and of what the Game Theory Society is.

Aumann: Game theory has become a big discipline, or rather a big *interdiscipline*. It is time to have a tool for gathering game theorists in all kinds of senses. Conferences, journals, the Web. When discussing my education, I mentioned that at City College there were a couple of tables reserved for the more dedicated math students. People would come between classes, sit down, have an ice cream soda, and talk about math. The Game Theory Society is the game theory table in the cafeteria that's called the world. It is a place where people can discuss game theory and exchange ideas, in various senses and various ways.

Hart: Do you have any thoughts on where game theory is going?

Aumann: It is difficult to tell. It is very hard to know where things are going. In the Presidential Address at the Game Theory Society Congress in Bilbao in 2000 [Aumann (2003a)], I discussed some directions for research in the future.

Let me say something of a more general nature. People are pushing in different directions; we are going to find a spreading of the discipline among different people. Some people go in a very strongly mathematical direction, very deep mathematics. We will see a separation of the more mathematical branches from the more applied branches like economic applications. We'll see a lot of experimental and engineering application of game theory. People in game theory will understand each other less in the future.

Hart: Do you expect a Tower of Babel syndrome to develop?

Aumann: It is not something that I would like, but it's a sign of maturity. Tower of Babel syndrome is a very good way of putting it.

Hart: What is definitely true is that from a small community where essentially everybody could understand everybody else, game theory has grown to a big "city," where people are much more specialized. As in any developing discipline, it's natural that everybody goes deeper into one

Figure 15.6 The blooming of game theory.

of the aspects and understands less and less of the others. Nevertheless, at this point there is still interplay between the various aspects and approaches, so everybody benefits from everybody else. Take physics or mathematics. I wouldn't understand what algebraic topology does nowadays. Somebody in combinatorics may understand something about probability, but wouldn't understand some of the things we do in game theory. Nevertheless, mathematics is a single discipline.

Would you like to say anything about the different approaches in game theory? For example, mathematical versus conceptual; axiomatic and cooperative versus strategic and noncooperative. Why is it that there are so many approaches? Are they contradictory or are they just different? And how about people who think that some approaches in game theory are valid, and other approaches are not?

Aumann: You are quite right that there is a group of people, working in noncooperative, strategic games, who think that cooperative (coalitional) game theory is less important, not relevant, not applicable.

Let me backtrack and describe what we mean by noncooperative or strategic game theory, vis-à-vis cooperative or coalitional game theory. Strategic game theory is concerned with strategic equilibrium—individual utility maximization given the actions of other people, Nash equilibrium and its variants, correlated equilibrium, that kind of thing. It asks how people should act, or do act. Coalitional game theory, on the other hand, concentrates on division of the payoff, and not so much on what people do in order to achieve those payoffs.

Practically speaking, strategic game theory deals with various equilibrium concepts and is based on a precise description of the game in question. Coalitional game theory deals with concepts like the core, Shapley value, von Neumann–Morgenstern solution, bargaining set, nucleolus. Strategic game theory is best suited to contexts and applications where the rules of the game are precisely described, like elections, auctions, Internet transactions. Coalitional game theory is better suited to situations like coalition formation or the formation of a government in a parliamentary democracy or even the formation of coalitions in international relations; or, what happens in a market, where it is not clear who makes offers to whom and how transactions are consummated. Negotiations in general, bargaining, these are more suited for the coalitional, cooperative theory.

Hart: On the one hand, negotiations can be analyzed from a strategic viewpoint, if one knows exactly how they are conducted. On the other hand, they can be analyzed from a viewpoint of where they lead, which will be a cooperative solution. There is the "Nash program"—basing cooperative solutions on noncooperative implementations. For example, the alternating offers bargaining, which is a very natural strategic setup, and leads very neatly to the axiomatic solution of Nash—as shown by Rubinstein and Binmore.

Aumann: These "bridges" between the strategic and the coalitional theory show that these approaches are not disparate. In order to make a bridge like that you have to define precisely the noncooperative situation with which you are dealing. One of the bridges that we discussed earlier in this interview is the Folk Theorem for repeated games. There, the noncooperative setup is the repeated game. When you have a bridge like that to the noncooperative theory, the strategic side must be precisely defined. The big advantage of the cooperative theory is that it does *not* need a precisely defined structure for the actual game. It is enough to say what each coalition can achieve; you need not say *how*. For example, in a market context you say that each coalition can exchange among its own members whatever it wants. You don't have to say how they make their offers or counteroffers. In a political context, it is enough to say that any majority of parliament can form a government. You don't have to say how they negotiate in order to form a government. That already defines the game, and then one can apply the ideas of the coalitional theory to make some kind of analysis, some kind of prediction.

You asked about the sociology of game theorists, rather than game theory. There is a significant group of people in strategic game theory who have an attitude towards coalitional game theory similar to that of pure mathematicians towards applied mathematics 50 years ago. They looked down their noses and said, "This is not really very interesting; we're not going to sully our hands with this stuff."

There is no justification for this in the game-theoretic sociology, just as there was no justification for it in the mathematics sociology. Each one of these branches of the discipline makes its contribution. In many ways, the coalitional theory has done better than the strategic theory in giving insight into economic and other environments. A prime example of this is the equivalence theorem, which gave a game-theoretic foundation for the law of supply and demand. There has been nothing of that generality or power in strategic game theory. Strategic game theory has made important contributions to the analysis of auctions, but it has not given that kind of insight into economics, or into any other discipline.

Another example of an important insight yielded by coalitional game theory is the theory of matching markets. This whole branch of game theory—and it is highly applied—grew out of the '62 paper of Gale and Shapley, "College Admissions and the Stability of Marriage." It is not quite as fundamental as the equivalence theorem, but it is a very important application, certainly of comparable importance to the work on auctions in strategic game theory, which is very important. There is no reason to denigrate the contributions of coalitional game theory, either on the applied or the theoretical level.

Hart: Indeed, Adam Brandenburger said that his students at Harvard Business School found cooperative game theory much more relevant to them than the noncooperative theory.

Let's switch to another topic. You have had an enormous impact on the profession by influencing many people. I am talking first of all about your students. By now you have had 13 doctoral students. I think 12 of them are by now professors, in Israel and abroad, who are well recognized in the field and also in related fields.

Aumann: Almost all the students eventually ended up in Israel, after a short break for a postdoc or something similar abroad.

Hart: That's not surprising since most of them—all except Wesley—started in Israel and are Israelis.

Aumann: There is quite a brain drain from Israel. A large proportion of prominent Israeli scientists who are educated in Israel end up abroad—a much larger proportion than among my students.

These are my doctoral students up until now: Bezalel Peleg, David Schmeidler, Shmuel Zamir, Binyamin Shitovitz, Zvi Artstein, Elon Kohlberg, Sergiu Hart, Eugene Wesley, Abraham Neyman, Yair Tauman,

Dov Samet, Ehud Lehrer, and Yossi Feinberg. Of these, three are currently abroad—Kohlberg, Wesley, and Feinberg. Also, there are about 30 or 40 masters students.

Each student is different. They are all great. In all cases I refused to do what some people do, and that is to write a doctoral thesis for the student. The student had to go and work it out by himself. In some cases I gave very difficult problems. Sometimes I had to backtrack and suggest different problems, because the student wasn't making progress. There were one or two cases where a student didn't make it—started working and didn't make progress for a year or two and I saw that he wasn't going to be able to make it with me. I informed him and he left. I always had a policy of taking only those students who seemed very, very good. I don't mean good morally, but capable as scientists and specifically as mathematicians. All of my students came from mathematics. In most cases I knew them from my classes. In some cases not, and then I looked carefully at their grades and accepted only the very best. I usually worked quite closely with them, meeting once a week or so at least, hearing about progress, making suggestions, asking questions. When the final thesis was written I very often didn't read it carefully. Maybe this is news to Professor Hart, maybe it isn't. But by that time I knew the contents of the work because of the periodic meetings that we would have.

Hart: Besides, you don't believe anything unless you can prove it to yourself.

Aumann: I read very little mathematics—only when I need to know. Then, when reading an article I say, "Well, how does one prove this?" Usually I don't succeed, and then I look at the proof.

But it is really more interesting to hear from the students, so, Professor Hart, what do you think?

Hart: Most doctoral students want to finish their thesis and get out as soon as possible. Aumann's students usually want to continue—up to a point, of course. This was one of the best periods in my life—being immersed in research and bouncing ideas back and forth with Professor Aumann; it was a very exciting period. It was very educating for my whole life. Having a good doctoral adviser is a great investment for life. There is a lot to say here, but it's your interview, so I am making it very short. There are many stories among your students, who are still very close to one another.

Next, how about your collaborators? Shapley, Maschler, Kurz, and Drèze are probably your major collaborators. Looking at your publications I see many other coauthors—a total of 20—but usually they are more focused on one specific topic.

Figure 15.7 At the GAMES 1995 Conference in honor of Aumann's 65th birthday, Jerusalem, June 1995. From left to right: Abraham Neyman, Bob Aumann, John Nash, Reinhard Selten, Ken Arrow, and Sergiu Hart.

Aumann: I certainly owe a lot to all those people. Collaborating with other people is a lot of work. It makes things a lot more difficult, because each person has his own angle on things and there are often disagreements on conceptual aspects. It's not like pure mathematics, where there is a theorem and a proof. There may be disagreements about which theorem to include and which theorem not to include, but there is no room for substantive disagreement in a pure mathematics paper. Papers in game theory or in mathematical economics have large conceptual components, on which there often is quite substantial disagreement between the coauthors, which must be hammered out. I experienced this with all my coauthors.

You and I have written several joint papers, Sergiu. There wasn't too much disagreement about conceptual aspects there.

Hart: The first of our joint papers [Aumann and Hart (1986)] was mostly mathematical, but over the last one [Aumann and Hart (2003)] there was some . . . perhaps not disagreement, but clarification of the concepts. The other two papers, together with Motty Perry [Aumann, Hart, and Perry (1997a,b)], involved a lot of discussion. I can also speak from experience, having collaborated with other people, including some long-standing collaborations. Beyond mathematics, the arguments are about identifying the right concept. This is a question of judgment; one cannot prove that this is a good concept and that is not. One can only have a feeling or an intuition that *that* may lead to something interesting, that studying *this* may be interesting. Everybody brings his own intuitions and ideas.

Aumann: But there are also sometimes real substantive disagreements. There was a paper with Maschler—"Some Thoughts on the Minimax Principle" [Aumann and Maschler (1972)]—where we had diametrically opposed opinions on an important point that could not be glossed over. In the end we wrote, "Some experts think A, others think 'Not A.'" That's how we dealt with the disagreement. Often it doesn't come to that extreme, but there *are* substantial substantive disagreements with coauthors. Of course these do not affect the major message of the paper. But in the discussion, in the conceptualization, there are nuances over which there are disagreements. All these discussions make writing a joint paper a much more onerous affair than writing a paper alone. It becomes much more time-consuming.

Hart: But it is time well consumed; having to battle for your opinion and having to find better and better arguments to convince your coauthor is also good for your reader and is also good for really understanding and getting much deeper into issues.

That is one reason why an interdisciplinary center is so good. When you must explain your work to people who are outside your discipline, you cannot take anything for granted. All the things that are somehow commonly known and commonly accepted in your discipline suddenly become questionable. Then you realize that in fact they shouldn't be commonly accepted. That is a very good exercise: explain what you are doing to a smart person who has a general understanding of the subject, but who is not from your discipline. It is one of the great advantages of our Rationality Center. A lot of work here has been generated from such discussions. Suddenly you realize that some of the basic premises of your work may in fact be incorrect, or may need to be justified. The same goes for collaborators. When you think by yourself, you gloss over things very quickly. When you have to start explaining it to somebody, then you have to go very slowly, step by step, and you cannot err so easily.

Aumann: That's entirely correct, and I'd like to back it up with a story from the Talmud. A considerable part of the Talmud deals with pairs of sages, who consistently argued with each other; one took one side of a question and the other took the other side. One such pair was Rabbi Yochanan and Resh Lakish. They were good friends, but also constantly taking opposite sides of any given question. Then Resh Lakish died, and Rabbi Yochanan was inconsolable, grieved for many days. Finally he returned to the study hall and resumed his lectures. Then, for everything that Rabbi Yochanan said, one of the sages adduced 30 pieces of supporting evidence. Rabbi Yochanan broke down in tears and said, "What good are you to me? You try to console me for the loss of Resh Lakish, but you do exactly the opposite. Resh Lakish would come up with 30 challenges to everything I said, 30 putative proofs that I am wrong. Then I would have to sharpen my wits and try to prove that he is wrong and thereby my position would be firmly established. Whereas you prove that I'm right. I know that I'm right; what good does it do that you prove that I am right? It doesn't advance knowledge at all."

This is exactly your point. When you have different points of view and there is a need to sharpen and solidify one's own view of things, then arguing with someone makes it much more acceptable, much better proved.

With many of my coauthors there were sharp disagreements and very close bargaining as to how to phrase this or that. I remember an argument with Lloyd Shapley at Stanford University one summer in the early seventies. I had broken my foot in a rock-climbing accident. Shapley came to visit me in my room at the Stanford Faculty Club, and I was hobbling around on crutches. This is unbelievable, but we argued for a full half hour about a comma. I don't remember whether I wanted it in and Lloyd wanted it out, or the other way around. Neither do I remember how it was resolved. It would not have been feasible to say, "Some experts would put a comma here, others would not." I always think that my coauthors are stubborn, but maybe I am the stubborn one.

I will say one thing about coauthorship. Mike Maschler is a wonderful person and a great scientist, but he is about the most stubborn person I know. One joint paper with Maschler is about the bargaining set for cooperative games [Aumann and Maschler (1964)]. The way this was born is that in my early days at the Hebrew University, in 1960, I gave a math colloquium at which I presented the von Neumann–Morgenstern stable set. In the question period, Mike said, "I don't understand this concept, it sounds wrongheaded." I said, "Okay, let's discuss it after the lecture." And we did. I tried to explain and to justify the stable set idea, which is beautiful and deep. But Mike wouldn't buy it. Exasperated, I finally said, "Well, can you do better?" He said, "Give me a day or two." A day or two passes and he comes back with an idea. I shoot this idea down—show him why it's no good. This continues for about a year. He comes up with ideas for alternatives to stable sets, and I shoot them down; we had well-defined roles in the process. Finally, he came up with something that I was not able to shoot down with ease. We parted for the summer. During that summer he wrote up his idea and sent it to me with a byline of Robert Aumann and Michael Maschler. I said, "I will have no part of this. I can't shoot it down immediately, but I don't like the idea." Maschler wouldn't take no for an answer. He kept at me stubbornly for weeks and months and finally I broke down and said, "Okay, I don't like it, but go ahead and publish it." This is the original "Bargaining Set for Cooperative Games" [Aumann and Maschler (1964)]. I still don't like that idea, but Maschler and Davis revised it and it eventually became, with their revision, a very important concept, out of which grew the Davis–Maschler kernel and Schmeidler's nucleolus. Because of where it led more than because of what it is, this became one of my most cited papers. Maschler's stubbornness proved justified. Maybe it should have waited for the Davis–Maschler revision in the first place, but anyway, in hindsight I'm not sorry that we published this. Michael has always been extremely stubborn. When he wants something, it gets done. As you say, Sergiu, coauthorship is much more exacting, much more painful than writing a paper alone, but it also leads to a better product.

Hart: This very naturally leads us to what you view as your main contributions. And, what are your most cited papers, which may not be the same thing.

Aumann: One's papers are almost like one's children and students—each one is different, one loves them all, and one does not compare them. Still, one does keep abreast of what they're doing; so I also keep an eye on the citations, which give a sense of what the papers are "doing."

One of the two most cited papers is the Equivalence Theorem—the "Markets with a Continuum of Traders" [Aumann (1964)]—the principle that the core is the same as the competitive equilibrium in a market in which each individual player is negligible. The other one is "Agreeing to Disagree" [Aumann (1976)], which initiated "interactive epistemology"—the formal theory of knowledge about others' knowledge. After that come the book with Shapley, *Values of Non-Atomic Games* [Aumann and Shapley (1974)], the two papers on correlated equilibrium [Aumann (1974, 1987)], the bargaining set paper with Maschler [Aumann and Maschler (1964)], the subjective probability paper with Anscombe [Aumann and Anscombe (1963)], and "Integrals of Set-Valued Functions" [Aumann (1965)], a strictly mathematical paper that impacted control theory and related areas as well as mathematical economics. The next batch includes the repeated games work—the '59 paper [Aumann (1959)], the book with Maschler [Aumann and Maschler (1995)], the survey [Aumann (1981)], and the paper with Sorin on "Cooperation and Bounded Recall" [Aumann and Sorin (1989)]; also, the Talmud paper with Maschler [Aumann and Maschler (1985)], the paper with Drèze on coalition structures [Aumann and Drèze (1975)], the work with Brandenburger on "Epistemic Conditions for Nash Equilibrium" [Aumann and Brandenburger (1995)], the "Power and Taxes" paper with Kurz

[Aumann and Kurz (1977a)], some of the papers on NTU-games [Aumann (1961, 1967)], and others.

That sort of sums it up. Correlated equilibrium had a big impact. The work on repeated games, the equivalence principle, the continuum of players, interactive epistemology—all had a big impact.

Citations do give a good general idea of impact. But one should also look at the larger picture. Sometimes there is a body of work that all in all has a big impact, more than the individual citations show. In addition to the above-mentioned topics, there is incomplete information, NTU-values and NTU-games in general—with their many applications— perfect and imperfect competition, utilities and subjective probabilities, the mathematics of set-valued functions and measurability, extensive games, and others. Of course, these are not disjoint; there are many interconnec- tions and areas of overlap.

There is a joint paper with Jacques Drèze [Aumann and Drèze (1986)] on which we worked very, very hard, for very, very long. For seven years we worked on it. It contains some of the deepest work I have ever done. It is hardly cited. This is a paper I love. It is nice work, but it hasn't had much of an impact.

Hart: Sometimes working very hard has two bad side effects. One is that you have solved the problem and there is nothing more to say. Two, it is so hard that nobody can follow it; it's too hard for people to get into.

We were talking about various stations in your life. Besides City College, MIT, Princeton, and Hebrew University you have spent a sig- nificant amount of time over the years at other places: Yale, Stanford, CORE, and lately Stony Brook.

Aumann: Perhaps the most significant of all those places is Stanford and, specifically, the IMSSS, the Institute for Mathematical Studies in the Social Sciences—Economics. This was run by Mordecai Kurz for 20 magnificent years between 1971 and 1990. The main activity of the IMSSS was the summer gatherings, which lasted for six to eight weeks. They brought together the best minds in economic theory. A lot of beautiful economic theory was created at the IMSSS. The meetings were relaxed, originally only on Tuesdays and Thursdays, with the whole morn- ing devoted to one speaker; one or two speakers in the afternoon, not more. A little later, Wednesday mornings also became part of the official program. All the rest of the time was devoted to informal interaction between the participants. Kenneth Arrow was a fixture there. So was Frank Hahn. Of course, Mordecai. I came every year during that period.

It was an amazing place. Mordecai ran a very tight ship. One year he even posted guards at the doors of the seminar room to keep uninvited people out. But he himself realized that that was going a little far, so that lasted only that one summer.

Another anecdote from that period is this: the year after Arrow got the Nobel Prize, he was vacationing in Hawaii at the beginning of July, and did not turn up for the first session of the summer. Mordecai tracked him down, phoned him and said, "Kenneth, what do you think you are doing? You are supposed to be here; get on the next plane and come down, or there will be trouble." The audacity of the request is sufficiently astounding, but even more so is that Arrow did it. He cancelled the rest of his vacation and came down and took his seat in the seminar.

The IMSSS was tremendously influential in the creation of economic theory over those two decades. And it was also very influential in my own career. Some of my best work was done during those two decades— much of it with very important input from the summer seminar at the IMSSS. Also, during those two decades I spent two full sabbaticals at Stanford, in '75–'76 and in '80–'81. This was a very important part of my life. My children used to say that California is their second home. Being there every summer for 20 years, and two winters as well, really enabled me to enjoy California to the fullest. Later on, in the nineties, we were again at Stanford for a few weeks in the summer. I told my wife there was a friend whom I hadn't seen in a year. She said, "Who?" and I said, "The Sierra Nevada, the mountains." We had been there a few weeks and we hadn't gone to the mountains yet. We went, and it was a beautiful day, as always. Many times during those years we would get up at 3 or 4 in the morning, drive to eastern California, to the beautiful Sierra mountains, spend the whole day there from 7 or 8 a.m. until 9 p.m., and then drive back and get to Palo Alto at 1 a.m.; exhausted, but deeply satisfied. We climbed, hiked, swam, skied.

The Sierra Nevada is really magnificent. I have traveled around the whole world, and never found a place like it, especially for its lakes. There are grander mountains, but the profusion and variety of mountain lakes in the Sierra is unbelievable. I just thought I would put that in, although it has nothing to do with game theory.

Hart: Getting back to the IMSSS summers: besides those who came every year, there were always a few dozen people, from the very young who were in the advanced stages of their doctoral studies, to very senior, established economists. People would present their work. There would be very exciting discussions. Another thing: every summer there were one or two one-day workshops, which were extremely well organized, usually by the very senior people like you; for example, you organized a workshop on repeated games in 1978 [Aumann (1981)]. One would collect material, particularly material that was not available in print. One would prepare notes. They were duplicated and distributed to everybody there. They served for years afterwards as a basis for research in the area. I still have notes from those workshops; they were highly influential.

In all the presentations, you couldn't just come and talk. You had to prepare meticulously, and distribute the papers and the references. The work was serious and intensive, and it was very exciting, because all the time new things were happening. It was a great place.

Aumann: You are certainly right—I forgot to mention all the other people who were there, and who varied from year to year. Sometimes people came for two or three or four consecutive years. Sometimes people came and then didn't come the next summer and then came again the following summer. But there was always a considerable group of people there who were contributing, aside from the three or four "fixtures."

Another point is the intensity of the discussion. The discussion was very freewheeling, very open, often very, very aggressive. I remember one morning I was supposed to give a two-hour lecture. The lectures were from 10 to 11, then a half-hour break, and then 11:30 to 12:30. I rose to begin my presentation at 10 in the morning, and it wasn't more than one minute before somebody interjected with a question or remark. Somebody else answered, and pandemonium broke loose. This lasted a full hour, from 10 to 11. After a few minutes I sat down and let the people argue with each other, though this was supposed to be my presentation. Then came the break. By 11:30 people had exhausted themselves, and I gave my presentation between 11:30 and 12:30. This was typical, though perhaps a little unusual in its intensity.

Hart: That was typical, exactly. There was no such thing as a 20-minute grace period. There was no grace whatsoever. On the other hand, the discussions were really to the point. People were trying to understand. It was really useful. It clarified things. If you take those 20 years, probably a significant part of the work in economic theory in those years can be directly connected to the Stanford summer seminar. It originated there. It was discussed there. It was developed there in many different directions. There was nothing happening in economic theory that didn't go through Stanford, or was at least presented there.

Aumann: We should move on perhaps to CORE, the Center for Operations Research and Econometrics at the Catholic University of Louvain, an ancient university, about seven or eight hundred years old. CORE was established chiefly through the initiative of Jacques Drèze. I was there three or four times for periods of several months, and also for many shorter visits. This, too, is a remarkable research institution. Unlike the IMSSS, it is really most active during the academic year. It is a great center for work in economic theory and also in game theory. The person

I worked with most closely throughout the years—and with whom I wrote several joint papers—is Jacques Drèze. Another person at CORE who has had a tremendous influence on game theory, by himself and with his students, is Jean-François Mertens. Mertens has done some of the deepest work in the discipline, some of it in collaboration with Israelis like my students Kohlberg, Neyman, and Zamir; he established a Belgian school of mathematical game theory that is marked by its beauty, depth, and sophistication.

Another institution with which I have been associated in the last 10 or 15 years is the Center for Game Theory at Stony Brook. The focus of this center is the summer program, which lasts two or three weeks, and consists of a large week-long international conference that covers all of game theory, and specialized workshops in various special areas—mostly quite applied, but sometimes also in special theoretical areas. The workshops are for smaller groups of people, and each one is three days, four days, two days, whatever. This program, which is extremely successful and has had a very important effect on game theory, has been run by Yair Tauman ever since its inception in '91. In the past I also spent several periods of several months each during the academic year teaching game theory or doing research in game theory there with a small group of top researchers and a small group of graduate students; that's another institution with which I've been associated.

I should also mention Yale, where I spent the '64–'65 academic year on sabbatical. This was after publication of the work with Frank Anscombe, "A Definition of Subjective Probability" [Aumann and Anscombe (1963)]; Frank was the chairman of the statistics department at Yale. At that time I was also associated with the Cowles Foundation; Herb Scarf and Martin Shubik were there. A very unique experience was the personal friendship that I struck up with Jimmy Savage during that year. I don't know how many people know this, but he was almost totally blind. Almost—not quite. He could read with great difficulty, and tremendous enlargement. Looking at his work there is no hint of this. I again spent about six weeks at Yale in the late eighties at the Cowles Foundation, giving a series of lectures on interactive epistemology.

One more place that influenced me was Berkeley, where I spent the summer of '64 and the spring of '72. There the main contact was Gérard Debreu, who was a remarkable personality. Other people there were John Harsanyi and Roy Radner. In addition to his greatness as a scientist, Gerard was also well known as a gourmet. His wife Françoise was a terrific cook. Once in a while they would invite us to dinner; Françoise would go out of her way to prepare something kosher. Occasionally we would invite them. It was his practice at a meal to praise at most one dish. Sometimes he praised nothing; sometimes, one dish. That totally transformed a compliment from Gerard from something trivial to something sublime. Nowadays, I myself cook and give dinners; when a guest leaves saying everything was wonderful, it means nothing. Though I allow myself to be kidded, it really means nothing. But when a guest leaves and says, "The soup was the most delicious soup I ever had," that says something. He doesn't talk about the meat and not about the fish and not about the salad and not about the dessert, just the soup. Or somebody else says, "This was a wonderful trout mousse." One dish gets praised. Then you know it's meaningful.

I also spent a month at NYU, in February of 1997. It was interesting. But for me, the attractions of New York City overwhelmed the academic activity. Perhaps Esther and I took the city a little too seriously. This was a very beautiful time for us, but what surrounds NYU was more important to us than the academic activity.

Hart: Maybe it's a good point to ask you, in retrospect, who are the people who have most influenced your life?

Aumann: First of all my family: parents, brother, wife, children, grandchildren. My great-grandchild has not yet had a specific important influence on me; he is all of one and a half. But that will come also. My students have influenced me greatly. You have influenced me. All my teachers. Beyond that, to pick out one person in the family, just one: my mother, who was an extraordinary person. She got a bachelor's degree in England in 1914, at a time when that was very unusual for women. She was a medal-winning long-distance swimmer, sang Schubert lieder while accompanying herself on the piano, introduced us children to nature, music, reading. We would walk the streets and she would teach us the names of the trees. At night we looked at the sky and she taught us the names of the constellations. When I was about 12, we started reading Dickens's *A Tale of Two Cities* together—until the book gripped me and I raced ahead alone. From then on, I read voraciously. She even introduced me to interactive epistemology; look at the "folk ditty" in Aumann (1996). She always encouraged, always pushed us along, gently, unobtrusively, always allowed us to make our own decisions. Of course parents always have an influence, but she was unusual.

I've already mentioned my math teacher in high school—"Joey" Gansler. On the Jewish side, the high school teacher who influenced me most was Rabbi Shmuel Warshavchik. He had spent the years of the Second World War with the Mir Yeshiva in China, having escaped from the Nazis; after the war he made his way to the United States. He had a tremendous influence on me. He attracted me to the beauty of Talmudic study and the beauty of religious observance. He was, of course, *khareidi*, a term that is difficult to translate. Many people call them ultra-orthodox, but that has a pejorative flavor that I dislike. Literally, *khareidi* means worried, scared, concerned. It refers to trying to live the proper life and being very concerned about doing things right, about one's obligations to G-d and man. Warshavchik's enthusiasm and intensity—the fire in his eyes—lit a fire in me also. He eventually came to Israel, and died a few years ago in Haifa.

The next person who had quite an extraordinary influence on me was a young philosophy instructor at City College called Harry Tarter. I took from him courses called Philo 12 and 13—logic, the propositional calculus, a little set theory.

Hart: So your work in interactive epistemology had a good basis.

Aumann: It was grounded in Philo 12 and Philo 13, where I learned about Russell's paradox and so on. We struck up a personal relationship that went far beyond the lecture hall, and is probably not very usual between an undergraduate and a university teacher. Later, my wife and children and I visited him in the Adirondacks, where he had a rustic home on the shores of a lake. When in Israel, he was our guest for the Passover Seder. What was most striking about him is that he would always question. He would always take something that appears self-evident and say, "Why is that so?" At the Seder he asked a lot of questions. His wife tried to shush him; she said, "Harry, let them go on." But I said, "No, these questions are welcome." He was a remarkable person.

Another person who influenced me greatly was Jack W. Smith, whom I met in my postdoc period at Princeton, when working on the Naval Electronics Project. Let me describe this project briefly. One day we got a frantic phone call from Washington. Jack Smith was on the line. He was responsible for reallocating used naval equipment from decommissioned ships to active duty ships. These were very expensive items: radar, sonar, radio transmitters and receivers—large, expensive equipment, sometimes worth half a million 1955 dollars for each item. It was a lot of money. All this equipment was assigned to Jack Smith, who had to assign it to these ships. He tried to work out some kind of systematic way of doing it. The naval officers would come stomping into his office and pull out their revolvers and threaten to shoot him or otherwise use verbal violence. He was distraught. He called us up and said, "I don't care how you do this, but give me some way of doing it, so I can say, 'The computer did this.'"

Now this is a classical assignment problem, which is a kind of linear programming problem. The constraints are entirely clear. There is only one small problem, namely, what's the objective function? Joe Kruskal and I solved the problem one way or another [Aumann and Kruskal (1959)], and our solution was implemented. It is perhaps one of the more important pieces of my work, although it doesn't have many citations (it does have some). At that opportunity we formed a friendship with Jack Smith, his wife Annie and his five children, which lasted for many, many years. He was a remarkable individual. He had contracted polio as a child, so he limped. But nevertheless the energy of this guy was really amazing. The energy, the intellectual curiosity, and the intellectual breadth were outstanding. A beautiful family, beautiful people. He made a real mark on me.

Let's go back to graduate days. Of course my adviser, George Whitehead, had an important influence on me. He was sort of dry—not in spirit, but in the meticulousness of his approach to mathematics. We had weekly meetings, in which I would explain my ideas. I would talk about covering spaces and wave my hands around. He would say, "Aumann, that's a very nice idea, but it's not mathematics. In mathematics we may discuss three-dimensional objects, but our proofs must be one-dimensional. You must write it down one word after another, and it's got to be coherent." This has stayed with me for many years.

We've already discussed Morgenstern, who promoted my career tremendously, and to whom I owe a big debt of gratitude.

The people with whom you interact also influence you. Among the people who definitely had an influence on me was Herb Scarf. I got the idea for the paper on markets with a continuum of traders by listening to Scarf; we became very good friends. Arrow also influenced me. I have had a very close friendship with Ken Arrow for many, many years. He did not have all that much direct scientific influence on my work, but his personality is certainly overpowering, and the indirect influence is enormous. Certainly Harsanyi's ideas about incomplete information had an important influence. As far as reading is concerned, the book of Luce and Raiffa, *Games and Decisions*, had a big influence.

Another important influence is Shapley. The work on "Markets with a Continuum of Traders" was created in my mind by putting together the paper of Shapley and Milnor on Oceanic Games and Scarf's presentation at the '61 games conference. And then there was our joint book, and all my work on nontransferable utility values, on which Shapley had a tremendous influence.

Hart: Let's go now to a combination of things that are not really related to one another, a potpourri of topics. They form a part of your worldview. We'll start with judicial discretion and restraint, a much-disputed issue here in Israel.

Figure 15.8 At the 1994 Morgenstern Lecture, Jerusalem: Bob Aumann (front row), Don Patinkin, Mike Maschler, and Ken Arrow (second row, left to right), and Tom Schelling (third row, second from left); also Marshall Sarnat, Jonathan Shalev, Michael Beenstock, Dieter Balkenborg, Eytan Sheshinski, Edna Ullmann-Margalit, Maya Bar-Hillel, Gershon Ben-Shakhar, Benjamin Weiss, Reuben Gronau, Motty Perry, Menahem Yaari, Zur Shapira, David Budescu, and Gary Bornstein.

Aumann: There are two views of how a court should operate, especially a supreme court. One calls for judicial restraint, the other for judicial activism. The view of judicial restraint is that courts are for applying the laws of the land, not making them; the legislature is for making laws, the executive for administering them, and the courts for adjudicating disputes in accordance with them.

The view of judicial activism is that the courts actually have a much wider mandate. They may decide which activities are reasonable, and which not; what is "just," and what is not. They apply their own judgment rather than written laws, saying this is or isn't "reasonable," or "acceptable," or "fair." First and foremost this applies to activities of government agencies; the court may say, "This is an unreasonable activity for a government agency." But it also applies to things like enforcing contracts; a judicially active court will say, "This contract, to which both sides agreed, is not 'reasonable,' and therefore we will not enforce it." These are opposite approaches to the judicial function.

In Israel it is conceded all around that the courts, and specifically the Supreme Court, are extremely activist, much more so than on the Continent or even in the United States. In fact, the chief justice of the Israeli Supreme Court, Aharon Barak, and I were once both present at a lecture where the speaker claimed that the Supreme Court justifiably takes on legislative functions, that it is a legislative body as well as a judicial body. Afterwards, I expressed to Mr. Barak my amazement at this pronouncement. He said, "What's wrong with it? The lecturer is perfectly right. We are like the Sages of the Talmud, who also took on legislative as well as judicial functions."

Hart: Do you agree with that statement about the Talmud?

Aumann: Yes, it is absolutely correct.

There are two major problems with judicial activism. One is that the judiciary is the least democratically constituted body in the government. In Israel, it is to a large extent a self-perpetuating body. Three of the nine members of the committee that appoints judges are themselves Supreme Court judges. Others are members of the bar who are strongly influenced by judges. A minority, only four out of the nine, are elected people—members of the Knesset. Moreover, there are various ways in which this committee works to overcome the influence of the elected representatives. For example, the Supreme Court judges on the committee always vote as a bloc, which greatly increases their power, as we know from Shapley value analyses.

In short, the way that the judiciary is constituted is very far from democratic. Therefore, to have the judiciary act in a legislative role is in violation of the principles of democracy. The principles of democracy are well based in game-theoretic considerations; see, for example, my paper with Kurz called "Power and Taxes" [Aumann and Kurz (1977a)], which discusses the relation between power and democracy. In order that no one group should usurp the political power in the country, and also the physical wealth of the country, it is important to spread power evenly and thinly. Whereas I do not cast any aspersions now on the basic honesty of the judges of the Israeli Supreme Court, nevertheless, an institution where so much power is concentrated in the hands of so few undemocratically selected people is a great danger. This is one item.

Hart: The court not being democratically elected is not the issue, so long as the mandate of the court is just to interpret the law. It becomes an issue when the judicial branch creates the law.

Aumann: Precisely. What is dangerous is a largely self-appointed oligarchy of people who make the laws. It is the *combination* of judicial activism with an undemocratically appointed court that is dangerous.

The second problem with judicial activism is that of uncertainty. If a person considering a contract does not know whether it will be upheld in court, he will be unwilling to sign it. Activism creates uncertainty: maybe the contract will be upheld, maybe not. Most decisionmakers are generally assumed to be risk-averse, and they will shy away from agreements in an activist atmosphere. So there will be many potential agreements that will be discarded, and the result will be distinctly suboptimal.

Hart: But incomplete contracts may have advantages. Not knowing in advance what the court will decide—Isn't that a form of incompleteness of the contract?

Aumann: Incomplete contracts may indeed sometimes be useful, but that is not the issue here. The issue is a contract on which the sides have explicitly agreed, but that may be thrown out by the court. *Ex ante*, that cannot possibly be beneficial to the parties to the contract. It might conceivably be beneficial to society, if indeed you don't want that contract to be carried out. A contract to steal a car *should* be unenforceable, because car theft should be discouraged. But we don't want to discourage legitimate economic activity, and judicial activism does exactly that.

Hart: The uncertainty about the court's decision may be viewed also as a chance device—which may lead to a Pareto improvement. Like mutual insurance.

Aumann: Well, okay, that is theoretically correct. Still, it is far-fetched. In general, uncertainty is a dampening factor.

In brief, for these two reasons—introducing uncertainty into the economy and into the polity, and its undemocratic nature—judicial activism is to be deplored.

Hart: Another topic you wanted to talk about is war.

Aumann: Barry O'Neill, the game theory political scientist, gave a lecture here a few months ago. Something he said in the lecture—that war has been with us for thousands of years—set me thinking. It really is true that there is almost nothing as ever-present in the history of mankind as war. Since the dawn of history we have had constant wars. War and religion, those are the two things that are ever-present with us. A tremendous amount of energy is devoted on the part of a very large number of well-meaning people to the project of preventing war, settling conflicts peacefully, ending wars, and so on. Given the fact that war is so, so prevalent, both in time and in space, all over the world, perhaps much of the effort of preventing or stopping war is misdirected. Much of this effort is directed at solving specific conflicts. What can we do to reach a compromise between the Catholics and the Protestants in Ireland? What can we do to resolve the conflict between the Hindus in India and the Moslems in Pakistan? What can we do to resolve the conflict between the Jews and the Arabs in the Middle East? One always gets into the particulars of these conflicts and neglects the more basic problems that present themselves by the very fact that we have had wars continuously. War is only apparently based on specific conflicts. There appears to be something in the way human nature is constituted—or if not human nature, then the way we run our institutions—that allows war and in fact makes it inevitable. Just looking at history, given the constancy of war, we should perhaps shift gears and ask ourselves what it is that causes war. Rather than establishing peace institutes, peace initiatives, institutions for studying and promoting peace, we should have institutions for studying war. *Not* with an immediate view to preventing war. Such a view can come later, but first we should understand the phenomenon.

It's like fighting cancer. One way is to ask, given a certain kind of cancer, what can we do to cure it? Chemotherapy? Radiation? Surgery? Let's do statistical studies that indicate which is more effective. That's one way of dealing with cancer, and it's an important way. Another way is simply to ask, what *is* cancer? How does it work? Never mind curing it. First let's understand it. How does it get started, how does it spread? How fast? What are the basic properties of cells that go awry when a person gets cancer? Just study it. Once one understands it one can perhaps hope to overcome it. But before you understand it, your hope to overcome it is limited.

Hart: So, the standard approach to war and peace is to view it as a black box. We do not know how it operates, so we try ad-hoc solutions. You are saying that this is not a good approach. One should instead try to go inside the black box: to understand the roots of conflict—not just deal with symptoms.

Aumann: Yes. Violent conflict may be very difficult to overcome. A relevant game-theoretic idea is that, in general, neither side really knows the disagreement level, the "reservation price." It's like the Harsanyi–Selten bargaining model with incomplete information, where neither side knows the reservation price of the other. The optimum strategy in such a situation may be to go all the way and threaten. If the buyer thinks that the seller's reservation price is low, he will make a low offer, even if he is in fact willing to pay much more. Similarly for the seller. So conflict may result even when the reservation prices of the two sides are compatible. When this conflict is a strike, then it is bad enough, but when it's a war, then it is much worse. This kind of model suggests that conflict may be inevitable, or that you need different institutions in order to avoid it. If in fact it is inevitable in that sense, we should understand that. One big mistake is to say that war is irrational.

Hart: It's like saying that strikes are irrational.

Aumann: Yes, and that racial discrimination is irrational (cf., Arrow). We take all the ills of the world and dismiss them by calling them irrational. They are not necessarily irrational. Though it hurts, they may be rational. Saying that war is irrational may be a big mistake. If it is rational, once we understand that it is, we can at least somehow address the problem. If we simply dismiss it as irrational, we can't address the problem.

Hart: Exactly as in strikes, the only way to transmit to the other side how important this thing is to you may be to go to war.

Aumann: Yes. In fact Bob Wilson discussed this in his Morgenstern lecture here in '94—just after a protracted strike of the professors in Israel.

Hart: Here in Israel, we unfortunately have constant wars and conflicts. One of the "round tables" of the Rationality Center—where people throw ideas at each other very informally—was on international conflicts. You presented there some nice game-theoretic insights.

Aumann: One of them was the blackmailer's paradox. Ann and Bob must divide 100 dollars. It is not an ultimatum game; they can discuss it freely. Ann says to Bob, "Look, I want 90 of those 100. Take it or leave it; I will not walk out of this room with less than 90 dollars." Bob says, "Come on, that's crazy. We have 100 dollars. Let's split 50–50." Ann says, "No." Ann—"the blackmailer"—is perhaps acting irrationally. But Bob, if he is rational, will accept the 10 dollars, and that's the end.

Hart: The question is whether she can commit herself to the 90. Because if not, then of course Bob will say, "You know what, 50–50. Now *you* take it or leave it." For this to work, Ann must commit herself credibly.

Aumann: In other words, it's not enough for her just to say it. She has to make it credible; and then Bob will rationally accept the 10. The difficulty with this is that perhaps Bob, too, can credibly commit to accepting no less than 90. So we have a paradox: once Ann credibly commits herself to accepting no less than 90, Bob is rationally motivated to take the 10. But then Ann is rationally motivated to make such a commitment. But Bob could also make such a commitment; and if both make the commitment, it is not rational, because then nobody gets anything.

This is the blackmailer's paradox. It is recognized in game theory, therefore, that it is perhaps not so rational for the guy on the receiving end of the threat to accept it.

What is the application of this to the situation we have here in Israel? Let me tell you this true story. A high-ranking officer once came to my office at the Center for Rationality and discussed with me the situation with Syria and the Golan Heights. This was a hot topic at the time. He explained to me that the Syrians consider land holy, and they will not give up one inch. When he told me that, I told him about the blackmailer's paradox. I said to him that the Syrians' use of the term "holy," land being holy, is a form of commitment. In fact, they must really convince themselves that it's holy, and they do. Just like in the blackmailer's paradox, we could say that it's holy; but we can't convince *ourselves* that it is. One of our troubles is that the term "holy" is nonexistent in our practical, day-to-day vocabulary. It exists only in religious circles. We accept holiness in other people and we are not willing to promote it on our own side. The result is that we are at a disadvantage because the other side can invoke holiness, but we have ruled it out from our arsenal of tools.

Hart: On the other hand, we do have such a tool: security considerations. That is the "holy" issue in Israel. We say that security considerations dictate that we must have control of the mountains that control the Sea of Galilee. There is no way that anything else will be acceptable. Throughout the years of Israel's existence, security considerations have been a kind of holiness, a binding commitment to ourselves. The question is whether it is as strong as the holiness of the land on the other side.

Aumann: It is less strong.

Hart: Maybe that explains why there is no peace with Syria.

Aumann: You know, the negotiations that Rabin held with the Syrians in the early nineties blew up over a few meters. I really don't understand why they blew up, because Rabin was willing to give almost everything away. Hills, everything.

Without suggesting solutions, it is just a little bit of an insight into how game-theoretic analysis can help us to understand what is going on, in this country in particular, and in international conflicts in general.

Hart: Next, what about what you refer to as "connections"?

Aumann: A lot of game theory has to do with relationships among different objects. I talked about this in my 1995 "birthday" lecture, and it is also in the Introduction to my *Collected Papers* [Aumann (2000)].

Science is often characterized as a quest for truth, where truth is something absolute, which exists outside of the observer. But I view science more as a quest for *understanding*, where the understanding is that of the observer, the scientist. Such understanding is best gained by studying relations—relations between different ideas, relations between different phenomena; relations between ideas and phenomena. Rather than asking "How does this phenomenon work?" we ask, "How does this phenomenon resemble others with which we are familiar?" Rather than asking "Does this idea make sense?" we ask, "How does this idea resemble other ideas?"

Indeed, the idea of relationship is fundamental to game theory. Disciplines like economics or political science use disparate models to analyze monopoly, oligopoly, perfect competition, public goods, elections, coalition formation, and so on. In contrast, game theory uses the *same* tools in all these applications. The nucleolus yields the competitive solution in large markets [Aumann (1964)], the homogeneous weights in parliaments (cf., Peleg), and the Talmudic solution in bankruptcy games [Aumann and Maschler (1985)]. The fundamental notion of Nash equilibrium, which a priori reflects the behavior of consciously maximizing agents, is the *same* as an equilibrium of populations that reproduce blindly without regard to maximizing anything.

The great American naturalist and explorer John Muir said, "When you look closely at anything in the universe, you find it hitched to everything else." Though Muir was talking about the natural universe, this applies also to scientific ideas—how we *understand* our universe.

Hart: How about the issue of assumptions versus conclusions?

Aumann: There is a lot of discussion in economic theory and in game theory about the reasonableness or correctness of assumptions and axioms. That is wrongheaded. I have never been so interested in assumptions. I am interested in conclusions. Assumptions don't have to be correct; *conclusions* have to be correct. That is put very strongly, maybe more than I really feel, but I want to be provocative. When Newton introduced the idea of gravity, he was laughed at, because there was no rope with which the sun was pulling the earth; gravity is a laughable idea, a crazy assumption, it still sounds crazy today. When I was a child I was told about it. It did not make any sense then, and it doesn't now; but it does yield the right answer. In science one never looks at assumptions; one looks at conclusions. It does not interest me whether this or that axiom of utility theory, of the Shapley value, of Nash bargaining is or is not compelling. What interests me is whether the *conclusions* are compelling, whether they yield interesting insights, whether one can build useful theory from them, whether they are testable. Nowhere else in science does one directly test assumptions; a theory stands or falls by the validity of the conclusions, not of the assumptions.

Hart: Would you like to say something about the ethical neutrality of game theory?

Aumann: Ethical neutrality means that game theorists don't necessarily advocate carrying out the normative prescriptions of game theory. Game theory is about selfishness. Just like I suggested studying war, game theory studies selfishness. Obviously, studying war is not the same as advocating war; similarly, studying selfishness is not the same as advocating selfishness. Bacteriologists do not advocate disease; they study it. Game theory says nothing about whether the "rational" way is morally or ethically right. It just says what rational—self-interested—entities will do; not what they "should" do, ethically speaking. If we want a better world, we had better pay attention to where rational incentives lead.

Hart: That's a very good conclusion to this fascinating interview. Thank you.

Aumann: And thank *you*, Sergiu, for your part in this wonderful interview.

REFERENCES

Aumann, R.J. (1956) Asphericity of alternating knots. *Annals of Mathematics* 64, 374–392.

Aumann, R.J. (1959) Acceptable points in general cooperative *n*-person games. In A.W. Tucker & R.D. Luce (eds.), *Contributions to the Theory of Games IV*, Annals of Mathematics Study 40, pp. 287–324. Princeton, NJ: Princeton University Press.

Aumann, R.J. (1961) The core of a cooperative game without side payments. *Transactions of the American Mathematical Society* 98, 539–552.

Aumann, R.J. (1964) Markets with a continuum of traders. *Econometrica* 32, 39–50.

Aumann, R.J. (1965) Integrals of set-valued functions. *Journal of Mathematical Analysis and Applications* 12, 1–12.

Aumann, R.J. (1966) Existence of competitive equilibria in markets with a continuum of traders. *Econometrica* 34, 1–17.

Aumann, R.J. (1967) A survey of cooperative games without side payments. In M. Shubik (ed.), *Essays in Mathematical Economics in Honor of Oskar Morgenstern*, pp. 3–27. Princeton, NJ: Princeton University Press.

Aumann, R.J. (1973) Disadvantageous monopolies. *Journal of Economic Theory* 6, 1–11.

Aumann, R.J. (1974) Subjectivity and correlation in randomized strategies. *Journal of Mathematical Economics* 1, 67–96.

Aumann, R.J. (1975) Values of markets with a continuum of traders. *Econometrica* 43, 611–646.

Aumann, R.J. (1976) Agreeing to disagree. *Annals of Statistics* 4, 1236–1239.

Aumann, R.J. (1980) Recent developments in the theory of the Shapley value. In O. Lehto (ed.), *Proceedings of the International Congress of Mathematicians, Helsinki, 1978*, pp. 995–1003. Helsinki: Academia Scientiarum Fennica.

Aumann, R.J. (1981) Survey of repeated games. In V. Böhm (ed.), *Essays in Game Theory and Mathematical Economics in Honor of Oskar Morgenstern*, Vol. 4 of Gesellschaft, Recht, Wirtschaft, Wissenschaftsverlag, pp. 11–42. Mannheim: Bibliographisches Institut.

Aumann, R.J. (1987) Correlated equilibrium as an expression of Bayesian rationality. *Econometrica* 55, 1–18.

Aumann, R.J. (1996) Reply to Binmore. *Games and Economic Behavior* 17, 138–146.

Aumann, R.J. (2000) *Collected Papers*, Vol. 1, xi + 786 pp., Vol. 2, xiii + 792 pp., Cambridge, MA: MIT Press.

Aumann, R.J. (2003a) Presidential Address. *Games and Economic Behavior* 45, 2–14.

Aumann, R.J. (2003b) Risk aversion in the Talmud. *Economic Theory* 21, 233–239.

Aumann, R.J. & F.J. Anscombe (1963) A definition of subjective probability. *Annals of Mathematical Statistics* 34, 199–205.

Aumann, R.J. & A. Brandenburger (1995) Epistemic conditions for Nash equilibrium. *Econometrica* 63, 1161–1180.

Aumann, R.J. & J. Drèze (1975) Cooperative games with coalition structures. *International Journal of Game Theory* 4, 217–237.

Aumann, R.J. & J. Drèze (1986) Values of markets with satiation or fixed prices. *Econometrica* 54, 1271–1318.

Aumann, R.J. & S. Hart (1986) Bi-convexity and bi-martingales. *Israel Journal of Mathematics* 54, 159–180.

Aumann, R.J. & S. Hart (eds.) (1992–2002) *Handbook of Game Theory with Economic Applications*. Amsterdam: Elsevier: Vol. 1, 1992, xxvi + 733 pp.; Vol. 2, 1994, xxviii + 787 pp.; Vol. 3, 2002, xxx + 858 pp.

Aumann, R.J. & S. Hart (2003) Long cheap talk. *Econometrica* 71, 1619–1660.

Aumann, R.J. & J.B. Kruskal (1959) Assigning quantitative values to qualitative factors in the naval electronics problem. *Naval Research Logistics Quarterly* 6, 1–16.

Aumann, R.J. & M. Kurz (1977a) Power and taxes. *Econometrica* 45, 1137–1161.

Aumann, R.J. & M. Kurz (1977b) Power and taxes in a multi-commodity economy. *Israel Journal of Mathematics* 27, 185–234.

Aumann, R.J. & M. Maschler (1964) The bargaining set for cooperative games. In M. Dresher, L.S. Shapley & A.W. Tucker (eds.), *Advances in Game Theory*, Annals of Mathematics Study 52, pp. 443–476. Princeton, NJ: Princeton University Press.

Aumann, R.J. & M. Maschler (1972) Some thoughts on the minimax principle. *Management Science* 18, P-54–P-63.

Aumann, R.J. & M. Maschler (1985) Game-theoretic analysis of a bankruptcy problem from the Talmud. *Journal of Economic Theory* 36, 195–213.

Aumann, R.J. & M. Maschler (1995) *Repeated Games with Incomplete Information*. Cambridge, MA: MIT Press, xvii + 342 pp.

Aumann, R.J. & L.S. Shapley (1974) *Values of Non-Atomic Games*. Princeton, NJ: Princeton University Press, xi + 333 pp.

Aumann, R.J. & S. Sorin (1989) Cooperation and bounded recall. *Games and Economic Behavior* 1, 5–39.

Aumann, R.J., R.J. Gardner & R.W. Rosenthal (1977) Core and value for a public goods economy: An example. *Journal of Economic Theory* 15, 363–365.

Aumann, R.J., S. Hart & M. Perry (1997a) The absent-minded driver. *Games and Economic Behavior* 20, 102–116.

Aumann, R.J., S. Hart & M. Perry (1997b) The forgetful passenger. *Games and Economic Behavior* 20, 117–120.

Aumann, R.J., M. Kurz & A. Neyman (1983) Voting for public goods. *Review of Economic Studies* 50, 677–694.

Aumann, R.J., M. Kurz & A. Neyman (1987) Power and public goods. *Journal of Economic Theory* 42, 108–127.

Shapley, L. & M. Shubik (1954) A method of evaluating the distribution of power in a committee system. *American Political Science Review* 48, 787–792.

16

Conversations with James Tobin and Robert J. Shiller on the "Yale Tradition" in Macroeconomics

Conducted by David Colander

MIDDLEBURY COLLEGE

Every graduate school has its own distinctive history that makes it unique in some way, but every graduate school is also part of the broader economics profession and reflects the currents in the profession. The following dialogue focuses on the question: Is it useful to distinguish a "Yale school of macroeconomics" from other schools of economics? The idea for this dialogue came from Bill Barnett in a discussion with Bob Shiller. Bill suggested to Bob some names of individuals who might conduct the "dialogue" and I was selected from that list. I happily agreed because, from my knowledge of the writings of the Yale faculty, I felt that there was a uniformity of ideas with which I was sympathetic, and which might deserve to be called a "Yale school"—a view shared with Bob Shiller. Exploring the issue further, I found that there was far less agreement on whether the macroeconomics work that currently goes on at Yale can be classified meaningfully as "the Yale school." The objections to specifying a separate Yale school were the following: (1) The term, Yale school, had been used in the 1960s to describe Jim Tobin's position in a debate with monetarists. Some felt it would be confusing to use the Yale school classification to describe a broader set of works that

Reprinted from *Macroeconomic Dynamics*, 3, 1999, 116–143. Copyright © 1999 Cambridge University Press.

are not connected to that earlier, more narrow, use. (2) Calling the work in macroeconomics currently done at Yale a "school" distinguishes it too much. The work that goes on in Yale is similar to the work that goes on in any top graduate economics program. It is not so clear how the work at Yale differs from, for example, MIT or Princeton. It would need to be more distinct to warrant calling it a "school." (3) There is a diversity of approaches that are used at Yale, and it is not clear that they actually fit together. For example, Chris Sims's work follows from a time-series statistics tradition with influences from real-business-cycle and calibration work; Shiller's work follows from a Keynesian tradition. Fitting them together requires a bit of a stretch. (4) The degree of continuity in the Yale school over time is not as great as I had first imagined. There was little linkage at Yale from Irving Fisher to Jim Tobin; thus the historical continuity needed for specifying a Yale school does not exist. These objections are elaborated in the dialogues below. After discussing these issues with a number of Yale faculty, I decided that there probably wasn't a Yale school of economics, but that there was a Yale tradition. We also decided to have a conversation with only two individuals—Jim Tobin and Bob Shiller—because they are major figures in maintaining what I believe is a Yale tradition. The conversations were held separately, although I asked many of the same questions to both, and focused much of the conversation on the issue of whether it is useful to distinguish a Yale school. Thus, the conversations discuss the work of other individuals at Yale more than a dialogue with another focus would have, and do not cover Tobin's or Shiller's current work as much as conversations with an alternative focus would have. The results are, I believe, interesting. They provide some useful insight into both the Yale tradition and current thinking and debates in macro.

A Conversation with James Tobin
Fall 1997

Colander: You went to Harvard as an undergraduate.

Tobin: That's right; I graduated in 1939. I didn't leave Harvard graduate school until two years after; it was 1941. I got the MA in one year because I had taken so many graduate courses when I was still an undergraduate.

Colander: At that point you were still working for your Ph.D., right?

Tobin: Yes. I was still taking more courses, more seminars, and so on. In the spring of 1941, I had taken a course with Ed Mason on the economics of defense. I was also teaching myself econometrics. The

Harvard economics department didn't have much in the way of modern statistics then. They had statistics courses, which I took, but they didn't have a course in econometrics as we now think of econometrics, and the teachers of economic statistics were not very enthusiastic about using statistics. Mainly, they were telling us the pitfalls of using statistics, so, aside from a seminar by a visitor, Hans Staehle from Switzerland, on demand analysis, we didn't have much going on at Harvard in this area. I took some mathematical statistics in the math department, and I took some advanced mathematical theory with Edwin B. Wilson, who was in the Public Health School but was, among other things, a first-rate mathematical economist.

In Mason's course, I had used the regression analysis that I'd been learning to estimate the demand for steel in the United States. Ed was involved in questions of mobilizing the economy for defense, so he suggested that I go to Washington and work in one of the new agencies which was supposed to be cutting down civilian uses of some of the potentially scarce metals like steel, aluminum, and nickel. They weren't prohibiting the civilian uses of these things; the point was to cut them down and then to allocate them to the civilian uses that were still to be allowed. This was one job of an agency called the Office of Price Administration and Civilian Supply, and I went to work in the civilian supply part in the summer of 1941.

I moved to a different agency, called the War Production Board, after the war started but, meanwhile, after Pearl Harbor I decided I would not want to spend the war doing this, so I enlisted in the Navy and then I was actually called to duty, duty being to go to school to learn to be an officer in 90 days, in April 1942. And then I was gone from economics until January 1946.

Colander: Then you went back to Harvard.

Tobin: Yes, I went back to Harvard. I got out of the Navy in the middle of December 1945, close to Christmas, and I went home. I had been on the same destroyer all that time; after I got my commission. I went home, and

Figure 16.1 James Tobin.

I had friends who were still in the government, and they were offering me jobs to come back to the government. I had been very successful as a government economist, and so those were attractive jobs. They paid a lot of money—what *looked* like a lot of money—so I didn't know what to do. Meanwhile I made inquiries about going back to Harvard. I wrote to Seymour Harris, whom I'd known extremely well at Harvard. He had taken an interest in me even though I had never been in one of his classes. I asked him if I could get a tutorship in one of the colleges—that would give me a room—and I asked the chairman of the department if I could get a job as a teaching assistant. I told these professors that I was considering whether to come back and finish the degree or to go back to Washington.

The chairman of the department was Harold Hitchings Burbank. He was a very conservative economist. He liked to run the department and chronically did. He replied by letter that he had been told by people who had examined me and people who had had me as a student that I had an unusually good chance of being a distinguished economist and therefore it would be a great mistake if I left academia. He and I hadn't been particular friends—we hadn't been enemies, but we hadn't been particular friends—but I was very much influenced by that letter, and I went back.

Colander: You got your Ph.D. in 1947 and you went to Yale in 1950. . . .

Tobin: Yes. Meanwhile, I had a Junior Fellowship at Harvard. It was actually my first job although it was not meant to be. It was meant to be a substitute for a doctor's degree, not a postdoctoral position. But they waived that requirement of the Junior Fellowship for veterans like me, because they could understand that the first thing I wanted when I got back was to get a degree. So the Junior Fellowship I got worked out as postdoctoral. I spent two years at Harvard, and the other year I went to England to Richard Stone's Institute, the Department of Applied Economics at Cambridge. *Then* I went to Yale.

Colander: Were you thinking of going any other place?

Tobin: I was away from the United States in the year before I was going to take a job, so a lot of the things had to be done by mail. I had been invited all over the country in the previous year—out to California, to Stanford, and all over the place. So I had a lot of opportunities. The best thing that had happened to me when I went back to graduate school in 1946 was that I met my wife. I met her in the spring of that year and we got married in the fall, and if I'd gone to Washington I wouldn't have. She said she'd go anyplace except New Haven, but we went to New Haven and she loved it.

Colander: I want to discuss a bit about the Yale school.

Tobin: I should say, in regard to Bob Shiller's contacts with Barnett, that I think there's a little bit of confusion between what is described as "the Yale school" and other informal institutions such as the eleven-o'clock coffee group, which meets most every day. This eleven-o'clock coffee group is not the Yale school—it includes people who might be identified as part of the old macroeconomic Yale school but it includes other people, too: Chris Sims, who's an advocate of real business cycles; Martin Shubik, a very interesting guy, but I don't think of him as a member of any particular school except his own; John Geanakoplos, who is sympathetic to my macro views but who wants to reconcile them to Arrow–Debreu; Herb Scarf, a math theorist; and T.N. Srinivasan, a tough neoclassical economist. I think that the people listed by Barnett and Shiller are part of this coffee group, but I would not classify them as being a Yale school. They are just a congenial and interesting subgroup of the Yale department.

Colander: How would *you* summarize the Yale school?

Tobin: I think that what people meant by the Yale school goes back to the 1950s. It is identified with my, and Art Okun's, macroeconomic and monetary views and teachings. (The importance of the late Art Okun, and the loss to all economists of his premature death, can't be exaggerated.) In our work we attempted to provide a reasonably systematic view of what Keynesian economics was, and what applications were possible. In monetary theory, the Yale school provided an alternative to monetarism. It involved the possible roles of monetary and fiscal policy. I was very much involved in that controversy with monetarists.

Around 1970, some Yale graduate students produced a T-shirt. On the back, it read "Yale School," an obvious counter to the much-touted "Chicago School." On the front it read "Q is all that matters." The latter was intended to be a parody of monetarism's "M is all that matters," which I had criticized, arguing that the most you could say is "M matters." I think this usage supports my view of the meaning of the term, Yale school. We of the Yale school were not the only macro- and monetary economists at Yale at the time. There were Willy Fellner, Henry Wallich, Robert Triffin, and Richard Ruggles, each with his own ideas and interests. We were all on good terms and learned from one another.

In retrospect, that controversy doesn't look as important as the one between Keynesian economics and *New* Classical macroeconomics—about whether or not the actual economy is best described as a continuous full-employment solution.

Colander: What would be the Yale school's position on that?

Tobin: Well, the Yale school position on that is that sometimes the economy is characterized as being at, or close to, or maybe above, full employment. In that case, the opportunity-cost logic of neoclassical economics applies. At other times, however, the economy is better described not as a perfectly competitive market-clearing situation, but as a situation with general excess supply (particularly in the labor markets). In this case it is possible for monetary and fiscal policy to increase aggregate demand and increase output. That doesn't mean that opportunity cost calculations are ruled out, but it does change the nature of the calculation. The macro-calculation concerns how you expand the economy. Since there are several different ways of getting to full employment from a situation of excess supply, one should apply welfare analysis to choose the appropriate path. For example, you might want to recover by monetary expansion rather than fiscal expansion, if you were trying to do something to improve long-term growth while you restore full employment.

I always regarded myself as a partner in crime, as Samuelson described me, in developing the so-called neoclassical synthesis. I don't think neoclassical synthesis is a good name for it, since it was a neoclassical/neo-Keynesian synthesis, but I guess it was a modification not of Keynes, but of some of the Keynesians whose view was that the economy was always at an under full-employment equilibrium, and that thus the neoclassical rules never apply. That was not the view of American Keynesians, myself included, in the early postwar years. It was, however, the view of many of Keynes's followers, especially in the U.K. They had no use for monetary policy at all in the early 1950s. I differed from that group in that I taught that monetary policy was a possible tool of macroeconomic policy and that to neglect it was a mistake.

Colander: One of the arguments against the neo-Keynesian portion of the neoclassical synthesis is that its interpretation of Keynesian economics is incompatible with the Walrasian model, but the neoclassical synthesis nonetheless forces it into that framework.

Tobin: Well, it doesn't do *that*—it just recognizes that that might be a good start for a model of a full-employment economy over a long period of time. In that sense, neo-Keynesian economics regards the business cycle as a departure from a Walrasian market economy, and explicitly says that that's what it is—situations of excess supply and excess demand at existing prices and wages. So I don't think it's guilty of doing that. It's just not throwing away the insights of neoclassical economics.

Colander: Most of the formalizations of neo-Keynesian economics assume pure competition in the goods market.

Tobin: Well, I don't have to assume that. It might make some difference for some things, but let's think about the question of whether, as Keynes assumed, the labor market is always on the marginal productivity curve, which is the neoclassical view. That implies that, given capital stock and technology, the lower the marginal productivity of labor, the greater the employment of labor, and therefore the lower the unemployment rate. So if we're going to have an increase in employment—a reduction of *un*employment—we're going to go down the marginal productivity curve and have a lower real wage. That's a kind of pure-competition result, applied to an environment where you wouldn't expect market clearing to be a part.

Why did Keynes do that? I think he did that because he wanted to make the point that his quarrel with classical economics was valid even though he accepted a large part of classical doctrine, this particular thing being a an important example.

Then, there was the empirical finding of several economists such as John Dunlop that, even in the late 1930s before the war, actual real wages did not move counter to the business cycle—but, instead, increased during cyclical recoveries.

I think it's a mistake to think that this real-wage observation requires some big correction of Keynes and that Keynes had made a serious error in this respect. It has seemed to me, always, that this actually just strengthened Keynes's case; it did not diminish its logic. Say you ask "What is the consequence of adopting Keynesian monetary or fiscal policies to eliminate unemployment?" If you say, "This can actually be done without a reduction in the real wage," so much the better; that just makes the case for Keynesian policies that much stronger. So it's not a devastating criticism of Keynes that he used this "classical" view of the demand function for labor in relation to the real wage. On the contrary, his case is strengthened. If it is true that, in the short run, the behavior of prices is not competitive, and that maybe there is not increasing marginal cost in the short run for the firm as he assumed, it actually strengthens Keynes's case.

Colander: When New Classicals really tried to force a microfoundation to the analysis, and assumed perfect competition in both goods and labor market in a Walrasian framework, they showed you can't really have a problem.

Tobin: Well, of course, but that's exactly what the Yale school believes. That's my view. The Walrasian solution doesn't apply in situations in which there's excess supply at existing prices, where prices are not moving rapidly enough, or correctly enough, to clear the market by price at every moment of time—whether it's monopolistic competition or pure competition. I think it's absolutely absurd, and contrary to a lot of empirical observation, to say that the observations we get during short-run business cycles are the result of price fluctuations and wage fluctuations which are always clearing the market. But that doesn't undermine the Walrasian model as something that is a useful way of looking at economies.

Colander: So you'd accept that the Walrasian model can still be used as the model in the long run.

Tobin: Yes. You can amend the Walrasian model to have a world of monopolistic competition in the long run also. That also could be a situation in equilibrium, where the firms in monopolistic competition with each other have no incentive to change the prices, or the wages, that they're offering to employees, so there is a long-run monopolistic-competition counterpart of market clearing.

Colander: John Geanakoplos has worked on microfoundations of an aggregate economy with multiple paths. He and others have argued that it might be useful to analyze the economy in a long-run model with multiple paths.

Tobin: I'm not persuaded that that's a useful way to go about macroeconomics in the sense that I'm interested in it, which has much to do with stabilization policy—macro policy in the short run. A lot of people have tried to save a combination of Walrasian economics and allegedly Keynesian outcomes by multiple equilibrium paths, but it seems to me not to be Keynesian in its consequences because, in every such equilibrium, there's no involuntary unemployment; there's no excess supply. There's market clearing in every equilibrium, so I don't think that that's a fruitful way of making a combination of neoclassical economics with market clearing and Keynesian results. It could be true that some of the results with multiple equilibria—that some of the equilibria are better than others for labor or for whomever. But none of them is a situation of involuntary unemployment, which is a situation in which there's not market clearing in any of the equilibria—not market clearing at the existing prices.

John Geanakoplos and other moving-equilibrium theorists also worry in a rather deep sense about phenomena like missing markets. If the modern theory of Walrasian economy is Arrow–Debreu equilibrium, then it's pretty obvious that there are all kinds of missing markets. Some markets are prohibited from existing—you can't sell yourself into slavery and that sort of thing. So people like John Geanakoplos like to look at all problems—including Keynesian problems—as examples of these funda-mental defects or departures from pure Walrasian outcomes. I say, more power to them. That's not the Tobin Yale school, though; the Tobin Yale school is more pragmatic than that, and, in a sense, much less fundamentally theoretical.

Colander: What's your view of the Clower–Leijonhufvud approach?

Tobin: I don't have anything against that; I just never found myself really instructed by it.

Colander: What's your view of the New Keynesian approach?

Tobin: I'm not sure what *that* means. If it means people like Greg Mankiw, I don't regard them as Keynesians. I don't think they have involuntary unemployment or absence of market clearing. It is a misnomer to call Mankiw any form of Keynesian.

Colander: How about real-business-cycle theorists?

Tobin: Well, that's just the enemy.

Colander: [*Hearty laughter*]

Tobin: That's what we've been fighting about all these years, and that's just a repetition of the conflict between Keynes himself and the economists he regarded as Classicals—not the best word to use for them. The New Classicals and the real-business-cycle believers are much more extreme than the people that Keynes was arguing with in his day, but it's the same argument over again. Actually, Pigou was a much more reasonable, plausible economist than Lucas and some of the other New Classicals.

Colander: What do you think of the recent Hahn–Solow book on Keynesians in a rational-expectations framework?

Tobin: I thought that book was the multiple equilibrium thing over again. It doesn't seem Keynesian to me, but maybe I'm missing something.

Colander: I was introduced to the Tobin Yale school when I studied your debate with Brunner and Meltzer. How would you respond to Brunner's comment that "the most serious and pervasive flaw is that the Yale monetary theory offers no rationale for money."

Tobin: I think that's ridiculous.

Colander: What is the rationale for money within this Walrasian system?

Tobin: First, what Walrasian system are you referring to? I don't understand *that*. I have a multiasset description of the financial sector; Brunner and Meltzer also have one, and I never did understand how at the same time they have multiasset substitutable assets and yet, in the end, they come to a monetarist result which seems to be inconsistent with the assumed substitutability among assets, including substitutability of some assets for money proper. I never understood how, then, they could combine having a similar multiasset framework with having a monetarist conclusion that depends on there not being substitutability of other assets for money. I never did understand that, so I don't understand how the Brunner–Meltzer framework has an explanation for the usage of money whereas my framework doesn't have it.

Saying that money is all-powerful is not an explanation of why it's there. The explanation of why it's there goes back to Jevons and the advantages of the society agreeing upon a common means of payment. Once that agreement has been reached, the advantage of accepting money as means of payment for goods and services is that you know you'll be able to use it again in another transaction, avoiding, as Jevons said, the double coincidence of wants. I have written a paper on money—just "Money." That's the title of it. It's in the Palgrave on money and finance, and I take up this issue that you've just referred to.

Colander: What if they mean—if one has money, one needs transactions in the model, and the model of each of the markets has to have a transactions cost?

Tobin: You're seriously saying that about *me?*

Colander: No. I'm saying that about the assumption of perfect competition, which underlies the Walrasian model.

Tobin: This isn't perfect competition. We're talking about the supply and demand for different assets. I have a paper, a well-read paper, on transaction costs for money, for moving money to interest-bearing assets, other assets than money assets, so I don't think I'm vulnerable to that particular criticism. I think the deeper kind of problem is why anybody holds money, because it doesn't have any value in the end, and so you say, "Well, nobody will have money on Judgment Day or an hour before Judgment Day, and if anybody held money an hour before Judgment Day they wouldn't want to hold it *two* hours before Judgment Day, so why do they want to have it *now?*" So, in some sense, if you want to get involved in this kind of philosophical argument, you could say that it must be that whatever date is guessed at for the end of the world, there's always some probability that it's going to last longer than that. So there's some reason to hold money because you're going to want to make transactions, or your heirs are going to make transactions beyond that. I can't get excited about that.

Colander: Of the people in the 11:00 a.m. coffee group, who would fall within the Yale school in the sense that you are talking about?

Tobin: I certainly don't want to appropriate for *myself* the adjective "Yale." There are lots of people in macroeconomics around Yale who wouldn't have been regarded as sympathizing in all respects or even some fundamental respect, with me and Art Okun, like William Fellner who was a good friend, but who had a quite different approach to macro. I learned a lot from him and we agreed on a lot of things, but we certainly didn't agree about Keynesian economics.

But who, now, at Yale would be regarded as sympathetic to my views in macroeconomics? That would be Ray Fair; Bill Brainard, who was a partner in developing a lot of what I did in the models we were just discussing; Bill Nordhaus, who was a student of mine, and a collaborator of mine not so much in macro but in other things like the MEW (the measure of economic welfare); and Bob Shiller, who's, again, not a student of mine or a collaborator, but who thinks about macroeconomic things in similar ways to me and Bill Brainard [see Figure 16.2]. That's probably it.

Colander: How about the Tobin school outside of Yale? Who would you include as its members?

Tobin: There's Gary Smith, who was at Yale before and who's now at Pomona. He did a lot of work with us when he was at Yale, so he certainly is one. I don't know; it's hard to answer that question without thinking about it a while. There are many people who tend to agree with me about the general thrust of macroeconomics, which included several people at MIT like Franco Modigliani, but I wouldn't say he learned anything from me—he had it all himself; Bob Solow and Paul Samuelson and younger people such as Stanley Fischer at MIT and Alan Binder at Princeton.

More directly involved with the Yale school is Janet Yellen who is currently chair of the Council of Economic Advisers and was my T.A. and collaborator, and George Akerlof, although I didn't have him as a student except maybe as an undergraduate. I'd also include Don Hester, my first R.A., now at Wisconsin; Don Nichols and Steve Durlauf, also at the University of Wisconsin; Jim Pierce, now at Berkeley; and Ralph Bryant at Brookings.

Colander: How would you explain a lot of the younger students choosing to work within a New Classical framework?

Tobin: Well, I think there was a counterrevolution against the Keynesian economics of the 1960s, and it occurred both within the profession itself and in the general opinion in the country, probably the result of the Vietnam War and the inflation that came as a result of that war and the price shocks in the 1970s. I think that Keynesian economics was erroneously blamed for the inflations of the Vietnam War period and especially erroneously blamed for the inflations of the 1970s and the early 1980s. I read the histories that some people write—what went on in the world— that attribute everything that happened in those years to bad monetary policy, without any recognition of the external shocks involved.

Within the profession itself, I guess there is a strong current for equilibrium solutions. There always has been. The rational-expectations New Classical real business theory also offered young economists of a mathematical bent a new outlet and challenge for their talents. I think some of the appeal of Keynesian economics in the 1930s, 1950s, was *that*, also, but, by 20 years later, those challenges had been exhausted, so if you were a young economist looking for something exciting to do, rational expectations was the thing. So, the idea that you should have microfoundations of everything you do, everything you say is going on in the economy, including short-run behavior, has a surface plausibility. Actually, I think there's not much possible content in trying to describe the behavior of every individual in the society as a solution of a dynamic programming problem so that you explain the whole of what is obviously to me, disequilibrium behavior—I think we don't have very much knowledge of how to model it, so that idea of microfoundations, I think, meant that it seems plausible. Then what it means is that you can't do any *macro*economics. The result of that is we have this schism between abstract academic theory and practical macroeconomics, which is done by the people who actually have to make decisions about these things— the Congressional Budget Office—the executive government, and central banks.

Colander: I would view the Tobin school as the foundation of practical macroeconomics.

Tobin: I would like to think of it that way, and as a field that progresses and uses methods spawned in the professional journals. It has to go on because there are practical problems that have to be addressed and solved. But meanwhile, graduate students are not going to be able to publish what they do unless they use the currently approved methodologies. That is creating a schism between academic professional training and the kinds of economics that are useful in policymaking. There's a lot of economics being written on practical problems these days and there's a lot of it that's very good stuff. It's not so much about macro policy that we're talking about, but a lot of important economic problems like Social Security, health care, and government budgets. I'm not saying the profession is going completely to the dogs; I'm just saying that it would be nice if there were a little more acceptance of different ways of looking at things in the macro area.

Colander: Now, again, we've said the Yale school didn't have a history, but if we're thinking about Yale over a longer period, Irving Fisher [Figure 16.3] clearly comes to mind. Would you see any connections there—Irving Fisher and you. Is there continuity in the "Tobin Yale school," or did it begin in 1950?

Tobin: There isn't much continuity, as a matter of fact. I have the greatest admiration for Irving Fisher's work. He made outstanding contributions to many subjects that have been of interest to me: transactions' demand for money, theory of interest and investment, multiperiod consumption, debt burdens, deflation, and depression. But Fisher

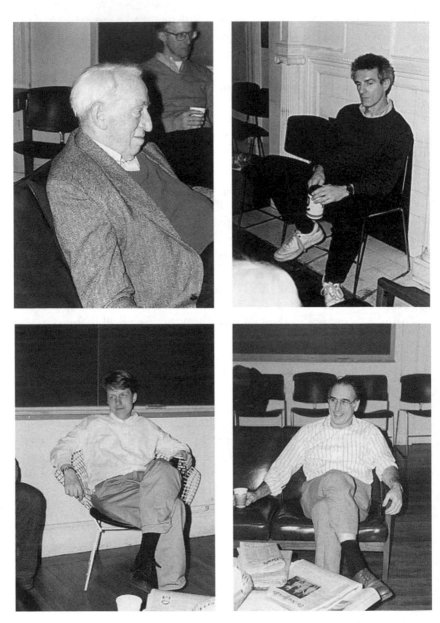

Figure 16.2 Participants in Yale Cowles coffee hour. Clockwise from top left: James Tobin and Bill Nordhaus, Ray Fair, Bill Brainard, and Robert Shiller.

was a quantity theorist, a monetarist, and had no use for Keynes or fiscal policy. His debt-deflation theory of depression was leading toward Keynesian macro. His views on monetary policy, gold, and reflation in the 1930s were unorthodox and correct. Fisher was an example for all economists, but there is not a continuity between his work and what is generally known as the Yale school.

Irving Fisher died in 1947 when he was 80 years old. By that time he had been formally retired for 15 years, or more, and before he formally retired he had not been teaching much at all and he had not had graduate students. Irving Fisher did not have a "school" created by his own teaching and scholarship because he didn't have any graduate students at all. He essentially withdrew from active participation in the department around 1925. He did all of his work in his house with his own research assistants. The only real Fisher disciple was James Harvey Rogers. He was a sort of Keynesian before Keynes in the 1920s and 1930s. He was not a slavish disciple of Fisher but he was a clear follower. He was a very good

Figure 16.3 Irving Fisher, circa 1945.
Source: Irving Fisher Papers, Manuscripts, and Archives, Yale University.

economist. He died in an airplane accident when he was, I think, around 50 years old. He was long gone when I got there so there was no continuity.

There were some young people who taught macroeconomics at Yale in the 1930s: for example, Richard Bissell, later of CIA fame and notoriety, and Max Millikin. They were young people and they were the Keynesian vanguard at Yale, but they went to the war and OSS and CIA and they were outside Yale and mostly out of economics after that. So there wasn't continuity from the prewar Yale to the postwar 1950s Yale and the prewar Yale, with Fisher's and Rogers's exception, was very conservative and not particularly good.

Colander: That's about all the time we have, and this is a good place to stop. Thank you very much.

A Conversation with Robert Shiller
May 1998

Shiller: You talked to Tobin already?

Colander: Yes, we talked last fall.

Shiller: I understand he is opposed to using the term "Yale school" broadly.

Colander: Yes, he felt the "Yale school" has a much narrower connotation.

Shiller: He may be right. Maybe we shouldn't use the term "school" to describe any department of economics. Yale's department of economics has changed in many ways over the years. Yale's department of economics, like almost all departments, is a grouping of people of diverse interests and approaches, and at any given time reflects the profession at large at the time much more than any one school of thought.

And yet, there are subtle differences in traditions, philosophies or in methods that do distinguish departments somewhat, and people actually care a lot about these differences. Subtle differences in approach to economics end up influencing students' decisions

Figure 16.4   Robert Shiller.

where to go to graduate school, and where to take a job thereafter. While these differences are hard to describe, they are actually more important than the rankings of departments that are given so much attention.

I think there is a tradition at Yale, call it the Yale school if you will, that precedes Tobin and goes beyond him. I see the Yale school in economics starting with Irving Fisher, carrying forward with the Cowles Foundation, and continuing with Tobin and beyond. Also, the tradition seems possibly to fit into a humanistic Yale tradition that extends beyond the department of economics.

Colander: For me, the Yale school is specific. I understood the term to describe Jim's position in reference to his debate with Brunner and Meltzer.

Shiller: There was a time when Jim was viewed as the counterpoint to Milton Friedman. Jim wrote a very critical review of the Friedman and Schwartz *A Monetary History of the United States* in the *American Economic Review* in 1965. When Friedman published his "theoretical framework" in the *Journal of Political Economy* in 1970, it was Jim who wrote a strong and widely noted rebuttal in 1972. So, from all this debate, it must have seemed to many, if there was a Chicago school, there must also be a Yale school. The public sense of a school of thought seems to be built around one or a few intellectual giants who take a strong public stand.

There are other historical reasons why some might easily arrive at a conclusion that there is at Yale an alternative to the Chicago school. The Cowles Foundation at Yale was taken from the University of Chicago in 1955 by Tjalling Koopmans after a dispute with the department of economics at Chicago, a department that did not at that time support the kind of quantitative research that Cowles represented. Koopmans was publicly critical of Friedman's methods too.

I am not sure how people view these debates today, so many years later. At times the Yale school must be thought of as politically much more liberal than the conservative Chicago school. Certainly, one hears from Tobin, Bill Brainard, and Bill Nordhaus more new ideas about new government initiatives than about ways of reducing the size of the government. Tobin's recent campaign for a tax on currency transactions, to put "sand in the wheels" of currency speculation, must seem antithetical to Chicago conservatism. But, overall, I would call the Yale school mostly apolitical, and certainly not associated with political parties.

To me, there is something else about this Yale tradition that should be noted. Tobin stands for an approach that is respectful both of solid economic theory and of difficulty in adapting it to the complexity of the real world. Tobin is a realist who knows the importance of studying institutions and history, and who has a deep motivation to see that economic policy really works as it is intended. One doesn't have to use the words Yale school to capture what he had in mind, but I've always thought that there is such a strength at Yale. I suppose you could use the term with caveats.

Colander: I agree. When I initially accepted Barnett's request, I felt that there was a broad methodological framework that would tie together the work of a number of people at Yale. I was thinking that there might be something called the New Yale school that I could juxtapose to the New Chicago school because I think Chicago is not the Chicago of old. Within that broad methodological framework, I saw three complementary lines of research.

One was highly theoretical and abstract. Martin Shubik's and John Geanakoplos's work fit in here. I think their theoretical work starts from a fundamentally different premise than does "new Chicago research." It requires what one might call a sociological face; for example, Shubik's work requires thinking about money in a different way than the profession has. I saw John Geanakoplos's work as possibly fitting into this broad theoretical framework.

On the empirical front, I saw Chris Sims's work fitting in this framework; it was trying to draw what one can out of the data without assuming, or not assuming, that markets clear. Finally, on the practical side, I saw Ray Fair's work as being another dimension to this; his econometric work is a nice middle ground. I also saw your work as nestled between the others, and a natural evolution of Tobin's approach.

Shiller: Well, there are some common elements here.

Colander: Yes. But it is clear that there was opposition to such a use of the term, so I will limit my discussions to you and Jim.

Shiller: I know. Some in our department were opposed to participating in these conversations, thinking that it would be more misleading than helpful if we tried to characterize the Yale school. They said that there is no more agreement here on tradition or method than there is in the profession as a whole, and that we should not misrepresent to people what they might find if they come here as students or faculty, but I am uncomfortable with their conclusion. If we followed their advice to the letter, and never discussed how one department differs from another in basic philosophy, then prospective students might have no advice for choosing among departments except those silly quantitative rankings based on popularity contests, published page counts, or the like. It is the intellectual traditions that really matter, and we have to try to characterize these traditions.

Interest in practical economic policy is an essential part of what I would say characterizes the Yale school, though its great interest in economic theory sets it apart from public policy schools per se. As departments of economics go, this department used to send a lot of people as advisers to Washington. It's a pretty good sign that economists are connected to the real world if they're being invited for advisory posts. Lately, this seems to happen much less often for Yale people. We do have a good representation of our economists in foreign countries, President Zedillo of Mexico was one of our economics Ph.D.'s, for example.

Colander: You have people like Truman Bewley. He changed his research program upon coming to Yale.

Shiller: Yes he was a great case of someone who changed fundamentally when he became a professor here, abandoning work in the most abstract of mathematical economics for empirical work on how individual wage setters make decisions. His forthcoming book, representing the results of over a hundred personal interviews with wage setters, resulted in a very deep understanding of a central issue for macroeconomics: why wages are sticky through time. I'm very impressed at what he's currently doing. So I think that either there's a subtle Yale influence on people or else Yale attracts people with certain kinds of emerging interests.

Colander: The question is: Does this influence warrant its classification as a separate school?

Shiller: As I said earlier, I think there is something distinctive about Yale that represents a long tradition. I see the Yale school going back to Irving Fisher. He was, in fact, the first person to receive a Ph.D. in economics from Yale, in 1891. He spent his entire career at Yale, until he died in New Haven in 1947. This spring we had a conference sponsored by the Cowles Foundation at Yale on the occasion of the 50th anniversary of Fisher's death. There will be a conference volume about his work. Most of our macroeconomics and theory faculty participated. If this isn't evidence of a departmental tradition I don't know what is.

Fisher is the man who gave the most convincing clarification of the theoretical role that the rate of interest plays in economic decisions, and his theoretical advances in capital theory influence much thinking even today. He is also the man who invented the term "money illusion" and who wrote an entire book on the subject, indicating an early awareness in him of the importance of behavioral economics. He is also the prime exponent of inflation-indexed bonds, which the U.S. Treasury just created last year. This indicates an awareness in him of the importance of institutional change. His work shows more vitality today than that of any other American economist from the first half of this century, and I think that it is elements of his approach that are responsible for this.

Such a tradition might continue to attract people to this department. Even if differences across departments of economics are in many ways subtle, a tradition represents a focal point where people of similar interests can converge, along lines that theorists have specified as a factor that can break multiplicity of equilibrium. Rather than choose a department randomly, students and professors can choose a department that involves some symbol that represents their approach or philosophy, thinking that others of like mind will tend to be attracted there. A departmental tradition can survive interruptions, I believe.

It's fairly rare that a department of economics will focus strongly on a particular approach. You had the University of Chicago, which shows a strong focus under Frank Knight, Milton Friedman, and others on advocacy of laissez-faire economics, and that period in Chicago history was a wonderful success, when judged from the legacy it left for us all. But even that Chicago tradition has changed now. It's quite different from what it was, much more technical and less practical-policy oriented. Now the Chicago approach is almost inseparable from a variety of other schools' approaches, and some argue that the old Chicago tradition is dead. But I would not agree. The symbols of Chicago's past will continue to influence the future of that department.

Colander: I think the key to answering the question "Is there a new Yale school?" is to discuss how Yale is distinct. Let me ask you the following: How does Yale differ from MIT, Princeton, and Harvard?

Shiller: That is so hard to answer briefly. There are so many different people and so many different dimensions, but each has a slightly different intellectual history which may tend to attract different people. Take MIT, for example. When you think of MIT, you may think of Samuelson, Solow, Modigliani, and Diamond. Because of them and others there, it has a wonderful intellectual tradition that attracts people who are motivated by any number of things in their work. Their legacy becomes a kind of a public focal point that helps to define their department, I think. At Yale I would still say that Irving Fisher and Jim Tobin would be a similar tradition.

Colander: So how would you contrast Samuelson and Tobin, for example?

Shiller: They are both great economists whom I admire. Both of them have very broad scope, beyond narrow economic models, and a commitment to social philosophy.

Colander: So you would characterize the Yale school as having a stronger focus on social philosophy.

Shiller: Maybe that's partly right. It's hard to be general about this. What image do we have of Tobin? To me, he comes through as a very moral person and who has genuine sympathy for others. That means he sees what other people are suffering and he wants to correct that. You get that sense more from him than from very many economists.

Colander: Could we distinguish what you have in mind about Yale by saying that there is a different motivation for theoretical work here? I'm thinking of your theoretical work. In my view, it starts from a different perspective—one that did not initially assume that markets work, but instead assumes that markets work because institutions make them work. It then tries to understand that interplay between institutions and theory. That seemed to me the epitome of what I felt characterized a broader Yale school. It included Jim Tobin's work, your work, and a number of others here.

Shiller: Yes, I think there is some difference in motivation here, though, as I have said, this motivation does not apply to everyone here. For me, it is central to my work. For the past decade, my work has been focused on improving economic institutions (as in my book *Macro Markets*, which proposed fundamental new financial markets), and on incorporating lessons from other social sciences, such as psychology and sociology, into economics.

Others here have shown a real interest in practical institutions and policy. Christopher Sims has been developing macroeconomic models for evaluating monetary policy. Giancarlo Corsetti has written a book (with Willem Buiter and Paolo Pesenti, both formerly here at Yale) about European monetary cooperation. Ariel Pakes has been studying index number theory, in connection with a differentiated products model, to try to understand how account should be made, in computing the consumer price index, of the changing quality and ever-increasing list of choices for consumers.

T.N. Srinivasan has been studying policy toward customs unions and regionalism in world trade. Bill Nordhaus and Robert Mendelsohn are deeply involved in applying economic theory to understand the economic dilemmas that will come due to global climate change. Of course, most departments have some people involved in practical policy, but I think Yale is one of the departments with a particular strength here.

In my view a department gaining a sense of identity is an accident of history. Things that happened long ago still tend to influence. I view Irving Fisher as part of the identity of this department even though he died in 1947. Another identifying aspect of the Yale department was having the Cowles Foundation here, which was a central early econometric mark.

Colander: I see the Cowles Foundation in some ways as playing a role in the abstract direction that macroeconomics went. My reading of that period is that some of the Cowles Foundation work that was done here really tried to provide a full scientific basis for the sets of models that were there. Thus, they were, in my view, claiming more for the macroeconometric models than what could be claimed. That's why I think Ray Fair's latest piece, talking about macro models in a different way, is important. They're workable models; they are not models that provide the grand scientific foundations for things. What macroeconometric models are trying to do is to understand things enough to handle policy. That seems to me fundamentally different from the approach the Cowles Foundation started out thinking about macro models. In some ways the picture I paint is not so pretty for the old Keynesians, because the old Keynesians in some ways were trying to have it all—both direct policy relevance and scientific basis.

Shiller: Yeah, I thought it was incredible hubris for Keynes to call his book the "general theory," suggesting associations with Einstein. Ray Fair has based his macroeconometric modeling work on a very practical, unglamorous, and commonsense approach, involving a careful testing of the predictive power of his models. He has explicit models that work as forecasters, out of sample, better than any simple model, as my work with Ray has demonstrated. I find it remarkable that there isn't more interest among academic economists in developing explicit macroeconomic forecasting models with a sensible account of real-world factors such as taxes and monetary policy and carefully testing the ability of the models themselves, without human intervention, to provide information about the future. There hasn't been much academic interest in getting into the practical minutiae of forecasting well in real time.

Colander: I think there were a number of different elements of Keynes's work; some were practical and some were theoretical. I actually think that Keynes's implicit theory is more general if it is interpreted as a multiple equilibria model. He never developed that but it's at the heart of my understanding of Keynes's theoretical contribution. That aspect of Keynes was quickly lost as researchers tried to fit Keynesian economics into a unique equilibrium Walrasian model. These two traditions, it seemed to me, were unmeshable. The Walrasian model left out of it all sorts of sociological and institutional issues that were central to Keynes's worldview.

Colander: Let's talk a little bit about you. How did you get into economics?

Shiller: When I was in college I was interested in just about everything. I thought choosing a field was an impossible decision to make but I had to make some decision. I can't say exactly what tipped me toward economics. I thought I wanted to help the world, and it seemed that economics was a good way to do that. I have very cosmopolitan interests and I could have ended up at any department at the university. I choose economics and went to MIT, where I worked under Franco Modigliani. I admired his approach to economics, and his commitment to moral and social issues. I remember that he and I were occupied with concern about the Vietnam War then.

Since then, I have done a lot of work in what may be called a behavioral economics mold, in both macroeconomics and finance. For a decade now, Richard Thaler and I have been organizing a series of seminars in behavioral finance, sponsored by the Russell Sage Foundation Roundtable on Behavioral Economics and by the National Bureau of Economic Research. George Akerlof and I have been organizing a series of seminars on behavioral macroeconomics for some years now. I have had a lot of support from my Yale colleagues for these endeavors, but these are more profession-wide seminars.

Colander: How would you characterize or differentiate the MIT–Modigliani approach from the Yale–Tobin approach?

Shiller: That's hard to do; I admire both these departments and people. In many ways, MIT represents to me the same tradition. To me, a lot of what I admire about the Yale school is carried forward also in another institution, the Brookings Panel on Economic Activity, with its publication, the Brookings Papers on Economic Activity. These were founded by Arthur Okun, a Yale economics professor very much in the Yale school tradition [see Figure 16.5]. The Brookings Panel, organized now by Yale's William Brainard and Brookings' George Perry, draws people doing this kind of practical, theoretically sound, policy-oriented research from many departments around the country.

Colander: If you can't separate Yale and MIT, doesn't that suggest that what we were talking about as the Yale school is really a broader school that goes beyond Yale and instead represents an "older Keynesian" tradition.

Shiller: It would often be Keynesian in a certain sense. It's an approach that is less methods bound than comes from Keynes. It is an approach than recognizes the richness and complexity of the real world. It is an approach that is responsive to reality and to inductive research, and sees sensible and effective policy formulation as the ultimate objective. It's an approach that involves being alert to, and open to, basic facts.

Colander: How would you respond to the argument that economics is trying to get underneath surface facts and observations, and get to the core motivating driving force of the economy?

Shiller: In my view, that argument reflects a false view of reality. There's kind of a group-think that develops in the profession that makes

Figure 16.5 Meeting of the Brookings Panel on Economic Activity in January 1978. Joe Pechman (left) was the Director of Economic Studies at Brookings. Art Okun (center) and George Perry (right) were co-founders of the Panel.

many economists think that there's a simple theme to human behavior, a single key that explains it all, such as expected utility maximization with a simple utility functional form that many economists use for no good reason. Human behavior is so much more complex, so we have to take our cue a lot from facts and do inductive work.

Colander: What percentage of the profession shares your approach?

Shiller: I don't know. I think in any profession, most of the people will be spinning their wheels, unfortunately. That is the nature of research, but I think that it also happens more than it should because people specialize too narrowly and define their research problems too narrowly. I wish a higher fraction of the economics profession were interested in history, psychology, sociology, institutions, and economic policy. In this, I don't mean necessarily day-to-day concern with politics. I'm not saying I want economists to be more like the kind of television-news sound-bite economists who are always ready to discuss what was said on the floor of the House yesterday.

Colander: Your view strikes me as having similarities with the Santa Fe complexity view. Would you agree?

Shiller: I have attended a couple of their conferences in New Mexico and found them very worthwhile. My view of the complexity of human nature (and, increasingly, the view of an enlightened segment of the economics profession, I think) reflects modern work in evolutionary biology. That work emphasizes that the human species is a product of natural selection, both genetic and cultural. That means that any little habit or pattern that was advantageous was reinforced, and any little habit or pattern that was not, was repressed. The outcome is a set of human motivations that is extremely complex. Lacking knowledge of evolutionary history, there is no underlying sense to it. We just have to accept these motivations in all their complexity. You have to understand this whole constellation of motives, desires, and behavior patterns that served us well as primitive hunter–gatherers, as isolated farmers, or as Victorian merchants, but which may not serve us well now. Trying to understand events that happened in very simple terms with very simple models is a fundamental method of our research, but we should not make the error of elevating these simple models too far.

Colander: How many people here at Yale share that point of view?

Shiller: I'm not sure.

Colander: How about Martin Shubik?

Shiller: He might agree; he also stresses incorporating the complexity of institutional facts into model building. He has shown how proper account of some of these facts about the circumstances we find ourselves in allows us to use game theory to provide insights not only into economic behavior, but also into such diverse fields as political science and social psychology.

Colander: What about Chris Sims? His empirical work seems to be challenging the way we pull information from data.

Shiller: Yes indeed. He had an article in 1980 called "Macroeconomics and Reality." I was very sympathetic to that article because he was pointing out some weaknesses in the profession's then-standard approach to macroeconometric modeling. This article is at least as important as Lucas is "Econometric Policy Evaluation: A Critique," which points out different weaknesses. The profession tends to develop a structure for modeling the economy, often not very well supported by any evidence, and focuses too much on the approach. Sims, in that article, was questioning these assumptions that are really without basis or fact and he was going back toward an econometric approach that was not driven by this unanalyzed structure.

Colander: But that article was written before he came to Yale, wasn't it?

Shiller: Yes, this was written before he came to Yale. His macroeconomic theory course to our first-year macroeconomics students today is very tightly focused on the mathematics of intertemporal optimization under rational expectations. I disagree somewhat with him about this focus. Students should certainly learn some of this material, but it excludes other things. Economic agents more often satisfice, to quote

Herbert Simon, than optimize, as a matter of simple fact, and the costs of calculation prohibit their behaving as represented in these optimizing models. Probably, however, our core macro sequence for first-year Ph.D. students at Yale works very well with both Sims and me in it, presenting different views.

John Rust has been worrying about the apparent unrealism of our economic models in their assumptions about agents' ability to compute. He has some results showing that massive parallelism, social memory, and decentralization can make it more plausible that people really can do these calculations, in effect. It is good that he is trying to confront these issues, though I am afraid that an aspect of unrealism will remain in many of these models.

Colander: Should there be a different methodology for macro than for micro?

Shiller: The terms macro and micro represent schools of thought as much as different subject matter. The terms suggest that macro is an aggregation of micro but in fact the differences between these schools of thought are perhaps as much in terms of method as of subject matter. The difference is a bit analogous to calculus and geometry in math. Geometry naturally seems to lend itself toward axiomatization, but calculus is rarely presented to students as an axiomatized system. I think that macro can be, in this sense, more like calculus. We start from some intuitive feeling; we build little models but they're not complete models; they don't work from first principles and so there's often been more willingness to introduce real-world complexity in human behavior in macro than in micro.

Colander: What's your view of the IS–LM model?

Shiller: Well I'm still teaching it although that's hardly the only thing I teach. The IS–LM model is not a complete model; it takes things as given. If that's all you know, you're far too limited.

Colander: Much of the work on the foundations of IS–LM has been done within the Walrasian general equilibrium model. What's your view on that work?

Shiller: It goes back to my fundamental thing: You say complexity; I say you can't reduce all human behavior to simple rules. We talk about IS–LM as the Keynesian model. But Keynes talks about so many different things, like envy or social comparisons, that go beyond the IS–LM story. I think of economic habits—patterns of behavior that are in our minds for no good reason. An example is money illusion. Money illusion is an important phenomenon. People have a preference for nominal quantities. This preference should be fundamental to macroeconomic theory.

Colander: Lets go back to the foundations people. Was it a natural step if you look at the evolution of macro? After IS–LM became standard, it started getting modified by Keynesians such as Modigliani and Tobin. It was a natural step from their works to providing simple micro foundations for the model's conclusions.

Shiller: Yes, it was a natural step because Keynes's book was a muddle. It was impossible to comprehend because there were all these loose ends trailing off.

Colander: But what I'm asking is whether the Neo-Keynesian work was a first step that started us down the micro foundations path. Was it the beginning of the assumption that you could provide simple explanations for complex things?

Shiller: Well, first of all, it's desirable to have simple explanations for complex phenomena—a physics model for economics. It would be nice to have it, but I think the physics methodology doesn't work as well in economics. We are not going to discover universal laws like $F = MA$ of the same importance in economics. I think the hope of finding such things has harmed some people's research in economics.

Colander: How do you see IS–LM fitting in with Walrasian general equilibrium theory? Are the two compatible?

Shiller: The Walrasian model is very abstract and would apply to civilizations on another planet or wherever. The IS–LM Keynesian model was designed for twentieth-century institutions and human behavior patterns. The IS–LM model is not really satisfying as a theoretical model; it is just an aid to thinking about some tentative conclusions from an intuitive theory.

Colander: What are your views of monetarism?

Shiller: Milton Friedman was the prime advocate of monetarism. I hope it is not seen as inconsistent with my philosophy that I am an admirer of him too. His *Monetary History*, written with Anna Schwartz, was a very interesting book, although the lack of stability of the money multiplier in recent years has blunted what they considered a major message of that book.

How can I be both an admirer of Friedman and of much in the Chicago school tradition, and yet also question the optimizing-model-based approach to macroeconomics that some would say is quintessentially Chicago? The answer is that what is really attractive about people's work is often not the dogmas that they choose to stress about them, and would have others adopt. One may be inspired by some of their work even while rejecting these dogmas. Milton Friedman is sometimes viewed as advocating exclusive reliance on certain kinds of rational-optimizing models, but I take a different perspective on his relation to this work.

Friedman wrote a book on methodology—his *Essays in Positive Economics*. The first essay in that volume has been used by many people to justify building elaborate economic models from counterfactual assumptions. He gives a story in that essay about how one would model the behavior of a skilled billiard player. The best way to do this might be to describe his plays as if he were solving an optimization problem in theoretical mechanics. It wouldn't be a criticism of this modeling method to point out that the billiard player cannot understand the mathematics of the theoretical mechanics. Thus his famous assertion that you cannot judge a model by the realism of its assumptions. Friedman is basically right about this, and this example does justify in a way the value of building optimizing models from counterfactual assumptions. Still, many who cite this example misapply this insight, as Koopmans forcefully argued.

I think we can't blame Friedman for all the misapplications of his methodology. In looking at his own method of research, you often see a lot of real strengths and good sense. His *Monetary History* with Anna Schwartz, for example, was one of the early examples of searching for natural experiments (they called them "quasicontrolled experiments") to sort out cause and effect, and not to rely exclusively on some enshrined method of model building as the only approach.

Colander: So you see some overlap between monetarism and Tobinesque macro?

Shiller: Well that's why we are having a problem with characterizing a Yale school. There's going to be overlap. The Chicago school isn't just at Chicago and what I might call the Yale school isn't just at Yale.

Colander: What's your view of the Clower–Leijonhufvud approach?

Shiller: I remember their works: That was an interesting literature years ago. I used to lecture about that but I haven't done that for a while. The ideas are mentioned in my course but only very briefly. I tell students about the difference between notional and effective demand, and about sticky prices. Their work evolved into a literature on disequilibrium, some of which was very important.

Colander: What's your view of New Keynesians?

Shiller: Acknowledging that wages and prices are sticky through time is extremely important for macroeconomics. There is also the related phenomenon of wage compression across types of people, which, Giuseppe Moscarini has shown, appears to account for the fact that less skilled workers tend to bear more of the brunt of macroeconomic fluctuations.

Colander: What would you say the relationship of the Yale school with Keynesianism is?

Shiller: Keynesianism is such an ill-defined thing now, and many people would say it's dead, not dead on the policy side, but on the theoretical side. However, as I said: Trying to build a model that captures a lot of observed phenomena rather than starting from first principles is important. Thus, I think there's a close relationship in terms of motivation and philosophy.

Colander: What is your view of the real-business-cycle approach?

Shiller: Real-business-cycle theory has been a prominent movement in macroeconomic theory ever since Kydland and Prescott's famous "time to build" piece in 1982. It has expanded through the profession and differentiated, so that it is not always recognizable as a distinct movement anymore.

The real-business-cycle modelers find basic facts about the macroeconomy, simple characterizations of the economy, such as which quantities and relative prices are changing over the business cycle and how these correlate with each other. They then try to relate these prices and quantity movements to a calibrated optimizing model of individual behavior. It is an attractive exercise to try to make sense of the basic facts this way.

We have a number of people at Yale who are pursuing what I would lump loosely under the heading real-business-cycle theory. Chris Sims, with Eric Leeper, Tao Zha, and others, has been doing time-series analysis of linearized dynamic stochastic general equilibrium models. Stefan Krieger builds business-cycle models with heterogeneous debt-constrained firms exposed to idiosyncratic production risk. George Hall models plant managers' capital utilization in terms of a dynamic programming model, and allows us to explain the behavior of production and inventories over the business cycle.

In the future, I would like to see more work combining the basic insights provided by this work with other information. The real-business-cycle theorists often limit themselves. There ought to be more recognition of the limited ability of people to calculate that I referred to above, their tendency to use rules of thumb, and the influence institutions have on their behavior. These theorists will say sometimes that, while they acknowledge these problems, they cannot see a good way to take account of these problems in their models. But it is very important to try.

Colander: I think we're running out of time, so we should probably end here. Thank you very much.